1299

D0490451

Social skills in interpersonal

'The book is well written and enjoyable to read. . . . It is likely to appeal to many professionals involved with a wide range of client groups. . . .? In addition, this text should be a valuable aid to industrial personnel such as managers, salesmen and market researchers.'

Behavioural Psychotherapy

'I would certainly recommend it to those therapists who are concerned with understanding more about the psychological aspects of therapy.'

Physiotherapy

'This most valuable book should be recommended to any therapist concerned to enhance their understanding of the communication processes inherent in their job. . . . The clarity of its presentation and structure and the comprehensive coverage of its research make it vital background reading for any therapist involved in staff training and development.'

Therapy Weekly

The subject of interpersonal skill has attracted enormous research interest in recent years. This third edition of *Social Skills in Interpersonal Communication* has been completely revised and rewritten to bring the book entirely up to date. New chapters have been added on the nature of skilled communication, and on interpersonal influence.

Social Skills in Interpersonal Communication is the leading book in this field and will remain the standard textbook for everyone studying interpersonal communication.

Owen Hargie, **Christine Saunders** and **David Dickson** are all at the Department of Communication, University of Ulster.

Social skills in interpersonal communication

Third edition

Owen Hargie,
Christine Saunders
and David Dickson

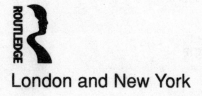

London and New York

First edition published 1981
Second edition published 1987
by Croom Helm Ltd
and Brookline Books

This third edition published 1994
by Routledge
11 New Fetter Lane, London EC4P 4EE

Simultaneously published in the USA and Canada
by Routledge
29 West 35th Street, New York, NY 10001

© 1994 Owen Hargie, Christine Saunders and David Dickson

Typeset in Times by
Ponting–Green Publishing Services, Chesham, Bucks
Printed and bound in Great Britain by
Mackays of Chatham PLC, Chatham, Kent

British Library Cataloguing in Publication Data
A catalogue record for this book is available from the British
Library.

Library of Congress Cataloging in Publication Data
Hargie, Owen.
  Social skills in interpersonal communication/Owen Hargie,
  Christine Saunders, David Dickson – 3rd ed.
      p.   cm.
  Simultaneously published in the USA and Canada.
  Includes bibliographical references and indexes.
  1. Social skills.   2. Interpersonal communication.
  I. Saunders, Christine.   II. Dickson, David, 1950–.
  III. Title.
  HM299.H36   1994
  302.3'4–dc20
                                    93–23616
                                     CIP

ISBN 0–415–11830–1 (hbk)
ISBN 0–415–08137–8 (pbk)

For Patricia, Ethel, Eric,
Rob, Anne and Mary

Contents

List of figures   viii
Preface to the third edition   ix

1 **Introduction**   1

2 **Interpersonal communication: a skill-based model**   9

3 **Nonverbal communication**   37

4 **Rewarding and reinforcing**   63

5 **Questioning**   93

6 **Reflecting**   120

7 **Set induction and closure**   142

8 **Explanation**   175

9 **Listening**   194

10 **Self-disclosure**   219

11 **Influencing**   246

12 **Assertiveness**   268

13 **Group interaction and leadership**   291

14 **Concluding comments**   316

Bibliography   318
Name index   357
Subject index   367

Figures

1.1   The social skill of reinforcement   5
2.1   Skill model of interpersonal communication   19
3.1   Seating preferences at a rectangular table   56
5.1   Types of questioning sequence   103
9.1   Selective perception process   197
9.2   Basic model of listening   200
9.3   Extended model of listening   200
9.4   Blocking tactics to listening   212
10.1   The Johari Window   233
12.1   Four styles of responding   273
13.1   Communication networks   302

Preface to the third edition

The importance of effective interpersonal communication in professional contexts is now widely recognised. Interpersonal skills training programmes have been reported in the literature for doctors, dentists, dietitians, nurses, health visitors, psychiatrists, pharmacists, radiographers, speech and language therapists, chiropodists, occupational therapists, opticians, physiotherapists, social workers, teachers, clergymen, counsellors, careers advisers, youth workers, policemen, military personnel, librarians, psychologists, selection interviewers, engineers and business personnel. In all of these occupations, the ability to communicate effectively at an interpersonal level is a vital part of the job, and it is therefore reasonable to expect that these professionals should have a knowledge of various types of social skills, and of their effects in social interaction. It is for this reason that interest in the study of social skills in professional contexts has mushroomed in the past few years.

It is seven years since the second edition of this book was published, and during this time we have received a considerable amount of feedback from tutors and trainees involved in interpersonal skills programmes, both within and without the University of Ulster, as well as from practising professionals. As a result of this feedback we have extended the coverage to include chapters on the model of interpersonal communication upon which our approach is based, and on the skill area of influencing. The theoretical base for the book was previously only accessible in some of our other books and its inclusion in this edition therefore makes the present text more self-contained. The second additional area, that of interpersonal influence, is one which is now recognised to be of vital importance to the work of many professionals. As well as adding these two new chapters we have updated available research information on all of the skills.

These are the main changes which have been made to this edition. The function of the book remains exactly the same, however, in that it has been designed and presented in such a fashion as to provide a useful reference for the study of social skills *per se* by interpersonal professionals. It is concerned with the identification, analysis and evaluation of a range of social skills which are employed widely in professional interaction. As such, this text should be of interest to qualified personnel and trainees in many fields. Detailed accounts are provided of thirteen social skill areas, namely: non-verbal communication, reinforcement, questioning, reflecting, set induction, closure, explaining, listening, self-disclosure, influencing, assertiveness, and interacting in, and leading, small group discussions.

In writing this book, the authors would like to acknowledge the assistance provided by the Faculty of Social and Health Sciences, University of Ulster. We would also like to thank all those members of staff at the University, and at other Centres in Northern Ireland, who have been involved in, and contributed to, the evolution of our Communication Skills Training programmes. The support, advice and encouragement of these colleagues is reflected in this third edition. The stimulation and invaluable feedback provided by trainees enrolled on our skills programmes are also recognised. A special word of thanks is given to Vivien Ward and Elisabeth Tribe at Routledge, for their help, support and expertise. Words of appreciation are also due to Philip Burch, Graphic Design Technician in the Department of Communication at the University of Ulster Jordanstown for his skill in producing the diagrams in this book; to Mrs Sadie Faulkner, Secretary in the Department of Communication, for all her help at various stages and for her enduring good nature; and to Mrs Lorraine Brownlie, Faculty typist, for her diligence and forbearance in typing the Bibliography. Finally, we are indebted to our families who provided the necessary motivation throughout the production of this book.

(It should be noted that where either the masculine or feminine gender is referred to throughout this text, this should be taken as encompassing both genders as appropriate.)

Owen Hargie
Christine Saunders
David Dickson
Jordanstown, 1994

Chapter 1

Introduction

In recent years increasing attention has been devoted to the entire spectrum of socially skilled interaction. Indeed, as Segrin (1992, p. 89) has noted, 'The concept of social skill has touched the interests of researchers working in virtually all fields of social science.' The fairly obvious observation that some individuals are better social interactors than others, has led to carefully formulated and systematic investigations into the nature and function of interpersonal interaction. This has occurred at three levels. First, theoretical analyses of how and why people behave as they do have resulted in various conceptualisations of socially skilled behaviour (see for example Ellis and Whittington, 1983; Trower, 1984). Second, research has been conducted into the identification and effects of different types of social behaviour. It is this level that the present book addresses. Third, several different approaches to training in social skills have been introduced in order to ascertain whether it is possible to improve the social performance of the individual (for a review of these see L'Abate and Milan, 1985; Dickson *et al.*, 1989).

THE NATURE OF SOCIAL SKILLS

At this stage, it is useful to examine exactly what is meant by the term 'social skill'. At first sight this may appear unnecessary, since the term has already been referred to and presumably the reader has understood what was meant by it. Social skills, in this global sense, are the skills employed when interacting with other people at an interpersonal level. This definition of social skill is not very informative, however, since it really indicates what social skills are used for rather than what they are.

Attempts to define the term 'social skill' proliferate within the psychological literature. In order to illustrate this point it is useful to examine some of the definitions which have been put forward by different theorists. Phillips (1978), in reviewing a number of approaches to the analysis of social skill, concluded that a person is socially skilled according to:

> the extent to which he or she can communicate with others, in a manner
> that fulfils one's rights, requirements, satisfactions, or obligations to a

reasonable degree without damaging the other person's similar rights, requirements, satisfactions, or obligations, and hopefully shares these rights, etc. with others in free and open exchange.

(p. 13)

This definition emphasises the macro-elements of social encounters, in terms of reciprocation between participants (although Phillips does point out that 'knowing how to behave in a variety of situations' is part of social skill). This theme is also found in the definition given by Schlundt and McFall (1985) who defined social skills as: 'the specific component processes that enable an individual to behave in a manner that will be judged as "competent". Skills are the abilities necessary for producing behaviour that will accomplish the objectives of a task' (p. 23).

These definitions tend to view social skill as an ability which the individual may possess to a greater or lesser extent. A somewhat different focus has been offered by other theorists, who define social skill in terms of the *behaviour* of the individual. Thus McGuire and Priestley (1981) regard social skills as 'those kinds of behaviour which are basic to effective face-to-face communication between individuals' (p. 6). Argyle (1981) extended this behavioural emphasis to encompass the *goals* of the individual when he stated, 'By socially skilled behaviour, I mean social behaviour which is effective in realising the goals of the interactors' (p. 1). Kelly (1982) added the dimension of *learning* by defining social skills as 'those identifiable, learned behaviours that individuals use in interpersonal situations to obtain or maintain reinforcement from their environment' (p. 3).

Michelson *et al.* (1983), in evaluating the defining features of social skill, derived six main elements as central to the concept. They noted that social skills:

1 are primarily acquired through learning;
2 comprise specific, discrete verbal and nonverbal behaviours;
3 entail effective, appropriate initiations and responses;
4 maximise social reinforcement from others;
5 are interactive in nature, and require appropriate timing and reciprocity of specific behaviours;
6 are influenced by environmental factors such as the age, sex and status of the other person.

In his review of definitions of skilled behaviour, Hargie (1986) also identified six main facets of social skill as comprising 'a set of goal-directed, inter-related, situationally appropriate social behaviours which can be learned and which are under the control of the individual' (p. 12). This is the definition adopted in this book. It emphasises six separate components of social skill.

First, socially skilled behaviours are *goal-directed*. They are those behaviours which the individual employs in order to achieve a desired outcome, and are therefore purposeful behaviours, as opposed to chance, or unintentional, behaviours. For example, if person A wishes to encourage person B to talk freely, he will look at B, nod his head when B speaks, refrain from interrupting B and utter what Richardson *et al.* (1965) termed 'guggles' ('hmm hmm'; 'uh huh', etc.) periodically. In this instance these *behaviours* are *directed* towards the *goal* of encouraging participation. In their discussion of interpersonal competence Spitzberg and Cupach (1984, p. 41) pointed out that 'skills may be considered as abilities focused on goal accomplishment, whether the goal is as specific as speaking without a trembling voice or is as general as learning to manage the greeting ritual in a variety of contexts'. A similar definition is propounded by Segrin and Dillard (1993, p. 76) who argue that 'social skill is the ability of an individual to achieve his or her interpersonal goals in a manner that is reasonably efficient and appropriate'.

Second, socially skilled behaviours must be *interrelated*, in that they are synchronised behaviours which are employed in order to achieve a particular goal. Thus the individual will employ two or more behaviours at the same time, for example, as mentioned previously, when encouraging B to talk, A may smile, nod his head, look directly at B and utter a guggle, and each of these signals will be interpreted by B as signs of encouragement to continue speaking. Each behaviour relates to this common goal, and so the behaviours are in this way interrelated and synchronised.

Third, social skills should be *appropriate* to the *situation* in which they are being employed. The socially skilled individual will be able to adapt his use of behaviours to meet the demands of particular individuals in specific social contexts. In this sense 'skilled communication relies upon the use of contextually appropriate and behaviourally facilitative means of relating effectively and efficiently to others' (Dickson *et al.*, 1993, p. 11). There is some evidence that professionals who develop a style of interacting for one aspect of their work may find it difficult to change this style if they have to move to another professional context. For example, teachers with considerable classroom experience may encounter such problems if they are additionally required to undertake a counselling role with pupils (Hargie, 1988).

Fourth, social skills are defined in terms of identifiable units of *behaviour* which the individual displays. The socially skilled actor must have: 'the ability to produce a number of different and appropriate behaviors. . . . Ultimately, one's social abilities must be exercised in a *behavioral performance*. . . . This is the observable feature of socially skilled communication' (Segrin, 1992, p. 92). We therefore judge whether or not people are socially skilled based upon how they actually *behave*.

As Argyle (1983b) has illustrated, socially skilled responses are hierarchically organised in such a way that large elements, like being interviewed, are composed of smaller behavioural units such as looking at the interviewer and answering questions. Argyle argues that the development of social skills can be facilitated by training the individual to acquire these smaller responses. Indeed, this technique is also used in the learning of many motor skills.

The fifth aspect of the definition adopted in this book is that social skills are composed of behaviours which can be *learned*. It is now generally accepted that most forms of behaviour displayed in social contexts are learned by the individual. This is evidenced by the general finding that children reared in isolation from other humans display distorted, socially unacceptable forms of behaviour, and do not acquire a language. At a less extreme level, there is evidence to suggest that children from a socially deprived home environment may also develop unacceptable social behaviours while children from a culturally richer home environment tend to develop more appropriate social behaviours (Eisler and Frederiksen, 1980).

Bandura (1986) has developed a social cognitive theory, which purports that all repertoires of behaviour, with the exception of elementary reflexes (such as eye blinks), are learned. This process of social learning involves the *modelling* and *imitation* of the behaviour of significant others, such as parents, teachers, siblings or peers. By this process, from an early age, children may walk, talk and act like their same-sex parent. At a later stage, however, the child may develop the accent of his or her peers and begin to talk in a similar fashion – despite the accent of parents.

A second major element is the *reinforcement*, by significant others, of behaviours which the individual displays. In childhood, for example, the parents will encourage, discourage or ignore various behaviours which the child displays. As a general rule, the child will tend to learn, and employ more frequently, those behaviours which are encouraged, while tending to display less often those behaviours which are discouraged or ignored. In this sense, feedback is crucial to effective performance. Indeed, Collins and Collins (1992, p. 5), in their discussion of skilled behaviour, point out that 'you may simply go on making the same mistakes unless you can also obtain accurate feedback on the quality of what you do. Without feedback of this kind skills will not continue to improve; there is even evidence that they may deteriorate.' (This issue will be discussed more fully in Chapter 2.)

The final element in the definition of social skills, and another feature of social cognitive theory, is that they should be under the cognitive *control* of the individual. Thus a socially inadequate individual may have learned the basic elements of social skills but may not have developed the appropriate thought processes necessary to control the utilisation of these elements in social interaction. An important dimension of control relates to the timing of social behaviours. If the use of a social skill is to achieve its desired effect, then the timing of behaviour is a very important consideration, in that socially skilled behaviours need to be employed at the most suitable juncture. For instance, to maximise their reinforcing potential, verbal statements of encouragement should be uttered as soon as possible in response to the utterances or actions of the other person that they are intended to encourage (this issue is fully discussed in Chapter 4). Indeed 'saying the right thing at the wrong time' would seem to be a characteristic of some social inadequates (Hargie and McCartan, 1986). It would, therefore, appear that learning *when* to employ social behaviours is just as crucial as learning *what* these behaviours are and *how* to use them.

EXAMPLE OF SOCIAL SKILL

In order to understand more fully these six basic elements of social skill, the skill of reinforcement (which will be reviewed in more detail in Chapter 4) can serve as a useful example. This skill is subdivided into verbal and nonverbal reinforcement techniques which can be employed in social interaction. These two subdivisions are in turn analysed in terms of the operational behaviours which are used to define and chart the use of the skill itself (see Figure 1.1).

Verbal reinforcers

These are the utterances made by individuals which serve the purpose of encouraging another person to continue with a certain behaviour or activity. There are three main categories of verbal reinforcement:

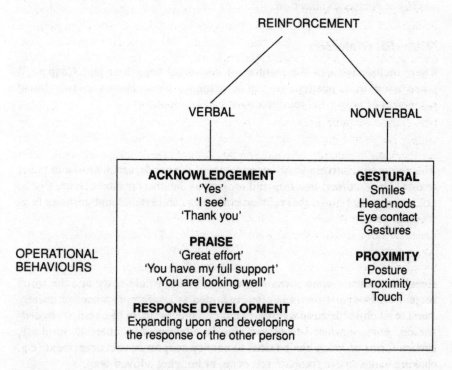

Figure 1.1 The social skill of reinforcement

Acknowledgement/confirmation

This refers to utterances which acknowledge or agree with what has been said or done by another. Examples of such reinforcers include: 'Yes'; 'That's right'; 'OK'. These words or phrases indicate to the speaker that his message has been received and comprehended.

Praise/support

This type of verbal reinforcement is stronger than the simple acknowledgement of what has been said, since it indicates overt support and encouragement for the speaker. Examples of such verbalisations are: 'You have done very well'; 'I agree with you entirely'; 'I love your dress.'

Response development

Here, reinforcement is provided by building upon and extending the topic raised by the speaker – in other words by developing the response. This is one of the most potent forms of reinforcement, since it indicates both that the listener must have been attending closely and also that what has been said is worthy of further exploration.

Nonverbal reinforcers

These include most of the features of nonverbal behaviour (see Chapter 3) when used in a positive or encouraging fashion. However, two broad categories of nonverbal reinforcement can be identified.

Gestural

This refers to relatively small movements of the hands, arms, head and facial region. Thus *smiling, nodding* and *looking* at the other person can usually be taken as signs of nonverbal reinforcement, as can certain hand *gestures* (e.g. 'thumbs-up').

Proximity

Here, the focus is upon gross movements of the whole body or substantial parts of it. Body *proximity* is often regarded as reinforcing since we usually stand or sit closer to those we like, or have an interest in. In like vein a *forward-leaning posture* when seated can signify attention and interest. Similarly, certain forms of *touch* can be used to convey support or encouragement (e.g. shaking hands to congratulate someone, or hugging a loved one).

The whole area of paralanguage is also important – how something is said as opposed to what is said (see Chapter 3). Saying 'that is very interesting' in a dull, flat voice may well negate any reinforcing value of the statement and would represent inappropriate use of paralanguage. In other words, for reinforcement to be skilled, oral statements should always be accompanied by apposite paralanguage in order to enhance the verbal content (saying 'That is very interesting' should itself sound interesting).

OVERVIEW

The factors discussed in this chapter, relating to the nature of social skills, should be borne in mind when examining each of the skills reviewed in the remainder of this text. It is recognised that the fluent application of these skills is a crucial feature of effective social interaction. In Chapter 2 a model of interaction is presented, which sets the study of interpersonal skill within the wider context of the social milieu. This illustrates how the appropriateness of social behaviour is determined by a number of variables relating to the context of the interaction, the roles of those involved and their goals, as well as personal features of the interactors (e.g. age, sex, personality, etc.). It is, therefore, impossible to legislate in advance for every social situation, in terms of what behaviours will be most successful to employ. The information about social skills contained in this book should rather be regarded as providing resource material for the reader. How these resources are employed is a decision for the reader, given the situation in which any particular interaction is taking place.

There are twelve main skill areas covered in this text, beginning with nonverbal communication in Chapter 3. This aspect of social interaction is the first to be examined, since all of the social skills which follow contain nonverbal elements and so an understanding of the main facets of this channel facilitates the examination of all of the social skills. Chapter 4 incorporates an analysis of the skill of reinforcement, while the skill of questioning is reviewed in Chapter 5. In Chapter 6, an alternative strategy to questioning, namely reflecting, is investigated. Reflection consists of concentrating on what another person is saying and reflecting back to him the central elements of his statements. Two important episodes in any action – the opening and closing sequences – are reviewed in Chapter 7, while the skill of explaining is focused upon in Chapter 8. The skill of listening is explored in Chapter 9, where the active nature of listening is emphasised. In Chapter 10, self-disclosure is examined from two perspectives; first, the appropriateness of self-disclosure by the professional, and second, methods for promoting maximum self-disclosure from clients. A skill area which has attracted growing interest in recent years, that of influencing, is covered in Chapter 11. Techniques for protecting personal rights are discussed in Chapter 12 in terms of the skill of assertiveness. Finally, in Chapter 13 the skills involved in interacting in, and leading, small group discussions are examined.

It should be realised that research in the field of social interaction is progressing rapidly and it is anticipated that, as our knowledge of this area increases, other important skill areas will be identified. The skills contained in this book do not represent a completely comprehensive list of all of the skills which have been identified to date, but they are generally regarded as being the central skills of interpersonal communication. In addition, it is recognised that, while these skills are studied separately, in practice they often overlap and seldom occur in isolation. Rather, the skills complement one another, and a knowledge of the repertoire of skilled behaviours outlined should enable the reader to extend and refine his own pattern or style of interaction.

Chapter 2

Interpersonal communication
A skill-based model

INTRODUCTION

What happens when two people meet and initiate a social encounter can be accounted for in different ways depending upon the particular theoretical perspective which one brings to bear upon such activity (Turner, 1988). One possibility, as we have seen, is to explain what transpires in terms of participants behaving skilfully in order to accomplish sought-after goals. Several performative features of skill in this sense were also outlined in the last chapter. In sum, this type of behaviour can be thought of as an efficient and effective way of achieving warrantable outcomes. Furthermore, behaving in this manner should be in keeping with the rules and conventions which govern acceptable conduct in that particular context. Let us take the example of a community nurse faced with the task of getting an elderly and somewhat recalcitrant patient to take medication as prescribed. Let us also assume that the nurse discovers that the most efficient (in terms of both time taken to complete the task and effort expended in so doing) and effective means (in terms of likelihood of success) of getting this particular patient to comply is by offering the threat of physical violence upon failure to do so. While the threat may be delivered with considerable aplomb, and have its desired effect, this type of 'patient management' would scarcely be sanctioned as a piece of highly skilled practice in the professional context within which it was embedded. Skilled behaviour must be appropriate given the situation.

Much of what has already been said has been about communication. It is difficult to imagine any type of sustained and meaningful interpersonal contact which is not premised upon those taking part communicating with each other. But what in fact is communication? The first part of this chapter will be given over to addressing this question. Having done so, a skill-based, theoretical model of the communicative process will be developed which highlights its transactional nature. What takes place when two people interact is presented as being undergirded by a complex of perceptual, cognitive, affective and performative factors operating within a person–situation framework. The activity is held to be energised and given direction by the desire to achieve set goals and is accomplished by the ongoing monitoring of both personal and environmental circumstances, including, of course, those represented by the other interactor sharing the encounter. Before proceeding with the model, however, we need to give more careful thought to the notion of communication.

COMMUNICATION AND INTERPERSONAL COMMUNICATION

At first blush, the term 'communication' seems commonplace and unproblematic. We can all readily recognise and attach meaning to it. But probing more deeply, what is the phenomenon being referred to? How does it operate? These are some of the questions to be taken up in this sub-section.

Picking up on the first question, maybe the most immediately striking feature of communication is its ubiquity – it appears to be everywhere and ever present (Dickson *et al.*, 1989). Consider part of the working day of Mr Topman, the Managing Director of a light engineering firm. His first task, upon arrival at work, is going through the morning's mail. He then dictates letters on matters arising, faxes some urgent material to suppliers in the USA, and makes several telephone calls before chairing the first meeting of the day with his executive team. After lunch, he and his financial adviser discuss the quarterly financial statement. At 2.30pm, his personal assistant informs him that the sales manager has just arrived for his appraisal interview. That over, he meets with Mrs Brightside who looks after the firm's public relations. An article which he had read in the local paper on his way to work that morning had troubled him. It hinted that the firm may be on the verge of shedding up to 25 per cent of its workforce with devastating effects for the local community. A press release is prepared and it is decided that Mr Topman should go on local radio that evening to quash the rumour. A truly busy day and all of it communication centred – but communication in many and diverse forms.

In this book our interest is largely restricted to interpersonal communication, i.e. communication which is face-to-face and involving few people (typically two) rather than large groups. Returning to Mr Topman, we can therefore largely disregard representational media (e.g. letters, reports, newspapers, files, etc.) and mechanical/electronic media (e.g. fax, radio, etc.) to concentrate primarily on the sorts of processes that characterised his encounters with his financial adviser, sales manager and public relations officer.

Ellis and Beattie (1986) describe communication as a 'fuzzy' concept with boundaries that are blurred and uncertain. This has created difficulties when it comes to reaching agreement over matters of formal definition. Holli and Calabrese (1991) attribute the problem to the vast range of activities that can be legitimately subsumed under this label. Indeed the *Journal of Communication* has published no fewer than fifteen different working definitions of human communication (Samovar and Mills, 1986). The fact that we are concentrating upon interpersonal communication simplifies things to some extent. What we have in mind can be essentially thought of, in the words of Brooks and Heath (1985, p. 8) as, 'the process by which information, meanings and feelings are shared by persons through the exchange of verbal and nonverbal messages'. (We will return to definitional issues later in this sub-section.) Several features of interpersonal communication are intimated in this definition. It is worthwhile exploring these, and several other commonly mentioned aspects, in greater detail.

Communication is a process

According to Holli and Calabrese (1991), one of the themes that the definitional variants share is the notion of communication as a process of sending and receiving messages. Wiemann and Giles (1988), for instance, place great emphasis on this aspect. Communication requires that at least two contribute to the ongoing and dynamic sequence of events in which each affects and is affected by the other in a system of reciprocal determination. As we shall see shortly, each at the same time perceives the other in context, makes some sort of sense of what is happening, comes to a decision as to how to react and responds accordingly.

 Being more specific, the components of the communicative process, in its simplest form, have been identified as including communicators, message, medium, channel, noise, feedback and context (Fiske, 1982; Gudykunst, 1991).

Communicators

The indispensability of communicators to the process is fairly obvious. In early models of how communication took place (e.g. Shannon and Weaver, 1949), one was designated the *Source*, the other the *Receiver*, and the process was held to commence when the former transmitted a message to the latter. More recently the over-simplicity of this thinking has been recognised. Communicators are at one and the same time senders and receivers of messages. While person A speaks, she is also typically monitoring the effects of her utterance and, in so doing, is receiving information from B. Likewise, person B, in listening to A, is also reacting to A's contribution, even if only to ostensibly ignore it. The notion of 'source-receiver' is therefore a more accurate representation of the role of each participant (DeVito, 1986).

Message

The message can be thought of as the content of communication embodying whatever it is that communicators wish to share. Gouran (1990, p. 6) describes it as, 'a pattern of thought, configuration of ideas, or other response to internal conditions about which individuals express themselves'. Such expression, however, presupposes some form of behavioural manifestation: thoughts and feelings, to be made known, must be encoded or organised into a physical form capable of being transmitted to others. Decoding is the counterpart of encoding whereby recipients attach meaning to what they have just experienced (O'Hair and Friedrich, 1992).

Medium

The medium is the particular means of conveying the message. As a system of symbols or codes it can take the form of morse code, semaphore or the English language, for instance. In the plural, 'media' has come to take on a rather special institutionalised meaning, referring to TV, radio, the press and such like.

Channel

Differences between this and the notion of medium are sometimes blurred in the literature. 'Channel' refers to that which 'connects' communicators and accommodates the medium. DeVito (1986, p. 8) describes it as operating like a 'bridge connecting source and receiver'. Fiske (1982) gives as examples light waves, sound waves, radio waves as well as cables of different types, capable of carrying pulses of light or electrical energy. Likewise, DeVito (1986) talks about the vocal-auditory channel which carries speech, the gestural-visual channel which facilitates much nonverbal communication, the chemical-olfactory channel accommodating smell and the cutaneous-tactile channel which enables us to make interpersonal use of touch.

These different channels may be utilised simultaneously, and typically are, in the course of face-to-face communication.

Noise

In this sense the word has a rather special meaning which is more than mere sound. It refers to any interference with the success of the communicative act thereby distorting the message so that the meaning intended is not that gleaned. As such, noise may originate in the source, the channel, the receiver, or the context within which participants interact. It may take the form of intrusive sound, which masks what is being said, or it may stem from the unique life experiences of the participants. It is, of course, in accordance with these life experiences that the processes of encoding and decoding messages are accomplished. Where ethnic or cultural differences intrude, meanings attached to particular choices of word or forms of expression can vary considerably causing unintended confusion, misunderstanding, insult or hurt

(Gudykunst, 1991). In sum, and as Kreps and Thornton (1992) remind us, meanings are ultimately in people rather than in words.

Feedback

By means of feedback, the sender is able to judge the extent to which the message has been successfully received and the impact that it has had. Monitoring receiver reactions enables subsequent communications to be adapted and regulated to achieve a desired effect. Feedback, therefore, is vitally important to successful social outcomes. It plays a central role in the model of skilful interaction to be elaborated in the second half of the chapter and more will be said about it then.

Context

All communication takes place within a context and is crucially influenced by it (Fisher, 1987). To be more accurate, communication takes place within intermeshing frameworks. An inescapable instance, geographical location, provides a physical setting for what takes place. People in lifts often behave in rather restrained ways which match the physical constraints of their surroundings, for example.

Then again, all encounters occur within a temporal context. A class may be held late on a Friday afternoon or early on Monday morning and the vigour and enthusiasm of the discussion may be influenced as a result. Individuals often describe themselves as 'morning', 'afternoon' or indeed 'evening people'. Some may even organise their workload, in as much as it is possible to do so, along these lines.

Relationship provides a further context for interaction. In a fascinating study of touch among opposite sex couples in public, Willis and Briggs (1992) found that males tended to initiate touch during courtship while, amongst married couples, females were more inclined to take the initiative. We can additionally think of a range of psychosocial factors such as status relationship, which constitute a different, but equally significant framework for communication.

So far, context has been depicted as exerting an influence upon communication. But it should not be overlooked that, in many respects, interactors, through communication, can also serve to shape aspects of their situation. The concept of context features prominently in the model to be developed shortly and will be returned to there.

Communication is transactional

As mentioned earlier, communication was viewed by early theorists, such as Shannon and Weaver (1949), as a fundamentally linear process, in that a message was formulated by the source and sent to the receiver. This view has given way to a more transactional conceptualisation which stresses the dynamic and changing nature of the process. Communicators affect, and are affected by each other, in a system of reciprocal influence (Myers and Myers, 1985).

Communication is inevitable

This is a contentious point. Communication is held, by those theorists who adopt a broad view of what constitutes the phenomenon (e.g. Watzlawick *et al.*, 1967; Scheflen, 1974), to be inevitable in social situations where those present are aware of one another's presence and are influenced in what they do as a result. For Carson (1969, p. 18), 'To the extent that one person's behaviour is contingent on that of another – to the extent that interpersonal influence, however slight has occurred – we will regard communication as having taken place between them'. Likewise, Watzlawick *et al.* (1967, p. 49) are responsible for the much quoted maxim that, under such circumstances, 'one cannot *not* communicate'. Imagine the situation where shy boy and attractive girl are seated opposite each other in the railway carriage. Attractive girl 'catches' shy boy eyeing her legs. She eases her skirt over her knees. Their eyes meet, shy boy blushes and they both look away in embarrassment. Has communication taken place between them or can their reactions be at best described as merely expressive or informative?

Others define communication in a much more restrictive manner. According to Ekman and Friesen (1969) communication presupposes conscious intention on the part of the encoder who behaves in such a way as to send a message to the receiver. But does the encoder have to be consciously aware of the intention? What if the decoder fails to recognise that the witnessed behaviour was enacted intentionally and reacts (or fails to act) accordingly? Has communication still occurred in this case? We will return to the issue of conscious involvement in the following sub-section.

Wiener *et al.* (1972) also restrict communication to a particular sub-set of behaviour, namely behaviour which is in keeping with some socially shared code according to which symbols take on meaning. But again, how widely shared must a code be for it to be accepted? How formally recognised must it be to count as a code?

Communication is purposeful

Another commonly cited characteristic of communication is its purposefulness. Those who take part do so with some end in mind; they want to effect some desired outcome (Berger, 1989). According to this functional view of the phenomenon, communication is far from idle or aimless but is conducted in the hope of making something happen, achieving a goal of some sort. It is this which both adds impetus and provides direction to the transaction.

A pivotal implication of casting communication as purposeful activity is, according to Kellermann (1992), that it must also be thought of as what she calls 'adjusted'. That is, communicators fashion what they say and do, on an ongoing basis, in response to the goals that they are pursuing and within the constraints which are operative. This stance is consonant with that of Winograd (1981) who proposed that everything uttered by a participant during the course of a social encounter was the final output of a design process with the object of realising a goal.

Adjusted performance presupposes the possibility of selection and choice amongst alternative courses of action. Following this line of argument further, making decisions on the basis of the estimated likelihood of effecting a sought-after outcome leads inevitably to the conclusion that communication is a strategic enterprise. For Kellermann (1992) this is one of its most characteristic attributes.

Is consciousness entailed by this line of thought? For Borden (1972) the answer is in the affirmative; purposive behaviour implies consciousness. Likewise, Klinger et al. (1981) believe that convictions of the existence of unconscious goals do not match the evidence, concluding that 'life would be far more chaotic than it is if substantial portions of people's goal strivings were for goals about which the striver was unconscious' (p. 171). Emmons (1989) has summarised this thinking by suggesting that it is commonly accepted that people have considerable access to their goals and can readily report them but are less aware of the underlying motivational basis upon which they are founded.

On the other hand it has been argued that much of communication is, to use the term employed by Langer et al. (1978), 'mindless'. They distinguished between *mindful* activity where 'people attend to their world and derive behavioural strategies based upon current incoming information' and *mindlessness* where 'new information is not actually being processed. Instead prior scripts, written when similar information was once new, are stereotypically reenacted' (p. 636). Kellermann (1992) argues vigorously that communication is at one and the same time purposeful/strategic *and* also primarily automatic. It is possible, she maintains, for intentional behaviour to be monitored outwith the stream of conscious awareness.

Pausing for a moment to reflect upon our own experiences, we can probably think of occasions when we are acutely mindful of 'thinking on our feet' as we try to formulate some coherent strategy for handling an awkward, threatening or perhaps simply unaccustomed situation. (Indeed we may become extremely aware of trying to decide what we should be trying to do in this situation – what our goal should be!) These occasions contrast sharply with more prosaic encounters, perhaps with old and familiar friends, when the evening just seems to slip 'mindlessly' past, for the most part, in relaxed and easy conversation with little awareness of the thought processes that lead to the introduction of topics or the interpretation of episodes.

Motley (1992) mentions circumstances under which we tend to become aware of customarily non-conscious encoding decisions. These include situations of conflict between two or more message goals; anticipations of undesirable consequences for a formulated or preformulated version of a message, thus requiring reformulation; some unexpected intervention (perhaps due to a failed attempt to 'take the floor' or experiencing the 'tip-of-the-tongue' phenomenon) between the initial decision to transmit a message and the opportunity to do so; and the goals of the communication being difficult to actualise or the situation troublesome in some other way.

The level at which cognitive processing is focused upon is also a factor in the likelihood of communication being found to be mindless. We may be very aware of considering alternative approaches to a problem but, once we have plumped for a line of attack, less so of the detail of the specific tactics which will be utilised. We will probably have very little awareness, if any (barring some of the special circumstances outlined above), of encoding decisions to do with choice of particular word in the implementation of these tactics. Likewise on the decoding side, we are more inclined to consider the gist of an important message consciously than, let's say, the nuances of its phonetic production (unless one happens to be a speech therapist interacting with a patient, of course).

In sum, describing communication as purposeful does not imply that the entirety of the communicative act must necessarily have prominence in the ongoing stream of consciousness. While intention, control and awareness are central to general conceptualisations of communication as skilled activity, it seems that many well-rehearsed sequences can be run off with only limited awareness (Berscheid, 1983). When skills are well-honed, they can often be executed on the 'back burner' of conscious thought. But the success of the encounter may be compromised as a result. Langer (1992) stresses that

> Without an awareness of the language choices I am making when I speak, I am left out of a process that would personally benefit me. Without an awareness of the choices I could make when I listen to others, the costs increase. . . . A mindful approach to language, where the individual is aware of alternative perspectives and conceptions of what is being said, would yield more control for the individual.

(p. 327)

Communication is multi-dimensional

Another significant feature of communication is its multi-dimensionality – messages exchanged are seldom unitary or discrete. Watzlawick *et al.* (1967) drew attention to the fact that the process takes place at two separate but interrelated levels. One concerns content and has to do with substantive matters – with discussing last night's TV programme, deciding which restaurant to go to, explaining the Theory of Relativity, and innumerable other similar quests. These issues form the topic of conversation and it is usually they that spring to mind when we think of what we do when communicating.

But this is seldom, if ever, *all* that we do when communicating. There is another, although less conspicuous side to the activity, involving such matters as identity projection together with relationship negotiation and how interactors define their association. In the choice of topic for discussion (and topics avoided), particular words and forms of expression adopted, manicured accents, speed of speech and a whole complex of nonverbal behaviours and characteristics, interactors work at what is sometimes called *self-presentation* or *impression management* (Goffman, 1959). This has to do with publicly presenting one's self in a positive light, as an essentially desirable type of person.

Succeeding in conveying the right impression can confer several sorts of possible advantage (Schlenker, 1986). It can lead to material rewards as well as social benefits such as approval, friendship and power. Goffman (1959) emphasised the importance of social actors maintaining *face*, which can be thought of as a statement of the positive value claimed for themselves – a public expression of self-worth. He observed that actors characteristically engage not only in self-focused facework but are careful not to invalidate the face being presented by their partner. In a highly influential book chapter, Brown and Levinson (1978) analysed how politeness operates as a strategy intended to reduce the likelihood of this being thought to happen.

Communication also serves relational ends in other ways by helping determine how participants define their association *vis-à-vis*, for instance, degree of affiliation, status relationship and the balance of power enjoyed. Status differences are often negotiated and maintained by subtle (and not so subtle) means. The two directives, 'Pass the salt' and 'I wonder would you mind passing the salt, please' are functionally equivalent on the content dimension – the speaker obviously wishes the person addressed to make the salt available – but a quite different type of relationship is presupposed in each case.

Power is also implicated. When people with relatively little social power, occupying inferior status positions, interact with those enjoying power over them, the former manifest their increased 'accessibility' by, among other things, being asked more questions, providing more self-disclosures, initiating fewer topics for discussion, being more hesitant in what they say, engaging in less eye contact while speaking, using politer forms of address, and being more likely to be touched than touching (Berger, 1985; Argyle, 1988). Sets of expectations are constructed around these parameters. It is not only the case that people with little power behave in these ways, there are norms or implicit expectations that they *should* do so. Failure to comply constitutes a contravention of an (usually) unspoken or unwritten 'rule' that governs social conduct and incurs 'penalties'. At the least the reputation of the miscreant will suffer; they will be seen to be less worthy social animals

(Harré, 1979). While it is perfectly acceptable for the teacher to praise a junior pupil for a commendable effort in class, were the pupil to address the teacher in like manner it would be seen as presumptuous or even discourteous – a just cause for a reprimand to be delivered.

These two communicative dimensions, content and relationship, are complexly interwoven and interrelated. Wilmot (1987) proposed that every statement has a relational significance and that the orchestrating of relationships is typically achieved in this 'indirect' way. While the relationship may become the topic of conversation, i.e. form the content of talk, this seldom happens. We will extend this line of thought when we come shortly to discuss the concept of goals.

Communication is irreversible

Simply put, once something is said it cannot be 'taken back'. It could be perhaps a confidence that was broken by a secret being revealed, but once that revelation has taken place it cannot be undone.

This is not to deny that the personal and relational consequences of the act can be retrieved. We can work at redefining what has taken place in order to make it more palatable and ourselves less blameworthy. The *account* is one mechanism which can be used to this end. Accounts can be regarded as explanations for troublesome acts. Two possibilities discussed by McLaughlin *et al.* (1983) are justifications and excuses. In the case of the latter the untoward action is attributed to the intervention of some external influence, e.g. that the information was extracted under threat or torture. Nevertheless, once information is in the public domain it cannot be privatised.

A SKILL MODEL OF INTERPERSONAL COMMUNICATION

Having spent some time outlining key characteristics of interpersonal communication, we will continue by exploring the crucial components and processes which underpin skilled dyadic (two-person) interaction. In so doing, we will build upon a conceptual model put forward by Hargie and Marshall (1986) and Dickson *et al.* (1993), based upon earlier theorising by Argyle (1983b).

The model presented in Figure 2.1 identifies six elements of skilled interpersonal interaction. These are:

1 person–situation context
2 goal
3 mediating processes
4 response
5 feedback
6 perception

By way of an overview, the model rests upon three basic assumptions. The first is that, as has already been claimed, people act purposefully. Second, that they are sensitive to the effects of their action. And third, that they take steps to modify subsequent action in the light of this information. In keeping with the model, dyadic interaction is depicted within a person–situation framework. What takes place when people come together and engage in communication is partly a feature of the particular attributes and characteristics that make each a unique individual, and partly due to the parameters of the shared situation within which they find themselves.

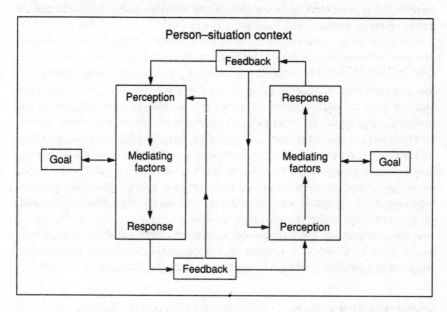

Figure 2.1 Skill model of interpersonal communication

One of the features of social activity is that it is goal-driven. Within this person–situation framework personal goals are established and pursued. What transpires is entered into in order to achieve some end-state even if this amounts to little more than the pleasure to be had from conversing. In a quest to realise the adopted goal, mediating processes are operationalised. Accordingly, possible strategies to actualise these outcomes may be formulated, their projected effects evaluated, and a decision on a plan of action derived. The implementation of this course of action will, in turn, be manifested in the responses which are made. The interactive nature of the process is such that each interactor, in reacting to the other, provides information of relevance in arriving at decisions on goal attainment. Additional to this mediated facility, each has a direct channel of feedback on performance enabling monitoring of self to take place.

While feedback makes information available, it can only be acted upon if it is actually received by the recipient. Perception is central to skilful interaction yet its intrinsically selective and inferential nature results, in many cases, in perceptual inaccuracy and miscommunication (Forgas, 1985; Hargie and Dickson, 1991). Notwithstanding, and by way of a summary, information stemming from perceptions of self, the situation and the other interactor, is considered in accordance with a complex of mediating processes the outcome of which is a plan to govern action. This plan of action, deemed to maximise opportunities for goal attainment under the prevailing circumstances, is represented in strategies to be behaviourally implemented in action, thereby determining individual responses.

It should be remembered that, first, due to the dynamic and changing character of communication, both participants are, at one and the same time, senders and receivers of information. Each is, even when silent, acting and reacting to the other. Second, as recognised by Trower et al. (1978), potential barriers to successful communication exist at each of the different stages outlined. This may be particularly pronounced when translated into a professional environment where, as noted by Barnlund (1976) with reference to health care, the complexities of problems faced, together with assessment, diagnosis and subsequent treatment, militate against the successful sharing of messages without ambiguity or information loss. Practitioners and patients typically differ in the language, concepts and knowledge base with which they respectively make sense of these matters.

A more detailed and systematic consideration of each of these components of the model will now be presented. Further information can be found in Hargie and Marshall (1986), Millar et al. (1992) and Dickson et al. (1993).

Person–situation context

As mentioned, that which ensues during interaction is partly due to participants and the personal 'baggage' that they bring to the encounter, including their knowledge, motives, values, emotions, attitudes, expectations and dispositions. The way in which they have come to regard themselves (their self-concept) and the beliefs that they have formed about their abilities to succeed in various types of enterprise (their feelings of self-efficacy) will also determine the sorts of encounters contemplated, how they are conducted and rewards derivable from them.

Interaction is also co-determined by parameters of the situation within which individuals find themselves, including role demands and the rules which pertain. Take, for example, a priest and a parishioner in the confessional. Each is personally unique, yet the respective roles offered by this highly restricted situation will mean that, regardless of the individuals involved, much the same sort of activity will be entered into by priests, on the one hand, and parishioners, on the other. Again, the implicit rules which dictate how both parties should conduct themselves under these circumstances will, by condoning certain actions and condemning others, regulate the interaction that unfolds.

Hargie and Marshall (1986) also discuss the potential effects which physical constraints of the environment, such as organisation of space and how it is adorned, can exert upon the communicative process.

These sources of influence are bi-directional. It is not only the case that personal characteristics and situational factors have a bearing on behaviour. What transpires during social contact can also effect changes in interactors. The manner in which the individual is typically reacted to by others, the interpersonal rewards that are enjoyed or punishments endured, can serve to mould how that person comes to regard herself. Thus involvement with others can lead to modifications in individual knowledge, beliefs and attitudes (indeed the success of educational and counselling endeavours typically depends on it) and can also, within limits, serve to redefine the social situation. Thus participants may decide to dispense with the customary formality surrounding certain situations such as the selection interview, summit meetings, etc., and turn the situation into a much more relaxed occasion. The successful relationship forged by Reagan and Gorbachev, which led to significant reductions in nuclear armaments and current improvements in East–West affairs, can be attributed to each being prepared and having the courage to countenance such a possibility.

Personal characteristics

Knowledge

Referring to the cognitive underpinning of communication, Hewes and Planalp (1987) distinguish between two basic interrelated components: first, cognitive processes, which have to do with the operations performed on incoming information including decoding meaning, memory storage, decision-making, etc.; second, knowledge structures, which are 'organised repositories of information about the world, including the social world, that inform experience and action' (p. 157). While the close interrelationship between them is acknowledged, it is only the latter that is relevant at this point. We will address the former when we come to discuss mediating processes.

Knowledge of our social world and how it operates, people and the circumstances in which they find themselves, together with shared communication codes, is fundamental to any contemplation of skilled interpersonal activity. Having relevant information upon which to draw is invaluable when deciding courses of action and pursuing them. Cody and McLaughlin (1985, p. 288) state that, 'The knowledge base concerning situations enables the individual to plan behaviour that may effectively produce a desired outcome.'

But the contribution of such an accumulated knowledge base is more wide-ranging. Indeed, it is drawn upon at every stage of the communication process from identifying goals which are likely to be within reach, through making sense of the situation and the actions of the other within it, to acting out a considered strategy. In relation to the latter, and within the context of conceptualisations of competence, a differentiation has been made between 'knowing that' and 'knowing how' (Fillmore, 1979). The latter is necessary for appropriate action to be conducted.

Psychologists and scholars of communication have made use of the notion of 'schema' in explaining how information is gleaned, stored, organised into a framework representing the world as experienced by the individual, and used to interpret current events (Roloff and Berger, 1982). Five main types of schemata have been identified; self-schemata have to do with our knowledge of ourselves (Markus, 1977); event schemata or scripts represent the sequences of events that characterise particular, frequently encountered, social occasions such as ordering a meal or buying a newspaper (Abelson, 1981); role schemata involve concepts according to which we expect people, based upon occupation, gender, race and so forth, to abide by certain norms and behave within set parameters of appropriate conduct (Brigham, 1991); causal schemata enable us to form judgements about cause–effect relationships in our physical and social environment, and to adopt courses of action based upon the anticipations which such schemata make possible (Tesser, 1978); people schemata are organised sets of knowledge about the features and characteristics of others and they therefore facilitate social categorisation.

A related, but somewhat more precise concept which has been used to explain how we structure information on others and categorise the social world in which we and they operate, is the prototype. Cantor (1981) defined it as 'an abstract set of features commonly associated with members of a category, with each feature assigned a weighting according to the degree of association with the category' (p. 27). Take the class of persons referred to as tramps. Our prototype might include looking dirty, dressing shabbily, being smelly, having unkempt hair, living on the street and begging. For any stranger whom we happen to meet on the street, the degree to which they concur with the prototype will determine whether we place them in this social category and view them as tramps.

Categorising others, and our social world, is inevitable. We simply would find it impossible to function if we regarded each and every person, object and occasion as unique and distinct. But placing people in categories can lead to the application of stereotypes, whereby individual characteristics are neglected and all members of the group are regarded, unjustifiably, in an undifferentiated manner, as sharing a set of generalised attributes. Such stereotypes may be widely held (social stereotypes) or peculiar to an individual (personal stereotypes) (Secord and Backman, 1974). Stereotypes can become self-fulfilling. If we regard all Germans as aggressive we may well act towards this German in a belligerent manner which could cause him to react in kind, hence confirming our stereotypical image.

Motives

Why do people do all of the things suggested as we have elaborated this model of skilled interaction? Why, indeed, take part in interaction at all? These are questions which address the issue of motivation. What directs and energises performance? What makes people do the things they do to, with and for others? A full consideration of these matters would take us well beyond the scope of this chapter. For our purposes, however, they can be scaled down to two vital and related issues. First, why do people adopt the goals that they do? Second, having done so, why do they continue to behave in accordance with them? The second question is probably easier to answer than the first.

Goals are taken to contribute both direction and impetus to the interactive process and therefore have inherent motivational implications. This basic proposition is embellished somewhat by Pervin (1989), in the suggestion that representations of end-states have both cognitive and affective features. The former specify the nature of that anticipated future state, while the latter address the extent and vigour of movement towards it. Persistence to achievement is an important characteristic of goal-directed behaviour and this motivational effect is perhaps the one that has received most attention from researchers. Once commitment to reach an outcome has been given, the normal development is for a course of action, designed to bring about that object or state of affairs, to be set in place and perpetuated, with continued checking to enable degree of success to be decided upon (Deci and Porac, 1978).

A number of theorists have invoked the concept of expectation in explaining why individuals persevere with action aimed at reaching a goal. According to expectancy-value theory, the strength of motivation is a joint feature of the value placed on the projected outcome together with the anticipation that that particular course of action will bring about the desired end-state. Vroom (1964) has tended to accentuate externally oriented benefits which will accrue following success, while others, including Atkinson and Raynor (1974) and Deci and Ryan (1985), have stressed the satisfaction of internally oriented needs such as feelings of achievement. Bandura (1986) takes a more extreme position proposing that it is not really goals *per se* that are the motivating factor but rather the individual's evaluation of performance against personal standards and the associated self-focused response of pride or self-criticism which results.

Not all goal aspirations, of course, are necessarily translated into action. Whether or not they are is dependent upon an appreciation of a variety of external and internal factors (Bandura, 1986). They include assessments of how conducive environmental circumstances are at that time to goal achievement together with judgements of self-efficacy which determine the extent to which individuals concerned believe that they have the abilities and resources at hand to succeed.

We have already touched on some of the proposed reasons why goals are formulated in the first place. Many accounts refer to the notion of need. Indeed, Guirdham (1990) regards motives as the internal responses to needs. Dillard (1990) believes, in turn, that goals reflect broad underlying motives. But what are these underlying needs that impel us to establish goals in directing our activities with others? Again, different classificatory systems exist. Emmons (1989), nevertheless, believes that in essence these can be rendered down to three basic concerns: the need to feel in control and to be able to predict events of which one is part; the need for a sense of belonging to and intimate involvement with others, making possible approval from them; and the need to exercise mastery and display competence in one's strivings thereby experiencing a sense of self-worth. These three fundamental needs have also been posited by other theorists to account for our dealings with others (Deci, 1992).

On a broader front, a range of physiological and safety needs can also be thought of as determining what we seek from our environment (Maslow, 1954). We are obviously motivated to meet our biological needs for food, drink, sex, etc. and to protect ourselves from physical harm.

Attitudes

We have considered the knowledge and motives with which individuals approach social encounters as influencing how they act and react and hence the patterns of communication which result. Attitudes held are another highly significant personal characteristic. One popular way of thinking about attitudes is in terms of three constituent elements – one cognitive, one affective and the third behavioural (Katz and Stotland, 1959). To be more precise, the cognitive aspect rests upon knowledge or beliefs about the target in question which may be a person, object, event or indeed any attribute of these. The affective component describes how one feels about the target, while the behavioural element has to do with one's predisposition to behave in a certain way towards it. I may have a particular attitude towards my next-door neighbour such that I believe that he is jealous of me and out to do me down (cognitive) which makes me dislike him (affective) so I avoid his company (behavioural). Note, however, that attitudes only define a tendency to behave in a particular way. In any situation there may not be a direct correspondence between attitude and actual behaviour. Attitudes interact with other personal characteristics including motives, values and other attitudes, together with situational factors, to determine behaviour (Brigham, 1991). Thus, while I have a certain predisposition to avoid my neighbour, in keeping with my attitude towards him, the fact that

I need to borrow his lawnmower and it is now spring may make me loath to shun him completely.

Personality

Personality is the complex of unique features of an individual which shape interaction with the environment and ability to relate to oneself and others (Harré and Lamb, 1986). Extroversion–Introversion is one frequently cited dimension which has been used to differentiate people (Eysenck and Eysenck, 1963) and which has implications for communicative behaviour. There is some evidence that introverts, compared to extroverts, tend to speak less, make more frequent use of pauses, engage in lower frequencies of gaze at their partners, are less accurate at encoding emotion and prefer to interact at greater interpersonal distances (Giles and Street, 1985).

Affect

So far it might seem that our view of the interactor is largely of a completely rational, information-processing automaton, completely devoid of any sort of emotional dimension to his or her existence. Affect is obviously central to interpersonal life. Just how emotion operates though, and the contributions of physiological constituents on the one hand, and social determinants on the other, is a matter of ongoing debate (Bowers *et al.*, 1985). In one often cited theory, Schachter and Singer (1962) proposed that visceral reactions had consequences for experienced levels of arousal. The individual attached meaning to these sensations by searching the environment for likely explanations. The identification of the emotional state was arrived at through this cognitive mediation and the appropriate behaviour enacted as a consequence.

Although, in the intervening years, this particular theory has attracted some criticism, many readily acknowledge that cognitive processes have a crucial part to play in emotional experiences. We cannot completely separate the affective and the cognitive – how we feel from how and what we think (Winton, 1990). Both are inextricably intertwined in thinking and feeling.

In an extremely informative review, Bowers *et al.* (1985) sketched the comprehensive impact of affect upon interpersonal communication, both in respect of isolated encounters and in the forming, maintaining and terminating of relationships. Much of this operates at the nonverbal level, intentionally and unintentionally, through paralinguistic and kinesic cues, and as such will be taken up in the following chapter.

Sociodemographic characteristics

A range of sociodemographic characteristics which also impact upon interpersonal behaviour and which include race/culture, age and gender, has been discussed by Giles and Street (1985), Hargie and Marshall (1986) and Millar *et al.* (1992). Much of this discussion has centred around effects on nonverbal behaviour and again will be explored in the following chapter.

Situational factors

It will be recalled that personal characteristics and situational factors operate to provide a contextual backdrop for communication. Acting conjointly they determine how people conduct themselves during social episodes. Witt (1991) discovered that whether telephonists presented a formal or informal public image when answering the telephone (according to self-reports) was a function of experienced mood (personal characteristic) and role ambiguity (situational factor). A more formal image was presented by those who experienced little role ambiguity and positive mood state.

Both features of the person and the situation may, within limits, be subject to change as a result of interaction. Having identified a number of key personal features that operate, we will now turn our attention to an analysis of the situation.

Several attempts have been made to delineate the essential constituents of situations. Perhaps the simplest is that by Pervin (1978) who proposed that (a) who is involved, (b) what is happening and (c) where the action is taking place, are what matter.

Moos (1973) provided a more elaborate taxonomy according to which six facets of situations or 'environments' can be isolated. These are (1) ecological dimensions, indicating geographical, meteorological, architectural and design aspects; (2) behavioural setting, which may be a classroom or a cathedral, and which encompasses both physical attributes and sets of expectations as to the appropriateness of courses of action; (3) organisational structure, such as number of employees, how they are organised in relation to each other, and the channels of communication available; (4) personnel, the personal and sociodemographic characteristics of those in the situation; (5) institutional climate, which covers such features as openness, participation, and trust; and (6) rewardingness, or the availability and patterns of distri-bution of rewards in the situation.

A more highly differentiated analysis of social situations, derived from extensive research, is that offered by Argyle *et al.* (1981). They identified no fewer than eight key features of the situations within which people interact. Many of these will be familiar, however, from what has already been said about the personal characteristics of situated individuals, again emphasising the close interrelationship between these two dimensions. The elements delineated by Argyle *et al.* (1981) will now be briefly outlined.

1 *Goal structure*. Situations have goal implications. Not only will we seek out situations with goal satisfaction in mind, but particular situations will place constraints on the goals that can be legitimately pursued.

2 *Roles.* In any situation individuals act in accordance with more or less clearly recognised sets of expectations centring upon their social position and status.

3 *Rules.* Situations are rule-governed. There are (often implicit) stipulations which govern what is acceptable conduct for participants. It is perfectly acceptable for two friends at a disco to wear revealing clothes, sing, dance and shout. Were such behaviour translocated to a cathedral service it would be in strict contravention of the contrasting rules which pertain in that situation.

4 *Repertoire of elements.* This refers to the range of behaviour which may be called upon for the situation to be competently handled.

5 *Sequences of behaviour.* In certain situations interaction may unfold in a quite predictable sequence of acts on the part of participants. We have already mentioned how people often function in highly routine instances according to scripts.

6 *Situational concepts.* Again we have come across this basic notion of individuals possessing knowledge which enables them to make sense of situations and perform appropriately in them, when we introduced the notion of a schema.

7 *Language and speech.* There are linguistic variations associated with social situations. Some, for example public speaking, require a more formal speech style than others, such as having a casual conversation.

8 *Physical environment.* The physical setting, as mentioned by Moos (1973), and including furniture, decor, lighting, layout, etc., may well influence who talks with whom, how they feel, how much they say and how the talk is regulated (Knapp and Hall, 1992).

Having considered the person–situation context of communication in some detail, it is time to move on to explore the other components of the model.

Goals

This concept has already been introduced in an earlier section when its motivational role was examined. Here we will extend that discussion. Following Dillard (1990, p. 70), we can think of goals quite simply as 'desired future states which an individual is committed to achieving or maintaining'. One of the assumptions underlying any goals-based account of human endeavour is, in the view of Dillard, that individuals are typically striving to actualise a multiplicity of outcomes in their dealings with their material and interpersonal environs, and often concurrently. Referring back to what was said earlier about the multi-dimensionality of communication, Tracy and Coupland (1990) believe that one of the most basic distinctions is that between *task goals* and *face goals* or *relational goals*. In certain situations it may be difficult to satisfy both and yet vitally important to do so.

In an interesting analysis of the talk between a female practitioner and those undergoing a routine gynaecological examination, Ragan (1990) identified what she labelled 'verbal play' episodes which were entered into at junctures during the procedure. These seemed to acknowledge and meet the face needs of both participants and 'serve to mitigate the intrinsic conflict between medical and face goals in the gynaecological exam' (p. 81).

The distinction accentuated by Kellermann (1992), on the other hand, is between goals which are intrinsic to the interaction and those which are extrinsic. Coordination of communication with the other is an example of the former, while the latter have to do with states of affairs that the participant is motivated to bring about as a result of communicating.

Along similar lines, Ruffner and Burgoon (1981) talk of goals which are instrumental and those which are consummatory. Instrumental goals are carried out in order to achieve some further outcome: e.g. a supervisor may reward effort to increase productivity. Consummatory communication, on the other hand, satisfies the communicator's goal without the *active* intervention of another: e.g. the supervisor may reward because it makes him feel good to distribute largesse.

Goals can be organised according to at least three dimensions. First, they can be hierarchically structured. This possibility is a common theme in the literature although some authors have formulated more complex arrangements than others. Indeed, and as recognised by von Cranach *et al.* (1982, p.7), 'The goal hierarchy is theoretically unlimited, but higher and highest goals in it may be of a more general nature, and, in life, are almost impossible to distinguish from "values".' Dillard (1990) believes that a three-level structure is adequate, with broad motives leading to goals which, in turn, govern sub-goals.

A second dimension along which goals can be placed is that of importance. Quite simply, more weight will be attached to some goals than others, and it will be these which have most impact upon action at any particular juncture. The processes involved in goal selection have been discussed by such as Deci and Porac (1978) and Locke and Latham (1984). Decisions reached depend very much on the psychological value attached to the accomplishment of that outcome, estimates of the likelihood of various anticipated courses of action being successful in this respect, projected immediacy of gratification, possible costs which may ensue, and so on. The value or valence of an outcome, as has been suggested, is ultimately a feature of the anticipated satisfaction of particular motives and the needs which give rise to them.

One implication of recognising that goals differ in importance, coupled with the assertion that interactors are typically pursuing several goals at the same time, is the need for a prioritising mechanism to regulate goal selection. There must be some form of ongoing assessment and reprioritising as certain outcomes are achieved, others possibly abandoned, and as circumstances alter. These circumstances, of course, include the participation of the interactive partner. In their investigation of goal management during contrived conversations between mainly strangers, one of the most striking outcomes reported by Waldron *et al.* (1990) was the greater importance of ongoing adjustment to changing circumstances rather than the deployment of fixed, predetermined plans.

Dillard (1990) mentions a third, temporal dimension to goals. This, together with hierarchical orderings, is in keeping with the views of Hargie and Marshall (1986) when they talk about long-term and short-term goals. The example they give is of a personnel officer interviewing a job applicant. The principal goal directing this activity is, of course, to reach a proper decision as to the suitability of the interviewee. An appropriate short-term goal might be to establish rapport and put the candidate at ease. Actions are generally under the immediate control of goals at this level although long-term goals must not be lost sight of (von Cranach *et al.*, 1982).

In discussing the nature of goals, Schlenker and Weigold (1989) make the further point that they may be quite precise and clearly specified or rather vague and indeterminate. Thus a junior nurse may have as a goal to be more assertive in transactions with other staff, or to politely but firmly refuse to swap shifts with Doreen the next time she asks! In the context of the identification of objectives for educational or therapeutic interventions, one of the commonly accepted recommendations is that they be precisely articulated in assessable terms (Millar *et al.*, 1992).

We have paid scant regard to the fact that, as suggested in the model in Figure 2.1, both parties involved in communication are likely to be acting in pursuit of goals. How these different goals relate has obvious and extremely important implications for the encounter and what transpires. Wilensky (1983) proposed that they may be either: (a) competitive, in which case they will be negatively related in that the goals of one interactor can only be satisfied at the expense of those of the other, or (b) concordant, where the relationship is positive and the achievement of one person's goal will facilitate the others.

An important part of the initial contact with clients in different professional settings is the business of locating, clarifying and establishing the suitability and compatibility of expectations (Saunders, 1986). Dinkmeyer (1971) called the creation of this framework of common purpose 'goal alignment', and without it little of benefit can be contemplated. In many instances, this agreement is formalised in the business of contracting (Lang and van der Molen, 1990).

Mediating processes

These mediate between the goal which is being pursued; perceptions of the situation, including the other interactor and events taking place, some of which may be occasioned by our preceding actions and hence provide feedback; and how we behave. They also, as we have seen, play a part in the formulation of goals, influence the way in which people and events are perceived and reflect the capacity of the individual to assimilate, deal with and respond to the circumstances of social encounters.

Some of the *intrapersonal* components of interpersonal interaction operating at this stage are discussed by Kreps (1988) in terms of the organisation, processing and evaluation of information, the formulation or reassessment of alternative ways of reaction, decision-making and the selection of action strategies. It is these action strategies, or plans for action, that Argyle (1983b) regards as the essential contribution of this stage to the overall process of interaction.

Hewes and Planalp (1987) have also deliberated on the cognitive processes that enable strategic action to be undertaken. It will be recalled that they differentiated between these processes and the sorts of knowledge structures discussed in the earlier section as instances of personal characteristics. (It should also be remembered that cognitive processes and knowledge structures are closely interdependent.) For them, one of the most basic properties of communication is impact. Unless A's behaviour has had an impact on B by making a difference to what B does, thinks or feels, communication cannot be held to have taken place. The impact of a message,

> depends on the degree to which it is the focus of attention, how it is stored and retrieved from memory, how it is integrated with other messages and prior knowledge, what inferences are drawn from it, how it is chosen from among possible alternatives and how it is implemented.
>
> (Hewes and Planalp, 1987, p. 161)

More specifically, the following processes have been identified by Hewes and Planalp as central. They are:

1 *Focusing* – the selective attention paid to certain messages or elements of a message.
2 *Integration* – the assimilation of information into existing knowledge structures of the physical and social world. In conversation, successful speakers often build cues into their message to reduce ambiguity and enable the listener to interpret the message as intended.
3 *Inference* – making use of existing knowledge and frames of reference to go beyond the given in the message to fill in 'the gaps', e.g. Jane goes to Janet's house to ask her out to play. She rings the bell. Janet's mother answers the door.

Jane: 'Can Janet come out to play?'
Mother: 'Janet hasn't finished her homework.'
Jane: 'OK, I'll call back later.'

4 *Storage* – for communication to have any enduring effect some sort of representation of it must be encoded in memory.

5 *Retrieval* – being stored is one thing, but we must be able to retrieve it. No doubt we can all reflect on instances where we were frustratingly unable to recall a piece of information that we 'knew'. Knowledge structures exert considerable influence on memory both in the initial storage and retrieval.
6 *Selection* – not all messages that are accessible will be acted upon. The selection of courses of action to pursue, and the decision-making that may be entailed, is one of the higher-order cognitive activities that form part of interaction.
7 *Implementation* – this refers to the carrying out of the chosen plan of action and will be considered when we come to discuss responses.

As noted, the cognitive processes identified by Kreps (1988) and by Hewes and Planalp (1987) differ in the demands made on thinking capacity. Some, such as paying attention and attaching meaning, are relatively low-order and typically take place automatically or 'mindlessly'. Indeed these simple features of the decoding of information are quite often discussed under the aegis of 'Perception' (Hinton, 1993), which we will come to shortly. Others, especially problem-solving or decision-making, are much more challenging, often take place at a conscious level and deserve further attention.

We can distinguish between descriptive and prescriptive models of problem-solving and decision-making, or between how decisions are arrived at and how they should be arrived at. According to Nelson-Jones (1989), a rational approach is recommended. The key steps to be followed include:

1 *Confront* – this includes recognising the need for a decision to be taken, clarifying what exactly it is that is hoped to be achieved and being open to the circumstances, both internal and external, of the decision.
2 *Generate options and gather information* – try to think of as many options as possible, without any attempt at this point to evaluate their chances of success. This may involve, time permitting, gathering additional information which can be drawn upon.
3 *Select an option* – this should be done with consideration for the anticipated consequences if each were selected. Projected advantages and disadvantages of each need to be thought through. One important consequence, of course, is the probability of that course of action successfully achieving the goal being pursued. Others have to do with judgements of self-efficacy – the belief in one's ability to successfully implement that strategy; implications for face – how one might be seen by the other or others; and personal costs – including the amount of difficulty and effort required. By reflecting upon the positive and negative features of each option according to these criteria, the best option under the circumstances can be logically and systematically revealed (Janis and Mann, 1977).
4 *Commitment to the decision* – here the person should strengthen her resolve to the course of action selected.

5 *Implement the decision* – timing of implementation is one of the important factors to bear in mind. Other features of implementation will be taken up when we move on to consider the Response element of the model.

The complexities involved at this stage of cognitive processing are still the subject of much speculation. In any case, we can be sure that they are under-represented in this brief overview. For instance, *metacognitions* are held by Hewes and Planalp (1987) to play a part. In order to interact successfully we must be able to think about and form an opinion on how others think and how they go about making sense of the world which they experience. The way in which messages are encoded by skilled communicators will reflect judge-ments along these lines.

Responses

Plans and strategies decided upon are implemented at this stage. A common categorisation of social action, and one which has already been referred to, is that which identifies the verbal and the nonverbal. While closely connected, verbal communication has to do with the purely linguistic message, with the actual words used. Nonverbal behaviour encompasses a whole range of body movements and facial expressions, together with vocal aspects of speech. This facet may be worth elaborating. Laver and Hutcheson (1972) differ-entiated between vocal and nonvocal, and verbal and nonverbal communi-cation. Vocal refers to language and accompanying vocalisations. Verbal communication, on the other hand, is taken to mean, as we have seen, only the actual words and language used. The nonverbal category, therefore, subsumes nonvocal behaviour in the form of what is sometimes called body language, i.e. gestures, posture, facial expressions, etc., together with vocal communi-cation such as moans and sighs and intonation features which are not verbal in the sense defined above. It is at this level, in words spoken, intonations used and gestures displayed, that the individual acts on and reacts to his or her environment. Here situated behaviour is manifest and messages transmitted. The remainder of this text is primarily concerned with an in-depth analysis of the response component of interpersonal communication.

Feedback

Feedback is a fundamental feature of communication and without it prospects of skilled engagement are denied. Having acted, individuals rely on knowl-edge of their performance together with outcomes that may have accrued in order to reach decisions as to what to do next and alter subsequent responses accordingly. In the model presented in Figure 2.1, two sources of feedback are depicted. The more direct channel acknowledges that we have access, through proprioceptive and kinaesthetic means, as well as visually (to a certain extent) and aurally (albeit with distortion), to what we say and do when communicating with others. Perhaps of greater interest is the thesis that, as interaction takes place, each member in pursing personal goals for the exchange is, at the same time, in what they say and do, providing the other with information which can act as feedback relevant to that other's goal quests. Haslett and Ogilvie (1988, p. 385) express it succinctly when they define feedback, in the interpersonal setting, as 'the response listeners give to others about their behavior. . . . Feedback from others enables us to understand how our behavior affects them, and allows us to modify our behavior to achieve our desired goals.' Gudykunst (1991) asserts furthermore that convergence towards mutual understanding and shared meaning is proportional to the degree to which feedback is put to effective use. Limited provision and/or reception increase the chances of divergence and misunderstanding.

Corresponding to the different aspects of responding, feedback can be provided verbally or nonverbally, the latter in nonvocal and vocal forms. Although both are typically implicated, nonverbal modes may be particularly salient when it comes to affective or evaluative matters, while cognitive or substantive feedback relies more heavily upon the verbal (Zajonc, 1980).

Fitts and Posner (1973) identify three possible methods by means of which feedback can operate to influence further behaviour. It may, first, contribute *knowledge* about the results of performance; second, it can serve to *motivate* continued effort to persist with a course of action; and third, it may provide *reinforcement* thereby strengthening the behaviour that led to it and increasing the chances that the individual will behave in a like manner in the future. Cairns (1986) has argued that the feedback concept in most theories of communication can be cast in this latter way, although this assertion is highly contentious. (The topic of reinforcement will form the content of Chapter 4.)

While it is relatively easy to distinguish conceptually between these three modes of operation, the practical problems of doing so in any specific instance will be recognised. Salmoni *et al.* (1984) conclude their discussion of the elusive functional mechanism of feedback, with the suggestion that, 'It acts in many ways simultaneously' (p. 382).

Perception

Not all information potentially available via feedback is perceived; not all information perceived is perceived accurately. But it is only through the perceptual apparatus that information about the internal and external environment, including other people and the messages that they transmit, can be decoded and acted upon through making judgements and decisions in relation to the goals being sought. We can think of the reception of information taking place at one of two interrelated levels – one narrow, focused and mainly content-based, the other broader involving the forming of impressions of others and making social judgements about them. Thus, on the one hand, we can think of the reception and decoding of specific messages or, on the other, the sorts of processes that lead to the conclusion that this person whom we have just met is cold and unfriendly. Since we have already touched on the former when we discussed mediating processes, the focus here will be on *person perception*.

Person perception is heavily dependent upon the knowledge structures of the perceiver. It is also one of the most significant yet complex challenges we face as social animals. Forgas (1985, p. 21) reminds us that, 'it is the first crucial stage in any interaction between people. We must first perceive and interpret other people before we can meaningfully relate to them.' There is a number of related processes that we need to take into account when reflecting upon perception and the part that it plays in social interaction. One of these concerns the business of *attribution*, whereby we locate the reasons for and causes of behaviour – our own and that of others.

Jones (1990) proposes that perceiving people is inextricably bound up with attaching meaning to them and what they do. Judgements have to be reached about what makes them act in the ways witnessed. Perhaps the two most fundamental alternatives are between identifying the cause as residing in the individual (i.e. she did it because she is that type of person) or in the situation and circumstances in which she found herself (i.e. she did it because she had no choice) (Heider, 1958). The resolution of this dilemma has tremendously pertinent consequences for the interpretation of action and our response to it. Whether or not we regard an action as praiseworthy, let's say, will depend on the personal and situational factors that are adjudged to have brought it about. To what extent was it due to luck, effort or ability? Was the actor a free agent? Would most others have acted in a similar manner if faced with that set of circumstances? Again, when others lavish praise on us it makes sense to establish the intentions underlying such largesse. Is it a genuine and spontaneous expression of appreciation and admiration? Is it a statement of solidarity or an attempt to guide and support? Or is it something altogether more sinister, a bid to control or manipulate? Answers to such questions will obviously offer different translations of the rewarding process and dictate contrasting courses of action in response.

How people are perceived is also a feature of the expectations that are entertained of them. We often see in others what we expect to find there. Jones (1990) points out that expectations can be category-based when we have little personal detail to go on. Prior knowledge of a name may bring out ethnic or religious presumptions. An address which locates the individual in a certain part of town may do likewise. Familiarity leads to these giving way to target-based alternatives when our expectations stem from all that we have come to know of that individual.

It has also been proposed that what we believe others to be like or what we think they will do, is mediated by *implicit personality theories* that we come to hold (Bruner and Taguiri, 1954). This refers to the grouping of traits and characteristics into internally consistent complexes. It could be that ambitious people are believed to be able, scheming, devious, ruthless and not to be trusted. With this view of how people operate, being rewarded, for example, by someone looked upon as ambitious will mean something quite different than would be the case were that person labelled in some other way.

In addition to perceptions of others, skilled interpersonal behaviour also requires accurate perceptions of self and of how one is being perceived, or *metaperception*. Being mindful of the public image portrayed must not be overlooked. We have already explored this dimension of communication. Snyder (1987) uses the term *self-monitoring* to refer to the observation, regulation and control of identity projected in public. While some endeavour to create and maintain an impression in keeping with the situation and to earn approbation, Snyder (1987) revealed that others were much less preoccupied by these concerns.

CONCLUSION

The ability to communicate is not unique to mankind, but we have a sophistication that far surpasses all other species. It enables us to move beyond events taking place at this time. We can share knowledge, beliefs and opinions about happenings in the distance past and possibilities for the future; about events here or in some other place; about the particular or the general; the concrete or the abstract. It also enables us to make meaningful contact with others through establishing, maintaining and terminating relationships.

Despite its significance, communication is a notoriously difficult concept to define precisely. Nevertheless, a number of attributes are readily recognised by many, if not all, of those who have deliberated on the topic. Interpersonal communication can be thought of as a process which is transactional, purposeful, multi-dimensional, irreversible and (possibly) inevitable.

Skilled interpersonal involvement can be accounted for accordingly in terms of notions of goals, perception, mediating processes, responses, feedback and person–situation context. All communication is context-bound. We can think of spatial, temporal and relational frameworks within which it is embedded. The personal characteristics of the participants together with features of the shared situation act to shape the interaction that transpires and both may be influenced, to some extent, in consequence. Likewise, goals pursued are determined by personal and situational factors. Plans and strategies to accomplish these derive from mediating processes and resulting tactics are enacted in manifested responses. A central premise of the model outlined is that, in interactive arrangements, participants are at one and the same time, in what they say and do, providing each other with information of relevance to decisions as to the extent of goal attainment. Without such feedback, skilled interaction would be impossible. Such feedback can only be acted upon, however, if it is perceived. As we have seen, perceptual processes, particularly those involved in personal perception, play a pivotal role in interpersonal transactions.

Chapter 3

Nonverbal communication

INTRODUCTION

Up until the early 1960s there were relatively few texts which were directly concerned with nonverbal aspects of human communication. However, more recently, a number of authors (Argyle, 1975; Scherer and Ekman, 1982; Bull, 1983; Feldman and Rime, 1991; De Paulo, 1992) have recognised that any study of the complete communication process must take account of both verbal and nonverbal channels which are found to a greater or lesser extent in all forms of communication. In practice, therefore, observations of everyday interactions in the home, street, classroom or at work profit from a detailed consideration of the verbal and nonverbal messages that govern and influence behaviour in different social settings.

In this chapter it is intended to map out briefly elements of nonverbal behaviour which should provide the reader with greater insight into and, therefore, some measure of control over communication processes. The selection of material, from what is now a very widely researched area, has been governed by its direct relevance to increasing the awareness, sensitivity and eventual skill preferences of people whose daily job is largely made up of 'dealing with others'.

The importance of appreciating the key role of nonverbal processes in communication is persuasively put by Birdwhistell (1970), one of the earliest authorities in the field, who claimed that the average person actually speaks for a total of only 10 to 11 minutes daily; the standard spoken sentence taking only about 2.5 seconds. In addition, he estimates that in a typical dyadic encounter the verbal components carry about one-third of the social meaning of the situation while the nonverbal channel conveys approximately two-thirds. Thus just as in the words of the song, 'It's not what you say but the way that you say it!', much of the information we are transmitting and receiving is being conveyed via the nonverbal channel.

WHAT IS NONVERBAL COMMUNICATION?

In order to define the concept 'nonverbal', it is useful to examine two important distinctions identified by Laver and Hutcheson (1972), namely verbal and nonverbal, and vocal and nonvocal. Vocal behaviour refers to all aspects of speech, that is, actual language used and accompanying verbal expressions such as tone of voice, rate of speech and accent, etc., whereas nonvocal behaviour refers to all other activities which have a communicative function such as facial expressions, gestures and bodily movements. Verbal behaviour, on the other hand, is taken to mean only the actual words or language used while nonverbal behaviour refers to all vocal and nonvocal behaviour which is not verbal in the sense defined above (this is discussed in more detail in Chapter 2). Thus, quite apart from the verbal content of what a person says, meaning is communicated by tone of voice, talk speed, volume of speech and intonation. In addition to the nonverbal aspects of speech, information is transmitted and received through a whole range of body movements such as the posture adopted when sitting in a chair – is it one of stiffness and uprightness suggesting tension or anxiety or is the person slumped down in the chair with perhaps his feet on a small table suggesting a feeling of relaxation or familiarity? Faces, too, play an important role in social encounters by giving expression to our inner thoughts, such as showing delight when presented with an unexpected gift or displaying sadness when told about the death of a close friend.

Before we open our mouths to speak our physical appearance conveys a great deal of information about our age, sex, occupation, status (if a certain uniform is worn) and personality. Indeed, Riggio and Friedman (1986) found that when people were engaged in public speaking, their physical attractiveness was an important factor in the audience's responses to them in terms of likeability, confidence and competence.

Not only are we concerned with the appearance and behaviour of the person involved in communication but, in addition, environmental factors such as architecture, furniture, decoration, smells, colour, texture and noise are extremely influential on the outcome of interpersonal relationships. These are only a few of the categories which nonverbal behaviour attends to. A more comprehensive range of nonverbal categories will be presented later in the chapter.

PURPOSES OF NONVERBAL COMMUNICATION

Nonverbal communication serves a number of purposes depending upon the context in which it is utilised. One of the most obvious functions it has is to totally replace speech. Consider at one extreme, the person who is deaf and dumb. He relies entirely on the use of hand and arm movements which have been developed universally to allow communication to take place. Sometimes, on the other hand, individuals are temporarily cut off from being able to communicate through speech, and so resort to using some form of body movements. This is particularly evident among deep-sea divers, mime artists, racecourse touts and individuals who suffer a temporary loss of voice. At a less extreme level, there are occasions when we do not always have to put into words what we want to convey and indeed to do so would be pretentious and too formal or forward. Thus a girl who meets a boy for the first time may give off signals through smiling or eye contact that she 'fancies' him and would like to explore this relationship further. In this sense, actions can speak louder than words. By and large, therefore, perceptive individuals can identify and interpret a wide range of nonverbal cues with a fair degree of accuracy and in so doing get the message over more effectively.

Nonverbal behaviour is also used to complement the spoken word. More particularly, specific nonverbal acts give the listener some idea of the affective state of the talker. Obviously not all oral statements are charged with the same degree of emotional content. For example, there is every likelihood that a person will not put the amount of feeling into the statement, 'It's lunchtime!' that she would into the phrase, 'My father has just died!' However, the words uttered by individuals experiencing some kind of emotional state, be it sadness, anxiety, fear, anger, frustration or affection, are usually elaborated on by the utilisation of accompanying nonverbal behaviour. We stamp our feet when we are angry, grin broadly when pleased and gasp when unexpectedly surprised.

It is also interesting to note, on the other hand, that nonverbal behaviour can on occasions contradict the verbal message. Consider, for example, the teacher who verbally invites pupils' questions and critical comments regarding the content of the lesson but who, in effect, makes it quite clear, via his nonverbal behaviour, that he will not be receptive to criticism. These subtleties can also be observed on TV. Witness the political leader who announces that he has every confidence in the measures he has taken for the good of the nation, while at the same time displaying nonverbal behaviour which indicates anxiety and lack of confidence. Where this contradiction exists it is generally thought that listeners place more credence on the nonverbal behaviours as they are considered harder to falsify (Ekman *et al.*, 1991). Such behaviours include blushing, sweating, trembling and tensing – which are spontaneous and outside the control of the individual. However, it is also recognised that, with practice, some people become extremely proficient at most forms of nonverbal deception as testified by the performances of top-class stage actors. Generally, though, complementary functions of nonverbal behaviour indicate attitudes, emotions and dispositions towards another person.

A third purpose of the nonverbal channel, and in a way related to the previous function, is that by accompanying speech it serves to illustrate more graphically what has been said although not necessarily linked with the emotional state. Friesen *et al.* (1980) refer to these gestural acts as illustrators and they will be examined later in the chapter under gestures. For instance, people, when asked to give an explanation to another concerning a route to travel, the shape of an object or the description of a particular job, usually illustrate what is said with movements and gestures. By observing people in conversations it can be noted that these accompanying movements actually facilitate speech where it is difficult to describe aspects of space and shape in purely verbal terms.

Fourth, nonverbal behaviour can help to emphasise parts of the verbal messages by being an integral part of the total communication process. When a speaker puts more stress on certain words than others, uses pauses between words to convey gravity or interest, varies the tone and speed of his utterances, he is underlining the importance of certain words or phrases in the mind of the listener. In a sense it is analogous to the writer who puts words in italics, underlines them or gives chapter headings. In addition, body movements are frequently used to add more weight to the verbal message. For example, the mother who wants to ensure and stress that her son listens closely to what she is saying may, in addition to saying, 'Listen to me', swing him round to face her closely and put both arms on his shoulders. These actions are all designed to add weight to the verbal message.

A fifth and equally important purpose of nonverbal behaviour is that it helps to regulate the flow of communication between speaker and listener. It becomes clear when observing two persons interacting, that they somehow seem to know when it is their turn to either speak or listen without actually stating to the other, 'Go on it's your turn now'. Duncan and Fiske (1977) have identified a number of nonverbal cues which offer a speaking turn to the other person. These are a rise or fall in pitch at the end of a clause, a drop in voice volume and termination of hand gestures. In addition, they found that if a speaker continued to use gestures such as hand gesticulation, it essentially eliminated attempts by the listener to take over the turn. Another line of research on turn-taking focused on the regulating functions of gaze (Duncan and Fiske, 1977). The findings of these authors, supported by later studies by Cappella (1985), show that turning the head away from the listener functioned as a turn-yielding cue. This aspect will be dealt with later in the chapter under the heading 'eye gaze'.

Linked with this fifth purpose is a sixth which contends that nonverbal behaviour can both initiate and sustain communication by providing an important source of feedback to the interactors. For individuals to proceed to interact with each other they need to be able to reach some kind of common understanding. To do this they must acquire as much information about each other as possible in order to be sensitive to the views and feelings of the other person. Interactors are constantly adapting and modifying their subsequent behaviour in the light of how they think their messages are being received. So the interviewer, entreating the client to describe how he feels about a controversial issue, who detects aspects of discomfort in his client's behaviour, may quickly change the subject or develop his line of questioning towards a less controversial aspect in order to ease any tension that might arise.

A seventh purpose of nonverbal behaviour is that it can have a considerable influence on other people by defining relationships without making them too explicit. If someone wants to influence another by being dominant over him he can manipulate his nonverbal behaviour in order to bring this about. The following behaviours are aspects of dominant nonverbal cues: a louder voice, greater amount of talk, choosing a focal position in a room, standing on a raised dais, sitting behind a desk, sitting at the head of the table, occupying a more impressive chair, interrupting successfully when another person talks, looking while speaking and using long glances to establish a dominant relationship. When individuals are negotiating and sustaining personal relationships it would be too disturbing for one to state openly that she did not like the other very much or that she thought she was more important than the other. Yet nonverbal cues can be emitted regarding these states without the sender being explicit. In addition, initial relationships can change over time so that an original dominant–submissive relationship can become one more equal in nature. Change would not come about as readily if persons had explicitly stated at the beginning how they felt towards each other. This alternative channel allows individuals to make up their minds slowly about others and change their views without being committed to define verbally a relationship which may vary with time.

Finally, nonverbal behaviour can help to define acceptable patterns of behaviour in a variety of social settings. All social settings, from the simple, such as Sunday lunch, the office Christmas party or a visit to the dentist, to the more elaborate, such as a graduation ceremony or a funeral, carry with them acceptable codes of conduct. If someone deviates from these common patterns of behaviour and so upsets the social scene, he is usually called upon either to apologise or offer an excuse or explanation for the deviant behaviour (Goffman, 1972).

These functions do not always occur independently. It is quite possible for complementing, illustrating and emphasising to occur simultaneously. It is also important to note that sometimes these functions can be fulfilled with a solitary nonverbal act, but more commonly a pattern of behaviours is used.

The remainder of this chapter will look more closely at the various components of behaviour which comprise the nonverbal channel. Since the challenge of the present chapter is to present and discuss those aspects of nonverbal behaviour which serve a communication function, the various behavioural elements will be classified into six dimensions, namely physical contact, kinesics (commonly referred to as 'body language'), proxemics (interpersonal spacing), physical characteristics of appearance, environmental factors and paralanguage (vocal part of speech such as voice pitch, volume and silences, etc.).

PHYSICAL CONTACT

This category of nonverbal communication has been included first because it is the earliest form of social communication which we experience. Our first contact with the outside world and what it is going to be like comes through tactile experiences. Some of these touch experiences include the doctor's hands as a baby is delivered and the mother's hands which feed, bathe, cradle, nurse and comfort the baby throughout his waking hours. Early tactile explorations appear to be of crucial importance to subsequent healthy behavioural development of young adults (Montagu, 1971).

Adler and Towne (1975), investigating child mortality rates during the nineteenth and early twentieth centuries from a disease then called *marasmus* (translated from the Greek meaning 'wasting away') noted that:

> In some orphanages the mortality rate was nearly one hundred percent, but even children from the most 'progressive' homes, hospitals and other institutions died regularly from the ailment. . . . They hadn't enough touch, and as a result they died.
>
> (pp. 225–6)

As a child grows up and enters adult life, touching is an area of behaviour that is susceptible to multiple interpretations since, as Heslin and Alper (1983) noted, 'It [touch] is complicated by social norms regarding who has permission to touch whom and what is considered to be an appropriate context for such behaviour' (p. 47). For instance, Sorensen and Beatty (1988) have noted that touching between women and men and also between women in our society is acceptable but touch among men tends to be frowned upon.

Touching serves a number of functions which are related both to the context in which touching occurs and to the relationship of the interactors. Heslin (1974) identified these functions, ranging from the most distant to the most intimate, as: functional/professional, social/polite, friendship/warmth, love/intimacy and sexual arousal. The first three categories only of this taxonomy will be discussed in this chapter since they are the most relevant to professional contexts. A number of professionals touch people in the normal course of their work: nurses, dentists, doctors, physical education teachers, health visitors, hairdressers and physiotherapists, to name but a few. However, touch in this sense does not carry connotations of social relationships but rather is seen as a necessary function of a particular job. Sometimes there is a tendency to decry the 'cool' manner in which professionals relate to their clients. However, such a manner is necessary if misinterpretations of touch contacts are not to be made.

Social/polite touching (especially hand-shaking) is an act that attempts to equalise status by signalling that the interactors are intending to acknowledge the 'human element' of the interaction rather than status differences. Friendship/warmth touch contacts such as a friendly pat, arm-linking, a comforting touch on the arm, aimed at establishing friendly relationships with others, can be very rewarding to individuals in terms of giving encouragement, expressing cares and concerns and showing emotional support and understanding (Wheldall *et al.*, 1986) Research into the influence that touch contacts can have shows that touching can help recipients talk to other people especially about themselves and their problems (Pattison, 1973). In addition, it would appear that persons are more likely to comply with requests and perform favours more readily when they are touched by the requester than when they are not (Kleinke, 1980; Willis and Hamm, 1980). This finding has implications for the medical profession who find it a constant struggle to get patients to comply with their instructions for the taking of medications. Finally, touching can communicate a feeling of warmth and caring and at the same time can make the recipient have a more positive attitude towards the toucher and the physical setting in which the touch contact took place. In an interesting study by Fisher *et al.* (1975) it was found that when men and women clerks in a university library briefly touched the hand of a reader returning identification cards, this less than half-second contact caused the women readers not only to like the librarian but also the library better than those who were not touched.

Henley (1977) was interested in investigating the link between touch and status, and concluded that individuals have certain expectations about touching and being touched by others in particular role relationships. For example, individuals expect to touch subordinates more than they touch superiors and to be touched more by superiors than subordinates. Thus it would be more likely that the doctor rather than the patient would be the touch initiator and similarly the teacher rather than the pupil.

Finally, it is important to be aware that there are groups within the community who very rarely touch other individuals; elderly people with no close relatives and widowed people receive little or no bodily contact designed to cater for their emotional needs. Professional helpers, such as teachers, social workers, nurses, health visitors and doctors, aware of this void, could employ appropriate touch contacts to redress this imbalance.

KINESICS

Kinesics or body motion, as the name suggests, includes all those movements of the body such as gestures, limb movements, head nods, facial expressions, eye gaze and posture. When we look at individuals or groups interacting, one aspect which is immediately striking is the amount of movement being displayed. People do not remain motionless when they are communicating. Instead, in general terms, information, attitudes, affective states or moods and status cues are being communicated through body movements. More specifically, Patterson (1983) suggested that there are five basic functions of body movements, namely, information giving, regulating interaction, expressing affective states, indicating social control and facilitating task goals. This typology is somewhat similar to that of Ekman and Friesen (1969) developed fourteen years earlier in which three categories, namely illustrators, affect displays and regulators, are directly related to Patterson's facilitating task goals, expressing affect displays and regulating interaction.

However, two other functions of Ekman and Friesen, emblems and adaptors, are alternative classification groupings. Emblems are those nonverbal behaviours which have a direct verbal translation, such as pointing to your wrist when you wish to 'know the time' or putting up the thumbs when you want to signify a win or some other success. These gestures are frequently used when the normal verbal channels are blocked or inadequate. According to Ekman and Friesen, adaptors are developed in childhood and tend to reveal personal orientations or characteristics towards the verbal messages. Many of the restless movements of the hands and fingers, and kicking movements of the legs and feet, may be acts of tension or anxiety, revealing more intense affective states than that portrayed merely by speech utterances. The remainder of this section will analyse these various functions in relation to the five main areas of kinesics: gestures, posture, head nods, eye gaze and facial expression.

Gestures

Kendon (1989) distinguished between gestures which totally replace speech (gestural autonomy) and gestures which complement speech (illustrators). Autonomous gestures or emblems, to use Ekman and Friesen's label, are employed every day where speech would be inadequate, for example in noisy environments (the floor of a busy factory) or over greater distances (policemen on point duty). Some instances of the vast range of hand and arm movements which are utilised every day and to which meaning is attached are:

Gesture	Inferences
hands outstretched	appealing
feet shuffling	impatience
moving hand	good-bye
shoulder shrugging	I don't know
drumming table with fingers	anxious
shaking clenched fist	angry
palms up and facing forward	stop, wait
thumbs up	success
thumbs down	loss
clenched fists	fear
rubbing eyes	bored
pointing arm and hand	go
clapping (fast)	approval
clapping (slow)	disapproval

It is interesting to note that forms of autonomous gestures tend to be different from one culture to another (Kendon, 1981) and that the cultures of the Mediterranean appear to be far richer in autonomous gestural forms than are the cultures of northern Europe (Morris *et al.*, 1979). Further comparative studies are needed, however, to reveal the origins of these systems and what purposes they serve.

Feldman *et al.* (1991) distinguish between gestures which are linked with speech (illustrators) and directed towards objects or events and those which are oriented towards the self. They suggest that the speech-linked hand gestures are intended to communicate, while the second group act as a form of tension release. Let us look more closely at the speech-linked hand gestures first. Hand gestures can be used to provide points of emphasis. For example teachers, when they are asking pupils to remember some important information, enumerate with their fingers the number of points to be remembered. This is borne out by research into teachers' use of nonverbal skills in the classroom where it was shown that gazing, mild facial expressions and hand gestures were the most commonly used nonverbal behaviours (Kadunc, 1991). It was also found that teachers most often utilised illustrators and least often used emblems. In addition, hand gestures can provide illustrations of the verbal content of a message. These illustrations can take the form of shaping, with the hands, actual objects or events being discussed, outlining pathways or directions which represent thought patterns, or employing some of the more generally agreed upon gestures listed previously in this section in conjunction with speech. Equally important is the need, on occasion, to use hand gestures in order to facilitate speech. It is fairly commonplace to observe speakers, struggling to find the appropriate words and phrases, using their hands to stimulate more rapid thought processes. Teachers, interviewers, public speakers and salesmen, who supplement their dialogue with good use of hand and arm movements, usually arouse and maintain the attention of their listeners, indicate their interest and enthusiasm, and tend to make the interaction sequence a stimulating and enjoyable experience for all participants.

Kendon (1984) focused on the various conditions under which individuals use the gestural expressive mode and concluded that the speaker divides the task of conveying meaning between words and gestures in such a way as to achieve either economy of expression or a particular effect on the listener. For instance, a gesture can be used as a device for completing a sentence that, if spoken, might prove embarrassing to the speaker. It can also be used as a means of telescoping what one wants to say, when the available turn space is smaller than one would like. Alternatively, gestures can be employed to clarify some potentially ambiguous word or as an additional component when the verbal account is inadequate to truly represent the information being shared. Further evidence that clarity and comprehension of an explanation or description can be increased by the use of gestural cues comes from a study by Rogers (1978) in which eight male and female students were asked to view various actions on a silent film, such as a tennis ball bouncing, or a car swerving, and then describe them to another person who was unable to view the film. These descriptions were subsequently video-taped and shown to another group of students either with sound and vision or with sound only. Results showed that comprehension was significantly increased in the audio-visual as opposed to the sound only condition.

Evidence that accuracy of understanding can be increased when gestural acts are used to complement the spoken word was provided in three studies by Riseborough (1981). First, she showed that persons were more able to identify objects from descriptions accompanied by appropriate gestures than those without gestures. Second, she found that subjects could recall a story more accurately when accompanying gestural behaviours were employed. Third, when the sound channel was obstructed by white noise, illustrative gestures increased comprehension.

If illustrators do complement speech acts, then it could be hypothesised that when people are restrained or restricted from using gestures, speech patterns would be hesitant and dysfluent. Graham and Heywood (1976) asked a group of British male students to communicate information about two-dimensional shapes, first with free use of hands and arms and, second, keeping their arms folded. The only significant result obtained was that pausing increased under the no-gesture condition.

Hand movements can also convey emotional states, although these are usually unintentional. One example is the highly nervous and anxious inter-viewee at a selection interview who exhibits his inner state by nervous wringing movements of the hands, fiddling with a ring or a watch or constantly moving the fingers and hands on his lap. These are all forms of 'social leakage' which can be avoided if interviewees are encouraged to 'anchor' their hands on either the arms of the chair or on their lap and only use the hands to illustrate or facilitate their speech content. (Alternative methods of ventilating tension during selection interviews include wriggling or curling of the toes, or tightening of the calf muscles on the legs. Such forms of 'leakage' are not so immediately apparent.) Hand gestures can also reveal other emotional dis-positions such as embarrassment – hand over the mouth; anger – knuckles showing white; aggression – fist clenching; shame – hands covering the eyes; nervousness – nail and finger biting. Professionals should be sensitive to these hand signals which, because of their often spontaneous nature, may reveal more about the client's feelings than words would permit.

Posture

Although there are three main categories of human posture, standing, sitting or squatting, and lying, in terms of interpersonal communication we are predominantly concerned with the position of the body when sitting and standing. Posture itself can signify differential status, a positive or a negative attitude, emotional level and persuasion.

Turning first to the role of status in postural communication, we need to differentiate between status related to subjects when they are standing and conversely when they are sitting. It has been noted that high-status individuals adopt a more relaxed position when they are seated (e.g. body tilting sideways; lying slumped in a chair) than low-status subjects who sit more upright and rigid in their chairs. In a standing position, the high-status subject again will appear more relaxed, often with arms crossed or hands in pockets, than low-status subjects who are generally 'straighter' and 'stiffer' (Mehrabian, 1972). To observe this factor the reader might like to switch the sound off next time when watching two individuals on an interview programme on television. Try to deduce from their postural positions which one is controlling the interview and which one is being interviewed.

Several researchers (Gatewood and Rosenwein, 1981; Rosenfeld, 1981; and Warner *et al.*, 1987) have identified the phenomenon of postural congruence, that is, those instances when two interactants exhibit the same behaviour at the same point in time. In other words, when your partner's behaviour is a mirror image of yours it is called 'mirroring'. These authors went on to suggest that 'postural mirroring' occurs during periods of more positive speech and is influential in creating rapport. Matched behaviours frequently displayed involve crossing the legs, leaning forward, head-propping and arm-crossing.

With regard to attitudinal state, a seated person who leans forward towards the other is deemed to have a more positive attitude towards both the subject and the topic under discussion than when she leans backwards, away from the person she is addressing (Siegel, 1980). When the people are standing, on the other hand, a more positive attitude is conveyed when an individual directly faces another rather than turns away. It is also interesting to note that most prolonged interactions are conducted with both participants either sitting or standing, rather than one standing and the other sitting. Where this situation does occur, communication usually is of a cursory (e.g. information desks) or strained (e.g. interrogation sessions) nature.

We should also be alert to the different, more intense, emotions that can be conveyed directly by postural positions. While earlier in the chapter it was noted that the face displayed information regarding specific emotions, bodily posture conveys the intensity of that emotion (Ekman, 1985). Clients who are temporarily emotionally aroused can adopt specific postures which speak louder than words. Extreme depression can be shown in a drooping, listless pose, while extreme anxiety can be seen in the muscularly tense, stiff, upright person. Focusing on patient behaviour, Fisch *et al.* (1983) found that posture was a significant indicator when differentiating between severely depressed and nearly recovered patients during doctor–patient interviews.

Finally, in an attempt to identify those nonverbal behaviours which had a persuasive impact on others, it was found that more upright postural positions or 'reduced reclining angles' along with intensity of voice and increased head-nodding were instrumental in achieving this goal (Mehrabian, 1972; Washburn and Hakel, 1973).

Head-nods

Head-nodding and shaking are in constant use during the interactive process and are related both to the role of the speaker and of the listener. In relation to the listener's role, there are two ways in which interest and enthusiasm for the speaker's message can be conveyed. Ekman and Oster (1979) suggested that interest shown towards a speaker is communicated by a tilting of the head to one side rather than conveyed from facial expressions. Additionally, head-nodding is a signal to continue talking and it is widely used by interviewers to encourage and motivate interviewees to speak at length. Duncan (1972) identified five cues, namely, sentence completions, requests for clarification, brief phrases such as 'uh-huh', 'yeah' and 'right', and head-nods and head-shakes, which indicated continuing attentiveness towards the speaker.

Examining the role of the speaker, Duncan and Fiske (1977) found that two cues, notably the head turning away from the other person and beginning to gesture, were significantly associated with wanting to take a turn to speak. Thomas and Bull (1981), examining conversations between mixed-sex pairs of British students, confirmed the findings of the previous two studies. They found that prior to asking a question, the students typically either raised the head or turned the head towards the listener; while just before answering a question the speaker turned his head away from the listener. This last finding may be due, as Beattie (1979) noted, to the effects of cognitive planning on the part of the listener prior to taking up the speaker's role.

When persons wish to bring a conversation to a close, there is evidence that head movements are instrumental in bringing this about in a smooth and synchronised way. Knapp et al. (1973) examined the behaviour of interacting pairs 45 seconds prior to leave-taking and found four frequently occurring nonverbal cues; breaking eye contact, pointing the legs and feet towards the door, leaning forward and head-nodding. The above authors conclude that, 'Nodding, smiling, and reinforcement may be viewed as behaviours which "politely" signal inattentiveness and lack of responsiveness on the part of the leaver' (p. 197). (This latter point is dealt with more fully in the discussion on 'Closure' in Chapter 7.)

Finally, the movements of the head also signify inner feeling states, such as cocked to one side showing interest or puzzlement, bowed low displaying depression or sadness, and tossed high in the air as a sign of defiance.

Eye gaze

Obsession with the eyes and their potent effects on human behaviour has been graphically documented down through the ages. This is exemplified by a number of phrases which are in common usage, including 'He's making eyes at me'; 'She gave him a look to kill'; 'His eyes seemed to bore right through me'; 'Don't look at me like that'; 'There's something about his eyes'. Musicians, artists and choreographers, too, have captivated the magic and mystique of the eyes in their various art forms. Indeed the epitome of the effects the eyes can have is the celebrated gaze of the Mona Lisa which has fascinated viewers for centuries. However, as students of human interaction, we are less concerned with the subjective impression which individuals make regarding the eye region of the face and more with the patterned movement made by the eyes as forms of signals or cues in any given interaction.

Gazing during social interaction can serve a variety of functions; one of the most important being related to turn-taking. Abele (1986) and Kleinke (1986b) both found that, in general, people looked more as they listened than as they spoke, and the duration of looking was longer during listening than talking. Mutual looking, that is eye-to-eye contact, was also examined and it was found that looking came in short bursts, so that as soon as eye-to-eye contact was made one or other of the interactors broke it. A typical interactive sequence would be: When person A comes towards the end of his utterance he looks at person B to signal that it is B's turn to speak. Person B, in turn, will tend to look away after he begins his response, especially if he intends to speak for a long time, or the material he is dealing with is difficult to understand. It is necessary, according to Beattie (1981), for the speaker under these conditions to blot out as many distractions as possible. Therefore, he effectively closes the visual channel. The listener, on the other hand, generally continues to look at the speaker unless the speech is very long, in which case he will look at the speaker only intermittently. It would appear that this pattern of gazing is a useful device to synchronise and control the flow of conversation between individuals and eliminates both the need verbally to state whose turn it is to speak and the habit of constantly interrupting each other. Most studies have used dyadic conversations when investigating this turn-taking pattern. Kalma (1992), on the other hand, studied triadic conversations and found that the persons with the highest ascribed influence gazed at the end of an utterance more often than the persons with the least influence. It would appear from this study that at the conclusion of speaking turns, gazing can be used to regulate the flow of interaction and it is dominant individuals who are good at it.

One group of researchers (Dovidio *et al.*, 1988) set up experiments with mixed-sex pairs of interactants in which the relative status of the interactants was deliberately manipulated. When there was a status difference between the interactants, the party having the higher status (whether male or female) had a longer gazing pattern. However, when status was not manipulated, men behaved in the 'visually dominant' way that high-status communicators display while women showed the less visually dominant behaviour typical of people in low-status roles.

Several studies (Russo, 1975; Rutter *et al.*, 1978; Hall, 1984) have confirmed that women tend to look more than men. Two possible explanations for this phenomenon appear to be that women display a greater need for affiliation than do men, and that desire for affiliation promotes more looking (Argyle and Cook, 1976). Alternatively, it is contended that eye contact is seen as less threatening to women than men, with the result that they are less likely to break eye contact in similar situations.

Eye contact is also a means by which we communicate the intensity of our emotions towards the other person, either of an affiliative or a threatening nature. We appear to make more and longer eye contact with people we like but this varies between males and females (Noller, 1980). Courting couples will spend a long time 'making eyes' at each other. Persons who are showing a great deal of hostility to each other will also persist in engaging in long periods of mutual gaze. However, it is usually easy to distinguish the two kinds of behaviour since subsidiary facial expressions, such as smiling in the affiliative situation and snarling in the threatening behaviour, are in evidence.

It is also important to remember from the previous chapter that individuals look for feedback on how their messages are being received: signs of approval and disapproval. This then makes it possible for interactors to modify their social behaviour so as to maximise sought outcomes. Kendon (1967) referred to this as the 'monitoring' function of gaze.

Gaze is also an important means by which counsellors convey interest and attention to their clients. Research indicates that counsellors are viewed more favourably when they look at their clients very often rather than seldom during a counselling interview (Fretz *et al.*, 1979; Kelly and True, 1980). In addition, counsellors who couple verbal reinforcers (see Chapter 4) with eye gaze can effectively reinforce their clients to express attitudes and feelings (Goldman, 1980).

Davidhizor (1992), in a review of eye contact, claimed that all health care personnel should have an understanding of the nature, functions and complexities of eye movement behaviour. Specifically he noted that 'It is through eye contact that patient needs are assessed, psychological support provided, and feedback response to care obtained' (p. 222).

Facial expressions

The face provides a rich source of information regarding the emotional state of an individual. In fact, some theorists regard facial expressions as the next most important source of information to language itself. Some evidence of this can be found in the amount of time and space authors, playwrights and script-writers give to describing in detail the facial movements of their characters.

Although facial cues are readily visible to us we frequently find it difficult to judge the emotional states being displayed. Ekman *et al.* (1971) drew our attention to the fact that we are dealing with a very complex phenomenon, pointing out that:

(1) one emotion is shown in one facial area and another is shown in another area – e.g. brows raised as in surprise, and lips pressed as in anger; (2) two different emotions shown in one part of the face – e.g. one brow raised as in surprise and the other lowered as in anger; and (3) a facial display produced by muscle action associated with two emotions but containing specific elements of neither.

(p. 53)

A later study, however, found that judgements about the content of a conversation could be made merely by observing and analysing the facial expressions of the participants. Dabbs (1985) asked two judges to view a video-tape, with the sound turned off, of thirteen male and thirteen female university students who had not previously met and who conversed in opposite-sex pairs for half an hour each. The subjects' faces were recorded and, from the findings, it was significant that judges could assess from facial expressions shown whether the respondents were talking at a social level (displaying nods, smiles or pleasing expressions) or an intellectual level (displaying thoughtful expressions and markedly less attention to each other).

It is commonly believed that facial expressions are a combination of innate and socially learned behaviour (Ekman, 1982). Some evidence seems to support the innate behaviour theory, in that a number of behaviours appear to be common across the different cultures of the world: behaviours such as one eyebrow raised, both eyebrows raised, yawning and lip-biting which suggest, in turn, concern, surprise, tiredness or boredom, and anxiety.

Often facial expressions and speech are at variance with each other, in which case we are apt to place more credence on what we see rather than what we hear (Zaidel and Mehrabian, 1969), although this varies with age, children and young adolescents paying more attention to visual components than older adolescents and adults (Bugental *et al.*, 1970). In addition, it is much easier to control speech behaviour than it is facial behaviour. A nervous twitch of the mouth in a crucial interview situation, blushing when attempting to hide embarrassment and seething with anger while trying not to show it, are only some of the many examples which account for this occurrence, particularly strong emotions being the most difficult to conceal. Recognising and understanding the various facial expressions would seem to be a useful skill for any student of human behaviour.

Two studies have focused on sex differences related to facial expressions (Duncan and Fiske, 1977; Bond and Ho, 1978). These studies found that during social encounters when subjects conversed with a person of the same or opposite sex, female subjects smiled significantly more frequently and spent a significantly higher proportion of time smiling than did males. Some feminist scholars in the USA see this difference as disadvantageous to women in that it would appear to put women in the lower-status or submissive role. As yet, no significant research has been conducted to confirm or refute that women's smiling is due to social weakness; indeed, one study on relative status in interactions found that lower-status persons smiled less (Halberstadt *et al.*, 1988).

Finally, it has been suggested (Buck, 1989) that people who are facially expressive may 'turn on' the expressive behaviour of others. In other words, their expressiveness encourages others to be open and frank in return; one person's level of self-disclosure is generally matched or reciprocated by the listener (see Chapter 10). The corollary, of course, is that inexpressiveness or face passivity dampens the expressiveness of others. For instance, normal people who interact with schizophrenics (expressively inhibited) are themselves less expressive than when interacting with other normal persons (Krause *et al.*, 1989). In addition, Jones *et al.* (1991) claim that even infants appear to be more expressive when their mothers are facially expressive rather than when they are reserved.

PROXEMICS

Proxemics refers to the role of space in behaviour. In particular there are three aspects, namely territoriality, proximity and orientation, all of which have a direct bearing on the communication process. Each will be discussed in turn.

Territoriality

Spatial behaviour is connected with 'territory', establishing it, invading it and defending it. Personal space is that space immediately surrounding the body, and it can be disturbing for individuals if this personal space is invaded. Professionals should normally avoid moving too close to their clients. If they do move too near to an individual this may result in a tendency for that person to move his head or body backwards. Personal territory, on the other hand, is a much larger area in which a person moves. This space often provides the individual with privacy or social intimacy. Examples of individuals creating their personal territory can be found every day in our general lives.

Thus members of a family usually occupy the same seats at meal-times, or specific seats when driving in the family car. Staff-rooms in schools, too, contain chairs which seemingly 'belong' to individual members of staff, as the student teacher often finds out to her embarrassment after occupying one of them on school placement! People in offices which are shared go to great lengths to place their desks in such a way as to create social barriers, or alternatively establish a status difference between themselves and clients. Booking personal territory in the form of leaving bags and coats on seats in libraries, restaurants and trains, are common everyday occurrences which we accept (Becker, 1973). Teachers arrange the desks in their classroom on occasion to establish a personal territory; rows of desks for pupils facing, at some distance, their own desk. However, if a teacher wants to break down the barriers between herself and the class it can often be achieved by rearranging the furniture. For example, she can arrange the chairs in a circle or semicircle to encourage whole-class discussion, or set up small groups of tables and chairs to encourage group cooperation exercises. Alternatively, she can remove the furniture completely to encourage totally free movement.

Finally, as with personal territory, individuals can sometimes feel threatened when their home territory is invaded. Examples of home territory are the house itself, cafés taken over by particular groups, pubs taken over by a sports team or even street corners frequented by gangs of youths. Social workers may be told very forcibly by their clients that they are not welcome in their home and any attempt by the social worker to establish entry may be severely criticised. Teachers, too, look upon their classrooms as private places and feel threatened and anxious on occasions when they are observed by other teachers, the headmaster, the inspectorate or educational researchers. Violence can often be the order of the day when home territories are invaded by rival groups. Witness two groups of rival supporters who have established their territory behind the 'home' team's goal. If the rival side attempts to invade their territory, the home side will defend it with violence. There is no doubt, therefore, that spatial behaviour is one of the important nonverbal social skills since seating positions, furniture arrangements, availability of space and positions of the interactors play an integrated part in determining both the amount and kind of interaction that will ensue.

Proximity

If individuals have freedom of choice regarding the position they take up in relation to each other, it can convey information about their relationship. More specifically, proximity refers to the interpersonal distance that individuals maintain when they are involved in interaction. The first distinction we can make is that generally we interact at a closer distance to people when we are standing rather than sitting. A sitting distance of 5 to 6 feet is common for discussion in a work situation while 8 to 10 feet appears to be the norm in a sitting-room or lounge. On the other hand, the usual nose-to-nose distance for ordinary conversation when we are standing is 3 to 4 feet. If a person violates these patterns of interpersonal distance by either placing herself within 2 feet or beyond 10 feet of our face when conversing we would feel uncomfortable and move ourselves either away from her or towards her until the appropriate distance is established. It is not difficult to appreciate that the narrowing of distance indicates a claim to a higher degree of intimacy and the increasing of the distance suggests coldness and aloofness (thus the expression 'she is very stand-offish').

Hall (1959, 1966) put forward, from his observation of North American society, that distance could be classified into four main zones depending on the purposes set for the interaction.

Intimate zone	–	Those who have an intimate relationship with each other will interact at a distance of approximately 18 inches.
Personal zone	–	Those who have a close personal relationship with other individuals will take up a distance of 18 inches to 4 feet.
Social/consultative	–	9 to 12 feet is an appropriate distance for professionals to interact with their clients and it can often be from behind a desk.
Public zone	–	Speakers on public occasions are usually placed at a distance of 12 feet or greater from their audience.

A study carried out by Baxter and Rozelle (1975) focused on a simulated police–citizen interview in which the distance between the officer and citizen was systematically varied according to Hall's first three distance categories. Briefly, as the interpersonal distance was decreased to within 2 feet of the two interactors, the citizen's speech time and frequency became disrupted and disorganised, eye movements and gaze aversion increased, more head movements (particularly rotating) increased, while foot movements decreased. These nonverbal behaviours, produced by manipulating the interpersonal distance zone, were strikingly similar to those identified by 'real' police officers describing behaviours indicating guilt, suspicion and deception. Thus it is important to be aware that the initiator can influence the other person's nonverbal behaviour and misconstrue the resulting consequences. Although this research was related to one professional group only, it has implications for other professional situations, such as selection, survey and counselling interviews.

In addition, status differences between individuals must be taken into account when observing interpersonal distances. People of equal status tend to take up a closer distance to each other than people of unequal status (Zahn, 1991). In fact, where a status differential exists the lower-status individual will allow the higher-status individual to approach quite closely, but will rarely approach the high-status individual with the same degree of closeness – witness the teacher who invariably moves round the classroom helping individual pupils with learning difficulties. In some subjects like physical education, drama, and art, the teacher may actually physically help a pupil to accomplish a task. Yet we would struggle to find instances where the pupil voluntarily approaches close to the teacher. Indeed, in a number of situations pupils prefer the greatest possible distance to be kept between the teacher and themselves. Another example of this occurs when students enter a lecture room – the area of the room that gets filled up first tends to be the back row.

Physical characteristics of participants also, to some extent, determine the amount of distance between interactors. Kleck and Strenta (1985), for example, found that persons communicating with physically deformed individuals chose a greater initial distance.

Professionals in their everyday working lives should be aware that whatever the position they take up in relation to their clients, it will have an effect on the kind of relationship they are hoping to achieve (Worchel, 1986).

Orientation

This aspect of nonverbal behaviour ought to be considered in relation to the previous component, proximity, since not only do individuals create interpersonal space, but the angle at which one person interacts with another affects the communication pattern. Orientation refers to the position of the body rather than the head and eyes only. It is useful to look at proximity and orientation together since it has been found that there is an inverse relationship between them – that is direct face-to-face orientation is linked to greater distance and sideways orientation linked to closer distance.

Sommer's early studies (1969) in North America of seating behaviour, replicated by Cook (1970) in the UK, point to some interesting differences in seating arrangements when individuals are given a choice of where to sit in different situations. Figure 3.1 will help to present some of these findings, the situations clearly indicating that a side-by-side position is considered to be cooperative in nature, while a face-to-face orientation usually conveys intonations of competitiveness. Conversation, however, appears to benefit from individuals taking up a 90° angle in relation to each other. At the same time, co-action would be a more conducive situation for studying or for children required to work independently at a task in the classroom.

PHYSICAL CHARACTERISTICS

Physical characteristics, as a potent aspect of the nonverbal channel cannot be over-emphasised, particularly in their influence in initiating some form of social contact. Before we even know what a person sounds like or what she has to say we are beginning to make judgements about her on the basis of physical appearance (see Chapter 7 for a further discussion on this issue). In our society physical attractiveness is one of the key dimensions of appearance, although we do manipulate our appearance on other occasions to signify a particular occupation, status or personality type. The importance of physical attractiveness is abundantly evident in both the amount and variety of artefacts, such as make-up, jewellery, wigs, false nails, perfume, after-shave,

Position of participants	Type of interaction	Suggested situations
X X ▭	Conversation	1 Counselling interview. 2 Employer interviewing an employee. 3 Some progressive job interviews.
X X ▭	Cooperation	1 Friends meeting in a pub. 2 Teacher helping a pupil in his work. 3 Staff cooperating on the same project.
X ▭ X	Competition	1 Some job interviews. 2 Headmaster interviewing a pupil. 3 Playing games such as chess, poker, etc.
X ▭ X	Co-action	1 Strangers in a public eating place. 2 Unfamiliar students working at same library table. 3 Strangers sharing a seat on a train.

Figure 3.1 Seating preferences at a rectangular table

high-heeled shoes, foundation garments, etc. which are readily available in the High Street shops. The potency of attractiveness was shown in an interesting study of trainee teachers by Hore (1971) who found that female student teachers who were considered 'attractive' by their male college tutors received consistently higher grades on teaching practice than those who were considered 'unattractive'. It would, however, have been interesting to find out if Hore would have obtained similar results from a survey of female tutors' grades of male student teachers.

In later writings, Berscheid and Walster (1978) found that physically attractive persons are consistently judged more favourably in initial inter-actions and suggest that the effects of physical attractiveness even outweigh the influence of expressive style. However, Riggio and Friedman (1986), in a study designed to identify those nonverbal and verbal cues which determined likeability, confidence and competence when persons were engaged in public speaking, found that physical attractiveness, although initially important, in the long term was less important than other social skills such as expressive facial behaviours and speech and gestural fluency. This finding was endorsed by Barnes and Rosenthal (1985), investigating the effects of physical attractiveness and attire in same and mixed-sex dyads. Results indicated that 'when actual people are used instead of photographs, the strong effect of physical attractiveness may become diluted by the amount of other information available' (p. 445).

These findings have implications for a number of professionals. For instance, McHenry (1981) argued that in the selection interview, a candidate may often be selected within the first 4 minutes of the interview and that interviewers are strongly influenced by physical cues such as 'physical attractiveness, beards, spectacles, height, clothes, etc., which have rather little correlation with the abilities being sought' (p. 19). The same author claimed that it is impossible to eliminate biased judgements completely but that by teaching an interviewer what to look for in a candidate, value judgements regarding appearance cues can be minimised.

In a recent study carried out by Melamed and Bozionelos (1992) the aim was to examine the relationship between physical height and managerial promotion among 132 British managers from the civil service. Analyses of the results suggest that even taking into account the personality traits of the managers, height was a more potent factor in determining who attained promotion. In other words, candidates were more likely to advance to higher grades in a short time if they were tall. Hitherto, research had suggested that height could affect selection decisions but not promotions (Mazur et al., 1984). These latter authors' rationale was based on the notion that physical attributes, such as height, influence and help to establish first impressions. However, if the managers are already familiar with the employee, as in a promotion decision, then the role of first impression is negligible. A possible explanation is that a process of self-fulfilling prophecy takes place. It is well established that tall people are perceived more positively than short people (Hensley and Cooper, 1987), and these expectations may reinforce behaviours associated with success in the work place and increase the likelihood of promotion.

In addition, Mayfield (1972) noted that factors such as physical attractiveness and being liked were related to sales effectiveness, especially when the salespersons had similar characteristics to the customers in terms of background (e.g. education and work history) and appearance (e.g. physique).

Hair, face, body shape and clothes can be manipulated by individuals and continually serve as a communication function. At the present time, length and colour of hair are important to certain groups of males in our society. Some adolescents, for example, favour keeping the hair long while many of their elders regard long hair as representative of a lack of both moral and social standards. More recently, shaving the head or wearing hair extremely short in 'skinhead' fashion or dyeing it in outrageous colours, depicts rebelliousness or a rejection of the present standards of society. Teachers in school, in a bid to get adolescents to conform to the cultural norm, often insist that a boy's hair must be cut when it reaches the shirt collar. Yet some young men find that to have long hair is more appealing to their young male and female counterparts. This is where the dilemma begins.

Facial expressions, as we saw earlier in the chapter, can tell us a great deal about a person but so also can the skin and the way it is decorated or left undecorated. Age can often be determined by the amount of wrinkles which are present on the face. We therefore get clues as to the kind of interaction which would be appropriate for certain age categories of persons. Women, especially, attempt to conceal signs of ageing by using make-up, or more drastically with face-lifts, yet generally men do not. Some interesting studies have found that people who wear spectacles are considered intelligent while girls who wear an abundance of make-up, particularly painted lips, are seen as more frivolous (Argyle and McHenry, 1971).

Not only do we learn a great deal about others from their body shape but we also like to find out what we think of ourselves – our self-image. As we grow we develop a picture of the ideal body type and this results in varying degrees of satisfaction with our own bodies in relation to that ideal type – particularly during adolescence. Generally, females consider that smallness and slimness are the most desirable states, while males are more satisfied with their shape when it is tall and muscular. Thus weight-watchers groups, health and beauty clubs and dance centres flourish to cater for women, while weight-training, body-building and rugby, football or other sports clubs flourish for men. Indeed, despite the influence of women's movements in recent years, there is little evidence to suggest that these sex differential patterns are changing rapidly.

Finally, although clothes basically serve to protect us from the cold, they also provide us with a great deal of information about the wearers. For example, personality characteristics can be reflected in the style of clothes, conservative individuals preferring more muted colours and conventional styles to more extrovert persons who tend to dress in the latest fashion and favour more flamboyant colours. It is interesting to note that persons who are going for a job interview often take great pains over choosing a sober shirt, tie and suit in order to appear conventional and serious, yet may favour 'gear' clothes in their non-work time. Social status, self-awareness and self-evaluation, too, can be inferred from the type of clothes worn (Solomon and Schopler, 1982). Thus schools may go to great lengths to impose school uniform on children, in an attempt to 'de-individualise', i.e. make pupils less aware of themselves as individuals. Uniforms, as well as occasionally protecting individuals from harm (e.g. deep-sea divers, firemen, grand prix drivers and test pilots), act as a means of identification and are immediately recognisable. Bickman (1974a) found that compliance with simple requests (i.e. putting a dime in a parking meter for someone else) was greatest when the asker was dressed in a uniform. These specific features may have a profound influence on resulting behaviour. The danger comes in stereotyping too closely those associated with a distinct physical appearance and dress. Research on impression management has long demonstrated that most people are willing to make inferences about the personal characteristics of others based upon scanty information (Schneider *et al.*, 1979). Professional interactors, especially in first encounters with clients, must examine the basis of their initial impressions of another since it will affect subsequent encounters and, more importantly, the expectations brought to future encounters.

ENVIRONMENTAL FACTORS

Most people will have had the experience of being invited to someone's home and feeling that the atmosphere was friendly and relaxed, the furniture arrangements pleasant and comfortable, and within no time feeling 'at home'. Conversely, most of us on another occasion will have been invited to a home which would not be unsuited to feature on the pages of *Vogue* but which appears stiff, unlived in and cold. We hesitate to sit down or touch anything lest we upset the neat, clean and tidy arrangement in any way. In other words, environmental situations appear to affect the type of interaction which will be obtained.

Interviewers, intent on relaxing their clients in an attempt to get them to converse more freely, should arrange the physical setting to produce this effect. Easy-type chairs set near a window, with pot plants on the ledge, and a coffee table placed near the chairs to hold ashtray and coffee cups, is much more conducive to a relaxed conversation-type interview than hard chairs, placed on either side of a desk in a room with metal filing cabinets and notice boards.

Haines (1975) referred to this essential element when identifying crucial communication skills for social workers. He stated that

> courtesy, kind words and gestures and attempts to ensure that clients are seated comfortably in an atmosphere that is warm both physically and psychologically are all aspects of reception that go far to create a sound basis for the development of effective communication.
>
> (p. 171)

Korda (1976) carried out research into the arrangement of furniture, particularly within offices, and identified two distinct areas; the zone around the desk he called the 'pressure area'; the semi-social area is the area away from the desk in which there are armchairs and a coffee table. According to Korda the effective businessman will select that area of the office more appropriate to the task he wishes to carry out with a particular client or colleague. Thus variations in the arrangements of environmental factors such as architectural style (modern or classical), interior decor, lighting conditions, colours, sounds, etc., can be extremely influential on the outcome of interpersonal communication (Canter and Wools, 1970; Smith, 1974). (See Chapter 7 for further information on the effects of the environment on initial perceptions.)

PARALANGUAGE

Paralinguistics is commonly referred to as that which is left after subtracting the verbal content from speech. The simple cliché, language is what is said, paralanguage is how it is said, can be misleading because frequently how something is said determines the precise meaning of what is said. This can be exemplified in the following statement: 'Mary's lending me her book.' If we decide to place more vocal emphasis on certain words we can alter the meaning of that statement:

  1 MARY's lending me her book.
  1a *Mary* is the one giving the book; no one else.
  2 Mary's LENDING me her book.
  2a Mary's *lending*, not giving or selling her book.
  3 Mary's lending ME her book.
  3a The receiver is *me* and no one else.
  4 Mary's lending me HER book.
  4a The book being lent is *not from another source*.
  5 Mary's lending me her BOOK.
  5a Nothing else is being lent, only her *book*.

Mehrabian and Ferris (1967) lend support to the notion that vocal cues assist in the total impact of any given message. In addition, paralinguistic features of speech also convey emotional features. Jaffe *et al*. (1979) noted that most persons can identify paralinguistic expressions such as rhythm of speech pattern, stress on individual words, rate of speech, pitch and volume, and define cultural meaning from their enactment. Scherer (1979) claimed that rate can be directly related to anger: 'hot' anger has a notably fast tempo while 'cool' anger is more moderate in pace. In addition, Scherer also noted that 'Extreme pitch variation and up contours produce ratings of highly pleasant active, and potent emotions such as happiness, interest, surprise and also fear. Down contours have similar effects but do not seem to contain elements of surprise or uncertainty' (p. 251). One emotional state which is likely to produce speech errors is apprehension. In the early stages of interaction with others, participants can be beset by 'speech dysfluencies'. However, as the participants become more familiar with the situation, the frequency of speech errors decreases (Scott *et al*., 1978).

Silence, and pauses in speech pattern, are common occurrences although the length or duration of pauses ranges considerably. Matarazzo *et al*. (1965) found that when an interviewer did not respond immediately to a statement by an interviewee, almost 60 per cent of the interviewees began to speak again. Newman (1982) contended that when silence occurs in the talk of strangers

and acquaintances, and there is no ongoing activity to account for it, s
is associated with discomfort and negative feelings. Hargie (1980) rep
results which indicated that by pausing after asking a question or after a pupil
responds, teachers can increase the level of pupil participation in classroom
lessons (this issue is further explored in Chapter 5).

[In addition to conveying meaning and emotions, changes in a speaker's
vocal pattern can be useful in gaining and maintaining the attention of
others.] We have all had experience of the guest speaker at 'Speech Days'
who speaks in such a dreary monotone that he can make the most interesting
material seem boring. Conversely, quite boring material can become interesting if delivered by someone who stimulates interest, by changing the pitch,
tone, speed and volume of vocal pattern.] Politicians and good public
speakers use these vocal techniques in order to emphasise points, stimulate
feelings and generally obtain and sustain the interest of their audiences
(Watzlawick, 1978).

OVERVIEW

As Knapp and Hall (1992) have stated, interactors need information about
other people's characteristics, attributes, attitudes and values in order to
know how to deal with one another. Direct measures of personality, intelligence, values and social status are often hard to obtain from the person
herself. Yet we often infer these states from the behavioural cues presented to
us. Of course the situation also works in reverse; not only do we gather
information about others from the way they present themselves to us, but we
ourselves go to great lengths to present others with a certain type of picture of
ourselves. This form of self-presentation does not take place all the time, only
when an individual is 'being observed' or is in the presence of others

Thus all of the situations which have periodically been referred to
throughout this chapter are the contexts within which people present, and
attempt to control certain aspects of, their self-image. The majority of signals
used to communicate these self-images are nonverbal in nature and range, as
we have seen, from appearance to posture, from clothes to facial expressions,
from paralinguistic features of speech to the environment itself. The potency
of the nonverbal aspects of behaviour cannot be underestimated and professionals should be sensitive to the kind of atmosphere they are creating, the
scene they are setting, and the parameters they are placing on an interaction
before they even begin to speak.

A knowledge of the various facets of nonverbal communication, and of
their effects in social interaction, can enable us to improve both our ability to
interpret the cues which are emitted by others, and our ability to control the
impressions which we are conveying to others. Many of the elements of
nonverbal communication which have been discussed in this chapter will
recur in the remaining chapters of this book. At the start of this chapter it was

emphasised that all social interaction is dependent upon the interplay, sometimes subtly conveyed, between the verbal and nonverbal messages. Therefore, all the remaining skills, from reinforcement outlined in Chapter 4 through to group interaction set out in Chapter 13, will contain some of the nonverbal aspects which have been discussed in this present chapter.

Chapter 4

Rewarding and reinforcing

INTRODUCTION

One of the basic principles governing behaviour is that people tend to engage in activities which are associated with some sort of positively valued outcome for them. Alternative courses of action that are thought, often from past experience, to produce little of consequence or, indeed, unwanted effects, are not maintained. Activities performed are, of course, enormously varied, as is the range of outcomes sought. Some of the more obvious examples of the latter pertain to physical well-being and include food, water, shelter, etc., while others, such as the company of an attractive partner, are less basic but still important. Events which are even less tangible, yet highly valued just the same, include such positive features of interpersonal contact as a friendly smile, word of praise from someone respected or an enthusiastic reaction from an attentive listener. As described by Argyle (1983b, p. 65), 'A person can be rewarding in a large variety of ways – by being warm and friendly, taking an interest in the other, admiring him, being submissive, showing sexual approval, helping with his problems, or by being interesting and cheerful.' The fact that such acts can influence the behaviour of the recipient is central to the concept of reinforcement as an interpersonal skill.

Faraone and Hurtig (1985) examined what those regarded as highly socially skilled actually did, compared to their low social skill counterparts, when they conversed with a stranger of the opposite sex. They found that the highly skilled were more rewarding in the way in which they reduced uncertainty, and therefore possible unease in the situation, and were more positive towards the other through what was said and topics introduced. Likewise in professional circles, the ability to reward and reinforce effectively during dealings with those availing themselves of the service on offer, has been heavily stressed.

REINFORCEMENT AND PROFESSIONAL PRACTICE

Those who have attempted to analyse how practitioners characteristically relate, frequently identify responding positively to those with whom they engage so as to reward and reinforce appropriately, as one of the core skills.

In education, for instance, Turney *et al.* (1983) included reinforcement in their anthology of basic teaching skills. They describe how teachers can increase pupils' attention and motivation, improve classroom behaviour and promote achievement by various verbal and nonverbal means including praise and encouragement, touch, gestures, adjusting physical proximity and making available the opportunity to take part in other activities such as playing class games with peers.

Shifting the focus from teaching to interviewing and counselling, Ivey and Authier (1978), in their quest to develop a taxonomy of microskills embodied in these activities, specified attending and listening as being of fundamental importance:

> The most basic unit of microcounseling is attending behavior, the careful listening to the client. The beginning counselor who is able to attend to and hear the client is equipped to start counseling sessions. Without the ability to attend, the helping interview – regardless of theoretical orientation – becomes an empty sham.

(p. 64)

Based on the premise that people will only talk about what others are prepared to listen to, they outline how clients can be encouraged to disclose issues of concern through the use of attending behaviour and the reinforcing effects in this endeavour of selective listening on the part of the counsellor. (See Chapter 9 for further information on listening.)

Reinforcement has also been identified as playing a prominent role in the practice of speech therapy. In a significant piece of research, Saunders and Caves (1986) undertook to unearth the key communication skills utilised by members of this profession in conducting therapy with both child and adult clients. Therapists were video-taped during consultations and this material was then subjected to peer analysis. From isolated positive and negative instances, the object was to reach consensus on a set of behavioural categories of effective practice. 'Using positive reinforcement' was one of the categories to emerge from interactions with children as well as adults. Verbal and nonverbal sub-types were specified. Using a similar methodology, Hargie *et al.* (1993) identified a number of rewarding behaviours which seem to be central to effective communication in community pharmacy practice.

Social rewards, including praise, make a potentially beneficial contribution to other and diverse areas of professional activity such as management and coaching. In the former setting there is some evidence that when properly programmed, improvements in absenteeism, motivation, job satisfaction and productivity can result (Davey, 1981; Rapp *et al.*, 1983). Sports coaches who employ these techniques have been found to be popular, especially with younger competitors, to enhance levels of skill and to improve results among those with whom they work (Martin and Hrycaiko, 1983; Smith and Smoll, 1990).

In the field of health care, DiMatteo and DiNicola (1982) and Raven (1988), among others, have recognised health worker social rewards in the form of attention, praise, approval, compliments, etc., as one (but only one) approach to increasing, for example, patient satisfaction and tackling the abiding problem of improving compliance with prescribed drug regimens and recommended courses of action. By taking steps to monitor patient behaviour and reinforce compliance when it does take place, health workers can go some way to ensuring that patients cooperate fully in their treatment. This may have particular impact in cases of adherence to difficult or stressful courses of action when, 'the here-and-now reward value of maintaining contact with a respected helper can tip the balance in favour of good intentions when the client is tempted to avoid the here-and-now costs and suffering' (Janis, 1983, p. 148). Both Janis (1983) and Raven (1988) emphasise that influencing change along these lines presupposes the prior establishment of a relationship of trust, acceptance and respect. It is only in this context that praise and approval are likely to be valued.

BEHAVIOUR AND ITS CONSEQUENCES

Since Ivan Pavlov, the eminent Russian physiologist, introduced the term (Pavlov, 1927), the concept of reinforcement has been the subject of much heated debate in psychology. One psychologist who was at the forefront of much of this during his long and highly active academic life was B.F. Skinner (1953, 1974, 1978). The application of reinforcement procedures in keeping with Skinnerian principles is known as *instrumental* or *operant conditioning*. The central tenet of this process focuses on the ability of the consequences of behaviour to modify the probability of subsequent manifestations of that behaviour (Schwartz, 1989).

For any particular piece of behaviour, we can think, first, of environmental stimuli which precede or accompany it and, second, of others which take place afterwards. Take the classroom example of a teacher asking the class a question to which a child raises his or her hand. As far as the child's act is concerned, the most conspicuous antecedent stimulus is obviously the posed question. The pupil's response also takes place within the context of a plethora of stimuli which constitute the classroom environment. Other stimuli follow on from it and are made available as a consequence of the behaviour having been performed, e.g. the teacher may react enthusiastically, the child may be offered the opportunity to display knowledge by answering, etc. The role of antecedent stimuli will be returned to, but for the moment those events which are the products of performance will be further considered.

In broadest terms, the relationship between a response and its consequences may be such that that type of response is subsequently either, (1) increased in frequency; (2) decreased in frequency; or (3) left largely unaffected – given that behaviour can have several predictable outcomes, it may be that some are of little importance one way or another to the person concerned and therefore of no functional significance. As to the first of these eventualities, reinforcement is the process taking place. Rewards or reinforcers serve to make preceding actions more likely to recur. (Skinner preferred the term 'reinforcement' to 'reward' due to the greater semantic precision which it afforded, together with its lack of mentalistic trappings. As such, a reinforcer, by definition, has the effect of increasing the probability of the preceding behaviour.)

Reinforcement can take a positive or a negative form, as will be explained shortly. Before doing so though, we will consider outcomes that serve to reduce the likelihood of similar actions being conducted.

Punishment

Punishment has the effect of suppressing behaviour thus making it less likely that those acts leading to it will be repeated. Indeed, it too can operate in either a positive or a negative way: the former through the administration of something unpleasant, a noxious stimulus, contingent upon the appearance of the targeted behaviour; the latter by withdrawing some benefit which, had the individual not acted in that way, would continue to have been enjoyed.

Attempts at control and influence through punishment are common in everyday interaction and may be subtly exercised. They can involve sarcasm, ridicule, derision, reprimands and threat, to specify but a few. A number of undesirable side-effects have been associated with punishment, some of which are summarised by Balsam and Bondy (1983). It can produce negative emotional reactions which can generalise beyond the response being punished to the punishing agent, say a teacher, to the subject taught, even to school itself!

Extinction

When actions previously reinforced cease, for whatever reason, to produce customarily positively valued outcomes, the likely long-term effect will also be a reduction in those activities. This occurs through the phenomenon of *extinction*. Thus while there are important differences between punishment and extinction, both serve to reduce the likelihood of a response (Hulse *et al.*, 1980).

Positive reinforcement

Reinforcement, as noted, can be engineered through positive or negative means. When behaving in a particular way leads to the introduction of some event that would not have occurred otherwise, any increase in this type of behaviour as a result is due to positive reinforcement. The pupil in the earlier example may have had his contribution to the lesson enthusiastically endorsed making it more likely that he would be prepared to make further contributions given the opportunity. It is positive reinforcement that is commonly acknowledged when reinforcement is talked of as a social skill, and it is therefore this type around which much of the chapter will be based.

Negative reinforcement

Here an act is associated with the avoidance, termination or reduction of an aversive stimulus which would have either occurred or continued at some existing level had the response not taken place. Negative reinforcement and punishment must not be confused despite the fact that the terms are sometimes treated interchangeably in the literature (Green, 1977). Although both involve aversive states, in the case of punishment this state is made contingent on the occurrence of the behaviour under focus and has the effect of making that behaviour *less* likely to recur. With negative reinforcement, behaviour resulting in the noxious stimulus being reduced, eliminated or avoided will be *more* probable.

The effects of people earning rewards of this negative kind for doing certain tasks have been well researched and documented but mostly as part of organised programmes of intervention in such institutional settings as mental hospitals, prisons and special schools. Allen and Stokes (1987) introduced this approach to manage the disruptive and uncooperative behaviour of children receiving restorative dental treatment. In this case children were asked to be 'Big Helpers' by lying still and being quiet while the dentist worked. This led to the temporary suspension of treatment. Gradually children had to be 'Big Helpers' for longer periods of time in order to have the dentist suspend treatment for a period. Not only were children markedly more compliant by the last visit but, from readings of heart rate and blood pressure, were significantly less stressed by the experience.

But opportunities in day-to-day interactions for controlling social behaviour through negative reinforcement can also be found. Bringing to an end as quickly as possible an interchange with someone found unpleasant, uninteresting or just difficult to relate to, could presumably be accounted for in this way (Cipani, 1990). Some evidence for this interpretation emerged from a laboratory-based experiment undertaken by Cramer *et al.* (1989), in which it was discovered that female subjects preferred males who espoused less traditional male values and attitudes. Within the experimental procedure, characteristics of females' switching as they changed from listening over an intercom to a 'macho' male, to listening to one who adhered less rigidly to the traditional male stereotype, was consistent with what would be expected if the former experience was aversive, making the negative reinforcement of switching behaviour possible. A similar explanation for the phenomenon of speaking in reply, especially in conversations where one's opinion has been challenged by the other party, has been put forward by Weiss *et al.* (1971) and Lombardo *et al.* (1973). Again, disagreement with one's point of view can be aversive; having the chance to subsequently defend it can bring relief and therefore make responding more likely.

Conversational 'repair' is a further feature of talk (McLaughlin, 1984). Apologies and disclaimers, as examples, are brought into play when participants unwittingly break a conversational or societal rule, thereby running the risk of losing face. Approaching this interpersonal activity from a behavioural perspective, Baldwin and Baldwin (1981) explain it in terms of negative reinforcement. Breaking the rule may cause embarrassment or discomfort which is assuaged by an apology or disclaimer thereby making it likely that these forms of repair will be relied upon in similar situations in future.

For negative reinforcement to work, there must be an existing state of unease or discomfort which can be reduced or eliminated through some action. What happens in situations where nothing that individuals do seems to bring relief, where the aversive stimuli to which they are subjected seem to be beyond their powers to control? According to Seligman (1975), when what we do appears persistently to bear no relationship to outcome, making it impossible to control unpleasant experiences to which we are subjected, *learned helplessness* often results. People become passive, apathetic and simply give up trying. Furthermore, and particularly when the cause is attributed to personal inability, this helplessness can generalise to other situations (Mikulineer, 1986), and give rise to stress (Glass and Singer, 1972) and depression (Seligman, 1975).

CATEGORIES OF POSITIVE REINFORCEMENT

The vast range of things that we do as we go about our daily lives gives rise to a multiplicity of differing outcomes, both physical and social. Many of these exert a controlling influence through the operation of positive reinforcement. Is it possible to begin to impose order on these innumerable instances of specific reinforcing event by classifying them according to some pertinent criterion? Among psychologists who respond affirmatively to this question, Sherman (1990) suggests that at least five categories can be identified.

Primary reinforcers

These can be thought of as stimuli, the positive value and reinforcing potential of which do not rely upon a process of prior learning. Ones that spring most readily to mind, some of which were mentioned in the introduction to the chapter, include food, drink, sex, etc. These are things that we depend on for survival due to our biological make-up. Despite their fundamental indispensability, the limitations of these as a direct means of influencing the complexities of interpersonal behaviour in modern society will be quickly appreciated. Here the rewards tend to be less basic.

Conditioned reinforcers

This grouping, which is also labelled **secondary reinforcers**, is in sharp contrast to the previous. It includes events that have no intrinsic worth but whose power to control behaviour is ultimately derived from an earlier association with primary reinforcers. Contrasting theoretical accounts of just how this happens are offered by Fantino (1977). Tokens, stickers, vouchers, stamps, badges, stars, etc., have been incorporated into organised programmes called *token economies* where they are earned for engaging in certain tasks and subsequently exchanged for something of greater appeal (Kazdin, 1988).

Under certain circumstances, an originally neutral stimulus can become associated with a plurality of primary reinforcers. Money, to cite one example, can be used to obtain food, drink, heat, sex, etc. Skinner (1953) gave the name *generalised reinforcers* to refer to this special class.

Social reinforcers

Social behaviour, by definition, presupposes the involvement of other people. In the main, the types of reward that govern and shape it are also contributed by those with whom we mix and intermingle. These rewards, Buss (1983) suggests, can be thought of as either process or content. The former are an inherent part of interpersonal contact and include, in order of increasing potency, the mere presence of others, attention from them and their conversational responsivity. An interesting observation is that too much or too little of these activities can be aversive; it is only at a notional intermediate level that they become reinforcing. This view is echoed by Epling and Pierce (1988), who comment that the attention given by a teacher to a pupil in the same environment may well change from being reinforcing to punishing as a function of the increase or decrease in frequency of delivery.

What takes place within interaction has also rewarding ramifications. Here Buss pays particular heed to the acts of showing deference, praising, extending sympathy and expressing affection. Unlike their process equivalents, these are thought to operate along unipolar dimensions and, additionally, presuppose a certain type of interpersonal relationship to be relevant and effective. We seldom praise or show affection to complete strangers, for instance. As well as process and content rewards, individuals can find variously reinforcing opportunities to compare themselves to others, compete, dominate or self-disclose, and may seek out situations and occasions to indulge themselves accordingly.

Skinner (1974) and Bandura (1986), among others, speak of individuals being moulded as social beings through the influence of the social milieu of which they are a part. As we have seen, the subtleties of the process make use of the judicious distribution, by significant members, of attention, interest, approval, affection and so on. It is these sorts of activities that lie at the heart of positive responding conceived of as an interpersonal skill. Through them one person can determine what another does without constant recourse to physical intervention. Furthermore, since many of the projects with which we concern ourselves are long-term, a great deal of initial effort may be expended with few tangible results to show in return. Here Bandura (1986) stresses the role of support from others in sustaining goal-directed performance.

According to Skinner, positive social reactions can be used to shape interpersonal behaviour because they serve as generalised reinforcers. Of 'approval' he wrote,

> A common generalised reinforcer is approval. . . . It may be little more than a nod of the head or a smile on the part of someone who characteristically supplies a variety of reinforcers. Sometimes . . . it has a verbal form 'Right!' or 'Good!'

(Skinner, 1957, p. 53)

Similarly, 'The attention of people is reinforcing because it is a necessary condition for other reinforcements from them. In general, only those who are attending to us reinforce our behaviour' (Skinner, 1953, p. 78).

For Lieberman (1990), among others, these aspects of social performance, in that they can be thought of at all as reinforcers in the Skinnerian sense, embrace both learned and unlearned dimensions. To be more specific, the suggestion is that some of the nonverbal features such as smiles and hugs may *not* depend upon prior experience to be positively valued.

Sensory reinforcers

One need only think of the attractions of, for example, listening to beautiful music, looking at a striking painting, attending the theatre or watching an exciting rugby match, together with the effort and expense that devotees will often sustain to do so, to appreciate that certain quantities and qualities of sensory stimulation can be rewarding.

This fact was exploited by Mizes (1985) in treating an adolescent girl who was hospitalised following complaints of chronic lower-back pain. The extent of this pain was such that she was virtually bed-ridden. Tests and examinations having failed to locate any physical cause, the case was treated as an abnormal behaviour disorder which was being inadvertently held in place through operant conditioning. When opportunities to watch TV, have access to the telephone and receive parental visits were made conditional upon demonstrably increased mobility, symptoms gradually subsided.

Activity reinforcers

According to David Premack, activities rather than things are reinforcing. It is eating, drinking, etc. that is of significance rather than food or drink, as such. Stated formally, the *Premack Principle*, as it is commonly known, proposes that activities of low probability can be increased in likelihood if activities of high probability are made contingent upon them (Premack, 1965).

Activity reinforcement can be a powerful means of organising work routines and maximising commitment in a diversity of professional settings including management, industry and education. Pupils may prefer practical classes to more didactic instruction but, given the freedom to choose, they would probably fill their time in some other way. This likelihood was put to good use by Hutchins *et al.* (1989), to improve low achieving secondary pupils' punctuality and readiness to begin lessons on time. The agreement was that if the entire class was present and prepared to begin work within 1 minute of the bell to signal the beginning of the period, the last 4 minutes would be set aside for members to do whatever they pleased. The effect of this group contingent free-time procedure was an average five-fold improvement in good time-keeping. Pupils also reacted favourably to it and teachers reported that more academic work got completed as a result.

The potential for these principles to enhance managerial effectiveness and raise output has been recognised by Komaki (1982). Increasing productivity was demonstrated by Gupton and LeBow (1971) through an internal rearrangement of the various types of task that workers carry out. In this case the workers were part-time telephone sales personnel in industry who sold both new and renewal service contracts. On average the success rate for attempts at renewals was more than twice that for new sales, so sales personnel tended to devote most of their energies to the former. As far as the firm was concerned this resulted in a general failure to attract new customers. By imposing the Premack Principle, five new calls were required before the representatives had an opportunity to make attempts at renewal sales. This contingency resulted in a substantial increase not only in the number of new contracts sold but renewals as well.

It should not be assumed, however, that only certain activities can reinforce. Premack stressed that any behaviour can increase the likelihood of any other provided that the former tends to occur more frequently and, in order to perform it, the latter has to be carried out. Instrumental and reinforcing actions are not intrinsically different: reinforcement is relative rather than absolute.

STIMULUS CONTROL

It was mentioned earlier in the chapter that behaviour can be set in a context of, on the one hand, preceding and accompanying stimuli and, on the other, consequent events. It must also be acknowledged that a particular response sometimes produces a rewarding consequence but at other times fails to. When a certain action only succeeds in eliciting reinforcement in the presence of particular accompanying stimuli then that piece of behaviour is said to be under *stimulus control* (Domjan and Burkhard, 1986) and those stimuli have become *discriminative stimuli* in respect of it. They signal the availability of a reinforcer for behaving in that way.

Many examples of stimulus control spring to mind. Fisher and Groce (1990) describe the doctor–patient consultation as a typically one-sided affair in which, 'Physicians solicit technical information from patients who provide the information requested, responding in a relatively passive fashion' (p. 226). Here the doctor is the one who asks the questions and introduces topics for discussion; blatant attempts by patients to negotiate their own agendas meet with little success. In this setting, doctor questions perhaps serve as discriminative stimuli indicating to patients when their contributions will be welcomed and when not! The perspicacious employee who learns to read the subtle cues that suggest the likelihood of his manager being receptive to new ideas, and accordingly picks his opportunity to propose some innovation, is also being influenced by stimulus control.

Discriminative stimuli, therefore, signal the occasion for particular behaviours to be reinforced and must not be confused with reinforcing stimuli. As stressed by Higgins and Morris (1985), the latter must always function as a consequence of the targeted behaviour while the former typically pre-date it.

VICARIOUS REINFORCERS

So far we have discussed the direct impact of positive outcome on the acquisition and regulation of the behaviour that brought it about. But the influence of rewards is more wide-ranging. Through observing our actions others learn not only how, but what to do; they benefit from our successes. Bandura (1986, p. 285) asserted that,

If a person experiences consequences in a group setting, the observed outcomes can affect the behaviour of the group as a whole. Even mild praise or reprimand can lead other group members to adopt praiseworthy acts and to avoid censurable ones. . . .

The implications of this fact for professional practice are far-reaching. Turney *et al.* (1983) highlighted the difficulty of a teacher, in a large and busy classroom, providing reinforcement on an individual basis, for appropriate behaviour and accomplishments. Under these circumstances an appreciation of how vicarious reinforcement can be put to good use, is particularly valuable.

In relation to management, the maxim of 'praise publicly–punish privately', cited by Prue and Fairbank (1981), articulates the potentially vicarious benefits of bestowing rewards in the presence of others. This practice was used effectively by O'Reilly and Puffer (1989) to enhance expressed motivation, satisfaction and productivity among a group of retail sales clerks, when the basis of reward allocation was seen to be fair. On a more cautionary note, however, it should be recognised that, first, praising in public can cause embarrassment for some and, if so, may produce negative rather than positive effects (Giacolone and Rosenfeld, 1987). Second, watching others persistently rewarded for something that the observer has done equally competently, but without comparable recompense, may cause resentment and demotivation. The latter has been referred to as the implicit effects of observed consequences and, as such, distinguished from vicarious facets, by Bandura (1986).

Rewards, vicariously experienced, can influence learning, motivation and emotions. In respect of learning, greater heed will probably be paid to what others do, and their action will be remembered for longer, when it is seen to succeed in gaining something desired. Indeed, when such learning is highly cognitively taxing, being freed from the behavioural reproduction and recognition of consequent elements which are part and parcel of direct reinforcement, is often a distinct advantage as far as the acquisition process is concerned. When it comes to regulating behaviour in the longer term though, directly experienced incentives are likely to prove more powerful (Bandura, 1977).

Seeing others rewarded for some action or behaviour can, therefore, act as a strong inducement for the observer to do likewise when it is inferred that similar outcomes will accrue. Furthermore, when the consequences of actions are socially mediated, a basis is established for reassessing the attractiveness of experienced outcomes through witnessing what happens to others under comparable conditions. Receiving recognition from a supervisor will probably mean much more once it is realised, from observations of interactions with others, that this person rarely acknowledges effort.

Receiving rewards and punishments is associated with the creation of pleasant and unpleasant emotional states. Awareness of these states and circumstances in other people can be emotionally arousing and this facility is believed, by Bandura (1986), to account for empathic responsivity to them. The ability to engage empathically with others is, of course, fundamental to effective counselling (Egan, 1986).

INTERPERSONAL EFFECTS OF SOCIAL REINFORCERS

A range of outcomes tend to be associated with social rewards and reinforcers. As listed by Dickson et al. (1993), these include:

1 Promoting interaction and maintaining relationships.
2 Increasing the involvement of the interactive partner.
3 Influencing the nature and content of the contribution of the other person.
4 Demonstrating a genuine interest in the ideas, thoughts and feelings of the other.
5 Making interaction interesting and enjoyable.

6 Creating an impression of warmth and understanding.
7 Increasing the social attractiveness of the source of rewards.
8 Improving the confidence and self-esteem of the recipient.
9 Manifesting power.

During social encounters we not only welcome but demand a certain basic level of reward. If it is not forthcoming we may treat this as sufficient grounds for abandoning the relationship in favour of more attractive alternatives. In a study undertaken by Jones *et al*. (1982), college students who were lonely, in comparison to their more gregarious peers, were found to be strikingly less attentive to conversational partners. Trower *et al*. (1978) have noted the marked lack of reinforcement which characterises the conversations of certain categories of mentally ill patient. It is suggested that their condition may be exacerbated by a lack of social rewards leading to reduced contact with others as relationships begin to crumble. Increased social isolation which results produces a further deterioration in their mental state with fewer opportunities for interpersonal involvement, thus creating a debilitating downward spiral.

For professionals who work mainly with other people, simply maintaining the interactive episode, while necessary, is not sufficient. It is important that the recipient of the service be encouraged to be fully involved in what takes place if the goals of the encounter are to be actualised. Promoting active participation in the classroom is a good example. Costs incurred by pupils, in the form of energy expended, lack of opportunity to devote time to competing activities, fear of getting it wrong, etc. must be offset by the availability of rewards. In some learning situations, e.g. acquiring a novel skill, intrinsic rewards from efficient task performance may be initially limited. Teacher reinforcement is therefore one method of increasing pupil commitment to what is taking place.

Apart from extending the general level of participation, rewards can be administered in a planned and systematic fashion to selectively reinforce and shape contributions along particular lines. When interviewing, the interviewee can be influenced in this way to continue with the detailed exploration of certain topics or issues to the exclusion of others regarded as being of lesser relevance or even counterproductive. In a medical setting, for instance, White and Sanders (1986) demonstrated how patients suffering from chronic pain conversationally focused more on their pain when the interviewer responded with attention and praise. Selectively reinforcing 'well talk', on the other hand, had the opposite effect. Using the same principles, teachers can increase the incidence of appropriate pupil behaviour in class (Wheldall and Glynn, 1989).

Before progressing, it should be acknowledged that, when worded in this way, there is little which is either original or profound in the proposition that people are inclined to do things that lead to positive outcomes and avoid other courses of action that produce unwanted consequences. This much is widely known. Indeed the statement may seem so obvious as to be trivial. But Lieberman (1990) makes the more interesting observation that, despite this general awareness, individuals are often remarkably unsuccessful in bringing about behavioural change both in themselves and in other people. The conclusion drawn is that, 'Clearly the principle of reward cannot be quite as simple as it sounds' (p. 157).

Many professionals make surprisingly poor use of this interpersonal skill. Cannell *et al.* (1977), investigating the performance of survey interviewers, disclosed that adequate or appropriate responses received proportionately less positive interviewer reinforcement than did less desirable reactions. Refusal to respond, the least desirable response, received proportionately the highest levels of reinforcement! Again Brophy (1981) has criticised teachers for failing to make proper use of praise in the classroom. Reviewing a number of studies, he concluded that its use is 'typically infrequent, noncontingent, global rather than specific, and determined more by students' personal qualities or teachers' perceptions of students' need for praise than by the quality of student conduct or achievement' (p. 8).

In addition to influencing what interactors say or do, providing rewards also conveys information about the source. Providers of substantial amounts of social reinforcement are usually perceived to be keenly interested in those with whom they interact and what they have to say. They also typically create an impression of being warm, accepting and understanding. Zimmer and Park (1967), for example, found that counsellors who created the impression of being warm were also more behaviourally attentive and used more supportive statements in their sessions with clients. By contrast those who, for the most part, dispense few social rewards are often regarded as cold, aloof, depressed, bored or even boring.

Extending this thinking, some investigators, including Lott and Lott (1968) and Clore and Byrne (1974), have made use of the concept of reinforcement in attempting to account for interpersonal attraction. Responses and pleasurable feelings which stem from receiving rewards become associated, it is proposed, with the provider, or even with a third party who happens to be consistently present when they are dispensed. Indeed, a number of studies have determined, perhaps predictably, that people like to receive praise, compliments and other similar positive evaluations and tend to like those who give them (Aronson, 1984).

Such attraction, though, is neither universal nor unconditional, depending, as it does, upon how what is taking place is construed by the recipient. The source is more likely to be found to be attractive if, for instance, the action being praised is regarded by the recipient as praiseworthy; praise from that individual is valued; and if it reflects a change from a more negative disposition by the source towards the recipient (Raven and Rubin, 1983). If, on the other hand, it is suspected that the source may have ulterior motives for lavish praise or compliments, and ingratiation or flattery are suspected, liking for that individual will probably suffer (Kleinke, 1986a). It is also improbable that such stimuli will have a reinforcing effect under these circumstances.

Positive reactions may not only produce more favourable impressions towards those who offer them (under certain conditions), but may also result in heightened feelings of *self-esteem* in the recipient. Self-esteem refers to the sense of personal worth that an individual entertains ranging from love and acceptance to hate and rejection. It can, in part, be based upon the persistent evaluations of significant others. Sullivan (1953) believed that one's concept of self develops out of the reflected appraisals of significant others. Thus positive rewarding experiences with parents and other key adults lead to favourable views of self, while experienced negativity including blame, constant reprimands, ridicule, etc. results in feelings of worthlessness.

However, it should not be assumed that people are merely in passive receipt of reactions from those with whom they interact. Rather they are in the business of presenting themselves in such a way as to attract a particular type of evaluative response from them (Backman, 1988). But what type of response? According to Tesser (1988) interactors seek to preserve a positive assessment of self and to be looked upon favourably. Attention, praise, approval and various other rewards already mentioned will be valued on these grounds. Others, including Swann *et al.* (1990), take a different line, arguing in support of a self-verification rather than self-enhancement position. It is not necessarily a positive evaluation that is being sought, they reason, but rather one that is consistent with the individual's existing self-referenced views and beliefs.

This line of thought has interesting and significant ramifications for rewarding and reinforcing. For those with a poor self-concept and low self-esteem, praise, and other positive reactions which are incongruent with how they regard themselves, may not be appreciated and fail to have a reinforcing influence. Indeed the opposite may be the case. Similarly, although for different reasons, Brokaw and McLemore (1983) cautioned against social reinforcement invariably being equated with friendly behaviour *per se*. They emphasised the complementarity between the social reinforcer and its targeted behaviour, discovering that confederate hostile-submissive responses to subjects' hostile-dominant statements produced a greater likelihood of that type of statement being repeated than did friendly-submissive utterances.

A further dimension of personality that is of functional relevance to social reinforcement is *locus of control* (Rotter, 1966). This term refers to the extent to which individuals regard themselves as having control over reinforcement received. Those who espouse internal control have the opinion that rewards gained are contingent upon their own performance and a reflection of their relatively enduring characteristics and qualities. At the other extreme, an external locus of control is typified by the idea that successes that may occasionally happen are due largely to chance, luck or some external influence. Kennelly and Mount (1985) assessed pupils' locus of control and found that internality, together with perceptions of teachers' reinforcement being contingent upon their behaviour, was predictive of good academic achievement and high ratings of pupil competence by teachers.

Finally, the possibility of the distribution of rewards as an exercise in power and authority should not be overlooked. Raven and Rubin (1983) mention this as one of six recognisably different forms of social power. (See Chapter 11 for further details.) Being in a position to determine whether or not another receives something valued confers on that person the ability to exert influence and determine the conditions under which rewards will be bestowed. When the giving of rewards is interpreted as an attempt at control, however, with the putative recipient valuing autonomy more highly than what is on offer, resistance to such manipulation may be provoked. O'Donnell *et al.* (1983) reported that subjects who realised what was taking place in a verbal conditioning experiment, but did not evince the expected increase in the reinforced response, tended to look upon what was happening as an attempt at social influence over them, to be resisted. This may be a manifestation of what Brehm and Brehm (1981) called *reactance*, or the attempt to assert personal freedom and autonomy when these are thought to be violated.

BEHAVIOURAL COMPONENTS OF SOCIAL REINFORCEMENT

It will be recalled that, in theory, anything which increases the frequency of the preceding piece of behaviour can be considered a reinforcer. Even if this list is restricted to elements of interpersonal behaviour, the resulting number of potential reinforcers could be extensive. We will, therefore, restrict coverage to the more widely recognised elements which have featured in the literature. In doing so, a conceptual distinction will be made between components which are essentially verbal and those that are nonverbal. While this is a convenient way of structuring the section, it should be recognised that in practice these two channels are closely interwoven.

Verbal components

The verbal channel of communication constitutes a powerful source of social reinforcement. Things said can provide feedback, validate self-views and strengthen feelings of self-esteem and self-worth, or have the opposite effect. Verbal components of reinforcement range in sophistication from simple expressions such as 'OK', to more elaborate responses which relate to some aspect of the functioning of the other.

Acknowledgement/confirmation

This category contains expressions, words and phrases which seem essentially to acknowledge, confirm or agree with what has been said or done. Examples include verbalisations such as 'OK', 'Yes', 'Right', 'Fine', 'I see', 'That's it', as well as nonlexical vocalisations like 'mm-hmm'. (Strictly speaking the latter would be more appropriately listed under the nonverbal heading but, since they have often been grouped along with the other verbal utterances exemplified, it is more convenient to include them here.) These listener responses are a common feature of conversations, being particularly noticeable when, for example, people talk over the telephone. It seems, in part, that they signal to the speaker that the message sent has been successfully received and understood, and that the listener is paying close attention (Rosenfeld, 1987).

From a counselling perspective, Ivey and Authier (1978) referred to these limited listener responses as 'minimal encouragers to talk' and, as part of a complex of basic attending skills which the counsellor should manifest, emphasised their role in helping the client to continue exploring areas of personal concern during the interview.

The reinforcing consequences of these attending utterances have been revealed in a number of experimental investigations, one of the most widely reported of which was that conducted by Greenspoon (1955). This researcher simply asked subjects to produce as many individual words as they could think of. By responding with 'mm-hmm', each time a subject gave a plural noun and ignoring all other types of words, the number of plural nouns mentioned by subjects increased considerably over the course of the experiment. A comparable finding was reported by Reece and Whitman (1962), who also selected plural nouns as the target response.

Attending behaviour of this type has also been found to enhance requests by interviewees for information during educational-vocational counselling sessions and, subsequently, to promote actual information-seeking activities outside of the interview setting (Samaan, 1971). Still in the area of vocational guidance and counselling, Oliver (1974) discovered that the career choices of male undergraduates could be steered in more realistic directions by selectively reinforcing, in a laboratory context, those choices that were in keeping with their occupational type, as determined by the Vocational Preference Inventory.

Not all investigations, though, have produced such positive outcomes. A study carried out by Siegman (1985), for instance, failed to corroborate findings by researchers like Matarazzo and Wiens (1972), and O'Brien and Holborn (1979) who documented the effects of a minimal encourager such as 'mm-hmm', on increasing the verbal contribution of respondents during interaction. Rosenfeld (1987) suggests that this failure may be accounted for by the fact that Siegman administered social reinforcers on a non-contingent basis (subjects were exposed to them regardless of whether they were engaging in lengthy speech turns). Incidentally, the lack of contingent application was also one of the reasons offered by Nelson-Gray et al. (1989), in explaining why no discernible increase in interviewee problem-related statements was brought about in their experimental investigation, by increasing the frequency of interviewer minimal encouragers.

Praise/support

Unlike the previous category, here listener reactions go beyond the simple acknowledgement and confirmation of, or agreement with, what has been said or done to express praise or support. Instances of this category of verbal reward range from one-word utterances, e.g. 'Good!', 'Excellent!' (and various other superlatives), through phrases like 'Well done!', 'How interesting!', 'Keep it up!', to more elaborate avowals of appreciation, as circumstances warrant. These are commonly employed by a broad spectrum of professionals when interacting with those to whom a service is offered. When appropriately administered, reinforcing consequences can be achieved. Professional domains where such effects have been examined are as diverse as organisational management, interviewing and coaching, but probably the most extensively researched area of application is in teaching.

Teaching is an activity where opportunities abound for putting praise and approval to good use in rewarding effort and accomplishment in the classroom. Educationalists are generally agreed that reinforcing appropriate pupil behaviour in this way is one of the hallmarks of effective teaching (Perrott, 1982).

Several reviews of research carried out over the years have featured this aspect of classroom interaction (Kennedy and Willcutt, 1964; Brophy, 1981; Lysakowski and Walberg, 1981; Cairns, 1986; and Wheldall and Glynn, 1989). The general consensus would seem to be that significant and beneficial changes can indeed be brought about. First, by rewarding on-task behaviour pupils are encouraged to spend more of their time in class doing the sorts of things that teachers expect, and less in irrelevant, unproductive or indeed disruptive activities. Second, pupils can have their motivation to learn strengthened when what they do evokes a positive teacher response. Third, and perhaps most importantly, levels of academic achievement may actually be elevated when teachers reinforce improving standards of work. Finally, it would appear that students who are receptive to teacher approval given for acceptable accomplishments in the classroom often experience greater feelings of self-esteem.

Kennedy and Willcutt (1964) summarised the early studies that they scrutinised by declaring that, 'Praise has been found generally to have a facilitating effect on the performance of school children' (p. 331). Some later reviewers, in contrast, tend to be more circumspect in their conclusions. As already mentioned, Brophy (1981) questioned the extent to which techniques such as praise are a prominent feature of the day-to-day classroom discourse of teachers and are used with reinforcing effect. Whether they are will depend upon a number of qualifying variables including features of the pupils such as reinforcement history, the type of task undertaken, the nature of the praise and the manner in which it is administered, together with characteristics of the source.

O'Leary and O'Leary (1977) suggest that the success of praise as a reinforcer can be increased by ensuring that, first, it is contingently applied; second, it specifies the particular behaviour being reinforced; and third, it is credible, varied according to the context and sounds sincere. Brophy (1981) develops this list by advocating that it be restricted to those students who respond best to it. Not all do, of course, with some finding it perhaps patronising or embarrassing when delivered in the presence of peers.

The influence of such factors as race, gender, age and socioeconomic status on children's susceptibility to reinforcers has been the subject of concerted inquiry. Socioeconomic status has attracted the attention of many researchers, leading Russell (1971, p. 39) to conclude that, 'One of the most consistent findings is that there is a social class difference in response to reinforcement.' Middle-class children have been held to respond better to less tangible reinforcers, including praise and approval, when compared with their lower-class compatriots. The latter, it is assumed, are less likely to be exposed to this type of reinforcement, especially for academic achievement, and are therefore unlikely to attach much value to it, favouring instead tangible rewards like money, food or toys. However, Schultz and Sherman (1976), having undertaken a comprehensive review of the area, were quite adamant that this view was ill-founded. They concluded that, 'social class differences in reinforcer effectiveness cannot be assumed in spite of our predispositions to do so' (p. 52). Cairns (1986), who also addressed this issue, concurred with the stance taken by these latter reviewers.

Relationships between these variables, if they do exist, are likely to be much more convoluted than those intimated by Russell. Miller and Eller (1985), for instance, reported significant increases in subsequent intelligence-test scores among lower- and middle-class white children following the praising of initial test performance, but gender differences played a part as well. Thus middle-class white females were more susceptible than their male counterparts. Praise also improved the performance of lower-class white males but not females. Furthermore, as far as Marisi and Helmy (1984) are concerned, age differences are implicated in determining how praise is reacted to. Comparing the effects of this incentive on performances of 6-year-old boys with those of 11 and 17 years on a motor task, they discovered that it was only with the youngest group that praise proved beneficial.

On the other hand, Wheldall and Glynn (1989) have shown that the behaviour of adolescents in class can be effectively managed by the teacher praising acceptable conduct in keeping with rules previously agreed by members, and largely ignoring minor infringements. Here, however, praise was contingently administered, unlike the procedure followed by Marisi and Helmy. Differences in the nature of the behaviour focused upon should also be appreciated. The boys in the study by Marisi and Helmy were engaged in the acquisition of a motor skill. Baumeister *et al.* (1990) point out that with certain skilled tasks, praise may not lead to improvements in performance but instead have the opposite effect. The most probable explanation offered by

Baumeister and his colleagues is that intervening in this way can distract attention from the task, to its detriment.

Other factors which have been found to mediate the reinforcing impact of praise and support include pupils' locus of control (Kennelly and Mount, 1985). As previously mentioned, people who are essentially internally set hold a belief in their own ability to extract reinforcers from the environment, whereas externals are inclined to put rewards that do come their way down to chance or luck. Internality of control and an appreciation of the contingency of teacher rewards was predictive of good academic achievement and teacher ratings of pupil competence in an investigation by Kennelly and Mount (1985). Alternatively, Baron *et al.* (1974) and Henry *et al.* (1979) have associated an external orientation with receptivity to verbal reinforcement.

A concept related to locus of control is that of attribution. Pupils' understanding of the reason for praise being given will determine what they make of it. So far we have assumed that praise, among other things, strengthens belief in ability and promotes self-esteem. Meyer *et al.* (1986) argued that just the opposite may sometimes occur and showed that those subjects praised for success at an easy task and not blamed for failure at a difficult task inferred that their ability for that type of work was low, when they had few other cues upon which to base judgements. When praise for success at the easy task was withheld and failure at the difficult task blamed, subjects assessed their ability as being much higher. Praise does not always carry positive messages, therefore, as far as inferences about ability levels are concerned.

Turning attention to characteristics of the reinforcing agent, Stock (1978) revealed that praise from the experimenter, compared to that given by a peer in the person of a student who assisted with the experiment, was much more influential in raising both quality and quantity of work carried out on the set task. This finding was in keeping with an earlier piece of research by Catano (1976) demonstrating the importance of the perceived expertness of the source. Thus praise from a peer looked upon as having relevant expertise was much more telling than that from an inexperienced colleague or no praise at all. According to results reported by Henry *et al.* (1979), boys were more responsive to peer feedback, while for girls praise given by adults led to faster problem-solving and greater perceptions of agent helpfulness. McGrade (1966) has also speculated that the socioeconomic status of the person praising may make a difference to reinforcing outcomes. More generally, evidence has been forthcoming that people have a greater susceptibility to being conditioned by those reinforcing agents that they find personally attractive (Sapolsky, 1960). Presumably attraction enhances their overall potential as sources of reward.

Still on the theme of factors that help determine the effects of praise and support, there is good reason to believe, at least with older individuals, that personality may play a salient role. In particular it seems that extroverts may be more receptive to the effects of praise while for introverts the punishment of inappropriate responses can produce better results (Boddy *et al.*, 1986; Gupta and Shukla, 1989). Susceptibility to the reinforcing influences of others seems to be strengthened among those who display a heightened need for approval and therefore have a predilection to act in ways that will increase the chances of others reacting favourably towards them (Crowne and Marlowe, 1964).

So far we have focused largely upon the classroom. While it is in this professional setting that their influence has been most extensively researched, praise and support have a wider applicability. In interviewing, the conditioning effects of interviewer utterances like 'Good', have been confirmed by a number of researchers. In an early study, Hildum and Brown (1956) invited respondents taking part in a telephone survey to give their reactions to a 15-item questionnaire designed to ascertain attitudes to an educational topic considered to be largely emotionally neutral. Each item had four possible responses ranging from strongly agree to strongly disagree. One group contacted had negative responses systematically reinforced using 'Good', while for a second, only positive reactions were treated in this way. In line with expectations, the expressed attitudes of respondents reinforced for responding negatively were markedly less favourable when compared with those influenced in the opposite direction. Goldman (1980) also demonstrated that attitudes elicited during survey interviews could be manipulated in this fashion by the interviewer. In this case, face-to-face interviews were conducted and attitudes had to do with intercollegiate athletic competition.

From a management perspective, praise has featured in work-place interventions designed, for example, to boost morale and improve productivity. One of the best-known is that implemented at Emery Air Freight (At Emery Air Freight, 1973). This company relied heavily upon large freight containers for transporting goods. An audit revealed the marked under-utilisation of these containers and identified this as the single most significant factor in depressing profits. A scheme was set in place to increase the use of empty container space. Warehousemen who had the responsibility for this task, were given daily feedback on their performance. Warehouse managers were also trained to praise and compliment the achievement of set targets. Workbooks given to managers suggested a huge variety of specific ways in which this might be put into practice, from a smile and nod of encouragement through to detailed praise for a job well done. As a result the company flew fewer containers that were less than half full, made savings of some $520,000 in the first year, and increased this to $2 million over a period of three years.

Response development

There is, in a sense, a progressive sequence of increasing involvement and acceptance which commences with the mere acknowledgement of a response, continues with the positive evaluation of it through praise, for example, and proceeds to the further exploration and development of the content. In this way, having an idea or action form part of the agenda for the ongoing discourse may, perhaps, be looked upon as the highest form of praise! It is quite easy for a teacher, manager, interviewer or coach to express a few perfunctory words of acknowledgement or commendation before continuing on a completely different tack, but the development of a response indicates, first, that the listener must have been carefully attending and, second, that the content must have been considered worthy of the listener's time and effort to make it part of 'the talk'.

A response can be developed in a number of ways. In the classroom, Perrott (1982) mentions how teachers may respond to pupil contributions, 'by accepting them, summarising them, applying them, building on them or asking questions based on them'. (p. 97). Here is a powerful means of providing reinforcement during a lesson, even if it is less frequently used than alternatives already considered. On the other hand, a teacher may develop a pupil's contribution by elaborating upon it herself. The potential reward for pupils of having their ideas form part of the lesson will be readily appreciated. In a group, members may be asked to contribute their suggestions and be reinforced by having their responses further explored by other members. In a coaching context, certain individuals can be selected to demonstrate a skill or technique to the other participants for them to develop. If tactfully handled this form of response development can be highly motivating and positively valued.

Clearly there is a whole range of possibilities for developing responses. Dickson *et al.* (1993) suggest that reflective statements (see Chapter 6) and self-disclosures (see Chapter 10) may function in this way and review some conditioning-type studies which have been carried out. In general though, research concerning the reinforcing effects of response development is less prevalent than that involving reinforcers included in the previous two categories.

Nonverbal components

The administration of reinforcement is not solely dependent upon the verbal channel of communication. It has been established that a number of nonverbal behaviours, such as a warm smile or an enthusiastic nod of the head, can also have reinforcing impact on the behaviour of the other person during interaction. Rosenfarb (1992) believes that positive change in client behaviour during psychotherapy, for instance, can be accounted for in this way. He explains how this might operate as follows:

Often, subtle therapeutic cues serve to reinforce selected aspects of client behavior. A therapist's turn of the head, a change in eye contact, or a change in voice tone may reinforce selected client behavior. . . . One therapist, for example, may lean forward in her chair whenever a client begins to discuss interpersonal difficulties with his mother. Another therapist may begin to nod his head as clients begin to discuss such material. A third may maintain more eye contact. In all three cases, each therapist's behavior may be serving as both a reinforcing stimulus for previous client behavior and as a discriminative stimulus for the further discussion of such relevant material.

(p. 343)

The fact that nonverbal cues can operate to so influence behaviour should not surprise us unduly if it is remembered (see Chapter 3) that the nonverbal channel of communication is frequently more important than the verbal channel with regard to the conveyancing of information of an emotional or attitudinal nature. Indeed, when information of this type resulting from one channel contradicts that carried by means of the other, greater credence is often placed on the nonverbal message. It would therefore seem that the nonverbal channel is particularly adept at communicating states and attitudes such as friendliness, interest, warmth, involvement, etc. Since such attitudes are frequently positively valued, behaviours which depict them are likely to have a reinforcing potential.

The selection of criteria to form a basis for the categorisation of nonverbal reinforcers is somewhat arbitrary. In the sections to follow we will consider, separately, gestural and proximity reinforcement.

Gestural reinforcement

This category includes relatively small movements of specific parts of the body. 'Gestural' in this sense is broadly defined to encompass not only movements of the hands, arms and head, but also the facial region. Concerning the last, two of the most frequently identified reinforcers are smiles and eye contact. Some research evidence exists to suggest that smiles can have a reinforcing effect. In one experiment, Showalter (1974) succeeded in conditioning affect statements through the selective use of this behaviour by the interviewer. Many studies have combined smiles with other nonverbal and verbal reinforcers. For example, Verplanck (1955) used a smile together with agreement and a paraphrase to increase the frequency of statements of opinion. Similarly, Krasner (1958) combined smiles with head-nods and 'mm-hmm' to increase the use of the word 'mother' by subjects. Pansa (1979) increased the incidence of self-referenced affect statements provided by a group of reactive schizophrenics, using a comparable procedure. Less positive results were obtained by Hill and Gormally (1977), Saigh (1981) and O'Brien and Holborn (1979). The last researchers suggested that the experimenter's smiles were misinterpreted by the subjects. It should be realised that smiles can convey scorn and contempt as well as warmth and understanding. The specific meaning attributed to this piece of behaviour is probably dependent upon contextual features including accompanying behaviour. The constant use of an isolated smile by an interviewer would undoubtedly seem rather strange and unnatural to an interviewee and therefore fail to serve as a reinforcer.

Eye contact is an important element of interpersonal interaction. The establishment of eye contact is usually a preparatory step when initiating interaction. During a conversation continued use of this behaviour may indicate attention, interest and involvement and its selective use can, therefore, have reinforcing consequences. Kleinke *et al.* (1975), in an interview-type experimental situation, instructed interviewers to (1) look at the interviewee constantly, (2) look at the interviewee intermittently or (3) refrain from looking. It was found that interviewees in the 'no gaze' condition, compared to the other two experimental treatments, made briefer statements and talked less. Interviewers in the 'constant gaze' condition were rated by interviewees as being most attentive, while interviewers who did not look at those they were interviewing were considered to be least attentive.

A positive relationship between interviewer eye contact and subjects' verbal productivity was also documented by, for instance, Klein *et al.* (1975), Duncan and Fiske (1977) and O'Brien and Holborn (1979). Goldman (1980) also reported that verbal encouragement could be used to reinforce expressed attitudes more effectively when coupled with eye contact. It should be appreciated that in certain situations, however, the over-use of eye contact or gaze can be threatening and therefore cause discomfort or distress. In this sense, eye contact could be punishing rather than reinforcing (although this did not seem to be the case in the Kleinke *et al.* study).

Certain movements of the hands and arms can signal appreciation and approval. Probably the most frequently used gestures of this type in our society are applause and the 'thumbs-up' sign. Head-nods are gestures which have a wider relevance. Their frequent use can be seen during practically any interactive episode, being commonly used to indicate acknowledgement, agreement and understanding. The reinforcing capability of this gesture has been emphasised by Forbes and Jackson (1980), among others. As with smiles, the majority of research studies which have exploited the reinforcing effects of head-nods, have combined them with various other nonverbal and verbal reinforcers. Matarazzo and Wiens (1972) found that the use of head-nods by an interviewer had the effect of increasing the average duration of utterance given by an interviewee. Although total verbal output of subjects increased significantly, Scofield (1977) obtained a disproportionately higher number of self-referenced statements following contingent application of interviewer head-nods combined with a paraphrase, restatement or verbal encouragement. Measures of interviewers' use of head-nods have also been discovered to predict successfully ratings of their competence by experienced judges (Dickson, 1981).

Proximity reinforcement

Unlike the previous category, the present one includes gross movements of the whole body or substantial parts of it. Proximity reinforcement refers to potential reinforcing effects which can accrue from altering the distance between oneself and another during interaction. A reduction in interpersonal distance usually accompanies a desire for greater intimacy and involvement. It is also more difficult to avoid attending to another when this distance is small and lack of attention is likely to be much more noticeable. However, while someone who adopts a position at some distance from the other participant may be seen as being unreceptive and detached, a person who approaches too closely may be regarded as over-familiar, dominant or even threatening. In the study by Goldman (1980), already referred to, attitudes of subjects were more successfully modified by means of verbal reinforcers when the interviewer stood at a moderate (4 to 5 feet) rather than a close interpersonal distance (2 to 3 feet). The optimal distance will depend upon a number of factors including the nature of the relationship, the sex of the participants and the topic of conversation. With these conditions in mind, a purposeful reduction in interpersonal distance, by signalling a willingness to become more involved in the interaction, can be used as a reinforcer (Rierdan and Brooks, 1978).

With participants who are seated, as professionals often are during encounters, it is obviously much more difficult to effect sizeable variations in interpersonal distance. However, this can be accomplished, to a certain extent, by adopting forward or backward leaning postures. Mehrabian (1972) reported that a forward leaning posture was one component of a complex of behaviours which he labelled 'immediacy' and which denotes a positive attitude towards the other person. Similarly, Nelson-Jones (1988) believes that this type of posture conveys acceptance and receptivity when used in counselling. As with some other nonverbal reinforcers, studies which have been conducted in part to establish the reinforcing effects of a forward leaning posture have combined it with several other reinforcers. However, there is some research evidence supporting the reinforcing effects which a forward leaning posture can have (Banks, 1972).

Touch represents a complete lack of interpersonal distance and, on occasion, can be used to good effect to encourage a partner to continue with a line of conversation. According to Jones and Yarbrough (1985), it can be construed in a number of ways to mean, among other things, affection, appreciation and support. Wheldall *et al.* (1986) found that when teachers of mixed-gender infant classes used positive contingent touch when praising good 'on-task' classroom behaviour, rates of this type of behaviour rose by some 20 per cent.

In many situations, however, touch is inappropriate, even socially forbidden and must be used with according discretion. (See Chapter 3 for further details.)

HOW DO REINFORCERS REINFORCE?

It is widely accepted that reinforcement modifies the future probability of the behaviour that led to it, as we have seen. There is much less agreement, however, about just how this is brought about. Miller (1963), reviewed nine contrasting theoretical attempts to explain the mechanism which is at the basis of the phenomenon. Some of these have since fallen from favour while other contenders have emerged to take their place. Furthermore, recent theorists have also shown a greater willingness to contemplate the possibility that the reinforcing outcomes of instrumental conditioning, under contrasting circumstances, may reflect different underlying processes (Davey, 1988). There may be no one correct answer to the question of how reinforcement has its effect.

Three possibilities will be briefly considered here. The first, favoured by the likes of Skinner (1953), is that reinforcers function essentially directly and automatically to bring about behavioural change. Two important implications stem from this view, each of which will be considered. The first is that the individual's awareness of what is taking place is not a prerequisite for reinforcement. The second concerns the nature of the relationship between the targeted response and the reinforcing event. The issue at stake here is whether reinforcement depends on the behaviour in question bringing about a positive outcome (contingency) or simply being followed in time by one (contiguity). A belief in contiguity as a necessary and sufficient condition for reinforcement to take place is commonly associated with its unconscious operation. Skinner (1977, p. 4), for instance, wrote that, 'Coincidence is the heart of operant conditioning. A response is strengthened by certain kinds of consequences, but not necessarily because they are actually produced by it.' This way of thinking about the operation of reinforcement is less popular now than it once was (Bower and Hilgard, 1981).

A second possibility is that reinforcers serve largely to motivate. The expectation of receiving a reward for succeeding in a task spurs on further efforts in that direction and makes it more likely that this type of task will be undertaken again. Such incentives may be external and represent the projected attainment of a tangible outcome (e.g. money, food, praise, etc.) or as Bandura (1989) stressed, be internal and derivable from anticipated positive self-evaluations at the prospect of succeeding in the task at hand. (Returning to the former type, in some instances external rewards can *reduce* motivation to engage in a set task. This has been explained in terms of the erosion of 'natural' intrinsic motivation to take part in that type of activity (Lepper and Greene, 1978).)

The third possibility to be considered here is that reinforcers function, in the main, by providing information on task performance. According to Dulany (1968), conditioning results can best be explained in terms of subjects trying to figure out the connection between what they do and the outcomes they experience in a sort of puzzle-solving exercise. Engineering further consequences then becomes a volitional activity. Conditioning studies with people are often arranged so that response-contingent points are allocated which can then be exchanged for back-up reinforcers like food or money. The material value of these are usually quite small. Wearden (1988), for example, draws attention to the fact that in some instances, subjects have worked diligently for, in real terms, as little as 5 pence an hour! When food is the reward, it is often left unconsumed, indeed sometimes discarded without being tasted and yet, at the same time, subjects continue to earn more. These findings are difficult to reconcile in motivational terms if money or food are thought of as the key inducements. A more plausible explanation offered by Wearden (1988) portrays the conditioning procedure as a problem-solving exercise in the eyes of the subjects. Points received for an appropriate move are prized, not hedonistically through association with money or food, but on account of the information they contribute to finding a solution to the 'puzzle'.

While conclusive proof is lacking to resolve these differences in position, the present consensus of opinion appears to be that, as far as social performance is concerned, probably little instrumental conditioning takes place without at least some minimal level of conscious involvement (Bower and Hilgard, 1981). While acknowledging exceptions, the effects of reinforcement seem to rely more upon a contingent than a mere contiguous association between behaviour and reward (Maier, 1989; Schwartz, 1989).

It can be concluded, therefore, that, in the main, rewards work best when the individuals involved are aware of a causal relationship between what they have done, or are doing, and the outcomes that are sought. According to such as Bandura (1977), those outcomes probably operate to motivate and inform, rather than to strengthen behaviour in an automatic and mechanistic fashion, although this is still a moot point.

GUIDELINES FOR THE USE OF THE SKILL OF REINFORCEMENT

In this section seven points concerning the use of the skill which tend to promote its effectiveness will be outlined.

Appropriate use

Throughout this chapter an attempt has been made to stress the fact that some stimuli which may have reinforcing properties in some situations may not have the same effects in others. It is, therefore, important that one remains sensitive to the characteristics of the situation, including the other people involved, when choosing the type of reinforcement to use. (This also applies to most of the other skills included in this book.) Thus some forms of praise which would be quite appropriate when used with a child, may seem extremely patronising if used with another adult.

Attention should, in addition, be paid to the reinforcement history of the individual. Sajwaj and Dillon (1977) remind us that while attention from others, as we have seen, usually has reinforcing potential, in the context of a history of associated punishment it may come to herald negative consequences and be actively avoided.

Not only is it the case that different people may prefer certain reinforcers to others, but the same individual on different occasions may find the same reinforcer differentially attractive.

Reinforcement given should also be appropriate to the task undertaken and the degree of success achieved. A consideration here has to do with the recipient's perception of equity. Lawler (1983) produced evidence that, at least with material rewards, less satisfaction is expressed when there are discrepancies between what is received and what is felt to be deserved, even when the inequity results in *higher* recompense than was thought to be merited. Furthermore, from an attributional point of view, people who receive praise for completing a relatively easy task may, if they have little else to go on, assume that it must be felt that they have low ability at this type of work (Meyer *et al.*, 1986)

Genuineness of reinforcement

It is important that reinforcement given is perceived as genuinely reflecting the esteem of the source. If not, as in the above example, it may come across as sarcasm, veiled criticism or perhaps a bored habit. Complementarity of verbal and nonverbal behaviour is important in this regard.

Contingency of reinforcement

In order for the various social behaviours reviewed in this chapter to function as effective reinforcers it is important that their application be made contingent upon the particular action which it is intended to modify. This does not mean that the random use of such behaviour will fail to produce an effect. It may well serve to create a particular impression, interpret the situation in a particular way, or as Saigh (1981) speculated, put the other person at ease. It is highly improbable, however, that it will selectively reinforce as desired.

In many situations, it may be prudent to specify, quite precisely, the behavioural focus of attention. Reference has already been made to O'Leary and O'Leary's (1977) recommendation that praise by teachers should specify the particulars of the behaviour being reinforced. If it is seen to be blatantly manipulative, however, and if the source is thought to harbour ulterior motives, the anticipated outcome of such application may not materialise.

Frequency of reinforcement

It is not necessary to reinforce constantly each and every instance of a specific response, for that class of response to be increased. It has been found that following an initial period of continual reinforcement the frequency of reinforcement can be reduced without resulting in a corresponding reduction in target behaviour. This is called *intermittent* reinforcement and has been found to increase resistance to extinction. It will be recalled that Brophy (1981) recommended that praise should be used sparingly to maximise its reinforcing efficacy. Accordingly, *Gain/Loss Theory* predicts that when the receipt of a reward is set against a backdrop of a general paucity of positive reaction from that source, its effect will be enhanced (Aronson, 1969).

Variety of reinforcement

The continual and inflexible use of a specific reinforcer will quickly lead to that reinforcer losing its reinforcing properties. If an interviewer responds to each interviewee statement with, for example, 'good', this utterance will gradually become denuded of any evaluative connotations, and consequently will rapidly cease to have reinforcing effects. An attempt should therefore be made to employ a variety of reinforcing expressions and behaviours while ensuring that they do not violate the requirement of appropriateness.

Timing of reinforcement

Based largely on animal studies and the principle of contiguity, it has been recommended that the reinforcing stimulus be applied immediately following the target response, since length of delay has been found to be inversely related to effectiveness. If reinforcement is delayed there is a danger that other responses may intervene between the one which the reinforcing agent wished to promote and the presentation of the reinforcer. With human subjects, though, it is unlikely that delayed reinforcement will be ineffective provided that the individual appreciates the contingent relationship between what was done and what it accomplished. This is not to overlook the fact that, from a motivational viewpoint, the availability of immediate recompense is likely to prove more attractive than the prospect of having to wait for some time for personal benefits to materialise.

Partial reinforcement

In this context partial reinforcement refers to the fact that it is possible to reinforce selectively certain elements of a response without necessarily reinforcing it in total. This can be accomplished during the actual response. Nonverbal reinforcers such as head-nods and verbal reinforcers like 'mm-hmm', are of particular relevance in this respect since they can be used without interrupting the speaker. Partial reinforcement can also be applied following the termination of a response. Thus a teacher may partially reinforce a pupil who has almost produced the correct answer to his question, with, 'Yes, Mary, you are right, Kilimanjaro is a mountain, but is it in the Andes?' By so doing he reinforces that portion of the answer which is accurate, while causing the pupil to rethink the element which is not.

Allied to this process, *shaping* permits nascent attempts at an ultimately acceptable end performance, to be rewarded. By systematically demanding higher standards for rewards to be granted, performances can be shaped to attain requisite levels of excellence. The acquisition of most everyday skills like swimming, driving a car, playing a violin, involve an element of shaping (Schwartz, 1989). If reinforcers were withheld until the full-blown activity was performed in accordance with more advanced criteria of excellence, learning could take a long time and be an extremely thankless task for the learner.

OVERVIEW

As a social skill, reinforcement is central to interpersonal interaction. What people do, what they learn, the decisions which they take, their feelings and attitudes towards themselves and others, indeed the sorts of individuals they become, can be shaped and moulded by the self-focused reactions of others.

While the basic notion that people tend to behave in ways that bring about positive outcomes for them is scarcely iconoclastic, it does seem that in many professional circles, reinforcement as a social skill is not well used. Brophy (1981), for example, questions whether teachers routinely use praise in the classroom in such a way as to be maximally reinforcing of desirable behaviour and achievement.

The sorts of social reinforcers which we have concentrated upon in this chapter can be divided, for convenience, into the verbal and the nonverbal. In practice, however, these two channels operate closely together. Verbal reinforcers include such reactions as acknowledging, confirming, praising, supporting and developing the other's responses by a variety of potential means. Nonverbally, gestures such as smiles, head-nods, and eye contact, together with grosser body movements, including reducing interpersonal distance, forward posture leans and touch, have been found to have reinforcing possibilities.

When utilised in accordance with the guidelines outlined above, reinforcement can serve to promote interaction and maintain relationships; increase the involvement of the interactive partner; make interaction interesting and enjoyable, demonstrate a genuine interest in the ideas, thoughts and feelings of the other; create an impression of warmth and understanding; enhance the interpersonal attractiveness of the source; and improve the confidence and self-esteem of the recipient. In relation to the latter, the possibility of praise for the completion of a task being attributed to a belief, by the source, in the performer's limited ability at such work should be acknowledged (Meyer *et al.* 1986). Interpreted in this way, it is unlikely that feelings of self-esteem will be promoted. The fact that dispensing rewards can be cast as a manifestation of power over the receiver should also be appreciated.

It is worth repeating that there is no implication that any of the verbal or nonverbal behaviours associated here with the skill of reinforcement *must* invariably have the reinforcing effects outlined. Nor is it assumed that only those ways of relating mentioned can have reinforcing potential. Whether or not reinforcement takes place will be determined by a complex of factors including those to do with the source, the recipient, the reward and the way in which it was delivered (Dickson *et al.*, 1993).

Finally, the issue of how reinforcement works was addressed. This matter is still largely unresolved. The three possibilities outlined were that it operates automatically and directly on behaviour, in accordance with the views of Skinner (1953); that it acts through increasing motivation; or that it provides information on performance and outcome. More recently the possibility of reinforcement operating in a plurality of ways has been entertained (Davey, 1988). However, the potency of reinforcement when used judiciously has been widely recognised in interpersonal contexts.

Chapter 5

Questioning

INTRODUCTION

Questioning is perhaps one of the most widely used social skills, and one of the easiest to identify in general terms. Together with the skill of reinforcement, questioning is one of the core skills in social interaction. Indeed, Strack and Schwarz (1992) contend that: 'A communication that is structured by questions and answers is probably the most important form of human interaction' (p. 173). In most social encounters questions are asked and responses reinforced – this is the method whereby information is gathered and conversation encouraged.

A question can be defined as a request for information, whether factual or otherwise. This request for information can be verbal or nonverbal. For example, a high-pitched 'guggle' such as 'hmmm?' after someone has made a statement, will usually indicate to the speaker that he or she is expected to continue speaking. Similarly, a nod of the head, after asking one member of a group a question, can indicate to another group member that her participation is desired also and that the question is being redirected to her. Questions, then, may be nonverbal signals urging another person to respond, or indeed they may even be statements uttered in an inquisitive fashion (e.g. 'You are coming to the party?'; 'Tell me more'). Statements which request information have been referred to by Woodbury (1984) as 'prosodic questions', and are defined as 'declarative sentences containing question cues that may be intonational, or these utterances are marked as questions by means of a variety of contextual cues' (p. 203).

Although a question can be posed nonverbally, most questions in social interaction are verbal in nature. At the same time, there are certain nonverbal signals which should accompany the verbal message, if a question is to be recognised as such. One of the main nonverbal accompaniments is the raising or lowering of the vocal inflection on the last syllable of the question. Other nonverbal behaviours include head movements, rapidly raising or lowering the eyebrows and direct eye contact at the end of the question accompanied by a pause. The function of these nonverbal behaviours is to emphasise to the other person that a question is being asked and that a response is expected.

The skill of questioning is to be found at every level in social interaction. The young child, exploring a new environment, seems to be naturally inquisitive, always seeking answers to an ever-increasing number of questions. At this stage questions play a crucial role in the learning and development process, as the infant attempts to assimilate information in order to make sense of his surroundings. The importance of the skill of questioning is, therefore, recognised from an early age.

The study of the nature and functions of questions has developed rapidly, with texts devoted to this topic in the fields of communication (Dillon, 1990), linguistics (Meyer, 1988), logic (Kiefer, 1982), counselling (Long *et al.*, 1981), psychology (Graesser and Black, 1985), survey interviewing (Sudman and Bradburn, 1982), teaching, (Dillon, 1988a), law (Kestler, 1982), interrogation (Gudjonnson, 1992) and journalism (Metzler, 1977). In addition, numerous papers, articles and book chapters have been written about the use and effects of questions.

Investigations into the use of questions in various professional contexts have been carried out for over half a century. An early study was conducted by Corey (1940) in which she had an expert stenographer make verbatim records of all classroom talk in six classes. It was found that, on average, the teacher asked a question once every 72 seconds. Some thirty years later, Resnick (1972) working with teachers and pupils in an infant school (serving 5- to 7-year-old children) in south-east London, found that 36 per cent of all teacher remarks were questions. Furthermore, this figure increased to 59 per cent when only extended interactions were analysed.

In a review of such studies, Dillon (1982) reported that 'teachers have been observed to ask an average of two questions per minute and their pupils all together two questions per hour, which yields a projected average of one question per pupil per month' (p. 153). When the teachers were surveyed about their use of questions, it was found that they actually asked three times as many questions as they estimated they had, and received only one-sixth the number of pupil questions estimated. However, as previously mentioned, reticence at asking questions is not the general norm for children. For example, Tizard *et al.* (1983) radio-recorded 4-year-old girls at home and at school and found that on average per hour the children asked 24 questions at home and only 1.4 at school. Interestingly, one major reason given by students for their reluctance to ask questions in class is fear of a negative reaction from *classmates* (Dillon, 1988b). Such findings indicate that teachers need to be aware of the many facets pertaining to classroom questioning.

A study of the use of questions by doctors has revealed parallel findings. As Fisher and Groce (1990, p. 230) concluded, following their study of medical interviews: 'It is doctors who ask most of the questions and patients who respond most of the time.' Indeed, West (1983) found that out of a total of 773 questions identified in twenty-one doctor–patient consultations, only 68 (9 per cent) were initiated by patients. This pattern and volume of doctor questions meant that patients had little scope to reply, let alone formulate a question. Furthermore, when patients did ask questions it was found that nearly half of these were marked by speech disturbances, indicating patient discomfort at requesting information from the doctor. Such discomfort can be overcome by sensitivity to patient needs and concerns. Parrott *et al.* (1992), in a study of paediatrician–patient communication, found that while paediatricians generally asked more questions than patients, during consultations in which they specifically addressed concerns raised by patients, more questions were subsequently asked by the latter. It would therefore seem that patient questions can be encouraged (and of course discouraged!) by the approach of the doctor.

In relation to community pharmacy, Morrow *et al.* (1993a) carried out a study in which they recorded a series of community pharmacist–patient consultations. They found that patients asked on average 2.5 questions per consultation compared with an average of 4.1 for pharmacists. This ratio of patient questions is much higher than that found in doctor–patient consultations. Interestingly, a number of the questions asked by these patients related to requests for clarification about what the doctor had previously told them. This suggests that either they felt more at ease asking questions of the pharmacist than indicating lack of understanding to the doctor, or that they had subsequently thought of questions they would have liked to have been able to ask the doctor. Morrow *et al.* argue that the public may have a view that since pharmacies are readily and easily accessible, pharmacists are probably 'approachable' professionals. Furthermore, the fact that in many instances clients are paying directly for the services they receive may mean that they feel more empowered to ask questions in community pharmacies.

There would seem to be a status and control differential in relation to the use of questions. Indeed, this was noted in a humorous fashion by Lewis Carroll in his book *Alice's Adventures in Wonderland* where a father responds to his child's questions as follows:

'I have answered three questions and that is enough',
Said his father 'don't give yourself airs!
Do you think I can listen all day to such stuff?
Be off, or I'll kick you down stairs.'

In most contexts it is the person of higher status, or the person in control, who asks the questions (perhaps the ultimate stereotype being the German SS officer in old war films, who shouts 'Ve vill ask ze questions!'). Thus the majority of questions will be asked by teachers in classrooms, by doctors in surgeries, by nurses on the ward, by lawyers in court, by detectives in interrogation rooms and so on. Indeed, it is for this reason that some counselling theorists would argue that counsellors should try not to ask any questions at all of clients, to avoid being seen as the controller of the interaction (Rogers, 1951). However, the type of question asked will be of importance in most settings, and this issue will be discussed later in the chapter.

Another facet of questioning is that the respondent in many instances experiences stress when being asked questions. This is certainly true in the above examples where stress and anxiety are often experienced by patients on the ward or in the surgery, by suspects in police stations, by pupils in classrooms and by defendants in court. Furthermore, in the latter two cases, the person asking the questions already knows the answers, and this makes these situations even more stressful and removed from normal interaction. In everyday conversation, we do not ask questions to which we already know the answers, or if we do we employ elaborate verbalisations to explain our behaviour (I was surprised to discover something. . . . Let me see if you can guess. . .).

In the courtroom where lawyers are advised to 'ask only questions to which the answers are known' (Kestler, 1982, p. 341), the creation of stress in witnesses is regarded as a legitimate tactic; such stress is also developed by a rapid-fire questioning approach. For example, the following is a 1-minute excerpt from the sequence of questions posed by the defence attorney, Mr Black, to the alleged rape victim in the Kennedy Smith trial in Palm Beach, Florida in December, 1991.

1 So then you parked the car again. Is that correct?
2 Did you lock the car while you were in it?
3 Did you remain in the car?
4 Were you in your car when Chuck and Ann arrived?
5 Did you get out of your car?
6 Did you get out of the car and go back into the house?
7 You have a relative that lives nearby, don't you?
8 Who is it that lives nearby?
9 How close does she live?
10 Doesn't Ann's sister live a couple of blocks away?

Such a sequence, where one question is asked every 6 seconds and the answers are already known by the questioner, would undoubtedly put most defendants under pressure. In the classroom, however, the heightened anxiety of pupils may be dysfunctional and detrimental both to learning and to pupil–teacher attitudes. Teachers should bear this in mind when asking questions in the classroom.

FUNCTIONS OF QUESTIONS

Stenstroem (1988, p. 304) pointed out that

It is difficult to imagine a conversation without questions and responses.

They do not only constitute a convenient means of starting a conversation but also make it a great deal easier to carry on and can be used for a variety of purposes.

The use of questions can indeed serve a number of functions, depending upon the context of the interaction. Thus salesmen ask questions to assess customer needs and relate their sales pitch to the satisfaction of these needs (Poppleton, 1981), negotiators ask questions to slow the pace of the interaction and put pressure on their opponents (Rackham and Carlisle, 1978), doctors use questions to facilitate diagnoses (Maguire, 1984) and so on. However, the main general functions of questions are as follows:

1 to obtain information;
2 to maintain control of the interaction;
3 to arouse interest and curiosity concerning a topic;
4 to diagnose specific difficulties a respondent may have;
5 to express an interest in the respondent;
6 to ascertain the attitudes, feelings and opinions of the respondent;
7 to encourage maximum participation by the respondent;
8 to assess the extent of the respondent's knowledge;
9 to encourage critical thought and evaluation;
10 to communicate, in group discussions, that involvement and overt participation by all group members is expected and valued;
11 to encourage group members to comment on the responses of other members of the group;
12 to maintain the attention of group members, by asking questions periodically without advance warning.

These are the chief functions which can be attained by employing the skill of questioning. It should be realised that the type of question asked can determine the extent to which each of these various functions of questions can be fulfilled. Indeed it is the responses made to questions which determine whether or not the objective has been achieved. In this sense, a question is only as good as the answer which it evokes.

TYPES OF QUESTION

Several different classifications of questions have been proposed. Once again, the context is important – whether it be interviewing, teaching, counselling, interrogating or merely engaging in social conversation, the type of questions used will vary accordingly. Rudyard Kipling (1902) put forward the following early categorisation of questions:

I keep six honest serving men,
(They taught me all I knew);
Their names are What and Why and When,
And How and Where and Who.

As will be seen, these lines reflect, to a fair degree, the different classifications of questions which have been identified.

Recall/process questions

This division of questions refers to the cognitive level at which questions are pitched. Recall questions are referred to as lower-order cognitive questions, while process questions are known as higher-order cognitive questions (Hargie, 1980). The distinction between recall and process questions is most commonly made within education, and can be found in classroom interaction research studies.

Recall questions

Recall questions, as the name suggests, involve the simple recall of information. In this sense, they are of a lower-order cognitive nature, since they only test the ability of the respondent to memorise information. Examples of recall questions would include; 'Where were you born?'; 'When was the Battle of Waterloo?'; 'What nationality was El Greco?'; 'Who wrote *Treasure Island*?' All of these questions have a specific answer, which is either correct or incorrect, and the respondent is asked to recall the answer in each case.

Recall questions serve a number of useful purposes in different settings. A teacher, for example, may employ recall questions at the beginning of a lesson in order to ascertain the extent of pupil knowledge about the lesson topic. Such questions provide information for the teacher and also serve to encourage pupil participation at the outset. Similarly, at the end of a lesson a teacher may use recall questions to determine the extent of pupil learning which has taken place as a result of the lesson, and also to highlight to pupils that this learning has occurred.

In interviewing contexts, recall questions may be employed at the beginning of an interview as a form of 'ice-breaker' to get the interviewee talking. Recall questions also form the basis of questioning by detectives of eyewitnesses at the scenes of crimes. In this instance the detective is either interested in building up a picture of a suspect or suspects, or in establishing the facts about what exactly occurred at the time the offence was committed. In the former case, the detective may ask questions such as 'How many people were in the car?'; 'What height was he?'; 'What colour was his hair?' In the latter case he may ask questions such as 'How fast was the car going approximately?'; 'Who fired the first shot?'; 'How close were you to the accident when it happened?' If a case goes to court, the eyewitness may be in the position of having to answer these questions again, and be asked to defend the answers.

These are but a few of the social contexts in which questions of a recall nature are employed. In medicine, recall questions are also of importance in the diagnosis of an illness. Thus a doctor will use questions such as 'When did the pain first begin?'; 'Have you had any dizzy spells?'; or 'Do you remember what you ate before you were sick?'

Process questions

Process questions are so called because they require the respondent to use some higher mental process in order to answer them. This may involve giving opinions, justifications, judgements or evaluations, making pre-dictions, analysing information, interpreting situations or making general-isations. In other words, the respondent is required to think, at a higher-order level, about the answer. Examples of process questions include: 'What might have happened if Japan had not bombed Pearl Harbour?' 'How do you think you could improve your relationship with your wife?'; 'Why should anyone who is fit and doesn't work receive money from the state?'; 'What do you think are the characteristics of a good manager?' All of these questions require the respondent to go beyond the simple recall of information and frequently there is no correct answer to a process question. Furthermore, process questions usually require longer responses and can seldom be answered in one or two words.

Process questions are employed in situations where someone is being encouraged to think more deeply about a topic. For this reason they are often utilised in order to assess the ability of an individual to handle information at a higher-order level. In executive-type selection interviews, process ques-tions are frequently used in this assessment function (e.g. 'What can you offer this company?'; 'How are imminent technological developments likely to affect the labour market?'). In addition, process questions can be usefully employed in teaching, whereby pupils are encouraged to think for themselves about the material which is presented to them.

Research reviews of questioning in the classroom context have con-sistently found that teachers ask considerably more recall questions than process questions (Gall, 1970; Hargie, 1983; Dillon, 1990). These are somewhat disconcerting findings, since the type of question asked by teachers will determine the degree of creativity or expressiveness available to pupils and process questions provide more scope than recall questions. In a world where technological advances move at a rapid pace, facts can rapidly become outdated and the ability to evaluate new information is of great importance. Given this situation, Hargie (1983) concluded that during training 'more attention should be given to means whereby teachers can increase their use of thought-provoking questions as opposed to factual or recall questions' (p. 190).

There is firm research evidence to support such a proposal, since Rousseau and Redfield (1980), in reviewing a total of twenty studies, concluded that 'gains in achievement over a control group may be expected for groups of children who participate in programmes where teachers are trained in questioning skills. . . gains are greatest when higher cognitive questions are used during instruction' (p. 52). However, caution should be exercised in attempting to generalise about the use of process as opposed to recall questions. Research evidence tends to suggest that process questions may be more effective in increasing both participation and achievement of individuals of high intellectual ability, whereas recall questions appear to be more effective in these respects with individuals of low intellectual ability. For teachers with mixed ability classes this general research finding poses some obvious difficulties with regard to questioning skills, in that the consistent use of process questions is likely to stimulate pupils with a high IQ but be inappropriate for, or confuse, pupils with a low IQ.

Closed/open questions

Another widely-used division of questions relates to the degree of freedom, or scope, given to the respondent in answering the question. Some questions place more restrictions on respondents than others. Questions which leave the respondent open to choose any one of a number of ways in which to answer are appropriately referred to as open questions, while questions which require a short response of a specific nature are referred to as closed questions. This distinction between open and closed questions is most commonly employed in a variety of interviewing contexts.

Closed questions

Closed questions are those questions wherein 'the respondent does not have a choice in his response other than those provided by the questioner' (King, 1972, p. 158). Closed questions usually have a correct answer, or can be answered with a short response selected from a limited number of possible options. There are three main types of closed question.

1 *The selection question*. Here the respondent is presented with two or more alternative responses, from which he is expected to choose. As a result, this type of question is also known as a forced-choice question. Examples of this type of question include: 'Do you prefer tea or coffee?' 'Would you rather have Fyfe, Cameron or Thompson as the next President?' 'Do you want to travel by sea or by air?'

2 *The yes–no question*. As the name suggests, this is a question which may be adequately answered by a 'yes' or 'no', or by using some equivalent affirmative or negative. Examples of this type of closed question include: 'Are you Irish?'; 'Did you go to university?'; 'Would you like some coffee?'; 'Has there been any bleeding?'

3 *The identification question*. This type of question requires the respondent to identify the answer to a factual question and present this as the response. While the answer to an identification question may involve the recall of

information (e.g. 'What is your maiden name?'; 'Where were you born?'), it may also be concerned with the identification of present material (e.g. 'What time is it?'; 'Where exactly is the pain occurring now?') or future events (e.g. 'Where are you going on holiday?'; 'When is your baby due?').

Closed questions have a number of applications. Most people will find closed questions easy to answer, and so by employing this type of question it is possible to get someone involved in an interaction at the outset. In fact-finding encounters, closed questions are of particular value and are often used in a variety of research and assessment type interviews. In the research interview it is the responses of subjects which are of importance, and responses to closed questions are usually more concise and therefore easier to record than responses to open questions; this in turn facilitates comparisons between the responses of different subjects. In many assessment interviews, the interviewer will have to ascertain whether or not the client is suitable for some form of grant or assistance and will have to find out whether the client meets a number of specified requirements (e.g. a social welfare official will have to ask a client about his financial affairs, his family background, etc. before deciding if he is eligible for state allowances).

In the Morrow *et al.* (1993a) study mentioned earlier it was found that almost all of the pharmacist questions were closed in nature and that 69 per cent of these were of the yes–no variety. Morrow *et al.* argue that pharmacists were following the clinical algorithm approach of eliminative questioning for diagnosis. While this approach, if carried out expertly, should result in the correct clinical conclusion, it is not without drawbacks in that important information may be missed. For example, one of the clients in this study was suffering from very severe toothache for which the pharmacist had recommended a product and was completing the sale when the client asked: 'What about if you've taken any other tablets? I've taken Paracodol.' This unsolicited enquiry provoked further questions and subsequently altered the pharmacist's dosage recommendations.

Closed questions can usually be answered adequately in one or a very few words. They are restricted in nature, imposing limitations on the possible responses which the respondent can give. They give the questioner a high degree of control over the interaction, since a series of closed questions can be prepared in advance in order to structure a given social encounter, and the possible answers which the respondent may give can usually be estimated. Where time is limited and a diagnosis has to be made, or information has to be gathered, closed questions may be the preferred mode.

Open questions

Open questions are questions which can be answered in a number of ways, the response being left open to the respondent. With open questions the respondent is given a higher degree of freedom in deciding which answer to give than with closed questions. Open questions are broad in nature, and require more than one or two words for an adequate answer. At the same time, however, some open questions will place more restriction upon respondents than others, depending upon the frame of reference subsumed in the question. Consider the following examples of questions asked by a detective of a suspect:

1 'Tell me about your spare time activities.'
2 'What do you do in the evenings?'
3 'What do you do on Saturday evenings?'
4 'What did you do on the evening of Saturday, 19 January?'

In these examples, the focus of the questions has gradually narrowed from the initial very open question to the more restricted type of open question. This could then lead into more specific closed questions, such as:

5 'Who were you with on the evening of Saturday, 19 January?'
6 'Where were you at 7.00 pm that evening?'

This approach, of beginning an interaction with a very open question, and gradually reducing the level of openness, is termed a 'funnel' sequence (Kahn and Cannell, 1957) (see Figure 5.1). Such a structure is common in counselling interviews, where the helper does not want to impose any restrictions on the helpee about what is to be discussed, and may begin a session by asking, 'What would you like to talk about?' or 'How have things been since we last met?' Once the helpee begins to talk, the helper may then want to focus in on certain aspects of the responses given. In the medical interview, Cohen-Cole and Bird (1991, p. 13) point out that:

A considerable body of literature supports the use of open-ended questioning as an efficient and effective vehicle to gain understanding of patients' problems. To be sure, after an initial nondirective phase. . . the doctor must ask progressively more focused questions to explore specific diagnostic hypotheses. This. . . . has been called an 'open-to-closed cone'.

An alternative approach to this sequencing of questions is to use an 'inverted funnel' sequence (sometimes referred to as a 'pyramid' sequence), whereby an interaction begins with very closed questions and gradually opens out to embrace wider issues. Such an approach is often adopted in careers guidance interviews in which the interviewer may want to build up a picture of the client (e.g. academic achievements, family background, interests, etc.) before progressing to possible choice of career and the reasons for this choice (e.g. 'Why do you think you would like to be a soldier?', 'What factors would be important to you in choosing a job?'). By using closed questions initially to obtain information about the client, the careers interviewer may then be in a better position to help the client evaluate possible, and feasible, career options.

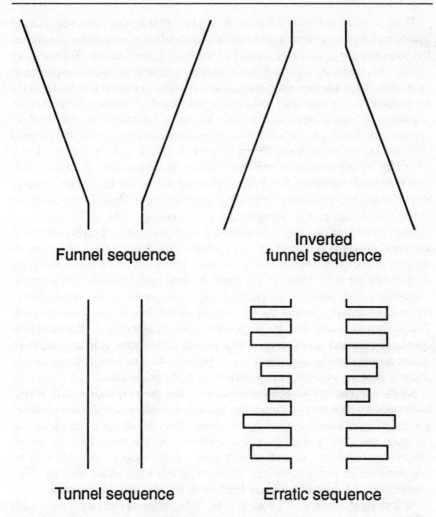

Figure 5.1 Types of questioning sequence

A third type of questioning sequence is referred to as the 'tunnel' sequence. In this type of sequence, all of the questions employed are at the same level and are usually closed. A series of closed questions may be used in certain types of assessment interview, wherein the objective is to establish a set of factual responses from the respondent. This type of closed tunnelling for information is often characteristic of 'screening' interviews, where the respondent has to be matched against some pre-set criteria (e.g. eligibility for some form of state welfare benefit or grant). A closed tunnel sequence of questions is also used by lawyers in court when they wish to direct a witness along a predetermined set of answers (as can be seen from the transcript of the Kennedy Smith trial cited earlier).

There is some research evidence to suggest that a consistent sequence of questions facilitates participation and understanding in respondents, whether the sequence be of a tunnel, funnel or inverted funnel nature. Turney *et al.* (1976), for example, highlighted the dangers of using an erratic sequence of open and closed questions (or of recall and process questions), as being likely to confuse the respondent and reduce the level of participation. Erratic sequences of questions (also known as rapid variations in the level of cognitive demand) are common in interrogation interviews where the purpose is to confuse the suspect and 'throw him off his guard' since he will not know what type of question to expect next. Indeed, in courtrooms, Kestler (1982) recommended that when lawyers wish to trap witnesses they should use an erratic sequence, involving 'a quick change of focus designed to catch the witness off-balance, with thoughts out of context' (p. 156).

Open questions are useful in allowing a respondent to express opinions, attitudes, thoughts and feelings. They do not require any prior knowledge on the part of the questioner, who can ask open questions about topics or events with which she is not familiar. For these reasons open questions are useful in exploring a wide range of areas. By using open questions, the respondent is encouraged to talk, thereby leaving the questioner free to listen and observe. This means, of course, that the respondent has a greater degree of control over the interaction and can determine to a greater extent what is to be discussed. It also means that the questioner has to pay attention to what is being said in order to indicate interest and attentiveness to the respondent.

Another advantage of open questions is that the respondent may reveal information which the questioner had not anticipated. Where a respondent has a body of specialised knowledge to relate, the use of open questions can facilitate the transmission of this knowledge. At the same time, however, where time is limited, or with over-talkative clients, open questions may be inappropriate in many instances. Answers to open questions may be time-consuming, and may also contain irrelevant, or less vital, information.

At first sight, there would appear to be little difference between the recall/process and the closed/open categorisations of questions, and indeed many closed questions are of a recall nature, while many process questions are also open questions. However, it is possible to have closed process questions and open recall questions. Consider a science teacher who has explained to pupils the chemical qualities of water and limestone, and then asks, 'What reaction will occur when I pour water on to a piece of limestone?' While the question is process, it is also closed. Similarly a question such as 'What did you do during the holidays?' is both open and recall. Thus there are differences inherent in these two classifications of questions and both are useful in varying contexts.

Several research studies have examined the relative effects of open and closed questions in different situations. Dohrenwend (1965), for example, found that, in research interviews, responses to open questions contained a higher proportion of self-revelation than did responses to closed questions when the subject matter under discussion was objective, and a lower proportion when the subject matter was subjective. This finding suggests that when concerned with self-disclosures, closed questions may be more effective in keeping the respondent to the topic of the question. (For more information on self-disclosure see Chapter 10.) Dohrenwend also found, however, that responses to open questions were about three times longer than responses to closed questions, as measured by amounts of verbalisation. Again, responses to subjective open questions were significantly shorter than responses to objective open questions, whereas length of response to closed questions did not vary with subject matter.

Generalisations about the relative efficacy of open or closed questions can be difficult, since the intellectual capacity of the respondent must be taken into consideration. There is evidence to suggest that open questions may not be as appropriate with respondents of low intellect. Schatzman and Strauss (1956) compared respondents who had not gone beyond the grammar-school level with respondents who had spent at least one year at college. They found that open questions tended to be more effective with the latter group than with the former group, as judged by the questioning behaviour of experienced interviewers who were given a certain degree of freedom about what type of questions to employ. The interviewers used more open questions with the respondents of higher education, than with those of lower education.

Dohrenwend concluded that closed questions offer more definite advantages than open questions in research interviews because they exert a tighter control over respondents' answers. Open questions, while answered in more detail, tended to result in responses which deviated from the topic of the question, whereas with closed questions the respondent was more likely to answer the question in a direct fashion. However, although closed questions may facilitate control, they also have disadvantages in research interviews. Dillon (1990) illustrates how the sole use of closed questions may result in missing or inaccurate information being gathered. Consider the following two questions.

Open: What three factors do you consider to be most important when buying a car?

Closed: Which three of the following factors are most important for you when buying a car?

Even if the factor a respondent considers most important is missing from the list attached to the closed question, this is not likely to be mentioned and some of the presented factors will be offered as the answer. The respondent will regard this as the expected behaviour. On the other hand, if only the open question is used, the respondent may simply overlook one or more important factors. Dillon therefore recommends the use of open questions with a range of respondents in order to produce an exhaustive list of alternatives for later inclusion in closed question format in survey interviews.

Research comparing the use of open and closed questions in counselling, has found that open questions are more effective in promoting interviewee self-disclosures, in producing more accurate responses, and increasing perceived counsellor empathy (Hargie, 1984). Thus most texts on counselling recommend that counsellors should concentrate on asking open questions while reducing the number of closed questions asked.

In a different context, Loftus (1982) found that in the questioning of eyewitnesses, open questions produce more accurate information, but less overall detail, than specific closed questions. As a result, she recommends that in the questioning of eyewitnesses, questions should be open initially ('Tell me what happened') to obtain accuracy of information, followed by specific closed questions ('What colour was his hair?') to obtain a fuller picture.

Another feature which needs to be taken into consideration in any examination of the relative effects of open and closed questions is the length of the question itself. There is evidence to indicate that duration of responses is related to length of questions, in that longer answers tend to be given to longer questions (Jucker, 1986). One explanation for this may be that as the length of a question increases it is likely to contain an increased number of propositions each of which then needs to be addressed by the respondent (Wilson, 1990).

Although the importance of determining the relative effects of open and closed questions has been recognised for some fifty years (Lazarsfield, 1944), more research is needed in this field to chart the impact of open and closed questions across situations. Such research will need to take cognisance of the linguistic context of questions. For example, Allwinn (1991) has demonstrated how closed questions can be elaborated on by skilled people through the use of pre-remarks ('I'm not very knowledgeable about this so could I ask you. . .') to indicate that a detailed response is required, despite the fact that the question could logically be answered in one or a few words. Also, in certain interactive sequences it is clear that although a question has been phrased in a closed fashion, an open reply is expected. Thus, research into the effects of questions needs to take cognisance of contextual factors which, as countenanced by the model of skilled interpersonal communication presented in Chapter 2, may influence behaviour.

Affective questions

Affective questions are questions which relate specifically to the emotions, attitudes, feelings or preferences of the respondent – that is to the *affective* domain. An affective question can be either recall, process, open or closed, depending upon which aspect of the client's feelings is being explored. Where an attempt is being made to ascertain the reactions of the respondent to a past event, a recall question may be employed (e.g. 'Who was your favourite teacher at school?'). On the other hand, when present feelings are being explored, a closed question may be used (e.g. 'Do you feel embarrassed talking about this?').

The utilisation of recall or closed questions, however, places restrictions upon respondents in terms of what they are expected to relate about their feelings. Where it is important that the client be given time and freedom to discuss emotions, open questions may be more advantageous. Open questions can relate to past emotions (e.g. 'How did you feel when your mother died?') or to the present emotional state ('What are your feelings towards your husband now?'). Open questions facilitate the expression of true feelings by the respondent.

In order to encourage a respondent to think more deeply about feelings, and about the underlying reasons for these feelings, process questions may be more applicable. Rather than merely asking for a report about underlying feelings, process questions require the respondent to evaluate the cause of these feelings (e.g. 'Why did you hate your father so much?', 'Why have your feelings towards your wife changed?'). This type of question encourages the respondent to interpret reasons for feelings and perhaps become more rational in exploring them.

As the examples used in this section illustrate, affective questions are particularly relevant in counselling contexts, where an individual visits a counsellor in order to seek help with some problem. The discussion of feelings is very important in such situations, and a variety of affective questions can encourage a client to verbalise feelings or emotions.

Affective questions are clearly relevant in many contexts. However, in certain situations these questions seem to be avoided. There is, for example, a growing body of research to indicate that the overwhelming focus of practitioner–patient interaction is task-centred, concerns the discussion of physical symptoms and tends to ignore the emotional aspects of the patient's well-being (Hargie and Morrow, 1990). Furthermore, Dickson *et al.* (1989, p. 106) argue that the 'dearth of questions which are related to the affective domain is the main reason for the poor rate of detection of psychosocial problems in patients'. Current changes in the training of health professionals, with an increased emphasis upon interpersonal skills, should help to rectify this deficit.

Leading questions

Leading questions are questions which, by the way they are worded, lead the respondent towards an expected response. This expected answer to a leading question is implied within the question itself, and may, or may not, be immediately obvious to the respondent, depending upon the phrasing of the question. There are four different types of leading questions.

Conversational leads

As the name suggests, these are leading questions which are used in everyday conversations. A normal conversation between two people contains a number of comments that anticipate a certain type of response. This would include comments such as 'Isn't this a lovely day?'; 'Have you ever seen my mother looking better?'; 'Isn't this meal really delicious?' As Dohrenwend and Richardson (1964) point out, these comments which 'stimulate the flow of conversation in social situations, not only anticipate the response, however, but usually anticipate it correctly' (p. 77).

Thus the conversational lead is intended to suggest the answer which the respondent would have given in any case, and thereby encourages the respondent to participate. This technique would seem to be useful, when applied expertly, in interviewing contexts. Dohrenwend and Richardson (1964) report research findings which indicate that, in interviews, conversational leads convey to respondents the impression of friendliness and strong interest on the part of the interviewer, but only when these leading questions accurately anticipate the respondent's answer. Correct conversational leading questions create the feeling amongst respondents that the interviewer is listening carefully and understanding what is being said. This, in turn, stimulates respondents to continue developing their ideas, feeling confident that the interviewer is paying attention and understanding their responses.

Simple leads

These are questions which are unambiguously intended to lead the respondent to give an answer which the questioner expects to receive. This type of leading question usually exerts a degree of pressure on the respondent to reply in a certain fashion. Unlike the conversational lead, the simple lead anticipates the answer which the questioner expects, as opposed to the answer which the respondent would have given in any case. The simple lead, then, takes less cognisance of the respondent's thoughts and feelings. Examples of this type of leading question include 'You do, of course, go to church, don't you?'; 'Surely you don't support the communists?'; 'Aren't the taxes in this country far too high?'

There is some evidence to suggest that the use of simple leads which are obviously incorrect, may induce respondents to participate fully in an interview in order to correct any misconceptions inherent in the question. Beezer (1956), for example, conducted interviews with East German refugees in which he found that simple leading questions that were clearly incorrect yielded more information from respondents than did questions which were not leading. Thus when respondents were asked, 'I understand you don't have to pay very much for food in the East Zone because it is rationed?', most respondents replied by trying to correct the interviewer's impressions about general conditions in East Germany.

Dohrenwend and Richardson (1964) suggested that the blatantly incorrect simple leading question serves to place the respondent in the position of expert *vis-à-vis* the misinformed interviewer. As a result, the respondent may feel obliged to provide information which will enlighten the interviewer. Some of this information may involve the introduction of new topics not previously mentioned by the interviewer. This may explain the finding reported by Richardson (1960) that leading questions were more likely to elicit volunteered information.

While these results tend to suggest that leading questions can be effective in encouraging participation, it is not possible to state how, and in what contexts, simple leading questions can be most gainfully employed. It may be that in certain situations, and with particular types of respondent, the use of simple leading questions could be counter-productive. As Loftus and Zanni (1975) point out, most authors of texts on interviewing have eschewed this form of question as being bad practice. Furthermore, in the courtroom, leading questions are not permitted in the direct examination of a witness by the counsel for the side calling him, although they are allowed during cross-examination of the other side's witnesses. Kestler (1982) has positively recommended the use of leading questions by lawyers during cross-examination since they 'permit control of the subject matter and scope of the response. The witness is constrained to answer "yes" or "no"' (p. 59). In other settings, however, such constraint on the respondent will not be so desirable, and simple leading questions will need to be used with caution, or avoided altogether.

Implication leads

These are questions which lead the respondent to answer in a specific fashion, or accept a negative implication if the answer given is contrary to that anticipated. This type of leading question exerts a much greater degree of pressure on the respondent to reply in the expected manner than does a simple leading question, and for this reason it is sometimes referred to as a 'complex leading question'. An example of this type of question would be: 'Anyone who cared for his country would not want to see it destroyed in a nuclear attack or invaded by a foreign power, so don't you think any expenditure on an effective defensive deterrent is money well spent?' In this case, a negative answer to this question places the respondent in the position of apparently being unpatriotic.

If a respondent disagrees with the anticipated response to this type of implication lead, some type of justification is usually expected by the questioner. For this reason, implication leads are often used by radio and television interviewers when interviewing political, or controversial, individuals. Similarly, in arguments and debates, implication leads are employed in order to put opponents under pressure, and emphasise a certain point of view. Loftus (1982) provided another example of an implication lead, namely 'Did you know that what you were doing was dishonest?' Again, the respondent is put under pressure to either accept the negative implication of dishonesty or respond at length.

Subtle leads

These are questions which may not be instantly recognisable as leading questions, but which nevertheless are worded in such a way as to elicit a certain type of response. They are also known as 'directional questions' in that the repondent is being directed towards a particular type of answer (Kunda and Fong, 1993). An example of how the wording of a question can influence the respondent to answer in a particular way was reported by Harris (1973). Subjects were informed that they were taking part in 'a study in the accuracy of guessing measurements, and that they should make as intelligent a numerical guess as possible to each question' (p. 399). Subjects were then asked either 'How tall was the basket-ball player?' or 'How short was the basket-ball player?' On average, subjects guessed about 79 inches and 69 inches, respectively, indicating the influence of the words *tall* and *short* in the respective questions. Other questions asked by Harris along the same lines produced similar results – thus the question 'How long was the movie?' resulted in average estimates of 130 minutes, whereas 'How short was the movie?' produced an average of 100 minutes.

Loftus (1975) reported similar findings in a study in which forty people were interviewed about their headaches and about headache products 'under the belief that they were participating in market research on these products' (p. 561). Subjects were asked either 'Do you get headaches frequently, and if so, how often?' or 'Do you get headaches occasionally, and if so, how often?' The *frequently* subjects reported an average of 2.2 headaches per week, whereas the *occasionally* group reported 0.7 per week. Loftus also asked either 'In terms of the total number of products, how many other products have you tried? 1? 2? 3?' or 'In terms of the total number of products, how many other products have you tried? 1? 5? 10?' Responses to these questions averaged 3.3 and 5.2 other products, respectively.

Findings such as these have been consistently reported in research investigations. Furthermore, 'researchers have long known that people tend to agree with one-sided statements, and that the same subject may agree to two opposite statements on different occasions' (Kunda and Fong, 1993, p. 65). This is referred to as the 'acquiescence effect' wherein respondents comply or acquiesce to the explicit or implicit direction of the question. Such acquiescence was found by Bless *et al.* (1992, p. 309), who carried out a series of studies which demonstrated that 'respondents report higher behavioural frequencies when the response scale offers high rather than low frequency response alternatives'. They also cite evidence to demonstrate that the more demanding the computation of a requested frequency response the more likely it is that respondents will be led by the alternatives suggested in the question.

In another study Loftus and Palmer (1974) had subjects view films of car accidents, and then questioned them about what they had seen. The question 'About how fast were the cars going when they smashed into each other?' produced higher estimates of speed than when the verb 'smashed' was replaced by 'hit', 'bumped', 'collided' or 'contacted'. One week later those subjects who had been asked the former question were also more likely to say 'yes' to the question 'Did you see broken glass?', even though no glass was broken in the accident.

In a similar piece of research Loftus and Zanni (1975) compared the effects of questions containing an indefinite article with the same questions containing a definite article. In this study 100 graduate students were told that 'they were participating in an experiment on memory' (p. 87). They were shown a short film of a car accident and then asked questions about this. It was found that questions which contained a definite article (e.g. 'Did you see *the* broken headlight?') produced fewer uncertain or 'I don't know' responses, and more false recognition of events which never in fact occurred, than did questions which contained an indefinite article (e.g. 'Did you see *a* broken headlight?').

This 'false recognition' was also reported in the Loftus (1975) study. She conducted four different experiments, each of which highlighted the way in which the wording of questions, asked immediately after an event, can influence the responses to questions asked considerably later. In one of these experiments 150 students were shown a video-tape of a car accident and asked a number of questions about the accident. Half of the subjects were asked 'How fast was the white sports car going when it passed the barn while travelling along the country road?', while half were asked 'How fast was the white sports car going while travelling along the country road?' Although no barn appeared in the film, 17.3 per cent of those asked the former question responded 'yes' when later asked 'Did you see a barn?', as opposed to only 2.7 per cent of those asked the latter question.

These findings have been confirmed in the sphere of interviewing suspects of crimes. Buckwalter (1983) pointed out that suspects are more forthcoming when asked to 'tell the truth' rather than 'confess your crime'. Similarly, in cases of murder, motives are given more readily to the question 'Why did you do it?' than to 'Why did you murder him?' Buckwalter advised interviewers to avoid terms such as 'kill', 'steal', 'rape', and replace them with words such as 'shoot', 'take', 'sex'.

In reviewing research findings relating to the use of subtle leads, Dillon (1986) concluded: 'It is obvious that the wording of a question affects the answer. . . . What is more, the wording of the question can influence people not only to over/under-report but also to give truly answers about non-existent things' (p. 107). The implications of these findings are likely to be of interest to many individuals, particularly those concerned with obtaining accurate recall of facts from others, including nurses, doctors, detectives, insurance investigators, lawyers and assessment interviewers.

Probing questions

Probing questions are questions which are designed to encourage respondents to expand upon initial responses and, in this sense, they are 'follow-up' questions. Once a respondent has given an initial answer, it can be explored further in a number of ways. Turney *et al.* (1976) have identified a number of different types of probing questions and these are as follows:

Clarification probes

These can be used in order to elicit a clearer, more concisely phrased response, in situations where the questioner is either confused or uncertain about the content or meaning of the initial responses. Examples of clarification probes would include 'What exactly do you mean?', 'Could you explain that to me again?' or 'Are you saying that you did not do it?'

Justification probes

These require respondents to justify initial responses by giving reasons for what they have said. Questions such as 'Why did you say that?', 'How did you reach that conclusion?' or 'What evidence have you got to support that?' all require the respondent to expand upon the initial response by giving a justification for having made it.

Relevance probes

These are questions which give respondents an opportunity to reassess the appropriateness of a response, and/or make its relevance to the main topic under consideration more obvious. This type of probing question enables the questioner to ascertain which relationships are being made by the respondent, between objects, people or events and in addition encourages the respondent to reflect on the validity of these relationships. Relevance probes include: 'How does this relate to your home background?', 'Is this relevant to what we discussed earlier?' or 'Why are you telling me this now?'

Exemplification probes

These require respondents to provide concrete or specific instances of what they mean by what may, at first, appear to be a rather vague statement. Asking a respondent to give an example to illustrate a general statement often helps to clarify the statement, by providing a definite insight into the thoughts of the respondent (see Chapter 8 for a discussion on the use of examples). Included here would be questions such as 'Could you give me an example of that?' 'Can you think of a specific instance of this?' or 'Where have you shown leadership qualities in the past?'

Extension probes

These can be used to encourage a respondent to expand upon an initial response by providing further information pertinent to the topic under discussion. An extension question is best employed in situations where it is felt that a respondent should be able to make further responses which will facilitate the development of the discussion. Examples of extension probes include: 'That's interesting, tell me more', 'Is there anything else that you can remember about it?' or 'And then what happened?'

Accuracy probes

These are questions which draw the respondent's attention to a possible error in fact that has been made in a response, and thereby offers the respondent an opportunity to adjust or restructure the response where necessary. Accuracy questions are most useful in situations where either it is absolutely vital that the respondent is certain about the accuracy of responses (e.g. an eyewitness being cross-examined in court), or where the questioner knows the correct answer and wishes to give the respondent a chance to reflect upon an initial response (e.g. a teacher questioning pupils). Accuracy probes include questions such as 'Are you quite sure about that?', 'You are certain that you could identify him?' or 'It definitely happened before 3.00 pm?'

Echo probes

These are so called because they are questions which 'echo' the words used by the respondent in the initial response, by containing these same words in the follow-up question. Echo probes are often employed in interpersonal interaction, but if these are over-used it is likely that they will be counter-productive, since if every answer given by the respondent is echoed, the respondent may soon become very aware of this procedure and, in all probability, will stop responding. Examples of echo probes are included in the following:

A: After the meal he became very romantic, and told me that he loved me.
Q: He told you that he loved you?
A: Yes, and then he took my hand and asked me to marry him.
Q: He asked you to *marry* him?!

Nonverbal probes

These are behaviours which are employed in such a manner as to indicate to the respondent a desire for further information. Included here would be the use of appropriate paralanguage to accompany expressions such as 'Ohh?!', or 'Never?!', together with inquisitive nonverbal behaviours (e.g. raising or lowering of eyebrows, sideways tilt of the head, and eye contact). The use of pauses following an initial response can also serve as a form of probe indicating a desire for further responses. Indeed, interviewer pauses can put pressure on an interviewee to respond in order to fill the silence.

Consensus probes

These are questions which give an opportunity for a group to pause in a discussion and for individual respondents to express their agreement or disagreement with an initial response. Asking consensus questions is a useful technique for a group leader to employ in order to gauge the extent of support within the group for any proposed idea or line of action. By asking 'Does everyone agree with that?' or 'Is there anyone not happy with that?' it is usually possible to evaluate the level of group consensus at any given time.

The ability to probe effectively is at the core of effective questioning. Fowler and Mangione (1990) assert that probing is one of the most difficult techniques for interviewers to acquire, while Millar *et al.* (1992, p. 131) note that: 'Novice interviewers often find that they have obtained a wealth of superficial information because they have failed to explore interviewee responses in any depth.' Attention should therefore be paid to the effective use of probing, by those who use questioning as a central technique during interpersonal encounters.

Rhetorical questions

A rhetorical question is a question which does not expect an answer, either because the speaker intends to answer the question, or because the question is equivalent to a statement (as in 'Who would not wish their children well?' to mean 'Everyone wishes their children well'). In the former case, rhetorical questions are often used by public speakers in order to stimulate interest in their presentation by encouraging the audience to 'think things through' with them. The use of rhetorical questions has been found to raise the level of audience attention and increase their retention of information (Bligh, 1971). As Turk (1985) put it: 'Asking questions is the best way to promote thought. . . . We are so conditioned to provide answers to sentences in question form, that our minds are subconsciously aroused towards an answer, even if we remain silent' (p. 75).

With large audiences, questions are usually not appropriate since only a few members of the audience would be given a chance to answer, and the rest of the audience may have difficulty in hearing the responses. For this reason, lecturers, politicians and other individuals, when addressing large groups of people, often employ rhetorical questions (Brown, 1982). An example of the use of such questions is contained in the following extract from a lecture on industrial economics:

> Although productivity agreements have been, and are being, applied quite widely in industry, they have not provided the solution to Britain's low level of productivity compared to other countries. Well, why should this mechanism have failed to provide a solution to Britain's problems? There are several reasons. . . .

Multiple questions

A multiple question is a question which is made up of two or more questions phrased as one. While a multiple question may contain a number of questions of the same type, quite often it comprises an open question followed by a closed question which narrows the focus (e.g. 'What did you do during the holidays? Did you go to Spain?'). Multiple questions may be useful where time is limited and it is important to get some answer from a respondent. For this reason multiple questions are often used by radio and television interviewers who have a given (often brief) period of time in which to interview a respondent.

In most situations, however, multiple questions are wasteful – especially where the questions subsumed within the multiple questions are unrelated. Such questions are liable to confuse the respondent, and/or the responses given by the respondent may confuse the questioner who may be unclear exactly which question has been answered. For example:

Q: Have you lived here long? Do you like it? I mean, what about the neighbours?
A: Yes.
Q: Yes, what?

In the classroom context, Wright and Nuthall (1970) carried out a study in which they observed seventeen teachers teaching three lessons each to eight children in schools in Christchurch, New Zealand. They found that the tendency on the part of a teacher to ask one question at a time was positively related to pupil achievement, whereas the tendency to ask more than one question at a time was negatively related to pupil achievement. While it is difficult to generalise from the results of one study, this research does highlight the possible disadvantage of using multiple questions in classroom interaction.

In the field of health, Walton and MacLeod Clark (1986) found that patients had difficulties in formulating a reply when asked multiple questions. Despite this, they report that nurses frequently employ multiple questions and provide several examples such as: 'Come on, take your trousers off. How do you like your pillows? Do you want the back rest out or not?' These questions serve to pressurise and confuse the patient and they also decrease the probability of receiving accurate information.

There are therefore dangers involved with the use of multiple questions in educational and health settings. However, the extent to which such disadvantages accrue in other situations has yet to be investigated.

RELATED ASPECTS OF QUESTIONING

In addition to the various types of questions discussed in the previous section and the objectives they serve in interpersonal interaction, there are a number of related aspects of questioning which anyone wishing to use this skill effectively should be aware of. These aspects are concerned with how questions are asked, rather than what questions can be asked, and include the following techniques.

Structuring

In certain social situations where a respondent is likely to be asked a large number of questions, it may be useful to structure the questions in such a way as to indicate to the respondent what questions are likely to be asked, and why it is necessary to ask them (e.g. 'In order to help me advise you about possible future jobs I would like to find out about your qualifications, experience and interests. If I could begin with your qualifications. . .'). By structuring the interaction in this way, the respondent knows why questions are being asked, and also knows what questions to expect. Once the respondent is aware of the immediate goals of the questioner, and recognises these as acceptable goals, it is likely that the interaction will flow more smoothly with the respondent attempting to give adequate answers (see also the skill of set induction in Chapter 7 for a fuller discussion of this type of structuring).

Prompting

Prompting is the technique which can be adopted to encourage a respondent to give an adequate answer, following either an unrelated answer, or no answer at all, to an initial question. Depending upon the hypothesised cause of the respondent's failure, the questioner may prompt in different ways. If it is thought that the respondent did not correctly hear the initial question, the questioner may simply restate the same question. If it is thought that the respondent did not understand the initial phrasing of the question, it may be rephrased either in parallel fashion, or at a simpler level. It may, however, be deemed necessary to prompt the respondent either by reviewing information previously covered (e.g. 'You remember what we talked about last week') or by giving a clue which will help to focus attention in the right direction. An example of this latter type of prompt is included in the following excerpt from a radio 'phone-in' quiz:

Q: With what country would you associate pasta?
A: Spain.
Q: No, think of Chianti. (*prompt*)
A: Oh yes, of course, Italy.

Pausing

The function of pausing as a form of probing question has already been mentioned. However, as well as pausing after receiving a response, it is possible to pause both before, and after, asking a question. By pausing before asking a question, it is possible to stimulate the attention of the listener and give the question greater impact. By pausing after asking a question, the respondent is given the distinct impression of being expected to give some form of response. The use of pauses after asking a question also reduces the likelihood of the questioner asking multiple questions. Finally, pausing after a respondent gives an initial response can serve to encourage the respondent to continue talking.

The importance of pausing has been investigated by Rowe (1969; 1974a, b). She found that when teachers increased the average 'wait-time' after pupil responses the length of these responses increased from seven words when the pause was 1 second to twenty-eight words when the pause was 3 seconds. Other positive benefits were that the teacher tended to ask more process questions, pupils asked more questions and those pupils who did not tend to say much started talking and produced novel ideas. The benefits of teacher pauses of a duration of 3 seconds have more recently been confirmed by Tobin (1987). Yet there is evidence to indicate that the average teacher pauses following a teacher question and a pupil response are 1.26 seconds and 0.55 seconds respectively (Swift *et al.*, 1988). The disadvantages of such a short wait-time are highlighted by Dillon (1990) who, in a review of research into the benefits of pausing across a range of professional contexts, concluded that pauses need to be of a minimum of 3 seconds duration in order 'to enhance the partner's participation and cognition' (p. 221).

Distribution

In group contexts, a group leader may wish to involve as many respondents as possible in the discussion. One method whereby this can be achieved is by distributing questions to all group members, so that all points of view can be heard. This is a useful technique to employ, especially with individuals who may be reluctant to express their views unless specifically given an opportunity to do so. The redirection of a question from one group member to another may be of particular value in achieving a discreet distribution of questions, without exerting undue pressure or embarrassing any one individual in the group.

Responses

Just as there is a wide variation in types of questions which can be asked, so too is there a wide variation in the range of possible responses which can be made. Dillon (1986) has identified a large number of possible answers to questions, the main types of which can be summarised as follows:

1 *Silence*. The respondent may choose to say nothing.
2 *Overt refusal to answer*, e.g. 'I'd rather not say'.
3 *Unconnected response*. The respondent may change the topic completely.
4 *Humour*. For example, to the question 'How old are you?', the respondent may reply 'Not as old as I feel!'
5 *Lying*. The respondent may simply give a false answer.
6 *Stalling*. Again, to the question 'How old are you?' the respondent may reply 'How old do you think I am?' Answering a question with a question is a classic stalling technique.
7 *Evading*. Wilson (1990) discusses several techniques used by politicians to evade having to answer questions directly. These include questioning the question, attacking the interviewer or stating that the question has already been answered. A good example of evasion occurred when a well known trade union leader being pressed by a TV interviewer to 'answer this important question' replied: 'Let me answer *my* important questions first, and then I'll answer yours'!
8 *Selective ambiguity*. Thus to the question about age, the respondent may reply 'Don't worry, I'll finish the marathon OK.' In other words, the respondent pretends to recognise the 'real' question, and answers it.
9 *Withholding and concealing*. In this instance, respondents will attempt to avoid disclosing information which may be damaging to them or those close to them. This is a problem commonly faced by investigators (criminal, insurance, etc.), but is also applicable to those professionals who have to deal with sensitive or taboo issues such as child abuse, incest, drug abuse and so on.
10 *Distortion*. Respondents in many instances will give the answers they think the questioner wants, or the answers that they feel are socially desirable, often without consciously realising they are so doing. Thus in survey interviews, respondents tend to overestimate voting, reading books and giving to charity, and underestimate illnesses, financial status and illegal behaviour (Bradburn and Sudman, 1980).

11 *Direct honest response*. Finally, in most instances the respondent will
give a direct, truthful answer to the majority of questions asked.

In any interaction, the professional will need to evaluate the responses
received, and make decisions about how to follow these up with appropriate
probing questions if necessary.

OVERVIEW

Although, at first sight, questioning would seem to be one of the simplest of
all social skills, upon further examination it can be seen that, in fact, the skill
is quite complex. As Dillon (1986) pointed out: 'It is easy to ask questions in
everyday situations. And it is easy to ask everyday questions in professional
practice. But it takes *great care* to prepare an educative question' (p. 112).
There would therefore seem to be a great deal of truth in the advice given by
Voltaire that we should 'Judge a man not by his answers but by his questions.'
   There is a large variety of different types of question which can be asked in
any given situation, and the answers received will be markedly affected by
both the wording, and the type, of question asked. However, no hard-and-fast
rules about which types of question to use in particular social encounters
exist, since much more situation-specific research is needed in order to
investigate the effects of aspects such as type of respondent and the nature of
the social context. Nevertheless, the categorisations of questions contained in
this chapter provide a useful starting point for the analysis of the effects of
questions in social interaction. Furthermore, the examples given, and the
research reviewed, should provide the reader with some insight into the
different modes of usage, and the accompanying effects, of different types of
question.

Chapter 6

Reflecting

INTRODUCTION

In the preceding chapter one technique which is commonly employed to gain information and conduct interpersonal exchanges was considered when central features of skilled questioning were outlined. Here an alternative procedure called reflecting will be introduced, although it should not be thought that the one must be used to the exclusion of the other. While sharing some of the functional features of questioning, reflecting differs in a number of important respects. Consider the following two short fictional interview transcripts. The first involves an excerpt from a survey interview conducted by a student (I) within the Faculty of Social Sciences at the local University of Newtown. The research project in which she is engaged is concerned with the effects of unemployment on population shifts. The interviewee (Ie), Mrs Dillon, has just recently moved to Newtown.

 I: How many people live here with you?
Ie: Just my husband at the moment. . . but the baby is due next month.
 I: Can I ask what age your husband is?
Ie: Oh, let me see. He's just turned 33.
 I: Uh-huh, and yourself?
Ie: I'm 28.
 I: OK, how long have you been living here in Newtown, Mrs Dillon?
Ie: It will be three years now next month.
 I: Is your husband employed at present?
Ie: Yes, thank goodness, although for how much longer is anyone's guess.
 I: Where does he work?
Ie: Down at Smiths. . . that's the shoe factory. . . . But it now seems certain that it's closing down. The main factory is in the South-East, you see. . . . We're ever so worried.
 I: What does your husband do there?
Ie: He's on the machines.

I: Right. . . . Do you work, Mrs Dillon?

Ie: No, we're relying totally on my husband's wage. It's the only money we have coming in and what with the mortgage and so on, we won't be able to cope without it.

I: Where did you live before coming to Newtown?

Ie: Smalltown.

I: Did your husband have a job there at the time of moving?

Ie: No, that's why we moved. He'd been unemployed since we were married, and then he got this job. So we moved . . . bought the house and all. It's been a bit of a struggle. . . .

The second interview again involves Mrs Dillon. A local health visitor has just called. Mrs Dillon has not been attending her GP for routine checks on her progress and dropped out of the antenatal classes at an early stage. The health visitor is keen to re-establish contact, find out if everything is all right, and again point out the benefits of attending for regular checks. We join the interview after the normal preliminaries:

Ie: No, as I said, it's not that I didn't find the classes useful. . . . It's just that somehow. . . . Oh, I don't know, I suppose I haven't really been out much at all this last while.

I: You've been spending most of your time at home.

Ie: Yes . . . come to think of it, I don't remember when I've been out last apart from doing the shopping. . . . It's not that I don't feel up to it. . . . I mean I could do it if I wanted to, I suppose. . . . I feel well enough. . . . But somehow. . . . Oh, I don't know. . . .

I: Although you feel fit enough be out and about, Jill, you seem reluctant to do so. There's been something keeping you indoors.

Ie: I think it's all to do with the baby, and Jonathan losing his job, and the mortgage. . . . Everything's beginning to really get on top of me. I don't know what we will do once Smiths closes. . . that's where Jonathan, my husband, works. We need that job . . . especially now.

I: You have enough on your plate just now with the baby coming but on top of that there's the worry of Jonathan being laid off work, and the stress of it is beginning to get you down.

Ie: That's it exactly. You see we took out the maximum mortgage when we moved here so we really haven't been able to save all that much and Jonathan won't get much redundancy because he hasn't been there long. I've got nothing for the baby yet.

I: Yes, losing a wage is bad enough at any time, especially when you are relying upon it totally and there is a large mortgage to pay, but with the baby due and the extra expense that that means, it makes it all seem so much worse.

Ie: This couldn't have happened at a worse time, really. I mean if we can't keep up the mortgage payments we might not even be here when the baby arrives. Although don't get me wrong, I want the baby, but somehow. . . .

I: Although now that the baby is almost here, you wouldn't want it any other way, but, let's say, the timing of it could have been better. The thought of having to find somewhere else to live with a new baby is an extremely worrying prospect for you just now.

Ie: This is my biggest dread. Sometimes I just sit and cry. You see I can't let Jonathan know how worried I am. He's been very depressed about the whole thing so I have to try to chivy him along. . . .

I: So you have been bearing this burden very much on your own so far, Jill.

Ie: Yes, you are the first person that I have really talked to about it. . . .

These two interviews, while involving the same interviewee, differ markedly in the approaches adopted by the interviewers. In the first situation the interviewer sought to obtain information on a number of pre-established topics relating to the interviewee's background circumstances, such as her age, whether or not she worked, the number of people sharing the house, her husband's employment, the length of time she had been living in her present abode, etc. The interviewer and the data which she required was very much the dominating feature of the interview with the interviewee merely providing this information. Questioning was the skill used exclusively to direct the interviewee from one topic to the next, and each question was often quite independent of the previous response. The interviewee was encouraged to furnish only information which was directly relevant to the needs of the interviewer and when she did begin to go further to reveal the impact of the anticipated loss of her husband's job, she was expeditiously redirected by means of another question.

The second interview, however, centred very much upon Mrs Dillon and the difficulties which she was experiencing, with the interviewer staying, conversationally, much more in the background. Rather than directly leading the interviewee to areas which the interviewer wished to explore, the health visitor gently guided the interviewee and facilitated Mrs Dillon's discussion of matters which seemed important for *her* – Mrs Dillon – to ventilate. Unlike the first interview, in the second case there were no questions asked by the interviewer. Rather her interjections took the form of statements – these statements were reflections.

While some inconsistencies have been identified by Dickson (1986) among the definitions which exist in the literature, reflections can be regarded as statements, in the interviewer's own words, which encapsulate and re-present the essence of the interviewee's previous message. Carl Rogers, the founder of non-directive or client-centred counselling (Rogers, 1951, 1961, 1980), is commonly credited with coining the term, although the technique can, of course, be used in other approaches to counselling (Ivey, 1988) and, indeed, in a variety of non-counselling contexts (Mills, 1991; Stiles and Putnam,

1992). An overview of definitional issues, together with contrasting theoretical perspectives on reflecting, is provided by Dickson (1986).

Returning to the contrasting interview excerpts, apart from contributing examples of the technique of reflecting, they serve to make two further points. First, that interviewing is not necessarily concerned with the asking and answering of questions although questions are commonly associated with this activity. Second, and related to this, the more general point that interviewers can differ markedly in the styles which they adopt.

STYLES OF INTERACTING

Style refers to the characteristic manner in which what is done is done. (A more thoroughgoing examination of the concept is provided by Norton, 1983.) A broad stylistic feature of interaction would seem to be that of directness, and approaches which differ in this respect have been commented upon in the contexts of teaching (Brown and Atkins, 1988), social work (Baldock and Prior, 1981), counselling and psychotherapy (Patterson, 1986) as well as interviewing (Stewart and Cash, 1991). Directness involves the degree of explicit influence and control exercised by, for example, the interviewer and, correspondingly, the extent to which the interviewee is constrained in responding. At one extreme of this dimension, the interviewer following a direct style will determine the form, content and pace of the transaction. At the other extreme these features will depend upon the concerns and predilections of the interviewee with the interviewer staying conversationally much more in the background, guiding and facilitating.

According to Benjamin (1987), the former style is typified by the use of interviewer leads, the latter by responses. Although acknowledging the difficulties of producing unambiguous definitions of these two terms, Benjamin (1981, p. 115) comments:

When I respond, I speak in terms of what the interviewee has expressed. I react to the ideas and feelings he has communicated to me with something of my own. When I lead, I take over. I express ideas and feelings to which I expect the interviewee to react. . . . When leading, I make use of my own life space; when responding, I tend more to utilise the life space of the interviewee. Interviewer responses keep the interviewee at the centre of things; leads make the interviewer central.

Reflections can be categorised as responses, in this sense, and are contrasted with questions, for instance, which tend to be a method of leading.

The particular style adopted by an interviewer is, in part, dependent upon the type of interview being conducted. A more direct, questioning style is most frequently adopted in circumstances where: the interviewee has accepted the interviewer's role as an interrogator; the information required is, basically, factual in nature; the amount of time which can be devoted to the interview is limited; a long-term relationship need not be established; and where the information is directly for the benefit of the interviewer. A more indirect, responsive style is used to best advantage when: the interviewee is the participant who stands to gain from the encounter; the information exchanged is affective; and, when the information is confused, fragmented and imperspicuous due, perhaps, to the fact that it involves a problem which the interviewee has never fully thought through before. Despite this distinction it would be inappropriate to assume that a more direct style of operating is never used under the latter conditions or that the question does not form part of the range of skills employed. Equally it would be erroneous to conclude that in the former circumstances a reflection statement should never be contemplated. Interviewers tend to vary in terms of the directness of their style depending upon the particular school of thought to which they adhere. Consequently some are likely to be more direct across a range of contexts than others. Nevertheless, as a generality, the above distinction holds.

While questions can be used within the second set of circumstances listed above, a reliance on this skill in a counselling-type interview was strongly discouraged by Boy and Pine (1963). Questions, they argued, are often unrelated to the client's needs, being derived from the counsellor's frame of reference, and are often posed in a routine, unthinking manner. This view has been echoed, more recently, by Mucchielli (1983), while Egan (1990) and Culley (1991) also draw attention to some of the shortcomings of a questioning approach in such a situation. Among these is the suggestion that questions socialise the interviewee to speak only in response to a question and to merely reveal information which is directly requested. They also encourage the interviewee to let the interviewer take complete responsibility for the interaction, and for finding a satisfactory solution to the problems or difficulties experienced by the interviewee. A further drawback is that their use is less likely to foster a warm, understanding relationship, conducive to the exploration of important, but perhaps intimate and, for the interviewee, potentially embarrassing details.

Similar comments have been made by Dillon (1990), when challenging the effectiveness of questions as a means of promoting pupil discussion in the classroom. Making comment on the outcomes of several case studies of this type of classroom activity, he concluded that, 'In all of these classes, it is as if we see discussion diminish in the face of teacher questions, resurging when alternatives are used, and again receding when the questions resume' (p. 234). Far from producing the desired outcome, pupils tend to become dependent and passive, reacting only to further teacher questions. The utilisation of the skill of reflecting, as an alternative in such circumstances, has been proposed.

A number of empirical studies have compared the outcomes of an indirect, reflective style with a range of alternatives. Unlike the above instance, most of this research has an interviewing or counselling orientation. In some cases attitudes of both interviewees and external judges to interviewers manifesting contrasting styles have been sought. Silver (1970), for example, found that low-status interviewees felt much more comfortable with interviewers who displayed a reflective rather than a judgemental approach. Ellison and Firestone (1974) reported that subjects observing a reflective rather than an intrusive interviewer who controlled the direction and pace of the interview in a particularly assertive manner, indicated a greater willingness to reveal highly intimate details. This interviewer was also perceived as passive, easy-going and non-assertive.

An interrogative approach in which further information was requested and a predictive style which required the interviewer accurately to predict interviewees' reactions in situations yet to be discussed, were the alternatives to reflecting examined by Turkat and Alpher (1984). Although impressions were based upon written transcripts, rather than actual interviews, those interviewers who used reflections were regarded as understanding their clients. Empathic understanding together with positive regard (two of the core conditions for effective counselling according to the client-centred school of thought) were related to the reflective style of interviewing in a study by Zimmer and Anderson (1968) which drew upon the opinions of external judges who viewed a video-taped counselling session. From the painstaking analysis of therapy sessions undertaken by Clare Hill and her colleagues (Hill et al., 1988; Hill, 1989), not only was reflecting discovered to be one of the most common of the identified techniques utilised by therapists, but clients reported that they found it one of the most helpful. They regarded it as providing support and seldom reacted negatively to its use. Such reflections assisted clients in becoming more deeply attuned to their emotional and personal experiences leading to more profound levels of exploration and greater insights into their circumstances and difficulties. One of the most marked outcomes was an association with significantly reduced levels of anxiety. Incidentally, and by way of comparison, closed questions, in particular, were regarded by clients as decidedly unhelpful when used by therapists. (It should be noted that 'reflecting' in these studies was actually labelled 'paraphrasing'. Since the latter encompassed a range of different types of reflective statement, this general use of the term paraphrasing contrasts with the rather specialised application to be encountered later in the chapter.)

Other researchers, rather than focusing upon attitudes, have investigated the effects of reflecting upon the actual behaviour of the interviewee. Some form of interviewee self-disclosure has commonly been measured. (For further information on self-disclosure see Chapter 10.) Powell (1968), for instance, carried out a study on the effects of reflections on subjects' positive and negative self-referent statements (i.e. statements about themselves). 'Approval-supportive' and 'open disclosure' were the comparative experimental conditions. The former included interviewer statements supporting subjects' self-references while the latter referred to the provision of personal detail by the interviewer. Reflections were found to produce a significant increase in the number of negative, but not positive, self-references. Kennedy *et al.* (1971), while failing to make the distinction between positive and negative instances, similarly reported an increase in interviewee self-statements attributable to the use of this technique.

Vondracek (1969) and Beharry (1976) looked at the effects of reflecting not only on the amount of subjects' self-disclosure but on the degree of intimacy provided. More intimate detail was associated with the reflective style of interviewing in both cases. However, the contrasting conditions of interviewer self-disclosure and use of probes were equally effective in this respect. A similar result was reported by Mills (1983) in relation to rates, rather than quality, of self-disclosure. Feigenbaum (1977) produced an interesting finding concerning sex differences of subjects. While females disclosed more, and at more intimate levels, in response to reflections, male subjects scored significantly higher on both counts in response to interviewer self-disclosure.

An investigation which actually featured marital therapists and couples undergoing therapy was conducted by Cline *et al.* (1984). A complex relationship emerged involving not only sex but also social status of subjects. Thus therapist reflectiveness was found to correlate positively with subsequent changes in positive social interaction for middle-class husbands but with negative changes for both lower-class husbands and wives. It also related positively to changes in expression of personal feeling for middle-class husbands and wives. When assessed three months after the termination of therapy, a positive relationship emerged between therapist reflections and outcome measures of marital satisfaction but for lower-class husbands only.

There seems to be little doubt now that there is a strong individual difference factor influencing reactions and outcomes to non-directive, reflective versus directive styles of engagement. In addition to demographic variables such as gender and class differences already mentioned, personality characteristics have also been researched. Some evidence reviewed by Hill (1992) suggests that locus of control, cognitive complexity, and reactance of clients may be important. Locus of control, it will be recalled from Chapter 4, refers to a belief in personally significant events deriving from either internal or external sources, while reactance is a predisposition to perceive and respond to events as restrictions on personal autonomy and freedom. Cognitive complexity relates to the conceptual differentiation and sophistication with which individuals make sense of their circumstances. Hill (1992) came to the conclusion that those high on internality of control, cognitive complexity, and low on reactance were more suited to less directive interventions such as reflecting.

In sum, these findings would suggest that attitudes towards interviewers who use a reflective style are largely positive. At a more behavioural level, this technique would also seem capable of producing increases in both the

amount and intimacy of information which interviewees reveal abou
selves although it would not appear to be significantly more effecti
alternative procedures such as interviewer self-disclosures or probes
actual therapeutic context there is some evidence linking reflecting with
positive outcome measures for certain clients. However, the intervening
effects of individual differences in demographic and personality factors
should not be overlooked.

FACTUAL AND AFFECTIVE COMMUNICATION

While some have regarded reflecting as a unitary phenomenon, others have
conceived of it as an 'umbrella' term encompassing a varying number of
related processes. These include reflection of content (Nelson-Jones, 1988),
reflecting experience (Brammer, 1988), content responses and affect responses (Danish and Hauer, 1973), reflecting meaning (Ivey, 1988) and
restatement (Auerswald, 1974). Perhaps the most commonly cited distinction
is between reflection of feeling and paraphrasing. Although sharing a number
of salient characteristics, these two skills have one important difference. In
order to appreciate fully this difference some preliminary considerations are
necessary.

It should, first, be appreciated that many of the messages which we both
send and receive provide different types of information. This is, of course,
an echo of an earlier point made in Chapter 2 when the multi-dimensionality
of communication was emphasised. One type of information is basically
factual or cognitive concerning ideas, places, people, objects, happenings,
etc. Another is predominantly feeling or affective concerning our emotional
states or attitudinal reactions to our environment. More accurately, messages vary along a continuum ranging from those which are factual to those
which are affective. An example of the former would be, 'It's 4.30', in
response to a request for the correct time (and providing, of course, that the
individual with the accurate timepiece does not suddenly realise that he or
she is late for an appointment!). An example of the latter might be 'Oh no!',
uttered by someone who has just been informed that a very close friend has
died suddenly. The utterance is not a denial that the unfortunate event has
taken place; it is simply an expression of shocked grief, and is therefore
fundamentally affective. The majority of messages, however, contain elements of both types of information. Consider the following statement: 'I
worked in the packing department at Hills. All I did from 9 o'clock until
5 was put tins into cardboard boxes, day after day after day.' The factual
element of this statement is that the speaker worked in the packing
department at Hills each day from 9 until 5 and the job consisted of packing
tins into cardboard boxes. The affective element, of course, is that it was
found to be routine and boring.

The affective component of a message can take three basic forms:

1 *Explicit*. Here the feeling aspect is explicitly stated in the verbal content. For example, 'I am so happy.'
2 *Implicit*. In this case feelings are not directly stated but rather the affective information is implicitly contained in what is said. Thus when a patient who has recently been bereaved says, listlessly, 'Some days I just don't get up . . . yet I am always tired. I don't have the energy to do anything. . . . I can't even concentrate to read. I keep thinking that I will never be able to manage on my own. Sometimes I think that it would have been better if I had been taken as well. . .', depression is a very obvious emotional message contained within the facts. Note, however, that there are no 'feeling words', as such, in the statement to label it.
3 *Inferred*. The affective component of a message can be inferred from the manner in which the verbal content is delivered – from the nonverbal and paralinguistic accompaniment. Research has shown that when the verbal and nonverbal/paralinguistic elements of an emotional or attitudinal message conflict as, for example, when someone says irately, 'I am not angry', we often, although not invariably, base our judgements on the latter source of information (Knapp and Hall, 1992). In the case of inferred feelings, unlike the previous two, the verbal content of the message does not play a part.

It is, on occasion, a rather perplexing activity trying to decode accurately the affective content when it has not been explicitly stated and, in these cases, caution is recommended. This would seem to be particularly good advice in the case of some types of nonverbal behaviour. While facial expressions are amenable to intentional manipulation, it has been discovered that they may be more accurate indicators of emotional state than certain body movements or paralinguistic cues (Ekman and O'Sullivan, 1991). Nevertheless, reflecting nebulous feelings expressed in these less obvious ways can often be not only more difficult but potentially more beneficial (Egan, 1990).

We thus convey and receive both factual and affective information. Paraphrasing involves mirroring-back, primarily, the factual content of a message while reflection of feeling, as the name suggests, focuses upon the affective element.

FUNCTIONS OF REFLECTING

Reflecting serves a number of functions, the most important of which will now be presented. Some of these have been identified by Pietrofesa *et al.* (1984), Brammer *et al.* (1989), and Culley (1991). They are:

1 To demonstrate an interest in and involvement with the interviewee.
2 To indicate close attention by the interviewer to what is being communicated.
3 To show that the interviewer is trying to understand fully the interviewee and what the latter is saying.

4 To check the interviewer's perceptions and ensure accuracy of understanding.
5 To facilitate the interviewee's comprehension of the issues involved and
   clarity of thinking on those matters.
6 To focus attention upon particular aspects and encourage further exploration.
7 To communicate a deep concern for that which the interviewee considers to
   be important.
8 To place the major emphasis upon the interviewee rather than the interviewer in the interview situation.
9 To indicate that it is acceptable for the interviewee to have and express
   feelings in this situation and to facilitate their ventilation.
10 To help the interviewee to 'own' feelings.
11 To enable the interviewee to realise that feelings can be an important cause
   of behaviour.
12 To help the interviewee to scrutinise underlying reasons and motives.
13 To demonstrate the interviewer's ability to empathise with the interviewee.

While a number of these functions are common to both paraphrasing
and reflection of feeling, some are more obviously relevant to one than
the other. These will be discussed further, as they apply more directly
to either paraphrasing or reflection of feeling, in the respective sections
which follow.

PARAPHRASING

Paraphrasing is sometimes also referred to as 'reflection of content'. It can be
defined as the process of mirroring or feeding-back to the interviewee, in the
interviewer's own words, the essence of the interviewee's previous statement, the emphasis being upon factual material (e.g. thoughts, ideas, descriptions etc.) rather than upon affect. There are three important elements of
the definition.

First, the paraphrase should be couched in the interviewer's own words. It
is not simply concerned with repeating what has just been said. It will be
remembered (from Chapter 5) that one type of probing technique, echoing,
involved the repetition of the interviewee's previous statement, or a part of it.
This, however, does not constitute a paraphrase. If, when paraphrasing, the
interviewer continually repeats the interviewee's words it can quickly lead to
the latter becoming frustrated. Brammer *et al.* (1989, p. 110), commenting on
this point, say that 'perhaps, the most glaring reflection error of the novice
counselor is to express the reflection in words already used by the client'.
Instead, the interviewer should respond using his own terms, perhaps using
synonyms, while not, of course, violating or misrepresenting the meaning of
the interviewee's communication.

Second, the paraphrase should contain the essential component of the previous message. This requires the interviewer to identify the core of the statement which is embedded in the verbiage – to ask himself, 'What is this person really saying?' It should, therefore, not be assumed that the paraphrase must encompass everything that has just been said, some of which may well be tangential.

Third, paraphrasing is fundamentally concerned with reflecting the factual information received. It largely ignores feelings which may also have been communicated. The word 'largely' is used purposefully, however, since it is often difficult to eliminate affective aspects entirely.

An excerpt from the transcript of an interview reported by Pietrofesa *et al.* (1984, pp. 305–6) neatly demonstrates how this skill can be used to good effect.

Client:　　　I am not sure that I should try to visit Shelly. She and I had a falling out not too long ago.

Counsellor:　You had an argument with her recently.

Client:　　　Well, I wrote to her and she didn't answer.

Counsellor:　So it is still unresolved.

Client:　　　I also wrote to Maureen, and she said that Shelly was in one of her moods of not communicating with anyone, even her mother. But I don't know.

Counsellor:　Sounds like Shelly has cut off a lot of people including you.

Client:　　　Yes, but . . . I did talk to her on the phone when I got back and she sounded friendly. . . but I still feel uneasy about seeing her, I don't know that she'd really want to see me because we broke apart.

Counsellor:　Even though she sounded okay, you still are not convinced she wants to see you.

Client:　　　Yeah, I dated a fellow that she had been going out with, but . . . I thought she was all through with him . . . but she got mad at me and I felt bad about it.

Counsellor:　She had stopped seeing him, so you thought it was okay to date him but you were mistaken.

The examples of paraphrasing included in this excerpt manifest 'in action' some of the defining characteristics of the skill mentioned previously. They also help to illustrate some of the functions of paraphrasing.

By demonstrating that he can accurately reproduce the fundamentally important part of the interviewee's statement, the interviewer 'proves' that he has been attending single-mindedly to the interviewee, that he feels it is important to understand fully what the interviewee is trying to relate, and furthermore has, in fact, achieved this understanding. By so doing, the interviewee is also made aware of the fact that the interviewer is interested in and accepts her and is quite prepared to become involved with any problems

which she may be experiencing. According to Dillon (1990, p. 186) responding with this type of reflective statement,

> permits the speaker (and other partners) to infer, rightly, that what he
> thinks and says *matters*. It confirms the speaker in his effort to contribute.
> It helps him to express thoughts gradually more clearly and fully. It assures
> him of understanding.

Hill (1989) discovered that one of the foremost uses of paraphrases by
therapists was to let clients know that they were being listened to.

From the interviewer's point of view the subsequent reaction of the
interviewee to his paraphrase also confirms (assuming that it is accurate) that
he is on the proper 'wavelength'. Indeed it seems that paraphrases are often
used for this very purpose as a check on accurate understanding of what the
interviewee has just said (Hill, 1989). Likewise in the classroom, teachers
may frequently paraphrase when, in response to a question, a pupil produces
a rather involved and, perhaps, disjointed response. By so doing teachers not
only establish that they have fully understood what was said, but they also
clarify the information provided for the rest of the class. Again, it is not
uncommon to hear someone who has just asked for and received directions of
how to get to a particular place, paraphrase back what he has been told, e.g.
'So I go to the end of the road, turn right, second on the left, and then right
again.' In this case paraphrasing helps both to check accuracy and promote
the memorisation of the data.

By encapsulating and unobtrusively presenting to the interviewee in a clear
and unambiguous manner a salient facet of that which the latter has previously
communicated, the interviewer also gently guides and encourages the con-
tinuation of this theme and the exploration of it at greater depth. Since the
interviewee's thoughts, especially when dealing with an apparently intractable
problem, are often inchoate and ambiguous, an accurate paraphrase, by
condensing and crystallising what has been said, can often help the interviewee to see more clearly the exigencies of the predicament. Paraphrasing
also enables the interviewer to keep the interviewee and his concerns, rather
than himself, in the forefront, by responding and guiding rather than leading
and directing. It indicates that the interviewer is actively trying to make sense
of what is being heard from the interviewee's frame of reference, rather than
insisting upon imposing his own (Hill, 1989). It has often been said that a good
referee is one who controls the game without appearing to dominate it. In
many situations the same holds true for a good interviewer. Paraphrasing is
one method of accomplishing this. The emphasis is firmly placed upon the
interviewee. Using Benjamin's (1987) terminology, the interviewer uses the
interviewee's life space rather than his own. By keeping the focus upon those
issues which the interviewee wants to ventilate, the interviewer also says,
metaphorically, that he acknowledges their import for the interviewee and his
willingness to make them his concern also.

Research relating to paraphrasing

The number of research studies which have centred upon the skill of reflecting in general, and paraphrasing in particular, is limited. The majority of the suggestions and recommendations concerning the skill have been based upon theoretical dictates and also the experiences of those practitioners who have employed and 'tested' the skill in the field. Some research investigations, however, have been conducted. For the most part these have been experimental in design, have been conducted in the laboratory and have sought to establish the effects of paraphrasing upon various measures of interviewees' verbal behaviour.

In some cases, though, paraphrases are defined in such a way as to include affective material (e.g. Hoffnung, 1969), while in others affective content is not explicitly excluded (e.g. Kennedy and Zimmer, 1968; Haase and Di Mattia, 1976). These quirks should be kept in mind when interpreting the following findings. Kennedy and Zimmer (1968) reported an increase in subjects' self-referenced statements attributable to paraphrasing, while similar findings featuring self-referenced affective statements were noted by both Hoffnung (1969) and Haase and Di Mattia (1976). According to Citkowitz (1975), on the other hand, this skill had only limited effect in this respect although there was a tendency for the association to be more pronounced when initial levels of self-referenced affect statements were relatively high. The subjects in this experiment were chronic schizophrenic inpatients and the data were collected during clinical-type interviews.

The distinction between the affective and the factual has been more explicitly acknowledged by others who have researched paraphrasing. Waskow (1962), for instance, investigated the outcome of selective interviewer responding on the factual and affective aspects of subjects' communication in a psychotherapy-like interview. It emerged that a significantly higher percentage of factual responses was given by those subjects who had their contributions paraphrased. Auerswald (1974) and Hill and Gormally (1977) produced more disappointing findings. In both cases, however, paraphrasing took place on an essentially random basis. Affective responses by subjects were also selected as the dependent variable.

The few studies which have considered the effects of this technique on attitudes towards the interviewer rather than behavioural changes on the part of the interviewee, have reported largely favourable outcomes. A positive relationship was detailed by Dickson (1981), between the proportion of paraphrases to questions asked by employment advisory personnel and ratings of interviewer competency provided by independent, experienced judges. A comparable outcome emerged when client perceptions of interviewer effectiveness were examined by Nagata et al. (1983).

It would therefore seem that when paraphrases are used contingently and focus upon factual aspects of communication, interviewees' verbal performance can be modified accordingly. In addition paraphrasing seems to promote favourable judgements of the interviewer by both interviewees and external judges. Counselling trainees have also indicated that this is one of the skills which they found most useful in their interviews (Spooner, 1976).

REFLECTION OF FEELING

Reflection of feeling can be defined as the process of feeding-back to the interviewee, in the interviewer's own words, the essence of the interviewee's previous statement, the emphasis being upon feelings expressed rather than cognitive content. The similarity between this definition and that of paraphrasing will be noted and many of the features of the latter, outlined in the previous section of the chapter, are applicable. The major difference between the two definitions is, of course, the concern with affective matters peculiar to reflection of feeling. Ivey and Authier (1978, p. 82) regard the most important elements of the skill to be:

(1) the direct labelling of the emotional state of the client and (2) some reference to the client via a name or personal pronoun; these may be supplemented by (3) present tense reflection of here and now states for more powerful experiencing (of course, past or future tense may also be used). . .

From the research carried out by Hill (1989), reflection of feeling was found to be the type of reflective response which was mentioned most often as being helpful in six of the eight psychotherapeutic cases examined.

A necessary prerequisite for the successful use of this skill is the ability to identify accurately and label the feelings being expressed by the interviewee. Unless this initial procedure can be adequately accomplished, the likelihood that the subsequent reflection of those feelings will achieve its desired purpose will be greatly reduced. A number of relevant distinctions to do with feelings have been drawn by Lang and van der Molen (1990). They point out that feelings can be simple or complex. It may be, taking the former, that essentially a single emotion such as anger or joy is being expressed. But it is more common for the emotional dimension of experienced problems to be multi-faceted. Anger may be tinged with feelings of guilt, shame, disappointment or despair. This fact makes the task of identifying and reflecting feeling that much more demanding. Again, and with respect to the object of feelings, they may be self-focused, directed towards the interviewer, or be vented on a third party, thing or event. Furthermore, feelings discussed may have been experienced in the past or be current in the here-and-how of the encounter.

It has already been mentioned, in an earlier section of the present chapter, that feelings may be explicitly stated, may be implied from what is said or may be inferred from nonverbal and paralinguistic cues. Concerning the latter, Ekman and Friesen (1975) described particular facial expressions associated with each of six basic emotions. These were: (1) happiness; (2) sadness; (3) fear; (4) anger; (5) surprise; (6) disgust. More recently, the same researchers reported cross-cultural evidence on agreement in the identification of a specific expression for contempt (Ekman and Friesen, 1986). Tomkins (1963), among others, suggested that a further two affective states, namely interest and shame, could be identified in a similar way but these have not been as consistently established.

Davitz (1964) conducted a number of experiments in which actors read verbally-neutral sentences in such a way as to convey different emotions. Tapes of these were presented to judges for decoding. One finding which emerged was that some emotions were more readily identifiable than others from nonverbal characteristics of speech. Fear and anger were two which were most easily recognisable. Research in this area has revealed that, in general terms, some people are more adept at identifying emotions from nonverbal features than are others. As a group, females tend to be more successful than males (Argyle, 1988). Cultural differences have also been noted (Giles and St Clair, 1985). It would also seem possible to train individuals to improve their performance.

While the terms 'feelings' and 'emotions' are sometimes used synonymously, feelings often refer to more subtle emotional or attitudinal states. For this reason they are typically more difficult to label accurately. It has been suggested that one cause of this difficulty, especially with the novice interviewer, is an insufficient repertoire of feeling terms which makes fine discrimination and identification problematic. Pietrofesa *et al.* (1984) have, therefore, recommended that interviewers memorise a number of broad categories of feeling words such as happy, sad, strong, weak, angry, confused and afraid. Each of these can be expressed at either a high, medium or a low level of intensity. Thus, for example, strongly expressed anger is rage; at a medium level it is being cross; and at a low level it is annoyance. By initially determining the broad category and then the intensity level, subtle feelings can more easily be deciphered and hence the process of reflecting them back facilitated. Lang and van der Molen (1990) stress the obvious importance of feelings expressed being reflected at the appropriate level of intensity in order for the helper to be fully in touch with the client. Failure to do so in the medical interview, through indicating levels of emotion deeper than the patient is yet prepared to acknowledge, can damage the physician–patient relationship, according to Cohen-Cole (1991).

As previously mentioned, the reflection of those nebulous feelings which are either implied or inferred, is typically more beneficial than those which are more obviously stated. The fact that the former are difficult for the interviewer to grasp, means that they are often equally difficult for the interviewee to comprehend fully. Focusing upon such feelings by means of reflection can, therefore, help the interviewee to obtain a more complete understanding of the affective states being experienced. Owing to the

possibilities of misunderstanding, however, it is often prudent for the interviewer to exercise caution in these cases.

The transcript of part of a counselling session reported by Pietrofesa *et al.*
(1984, p. 310) provides some useful examples of the skill of reflection of
feeling in practice. A brief excerpt follows:

Client (1):	I guess I've always lived in someone else's shadow. New interests were more or less forced upon me. Their hobbies were my hobbies. That type of thing. I don't even know what my hobbies are (heavy laughter). . . and that to me is really sad.
Counsellor (1):	You feel separated from yourself and sad about it.
Client (2):	Yeah. . . . Their ideas and so forth. . . and now, oh boy, I really feel lost.
Counsellor (2):	You seem confused about who Judy is. . .
Client (3):	I've wondered about that. It didn't really. . . what I felt and what I thought really didn't seem to matter to the most important people in my life . . . and maybe that's the part that really hurts. Whenever I tried to exert myself, I always got – phew – squashed down.
Counsellor (3):	You felt squashed and hurt by people closest to you.

The reader should compare the counsellor responses in this excerpt with the
examples of paraphrases provided in the previous section. It will be noted that
in the present case the counsellor's primary focus is upon the feelings being
conveyed by the client. The intent is to encourage further exploration and
understanding of them.

While the above examples were drawn from a counselling session it
should, of course, be realised that the use of this skill is not confined to that
context. It will be recalled that one type of question used by teachers, doctors,
nurses and careers guidance personnel, among others, relates to the affective
domain. In all of these circumstances feeling states could be explored using
the reflective technique. Mills (1991) also sees a role for this skill in the
negotiating process – particularly in 'win-win' situations where both parties
have recognised possibilities for *mutual* gain. Here reflecting the feelings of
the other party assists in the process of exploring their needs and, at the same
time, builds rapport and mutual respect. Reflection of feeling is therefore
applicable in a broad range of circumstances as a means of promoting further
examination of feelings, emotions and attitudes.

The skill of reflection of feeling shares a number of functions in common
with the skill of paraphrasing. Thus by reflecting feeling the interviewer
demonstrates attention to, and interest in the interviewee. The use of the skill
helps the interviewee to feel understood, to feel that both she and her
concerns are important and respected. It also acts as a means whereby the
interviewer can check for accuracy of understanding. Going beyond these

common functions, however, reflection of feeling indicates to the interviewee that it is acceptable to have and express feelings in that situation. This is important, since in many everyday conversations the factual element of communication is stressed to the neglect, and even active avoidance, of the affective dimension (Lang and van der Molen, 1990). In our society it is normally considered inappropriate to express deep personal feelings to any but very intimate acquaintances.

By reflecting the interviewee's feelings an interviewer acknowledges the other person's right to have such feelings and also confirms the acceptability of expressing them during that particular interaction. When performed accurately the skill further serves to encourage exploration and promote understanding of aspects of the interviewee's affective state. Reflecting back the central feeling element of his previous statement enables the interviewee to think more clearly and objectively about issues which previously were vague and confused.

Another function of reflection of feeling mentioned by Brammer *et al.* (1989) is to help the interviewee to 'own' feelings – to appreciate that ultimately she is the source of, and can take responsibility for them. Various ploys commonly used in order to disown feelings have been outlined by Passons (1975). These include speaking in the third rather than the first person (e.g. 'One gets rather annoyed.'). Because reflections frequently take the form of a statement beginning, 'You feel that. . .', interviewees are helped to examine and identify underlying reasons and motives for behaviour which they may not, previously, have been completely aware of. They are also brought to realise that feelings can have an important causal influence upon action (Nelson-Jones, 1988). Thus someone who, for example, holds a strong negative attitude towards members of a particular ethnic group is likely to behave uncompromisingly towards them. This effect can also be mediated by selective perception, since such a prejudiced person is less likely to 'see' examples of laudable actions by this section of the community which would negate their jaundiced attitude. Rather, they are more inclined to perceive and believe reports of despicable behaviour which reinforce their negative feelings towards this particular minority group. Again, if ever in the company of a member of the outgroup, the effects of such feelings may influence the latter to be less than cordial, supporting the feeling held which, in turn, will further affect perception and behaviour. Allowing such prejudiced individuals to examine their feelings by means of reflection can, therefore, enable them to realise how much feelings can influence not only their own, but other people's behaviour.

The use of this skill can also serve to foster a facilitative relationship with the interviewee. It is widely held that interviewers who reflect feeling accurately tend to be regarded as empathic (Nelson-Jones, 1988; Lang and van der Molen, 1990). (Although, it should also be acknowledged that others, such as Egan (1990), regard being empathic as involving much more than reflecting.) With such an interviewer, the interviewee feels deeply understood, sensing that the interviewer is with him and is able to perceive the world from his, the interviewee's, frame of reference. The interviewee in such a relationship is more likely to be motivated to divulge information which is important and personally meaningful.

Reflection of feeling is, therefore, a very useful skill for any interactor, professional or otherwise, to have in his repertoire. It is, however, one which many novices initially find difficult to master. Brammer *et al.* (1989) have listed some problems associated with it. Anyone attempting to use the skill should be aware of the dangers of reflecting inaccurately. By reflecting feelings which were not expressed, the difficulties experienced by an interviewee may be compounded and, for example in crisis intervention, this may have serious consequences. Another practice which should be avoided is bringing interviewee feelings to the surface but not assisting the interviewee to examine them in further detail. This can sometimes happen at the end of an interview when the interviewer leaves the interviewee 'in mid-air'. This can be avoided by applying proper closure procedures (see Chapter 7).

There is a tendency among many inexperienced practitioners to begin their reflection consistently with a phrase such as 'You feel. . .'. The monotonous use of some such introduction can appear mechanical and indeed 'unfeeling' and can have an adverse effect on the interviewee. For this reason a greater variety of types of statement should be developed. Other malpractices include an over-reliance upon the words of the interviewee by simply repeating back what he said. This is called *parroting* and should be distinguished from reflecting. Mills (1991, p. 74) underscores the functional difference in that, 'Parroting stunts conversations, whereas reflecting encourages discussion.' At the same time, while using her own words, the interviewer should be careful to ensure that the language which she uses is appropriate to the interviewee and the situation. She should also guard against going beyond what was actually communicated by including unwarranted suppositions or speculations in her reflection. Conversely, the reflective statement should not neglect any important aspect of the affective message of the interviewee.

Perhaps one of the most difficult features of the skill is trying to match the depth of feeling included in the reflection to that initially expressed (Brammer, 1988). If the level of feeling of the reflection is too shallow the interviewee is less likely to feel fully understood or inclined to examine these issues more profoundly. If it is too deep the interviewee may feel threatened, resulting in denial and alienation. This, together with the other potential pitfalls mentioned above, can only be overcome by careful practice coupled with a critical awareness of one's performance.

Research related to reflection of feeling

As with paraphrasing, the various recommendations concerning the use of reflection of feeling have, for the most part, been based upon theory and practical experience rather than research findings. Again, studies which have featured this skill can be divided into two major categories: first, experiments, largely laboratory-based, designed to identify effects on subjects' verbal behaviour; second, those which have attempted to relate the use of the technique to judgements, by either interviewees or observers, of interviewers in terms of such attributes as empathy, warmth, respect, etc. In many instances both types of dependent variable have featured in the same investigation.

A significant relationship between reflection of feeling and ratings of empathic understanding emerged in a piece of research conducted by Uhlemann *et al.* (1976). These ratings were provided by external judges and were based upon both written responses and audio-recordings of actual interviews. Interviewers who reflected feelings not yet named by the interviewee were regarded by them as being more expert and trustworthy, according to Ehrlich *et al.* (1979). A similar procedure, labelled 'sensing unstated feelings' by Nagata *et al.* (1983), emerged as a significant predictor of counsellor effectiveness when assessed by surrogate clients following a counselling-type interview.

However, not all findings have been as positive. Highlen and Baccus (1977) failed to reveal any significant differences in clients' perceptions of counselling climate, counsellor comfort or personal satisfaction between clients allocated to a reflection of feeling and to a probe treatment. Likewise, Gallagher and Hargie (1992) failed to report any significant relationships between ratings of counsellors' reflections, on the one hand, and, on the other, separate assessments by counsellors, clients and judges of empathy, genuineness and acceptance displayed towards clients. As acknowledged, the small sample size may have been a factor in the outcome of this investigation.

The effects of reflections of feeling on interviewees' affective self-reference statements have been explored by Merbaum (1963), Barnabei *et al.* (1974), Highlen and Baccus (1977), and Highlen and Nicholas (1978), among others. With the exception of Barnabei *et al.* (1974), this interviewing skill was found to promote substantial increases in affective self-talk by subjects. Highlen and Nicholas (1978), however, combined reflections of feeling with interviewer self-referenced affect statements in such a way that it is impossible to attribute the outcome solely to the influence of the former. One possible explanation for the failure by Barnabei *et al.* (1974) to produce a positive finding could reside in the fact that reflections of feeling were administered in a random or non-contingent manner. It has already been mentioned that paraphrases used in this indiscriminate way were equally ineffective in producing increases in self-referenced statements. A fuller review of research on reflecting feeling and paraphrasing is provided by Dickson (1986).

OVERVIEW

The following points, which should be remembered when adopting a reflective style, apply both to the skills of paraphrasing and reflection of feeling. Some of them have already been mentioned but their importance makes it unnecessary to apologise for their repetition. The basic guidelines for reflecting are as follows.

First, use your own words. Reflecting is not merely a process of echoing back the words of the interviewee. The interviewer should strive rather to reformulate the message in his own words.

In addition, Ivey (1988) recommends using a sentence stem which includes, as far as possible, a word in keeping with the other's characteristic mode of receiving information. For example, assuming that the other is a 'visualizer', it would be more appropriate to begin a reflection, 'I notice that you. . .' or 'It appears to me that. . .', rather than 'I hear you talk about. . .' or 'Sounds to me as if. . .'.

Second, do not go beyond the information communicated by the interviewee. Remember, reflecting is a process of feeding-back only information already given by the interviewee. Brammer *et al.* (1989, p. 115) are adamant that 'the counselor not add or take away from the meaning of the client's statement'. For this reason, when using the skill, the interviewer should not include speculations or suppositions which represent the interviewer's attempt to impose his own meaning on what was communicated, and while based upon it, may not be strictly warranted by it. The interviewer, therefore, when reflecting, should not try to interpret or psychoanalyse. Interpretation may be useful on occasion, but it is not reflection (Ivey, 1988). For example:

Interviewee: I suppose I have never had a successful relationship with men. I never seemed to get on with my father when I was a child. . . . I always had problems with the male teachers when I was at school. . .

Interviewer: You saw the male teachers as extensions of your father.

Note that this statement by the interviewer is not a reflection. It is an interpretation which goes beyond what was said by the interviewee.

Third, be concise. The objective is not to include everything which the interviewee has said but to select what appear to be the most salient elements of the message. It is only the core feature, or features, which the interviewer should strive to reflect – the essence of what the interviewee has been trying to communicate. Reflections tend to be short statements rather than long, involved and rambling, although the actual length will obviously vary depending upon the information provided by the interviewee.

Fourth, be specific. It will be recalled that one of the functions of reflecting is to promote understanding. Frequently an interviewee, perhaps because he has never previously fully thought through a particular issue, will tend to express himself in a rather vague, confused and abstract manner. It is more beneficial if, when reflecting, the interviewer tries to be as concrete and specific as possible, thereby ensuring that both he, and indeed the interviewee, successfully comprehend what is being said.

Fifth, be accurate. The inclusion of a 'check-out' statement as part of the reflective utterance has been strongly advised as a means of assessing accuracy of understanding (Ivey, 1988). For instance, 'Deep down I sense a feeling of relief, would you agree?' In addition to inviting corrective feedback, by offering the opportunity to comment on the accuracy of understanding, the interviewer avoids giving the impression of assumed omniscience or of imposing meaning on the interviewee. If an interviewer is frequently inaccurate in reflections proffered, the interviewee will quickly realise that further prolongation of the interaction is pointless, since the interviewer does not seem able to grasp what he is trying to convey. This does not mean that the occasional inaccuracy is disastrous. In such a case the interviewee, realising the interviewer's determination to grasp what he is trying to relate, will generally be motivated to provide additional information and rectify the misconception. Accuracy depends upon careful listening (see Chapter 9). While the interviewee is talking the interviewer should be listening single-mindedly rather than considering what to say next or engaging in other thoughts less directly relevant to the interview.

Sixth, do not over-use reflections. It should not be thought that reflections must necessarily be used in response to every interviewee statement. To attempt to do so may restrict the interviewee rather than help her forward. Reflections can be used in conjunction with the other skills which the interviewer should have at her disposal (e.g. questioning, reinforcing, self-disclosure, etc.). In some instances it is only after rapport has been established that reflection of feeling can be used without the interviewee feeling awkward or threatened.

Seventh, reflections of feeling and paraphrases typically reflect what has been contained in the interviewee's immediately preceding statement. It is possible, and indeed desirable on occasion, for reflections to be wider-ranging and to cover a number of interviewee statements. The interviewer may wish, for example, at the end of the interview, to reflect the facts and feelings expressed by the interviewee during it. Reflections such as these, which have a broader perspective, are called *summaries of content* and *summaries of feeling*, and are a useful means of identifying themes expressed by the interviewee during the interview, or parts of it.

Finally, it has been stated that reflection contains two essential component skills – reflection of feeling and paraphrasing. It is, of course, possible to combine both factual and feeling material in a single reflection if the interviewer feels that this is the most appropriate response at that particular time. Carkhuff (1973) suggests that by combining both feelings and facts in a format such as, 'You feel ... because ...', one type of information complements the other and enables the interviewee to perceive the relationship between them. Moreover, Ivey (1988) identifies how, in this way, deeper meanings underlying expressed experiences can be located and sensitively surfaced. He refers to this more profound process as *reflecting meaning*.

Chapter 7

Set induction and closure

INTRODUCTION

Beginnings and endings are equally important parameters within which social interaction takes place, in that they are structured, formalised sequences during which interactors have a greater opportunity to make important points or create an effective impact on others. How we greet and part from others has long been recognised as crucial to the development and maintenance of relationships (e.g. Roth, 1889).

Although in this chapter set induction and closure will be discussed separately, these are complementary skills within any interaction. This can be exemplified by examining the behaviours identified by Kendon and Ferber (1973) as being associated with the three main phases involved in both greetings and partings between friends:

A Distant phase. When two friends are at a distance, but within sight, the behaviours displayed include hand waving, eyebrow flashing (raising both eyebrows), smiling, head tossing and direct eye contact.
B Medium phase. When the friends are at a closer, interim distance, they avoid eye contact, smile and engage in a range of grooming (self-touching) behaviours.
C Close phase. At this stage the friends will again engage in direct eye contact, smile, make appropriate verbalisations and may touch one another (shake hands, hug or kiss).

During greetings the sequence is ABC, while during partings the reverse sequence CBA, operates. At the greeting stage the sequence underlines the availability of the participants for interaction, whereas during parting it signals the decreasing accessibility for interaction (Goffman, 1972).

Many animals also have greeting rituals, some of which are very elaborate. Indeed, nesting birds have greeting displays each time one of them returns to the nest with food. Chimpanzees are most similar to humans in that they touch hands, hug and kiss when they meet. However, in his analysis of greetings and partings Lamb (1988, p. 103) pointed out:

Interestingly there seems to be no ritual of parting among other animals – they presumably do not have any conception of the future of their relationships and therefore do not need to reassure each other that there will be such a future or that the past has been worthwhile.'

For humans, however, the sense of temporal and relational continuity means that both beginnings and endings of interactions are seen as being important.

SET INDUCTION

Anyone who is familiar with the world of athletics will be aware of the instructions given by the starter to the competitors before a race – 'On your marks. Get set. Go!' By telling the athletes to get set, the starter is preparing them for his final signal, and allowing them to become both mentally and physically ready for the impending take-off, which they know is about to follow. This simple example is a good introduction to the skill of set induction.

Set induction is the term used by psychologists to describe that which occurs when 'an organism is usually prepared at any moment for the stimuli it is going to receive and the responses it is going to make' (Woodworth and Marquis, 1949, p. 298). In other words, set induction establishes in the individual a state of readiness, involves gaining attention and arousing motivation, as well as providing guidelines about that which is to follow.

Set induction is a skill which is widely used, in various forms, in social interaction. At a simple level it may involve two people discussing local gossip, where, to stimulate the listener's attention, they may use phrases such as: 'Wait until you hear this. . .'; 'You'll never believe what happened today. . .'; 'Have you heard the latest. . .'.

At another level, on television and at the cinema, there are usually 'trailers' advertising forthcoming attractions in an exciting and dramatic fashion, and here again the object is to arouse interest in what is to follow. Indeed, television programmes usually contain a fair degree of set induction in themselves, employing appropriate music and accompanying action, to stimulate the viewer to stay with the programme. Other examples of set induction in the media include newspaper headlines, the front cover of magazines indicating what stories appear inside and quotations from press reviews on the back cover of books.

The term 'set' has many applications in our everyday lives. For example, how a table is set will reveal quite a lot about the forthcoming meal – how many people will be eating, how many courses there will be and how formal the behaviour of the diners is likely to be. Other uses of the term set include 'It's a set up', 'Are you all set?' and 'Is the alarm set?' In all of these instances, preparation for some form of activity which is to follow is the central theme, and this is the main thrust of the skill of set induction.

In relation to social interaction, the induction of an appropriate set can be defined as the initial strategy utilised in order to establish a frame of reference, deliberately designed to facilitate the development of a communicative link between the expectations of the participants and the realities of the situation. Set induction can therefore be a long, or a short, process depending upon the context of the interaction. It can involve establishing rapport, arousing motivation, establishing expectations and evaluating these in relation to realistic outcomes, and outlining the nature and purpose of the forthcoming interaction.

Functions of set induction

Set induction involves more than simply giving a brief introduction at the beginning of a social encounter. It may involve a large number of different activities, depending upon the context in which set is to be induced. However, the main purposes in employing this skill in interpersonal interaction can be listed as follows:

1 to induce in participants a state of readiness appropriate to the task which is to follow, through establishing rapport, gaining attention and arousing motivation;
2 to ascertain the expectations of the participants and the extent of their knowledge about the topic to be considered;
3 to indicate to participants what might be reasonable objectives for the task to follow;
4 to explain to participants what one's functions are, and what limitations may accompany these functions.
5 to establish links with previous encounters (during follow-up sessions);
6 to ascertain the extent of the participants' knowledge of the topic to be discussed.

These are the main generic functions of the skill of set induction. However, depending upon the nature of the interaction, the functions of set induction will vary, so that different techniques will accordingly be employed in order to achieve them. Thus, for example, a helper will use different behaviours to open a counselling session from a teacher introducing a classroom lesson. There are several types of set which can be put into operation, and each type will be more relevant and effective in one social situation than another. These types of set induction are outlined in the following section.

The process of set induction can take an infinite variety of forms both between, and within, social settings. The set used will be influenced by, amongst other things, the subject matter to be discussed, the amount of time available, the time of day, the location of the encounter and the personality, experience and socioeconomic background of the interactors. These factors should all be borne in mind when evaluating the main techniques for inducing set.

Motivational set

The skill of set induction can be employed in order to gain attention and arouse motivation at the beginning of an interaction. Professional entertainers are well aware of the power of motivational set. For example, the singer Lionel Richie gives the following advice:

> when you walk out on stage – whether you sing, dance, fly – whatever you do, do it in the first song. Drop it on them. Then, people will stick around for the second. And then you do it again to them. And only after the third song do you stop and say, 'Good evening everybody and welcome to the show.'
>
> (*The Independent*, 6 June 1992)

In many situations, particularly in learning environments, it is very important to gain the attention of participants at the outset, so that the task may proceed as smoothly as possible. Otherwise the main objectives of the interaction may be more difficult to achieve. Garramone (1984), for example, found that the way individuals perceive and assimilate information is affected by their initial motivation to attend. A number of methods can be used to induce motivational set.

The use of novel stimuli

Psychologists have long recognised the potency of a novel, or unusual, stimulus as a method for gaining the attention of individuals and there is well documented research evidence to indicate that the introduction of novel stimuli is an effective technique for arousing interest with widely differing populations (Hargie *et al.*, 1981). Thus, a new or unusual stimulus will be effective both in gaining attention and in increasing retention of information. For example, in the sphere of selling, Busch and Wilson (1976) found that when the salesperson had a product which was new or unique, it was easier to secure a sale.

Producers of TV news programmes, aware of the value of stories involving violence in obtaining the attention of viewers, have a maxim regarding opening items of 'If it bleeds, it leads.' Furthermore, Cameron *et al.* (1991) have investigated the effects on viewers of TV news teasers, which they describe as follows: 'In a teaser, the news anchor describes or sometimes previews an upcoming news item to captivate the audience' (p. 688). They discovered a primacy–recency effect in that news teasers served to enhance memory for the first and last of the set of three commercials immediately following the teaser (see Chapter 11 for further discussion of the primacy–recency effect). It has also been shown that viewers pay more attention to news stories which have been teased (Schleuder and White, 1989). Thus, these teasers, which usually emphasise the novelty value of the upcoming item, are effective in persuading viewers to attend more closely to the TV coverage.

The implications of these results for learning are fairly obvious. There are many aids which can be used in order to arouse motivation. These may be diagrammatic, real objects or audio-visual recordings. By focusing on any of these aids at the outset, the learning environment should be enriched accordingly. A word of caution is needed here, however, in that the stimulus utilised should be related to the task in hand. As Turney *et al.* (1976, p. 92) pointed out, 'Gimmickry is to be avoided, for unconnected novelty may secure short-term attending . . . but fail to establish an appropriate set enduring for the task.'

The posing of an intriguing problem

Employed at the beginning of an interaction sequence this can engage listeners' interest immediately and hold it for a long time if they are required to solve the problem. For example, a science teacher at the start of a lesson places a container full of water in front of the pupils. He then holds a brick over the container, telling pupils to observe carefully what is about to take place. The brick is slowly immersed in the container, and the displaced water collected in a separate vessel. He then asks pupils to explain what has happened, and why. This then leads to a discussion of Archimedes' Principle.

Studies have shown that the use of thought-provoking problems at the beginning of lessons is related to increased pupil achievement (Saunders, 1986). However, this technique can be applied to many settings, and is equally applicable whether the problem posed is a technical or a social one. Furthermore, it does not really matter whether or not the problem has a correct solution. The idea here is to establish immediate involvement and participation at either an overt or covert level. The use of case histories can be particularly relevant in this respect, providing the case outlined is applicable to the audience addressed. Thus, for example, a tutor of trainee counsellors may relate the problems presented to him by a difficult client, and ask the trainees how they would have handled the situation which he has described to them.

Making a controversial or provocative statement

This can also serve quickly to encourage participation. For example, at the beginning of a sociology seminar, incorporating both males and females, the lecturer announces that in his view married women should only be allowed to obtain employment once male unemployment has been eliminated. In any case, he continues, the women's natural place is in the home. This then leads to a discussion of the role of women in society.

Following the lecturer's statement it is very likely that some females will feel motivated to respond immediately, and in this way discussion can be encouraged. However, this method of inducing set must be carefully thought out, since the object of the exercise is to provoke comment, rather than aggression, on the part of the listener. With very sensitive topics or volatile audiences, great caution should be exercised when using this technique!

The initial behaviour of the interactors

This will influence the set which is induced. The adoption of unexpected or unusual behaviour can be a powerful method for gaining attention. For example, a teacher may sit with the class, move about the room without speaking, or act out a short story with conviction and expression, in order to stimulate pupils to attend to his lesson. The 'initial behaviour' needs to depart from the normal pattern to be most effective. All humans have a basic cognitive structure which will strive to accommodate new information of an unexpected nature. It is, therefore, the element of behavioural surprise which is central to the efficacy of this method, since this stimulates the individual's attentiveness, and hence facilitates the process of assimilation.

Indeed all of the methods for inducing motivational set will involve an aspect of curiosity arousal. The novelty of a stimulus will influence its degree of effectiveness in gaining attention. Another factor which will determine the efficacy of a stimulus in gaining attention is its intensity. A strong stimulus is more likely to be noticed than is a weak one. Hence a loud noise, a bright light or a large object will usually stimulate attention much more quickly than a faint noise, a dim light or a small object.

Finally, in relation to motivational set, it should be remembered that to catch attention is one thing, but to hold it for an extended period of time is another. As was mentioned earlier, any technique or device employed to induce motivational set should be appropriate to the task in hand. Gimmickry will quickly lose appeal, if it is unrelated to any underlying and enduring theme which will be of interest to those in whom set has been induced. Thus the follow-up to motivational set should be carefully planned to capitalise on the initial attentiveness of participants.

Social set

In order to establish a good rapport with another person, before proceeding with the main business of the interaction, it is usually desirable to employ a number of 'social' techniques. Such techniques serve to introduce a 'human' element into the encounter, and often facilitate the achievement of the main objectives involved. The induction of an appropriate social set is, therefore, often an important preliminary to the more substantive issues which are to be discussed later, in that it serves to establish a good, amicable, working relationship between the participants at the beginning of the interaction. The main techniques which can be employed in order to induce a good social set are as follows.

The initial approach of an individual

This will induce a certain type of set in the other participants, depending upon what this approach is. The use of social reinforcement, in a friendly manner, will serve to make the other person feel more at ease in most situations. Social reinforcement techniques include a handshake, smile, welcoming remarks, tone of voice and eye contact. Kendon and Ferber (1973) pointed out that 'In the manner in which the greeting ritual is performed, the greeters signal to each other their respective social status, their degree of familiarity, their degree of liking for one another, and also, very often, what roles they will play in the encounter that is about to begin' (pp. 592–3).

Thus the manner in which professionals greet their clients is of considerable importance. Krivonos and Knapp (1975) found that the use of appropriate greeting behaviour has a considerable influence on the success of the ensuing interaction. An important aspect here is the use of the client's name, which leads to a more favourable evaluation of the interviewer by the client (Dell and Schmidt, 1976; Rackham and Morgan, 1977). There is some evidence from the medical field that professionals could improve their greeting behaviour. Studies of health visiting have shown that patients often did not know the name of their health visitor (Robinson, 1982), and that patients complained about the lack of welcome given by health visitors during visits to clinics (Field et al., 1982). Likewise, Maguire and Rutter (1976) found that doctors frequently failed to introduce themselves at the beginning of an encounter with a patient.

It is difficult to be prescriptive about the greeting ritual, however, since this is influenced by factors such as the acquaintance of the people involved, their respective roles, the function of the interaction, the location, and the sex of the interactors. For example, Greenbaum and Rosenfeld (1980) conducted an observational study of 152 greeting dyads at Kansas City International Airport and identified that bodily contact was observed in 126 (83 per cent) of the greetings. The types of contact observed were (a) mutual lip-kiss, (b) face-kiss, (c) mutual face contact, excluding kiss, (d) hand-shake, (e) hand-holding, (f) hand to upper body (touching the face, neck, arm, shoulder or back) and (g) embrace. Female greeting behaviour was very similar with both males and females, whereas males used markedly different greetings with females as opposed to males. Male same-sex dyads had a significantly higher frequency of hand-shaking, whereas dyads containing a female had significantly more mutual lip-kisses and embraces.

The use of non-task comments

Following the initial greeting, this is also a common technique which is employed in order to 'break the ice' in social encounters. This process of 'ice-breaking' is usually a preliminary to the exchange of information at a more substantive level. Statements relating to the weather or non-controversial current affairs are quite common general opening remarks, coupled with comments relating to the specific situation (e.g. the price of a drink in a bar). In their analysis of 'phatic communion', or small talk, Coupland *et al*. (1992) discuss the function of the HAY (How are you?) question in openings. They point out that it serves to signal recognition for and acknowledgement of the other person and is not expected to produce any self-revelations from the respondent. They use the following joke to illustrate how it is an empty question with no length of response expected.

A: How are you?
B: I have bursitis; my nose is itching; I worry about my future; and my uncle is wearing a dress these days.

Kleinke (1986a) reported the results of studies he conducted to determine the least, and most, preferred opening lines for men meeting women, or women meeting men, in situations such as a bar, supermarket, restaurant, laundromat, beach or general situations. He found that the use of 'innocuous' openings (e.g. 'I feel a little embarrassed about this, but I'd like to meet you') was preferred to smart or 'flippant' openings (e.g. 'Didn't we meet in a previous life?') by both males and females. This is important, since the success of the opening comment can determine whether further interaction will take place.

Shuy (1983) has recommended the use of non-task comments by doctors, pointing out that:

> The medical interview can be cold and frightening to a patient. If the goal of the physician is to make the patient comfortable, a bit of personal but interested and relevant chitchat, whatever the cost in precious time, is advisable. The patients are familiar with normal conversational openings that stress such chitchat. The medical interview would do well to try to move closer to a conversational framework.
>
> (p. 200)

The use of non-task comments is useful in a range of situations. Salesmen are usually trained to employ such comments before attempting to secure a sale. An insurance salesman, for example, should avoid entering a house and immediately proceeding to discuss the benefits of particular policies. Rather, insurance salesmen are usually trained to use non-task comments, and to relate these to some possession of the householder (e.g. 'That's a lovely piece of stereo equipment you have') before progressing gradually towards the sale. However, a note of caution was sounded by Sullivan (1954) who warned against the use of non-task comments (which he referred to as 'social hokum') in the psychiatric interview. In this setting, Sullivan emphasised the importance of 'getting started' on substantive issues as soon as possible. Thus, as Saunders (1986) pointed out, 'in a professional context, establishing rapport by the use of non-task comments needs to be carefully considered and genuinely delivered' (p. 179).

The provision of 'creature comforts'

This is another aspect of social set. Creature comforts refer to those items which can be employed in order to make someone feel comfortable in any given situation. This would include: a soft or 'easy' chair on which to sit; an offer of a drink, whether alcoholic or a cup of tea or coffee, which gives the person something to focus upon and also creates further non-task comments (e.g. 'Do you take sugar?'); an offer of a cigarette or cigar; and reasonable lighting and temperature in the room.

All of these creature comforts can be designed to establish a good social set. This is clearly demonstrated by the fact that they are often taken away in situations where an individual is being subjected to stress. A suspect being interrogated by detectives is usually seated on a hard chair and may have a bright light shining into his eyes. These 'tough guy' tactics may, however, be alternated with 'nice guy' tactics where one detective gives the suspect a cigarette, coffee and sympathy, so that he may see him as a friend in whom he can confide. At a lesser extreme a candidate at a difficult selection interview may well be seated in such a way that he is facing the window, and may also be given a chair which is difficult to settle into (e.g. an easy-chair without arms).

In some settings, however, the professional may have little control over the environment. As Nelson-Jones (1988, p. 34) pointed out, quite often: 'counselling interviews are conducted in less than ideal conditions through no fault of the counsellor, who is then faced with minimizing the impact of adverse working conditions'. In other words, the setting for an interaction should be as conducive as possible, but the behaviour of the professional can help to overcome the lack of certain creature comforts.

These are the main methods which are used to induce social set, and thereby establish a good relationship at the start of social encounters. They include the ritualised, nonverbal indicators of greeting, such as eye contact and raised eyebrows, a nod of the head, smile and hand-shake. Verbally, the use of non-task comments serves to break the ice and establish friendly communication sequences, thereby creating the impression of personal interest, as opposed to more formal interest in the main function of the transaction. The provision of creature comforts also helps to underline a consideration for the other person as a fellow human, and facilitates the development of rapport. If these techniques are used to good effect, they should result in the induction of an appropriate social set.

Perceptual set

The initial perceptions which are received in social situations will influence the expectations of participants. How someone 'sees' a situation will depend upon a number of factors relating to his immediate surroundings. Although it is often true that first impressions can be deceptive, most people, to a greater or lesser degree, will make some judgement about a book, based upon its cover. As Lamb (1988, p. 103) noted:

> Infants develop fear of strangers at between seven and eight months, when they begin to make the distinction between who they know and who they do not. We never outgrow this uncertainty about people outside our established circle. As adults we worry about the first impressions we make, finding ourselves at the mercy of someone who is bound to form judgements on the basis of very little genuine knowledge about us.

It has been found that important decisions, such as whether or not to offer someone a job, are indeed affected by the first impressions of the candidate gleaned by the interviewer (Arvey and Campion, 1984). Perceptual set will be influenced both by the environment and the participants.

The nature of the environment

When an individual enters a room for the first time, he will receive information concerning the layout of tables, chairs and other furnishings. Depending upon the nature of these perceptions, he will in turn translate them into a set of expectancies about the format for the interaction which is to follow. For example, a table and upright chairs will usually convey an impression of a business-like environment, whereas a coffee-table and easy-chairs will suggest a more social or conversational type of interaction. Thus an individual attending a selection interview may be somewhat taken aback if confronted with the latter type of setting, since this will be contrary to his expectations.

Situations which are not relished by most people in general, however, are visits to the doctor or dentist. Such visits are not made any more comforting by the nature of the waiting rooms in most surgeries. Inevitably these tend to be composed of rather bleak furnishings, with an uncomfortable layout of chairs – usually around the walls – which makes conversation rather awkward. Yet a very different perceptual set could be induced in patients, by providing easy-chairs laid out in small groups to encourage social interchange, coupled with appropriate lighting and soft music. While such a change may not completely allay the fears of patients, it would certainly make the period of waiting much more acceptable and less stressful. It would also help to humanise the process of receiving treatment. The layout should, of course, also accommodate those who do not wish to engage in conversation.

The nature of the environment in terms of affluence may also affect initial impressions. Dittmar (1992) carried out a study in which she filmed a young male and a young female individually in a relatively affluent and in a fairly impoverished environment. She then showed the 5-minute videos of these individuals moving about their home to fifty-six pupils aged 16–18 years at a prestigious public school, and to fifty-six pupils of the same age at a working-class comprehensive school, in England. She found that the 'wealthy' people were seen as more intelligent, successful, educated and in control of their lives than the 'impoverished', whereas the latter were rated as warmer, friendlier and more self-expressive. No significant differences emerged between the two socioeconomic groups of judges on these evaluations. One gender effect did emerge in that 'The female video character was viewed as less autonomous and self-reliant when poor than wealthy, whereas the reverse was found for the male character' (p. 388).

Many professionals spend their working lives interacting with clients in institutional settings (e.g. hospitals, prisons, schools), and this has a marked effect on interpersonal communication. Burton (1985) described hospitals as 'strange places where strange things happen to people . . . the strangeness of the hospital setting is so immense that it almost defies analysis' (p. 86). He argued that attempts should be made to restructure the hospital environment to allow the patient more dignity, privacy, respect, autonomy and choice. There is evidence that the restructuring of the furniture and fittings of an old people's home (Blackman *et al.*, 1976) and a psychiatric hospital (Holahan, 1979) resulted in greater interaction between the individuals within these settings. These findings also demonstrate that the environment can be manipulated in ways which either facilitate or discourage client participation.

The personal attributes of the participants

This will also have an influence upon the expectations of the perceiver. The age, sex, dress and general appearance of the other person will all affect the initial perceptual set which is induced. Generally, older, more mature professionals are often viewed as being more experienced and competent than newly qualified professionals, who may therefore find it more difficult to inspire confidence in clients. However, this is dependent upon the professional context, and the age of the client.

For example, Foxman *et al.* (1982) found that young mothers were less happy with older health visitors, and a similar finding was reported by Simms and Smith (1984) in a study of teenage mothers. In these instances the young mothers would find it difficult to identify with the older health visitors and, as Foxman *et al.* point out, may have felt 'threatened' by their own lack of experience in comparison to the health visitor. Thus the ages of both the professional and the client are important considerations which can affect expectations and behaviour.

During social interaction we also tend to respond differently to, and hold differing expectations of, the behaviour of individuals depending upon their gender (Mayo and Henley, 1981). Females tend to be touched more, smile more frequently, require less interpersonal space, use more head-nods and engage in more eye contact. Males are likely to be more positively evaluated if they are regarded as being competent, assertive and rational, whereas females are viewed more positively if they portray traits such as gentleness, warmth and tact. Presumably these expectations influence the career choices of females and males, so that in professions such as nursing there is a high preponderance of females.

Another important factor is the attractiveness of the participants. Individuals are judged on level of attractiveness from a very early age, since it has been shown that nursery school children exhibit an aversion to chubby individuals, and a greater liking for physically attractive peers (Stewart *et al.*, 1979). In examining the relevance of attractiveness in interpersonal interactions, Altman (1977) pointed out that persons rated as being highly attractive tend to receive more eye contact, more smiles, closer bodily proximity and body accessibility (openness of arms and legs) than individuals rated as being unattractive. Cook (1977, p. 323), in reviewing a number of facets of interpersonal attraction, particularly during initial social encounters, and in emphasising the importance of first impressions, pointed out that:

The first impression takes in a number of things. In most but not all relationships people look for someone who is attracted to them. . . . Some preliminary assessments of personality, outlook, social background – an attempt to 'place' the other – will be made. . . . A relatively unattractive or unpopular person who tries to make friends with – or a sexual partner of – someone much more attractive or popular is likely to suffer a rebuff.

In terms of the physical attractiveness of an individual, it would therefore seem that this is an important aspect of perceptual set. It is likely that someone regarded as being very attractive will also be seen as being popular, friendly and interesting to talk to. This, in turn, will influence the way in which the attractive individual is approached by another person, thereby probably creating a self-fulfilling prophecy (Duck, 1977). However, interpersonal attractiveness is usually more than mere physical make-up, since factors which are relevant here include cleanliness, dress, rewardingness, personality, competence and similarity of attitude. In first meetings with another person the former two variables will obviously be more accessible to evaluation than the latter two. Personality judgements can only be made following an encounter with the other person, while judgements about competency are situation-specific (Rosenblatt, 1977). These findings would suggest that a physically unattractive professional may be successful and popular with clients by ensuring that he has a good interactive style and a professional approach.

People are frequently evaluated on the basis of their mode of dress. The reason for this is that the style of dress which one adopts is often a sign of the group with which one identifies. Thus certain professions have become associated with a particular style of dress, with the deliberate intention of conveying a definite public image. This is exemplified by the adoption of uniforms by members of many institutions and organisations, who may want to present a consistent image, or be immediately identified in their job function. Policemen, soldiers, nurses, hospital doctors, priests and traffic wardens all immediately induce a certain type of set in the observer. At another level, however, business executives, civil servants, salesmen, solicitors and estate agents have a less formal type of 'uniform' – namely, a suit, shirt and tie. Indeed, Forsythe (1990) found that female job applicants received more favourable hiring recommendations from experienced male and female business personnel when they were wearing more masculine clothing (e.g. a dark navy suit) than when wearing distinctly feminine attire (e.g. a soft beige dress).

Numerous research studies have been conducted into determining the effects of dress, and physical attractiveness, upon evaluations of counsellors. In summarising the findings from these studies, Kleinke (1986a) concluded that counsellors who dress formally enough to portray an impression of competence and whose dress is in style rather than old-fashioned, are preferred to those who dress very formally and are consequently seen as 'stuffy' or unapproachable. Likewise, physically attractive counsellors are preferred to unattractive counsellors.

These are the main facets of perceptual set linked to personal attributes. However, as discussed in Chapter 3, judgements about individuals may also be influenced by other features such as height, overall body shape, the use of cosmetics and perfumes, whether a male has a moustache or a beard and whether or not glasses are worn. Some of these aspects can be manipulated in order to induce a certain type of set in another person. In relation to the latter dimension, Harris (1991) found that subjects judged people to be more intelligent, intense and appropriately sex-typed when wearing glasses, and generally attributed to them a positive overall stereotype. Furthermore Harris also reported that 'men saw glasses as making women appear more attractive and sexy, whereas women thought that glasses would make them less so' (p. 1674). This finding therefore seems to run contrary to the well-known adage as espoused by Dorothy Parker in *The Portable Dorothy Parker* that 'Men seldom make passes at girls who wear glasses'!

However, supporting evidence for other aphorisms related to appearance have been reported in a study into female hair colour by Weir and Fine-Davis (1989). They presented male and female subjects with photographs of equally attractive females wearing different coloured wigs of identical style. They found that blondes were seen by both sexes as being significantly more popular than redheads and were also rated as being significantly less intelligent than brunettes by male judges, but not by female judges. Redheads were rated by both females and males, in line with the 'fiery' stereotype, as being significantly more temperamental and aggressive than blondes or brunettes. These findings confirm what Weir and Fine-Davis illustrate to be a continuing stereotype of the fun-loving, dumb, blonde. For example, the Greek poet Menander wrote that 'no chaste woman should make her hair yellow', while in Ancient Rome the hallmark of a prostitute was her dyed blonde hair. Hollywood actresses such as Marilyn Monroe and Jayne Mansfield were blondes who were portrayed as beautiful, sensuous, yet mindless, individuals. More recently, the pop star Madonna, who dyed her hair blonde, has shocked society with explicit songs, book and videos.

In one study into the accuracy of first impressions, Hargie and Dickson (1991) showed first-year undergraduate students a series of people on video for one minute with the sound turned off and asked them to judge a number of attributes and provide reasons for their choices. It was found that the students were accurate in estimating age but not in making judgements of marital status, socioeconomic status, personality and religion. One fascinating aspect of this particular study was the fact that the observers believed they *had* the ability to make such judgements. Furthermore, they readily gave reasons as to why they believed their judgements were accurate! Perhaps these students believed the view of Oscar Wilde when he argued: 'It is only shallow people who do not judge by appearances'! They also illustrate the fact that we all readily make judgements about other people whom we have just met.

While it is clear that first impressions are important in influencing our attitudes to others, more research is needed to ascertain how combinations of factors influence our judgements. For example, what effect does wearing glasses, dressing in 'masculine' clothes and appearing to be wealthy have upon male evaluations of blonde females?

Cognitive set

The main purpose of many social encounters is concerned with substantive issues of fact. Before proceeding to these issues, however, it is important to ensure that the terms of reference are clearly understood at the outset. In order to achieve this objective, it is often necessary to draw up a 'social contract' with the individuals involved so that all parties are in clear agreement as to the nature and objectives of the ensuing interaction. In other words, it is important to induce an appropriate cognitive set in the participants, so that they are mentally prepared in terms of the background to, and likely progression of, the main business to follow, which should as a result flow more smoothly. As Millar *et al.* (1992, p. 125), in their analysis of interviewing, noted:

> During the initial few minutes of an interview the client will be searching for cues or indicators which will either confirm or alter his expectations, and which will signal how to behave, how to relate to the interviewer, what

to say and what not to say. The interviewer, therefore will have some opportunity to create constructive and realistic expectations.

There are several factors which are pertinent to the induction of an appropriate cognitive set, and these are as follows:

Prior instructions

It has long been known that prior instructions, such as techniques to use in solving a problem or special items to be aware of, have been found to improve performance. For example, Reid *et al.* (1960) found that serial learning was speeded up by providing instructions to subjects about how to approach the learning task. In reviewing research into prior instructions, Turk (1985) concluded that telling individuals what they will hear actually biases them to 'hear' what they have been encouraged to expect, regardless of what message they actually receive. As Turk puts it 'Telling people what they are about to perceive will radically affect what they do perceive' (p. 76). The effect of prior instructions was also borne out in a study by Simonson (1973), who found that subjects told to expect a 'warm' counsellor actually disclosed more than those who were told they would be seeing a 'cold' counsellor, regardless of the actual behaviour of the counsellor.

In a more recent study, Park and Kraus (1992) had a group of subjects ask one question each to a person they did not know. They found that when the questioners were instructed to obtain as much information as possible about traits of the respondent such as intelligence, honesty, truthfulness and dependability, they were able to do so successfully. Park and Kraus concluded that it is possible to 'obtain a greater amount of verbal information relevant to difficult-to-judge dimensions when instructed to do so' (p. 445). On the basis of their results they recommend that personnel officers and selectors at employment interviews should be instructed in advance to search for specific information about candidates. Such an approach may help to overcome the problem whereby decisions may be made by selectors before the interview. Eder *et al.* (1989, p. 28), in their review of research into the employment interview, concluded that 'Cognitive schemas developed by the interviewer after a brief review of the candidate's resume and application materials likely guide the interview process and predetermine its outcome.' This finding also underlines the importance of candidates devoting concerted attention to the application form and CV!

Reviewing previous information

This is also very useful in preparing individuals for the activity which is to follow. Aubertine (1968), for example, found that teachers who introduced new material by linking it with knowledge already familiar to pupils, were rated by pupils as being more effective. This process, of linking that which is known with the unknown material to follow, has also been shown to be an effective teaching procedure, in facilitating the understanding and retention by pupils of new information (Novak *et al.*, 1971).

It is also important to ascertain the extent of knowledge which participants may have regarding the subject to be discussed. This information, when gathered at an early stage, enables decisions to be made about an appropriate level for any ensuing explanations and whether or not to encourage contributions. These points are pertinent when addressing a person or persons on a new topic for the first time.

In many interpersonal transactions, one encounter will be influenced by decisions made and commitments undertaken in the previous meeting. Again, it is important to establish that all parties are in agreement as to the main points arising from prior interactions and the implications of these for the present discussion. If there is disagreement, or confusion, at this stage it is unlikely that the ensuing encounter will be fruitful.

This problem is formally overcome in many business settings, where minutes of meetings are taken. The minutes from a previous meeting will be focused upon, and will have to be agreed at the outset, before the main agenda items for the current meeting can be discussed. This procedure ensures that all participants are in agreement about what has gone before, and have therefore a common frame of reference for the forthcoming meeting. In addition, agenda items are usually circulated prior to the meeting, and this in itself is a form of cognitive set, allowing individuals to prepare themselves for the main areas to be discussed.

Ascertaining the expectations of individuals

This is a useful technique to employ at the beginning of an interaction. Individuals approach social encounters with certain expectations, which they expect to have fulfilled. If these expectations are unrealistic, or misplaced, it is important to make this clear at a very early stage. One common problem facing social workers, for instance, is that clients often expect the social worker to be able to offer instant financial, or other material, aid. In most cases the social worker is unable to fulfil these expectations and will have to ensure that the client is aware of this.

If the expectations of individuals are not clearly ascertained initially, the conversation may proceed for quite some time before these become explicit. In some instances this can cause frustration, embarrassment or even anger, where people feel their time has been wasted. It can also result in the discussion proceeding at dual purposes, and even terminating, with both parties reading the situation along different lines. By ascertaining the immediate goals of the other interactors, such problems can often be overcome. This can be achieved simply by asking the other person what he expects from the present encounter. Once his goals are clarified, it is probable that his behaviour will be more easily understood.

Outlining functions

This is another important facet of cognitive set. It may involve the outlining of professional job functions. If someone holds false expectations, as was discussed in the previous section, it is vital to make this clear, and to point out what can and cannot be done within the limitation of professional functions. Thus the social worker faced with a client expecting an immediate 'hand-out', may have to explain why this is not possible, by outlining the functions of the social worker as applied to this specific situation. At the same time, the social worker could also explain how he might be able to help the client obtain financial assistance. Part of this explanation may involve outlining the functions of other related helping agencies and their relationships with the social work service.

Thus, the expectations of the client should be related to the functions of the professional. Once this has been achieved the interaction should flow more smoothly, with both participants aware of their respective roles. As Pope (1979, p. 515) observed

> Another task of the beginning segment of the interview is the mutual adjustment of role expectations that each participant has of the other. If such expectations are not in synchrony with each other, it is not possible to move ahead to the second or main segment of the interview. Unless these expectations complement each other the dyad lacks stability and communication remains inhibited.

Nelson-Jones (1988) used the term 'structuring' to refer to the process by which counsellors make their clients aware of their respective roles in the counselling interview, and argued that the most important juncture for outlining functions is at the contracting stage of the initial session. At this stage the counsellor has to answer the implicit or explicit client question 'How are you going to help me?' Nelson-Jones also observed that counsellors will answer this question in different ways, depending upon their theoretical perspectives, but suggested one exemplar response as: 'I see my role as more to support and help people as they make sense out of their own lives rather than to come up with ready-made solutions' (p. 85).

Outlining the goals of the forthcoming interaction

This is a useful method for structuring a social encounter. It is not possible in many contexts, notably during client-controlled counselling sessions where the client is allowed to structure the interaction and decide what should be discussed (Rogers, 1977). However, in those situations where it is possible, it is helpful to state clearly the goals for the present interaction, and the stages which are likely to be involved in pursuit of these goals.

Indeed the ability of the teacher to structure lesson material in a logical, coherent fashion would appear to be a feature of effective teaching. In his comprehensive review of research into the relationship between teacher behaviour and pupil achievement, Rosenshine (1971) found a positive correlation between the ability of the teacher to structure the introduction of new material, and increases in pupil achievement. This is exemplified in a study by Schuck (1969), who found that student teachers when given training in the skill of set induction received significantly higher ratings from pupils, and effected significantly greater gains in pupil achievement, than a comparable group of student teachers who received no such training. Schuck concluded from this study that set induction 'is a powerful variable in determining the kinds of learning that will occur in the classroom' (p. 785).

There are many other situations where it is desirable to structure interaction by providing guidelines about that which is to be discussed and the stages through which the discussion will proceed. A careers officer interviewing a young person for the first time will usually indicate what he hopes to achieve by the end of the interview, and state what areas he is going to ask questions about and why (e.g. school subjects, interests and hobbies, work experience). In the medical sphere, Cohen-Cole (1991, p. 53) points out that 'effective interviews begin with an explicit statement or acknowledgement of goals. Sometimes these may need to be negotiated between the doctor and the patient if there are some differences in objectives.'

The importance of negotiating the agenda has also been recognised in the counselling context by Lang and van der Molen (1990). They noted that as early as possible in the helping interview

> the helper is advised to inform the client straightaway about his way of working, and then see if the client agrees with that, or whether he has other expectations. The helper can then consider these expectations and see if they are realistic and if they fit in with his way of working.
>
> (p. 93)

Similarly a survey interviewer, as well as explaining the purpose of the survey being conducted, should tell subjects the particular areas he will be focusing upon during the interview and obtain explicit agreement about these before proceeding. In behaviour therapy, better relationships have been found between therapist and client when the therapist clarified his functions and outlined the goals of the interaction at the outset (Goldfried and Davison, 1976).

This technique, of providing guidelines about the probable content of a forthcoming interaction, allows participants to set themselves fully. They will therefore be mentally prepared for the topics to be discussed, and will be thinking about possible contributions they may be able to make. It also means that the individual often feels more secure in the situation, knowing in advance what the purpose of the interaction is, what the main themes are likely to be, how the sequence of discussion should proceed and the anticipated duration of the interaction.

The purpose of cognitive set is therefore to prepare someone for the main substantive, factual part of an encounter. This may involve giving instructions about the nature of a task and how best to approach it. It may also involve reviewing previous information, or highlighting previous encounters, in order to remind the person of what has gone before. Where appropriate, the expectations of the participants should also be ascertained so that these may be taken into account, and related to the realities of the situation. Finally, it involves outlining the goals of the interaction, and how these are to be achieved. These functions of cognitive set can partly be summarised as the process of informing participants where they have been, what stage they are now at and where they are going.

Overview of set induction

Set induction is, therefore, a very important process in interpersonal interaction. It is of particular importance during initial social encounters – hence the expressions 'well begun is half done' and 'start off as you intend to go on'. Where individuals have been interacting with one another over a period of time, certain expectations about behaviour will be built up. Thus different people may be classified as talkative, quiet, nasty, warm, cold, humorous and so on. Having been allocated a label, people are then expected to behave as categorised. If someone behaves 'out of character' this will usually be noticed and commented upon (e.g. 'You are very quiet tonight'). However, the expectations of other people can be modified if a person changes his style of interacting and this new style is adopted over a prolonged interval (e.g. 'He used to be very shy before he joined the army'). In this way, people can be encouraged to alter their set for any particular individual.

In the case of first encounters, set induction will vary in length, form and elaborateness depending on the context of the interaction. Motivational set involves the gaining of attention and the arousal of curiosity in order to encourage people to 'sit up and take notice'. Social set involves (verbally and nonverbally) welcoming people, providing creature comforts and generally making them feel settled. Perceptual set refers to the effects of the initial impression formed by people based upon the nature of the environment and the personal attributes of the other interactors. Cognitive set involves establishing expectations and outlining goals for the interaction.

Schuck (1969) neatly summarised the skill of set induction as consisting of four main processes, namely:

1 *Orientation.* This involves welcoming people, settling them down, and gaining attention.

2 *Transition*. Links with previous encounters should be made. The expectations of the people involved should be ascertained and the functions of the participants should be clarified.

3 *Evaluation*. Following the process of transition, an evaluation should be made of the relationship between the expectations of the participants and the realities of the present situation, so that a smooth interaction can follow. If discrepancies arise between expectations and reality, then these must be clarified. Similarly if disagreement or uncertainty exists about previous encounters, past decisions or material already covered, this must be clarified as well.

4 *Operation*. Only when the processes of transition and evaluation have been satisfactorily completed should the operational stage be implemented. This involves informing people of the goals for the immediate interaction (or deciding jointly upon goals where appropriate), explaining why these are the goals which have been decided upon, and pointing out the likely nature, content and duration of the forthcoming interaction.

CLOSURE

Closure is in many ways complementary to the skill of set induction in that while there are social norms for opening an interaction sequence there are also common interaction rituals for closing an encounter. However, there are some differences between the two skills. First, at a social level, while a person may contemplate and plan the best way to greet someone, particularly when that person is a stranger or a comparative stranger, he will seldom think about the appropriate way to say goodbye to that person. In general social terms, therefore, closure can be seen more as an impromptu action than a planned one. However, it will be argued in this chapter that unplanned closures are the least effective way to achieve formal closure since, as Bakken (1977) observed, goodbyes or parting rituals may serve to regulate and maintain relationships. In other words, how we take our leave of another person will to a great extent determine our motivation for meeting that person again.

A second major difference, suggested by Goffman (1972), is that 'greetings mark a transition to increased access and farewells to a state of decreased access' (p. 79). Perhaps this anticipation of lack of access is one of the factors that contributes to some of the difficulty that many of us have experienced in leave-taking. Many people prolong an interactive sequence simply to avoid being the first to indicate closure markers for fear of seeming to end a relationship. These periods of 'decreased access' signal a change in the amount of contact interactants will have with one another. If the probability of future meetings is very high then phrases such as 'See you soon', 'Bye for now', may well be employed. On the other hand, if the departure is of a more permanent duration, something more dramatic is likely to be said, such as

'Goodbye' or 'Bon voyage'. The parting terms appropriate in the former situation would be totally inappropriate in the latter and vice versa.

Simply to stop talking is not always an effective method of closing an interpersonal encounter, and in fact any attempt to close in this way could often be interpreted as anger, brusqueness or pique. Instead, closure can be defined more appropriately as the ability to 'organise the simultaneous arrival of the conversationalists at a point where one speaker's completion will not occasion another speaker's talk, and that will not be heard as some speaker's silence' (Schegloff and Sacks, 1973, p. 295). In other words, closure can be seen as drawing attention to the satisfactory completion of an interaction sequence.

At a simple, conversational level, short terminal exchanges such as 'Cheerio', 'All the best' or 'So long' will suffice and indeed research on conversational analysis has shown that this type of talk is closed in this conventional way (Button, 1987). At a more complex level, where a great deal of information and ideas have been exchanged, it is usually necessary to provide a more structured closure, perhaps in the form of a summary immediately preceding the final social exchange. Agar (1985) describes the latter terminal exchanges as those most commonly found in institutional or work contexts and notes that while detailed analysis of the discourse is highly structured in nature, very little attention has been given to how such discourse is closed. Indeed Hartford and Bardovi-Harlig (1992), utilising thirty-one academic advising session interviews, show that institutional conversations differ from natural conversations with respect to their closings. In addition, leave-taking can have an important supportiveness function often taking the form of an expressed desire to continue the interaction at a later date. After all, as Knapp *et al.* (1973) put it, 'What could be more supportive than doing it all again?' (p. 185). Bardovi-Harlig and Hartford (1990) call this aspect of closure the 'expression of gratitude' phase in which the speaker uses phrases such as 'Thanks a lot', 'Nice to meet you', 'Okay! (smiles) That completes everything.'

Drawing upon these findings, closure, in relation to social interaction, can be defined as directing attention to the termination of social exchange by summarising the main issues which have been discussed, drawing attention to what will happen in the future and, finally, breaking interpersonal contact without making participants feel rejected or shunned.

Functions of closure

The main functions in employing this skill in a wide range of interactive sequences can be listed as follows:

1   to indicate to participants that a topic has been completed, at least for the moment;

2   to focus the participants' attention on the essential features of the material covered;
3   to assist in consolidating for participants the facts, skills, concepts or arguments covered in previous episodes;
4   to give participants a sense of achievement (if a successful conclusion has been arrived at);
5   to indicate to participants the possibilities of future courses of action;
6   to assess the effectiveness of the interaction, particularly in relation to participants' knowledge;
7   to establish a conducive relationship so that participants look forward to a future encounter.

Although these are the main general functions of the skill of closure they are not all appropriate in every interactive situation. Some are more important than others depending upon the context in which the skill of closure is being employed. Those employed in the 'helping' professions may lay more stress on establishing a conducive relationship in their closure than in consolidating facts and information which are sometimes at a minimum in this type of encounter. On the other hand, where the interactors are concerned with exchanging facts and information (teachers, judges, barristers, television presenters, salesmen and public speakers, etc.) there may be greater emphasis on summarising and consolidating information for the benefit of their less informed clients.

In addition, the skill of closing, as with opening, can manifest itself in a number of ways depending upon, for example, the number of participants involved, the purpose of the encounter, location and time of day as well as personal characteristics of participants such as personality, intellect, experience and socioeconomic background. Therefore, it is crucial, when assessing the effectiveness of the skill of closing, to consider those factors which directly influence any evaluation thereof.

The remainder of the chapter will focus upon four main types of closure which can be commonly executed, namely, factual, motivational, social and perceptual. The following sections will set out in more detail the different types of closure which can be applied and illustrate how each type may be more appropriate in one social context than another.

Factual closure

Factual closure may be used a number of times within social interaction, following the presentation of facts, information, skills, ideas, opinions, feelings or problems. Thus while factual closure is important at the end of an encounter, it can be used intermittently throughout, particularly if the interaction is of a lengthy duration. In this way the essential features of any sequence can be highlighted in a brief, coherent fashion in order to crystallise for individuals what has been discussed, as well as encouraging them to relate this material to more general, conceptual issues. In addition, it is essential that any new facts or information that have been assimilated should be related both to previous knowledge and to similar examples and cases covering new situations where possible. In other words, participants should be commended to use the knowledge they have gained to plan and execute future courses of action.

Factual closure can be achieved in a variety of ways depending upon the social context. Among the techniques which are available can be included the following.

Summary

Writing about some of the main functions of speech conclusions, Aristotle, in the fifth century BC, claimed that recapitulation of the main points of an argument or speech helped to dramatise or draw attention to the speaker's case. Many centuries later, our thinking does not appear to be radically different.

Reynolds and Glaser (1964), in research into biology teaching, found that regular summaries, or 'spaced reviews' as they called them, increased pupils' knowledge of the subject area, the implication being that regular and progressive summing up at various intervals facilitates the retention of knowledge. Wright and Nuthall (1970) confirmed this finding when they found from their research that concluding remarks by teachers were positively correlated with pupil achievement. Although teachers find this a worthwhile skill to achieve in the classroom, other professional interactors should attempt to incorporate it into their repertoire of skills, particularly when a range of ideas and information is being discussed. Testimony to this is the study carried out by Rackham and Morgan (1977) to assess the skills of chairpersons. They noted that group members felt that meetings lacked clarity and structure when the chairperson did not summarise at the end. More recently Dickson *et al.* (1989), from their review of research into practitioner–patient communication concluded that patient understanding and recall could be improved when instructions were repeated at intervals throughout the consultation. Bearing this in mind careers officers, who may be giving pupils information on a range of job opportunities, can usefully employ transitional summaries. Nurses and community care workers, too, when advising patients about the most suitable way to dress a wound, feed a baby, administer an injection, etc., can quickly and effectively recap the main points of the process to ensure the patient's understanding. However, it must be stressed that brevity is the order of the day. The repetition in a more concise form of the essential elements involved, helps to cement them in the listener's memory. Morrow *et al.* (1993b) reviewing research into health care communication endorse this point by noting that simplification of information enhances recall.

Marshall *et al.* (1982) identified the 'influencing' summarisation skill in a counselling context. They contended that 'the summarization skill of influencing has the additional component of informing the client of the helper's expectations, whether they be merely the scheduling of the next visit or the completion of some homework assignment' (p. 98). However, in addition they also point out that the influencing summary can serve as a perception check, as well as a means of consolidating and redirecting.

Another function of making an explicit summation, either at the end of an interview or at the termination of a particular topic, was put forward by Benjamin (1981) who feels that it gives both the interviewer and interviewee the chance to check if each has understood the other. Thus, for example, a helper could end with the words, 'Before you go, I just want to make sure I understand your position. . . . Have I left anything out or does that appear to be the right position?' Munro *et al.* (1983) agree that this is a useful technique for counsellors to use but, as an alternative, claim that it is also effective to have the client summarise what has taken place or been discussed in order that the counsellor gets a better understanding of the client's view of things as well as helping the client to assess what progress has been made.

Byrne and Long (1976), in an analysis of doctor–patient interactions, noted that towards the end of an interview a patient will frequently introduce new and often vital information. They termed this the 'By the way . . .' syndrome. Obviously this can cause major problems for doctors in making a decision as to whether to continue with the interview or arrange a further consultation. Livesey (1986) also recognised this as a problem with some general practitioners and suggested that the 'By the way . . .' syndrome could be avoided by encouraging patients to interact fully and freely throughout the entire consultation.

In conclusion it would appear that the summary is a useful technique to employ when achieving closure, although Knapp *et al.* (1973) warned that it can be overlooked in practice. In a study designed to identify functions and elements of leave-taking in an information-seeking interview situation, they found the act of summarising was not evident. However, they speculated that this could have been the limited time available to the subjects in the experimental interviews. Cohen-Cole (1991) refers to this summary aspect of the medical interview as 'checking' and warns that although it is a key data-gathering skill for medical practitioners, more often than not it is overlooked. Checking should take the form of a summary allowing the doctor a chance to check for accuracy of what a patient has just said, correct any misunderstandings and also communicate to the patient that he is listening and trying to understand. More recently Saunders and Saunders (1993), in a study of university lecturers' teaching, found that while lecturers claimed that all modes of teaching should conclude with an appropriate closure sequence, in practice, none were included in the lecturers' own video-taped teaching sessions. Generally speaking, the lecturers admitted to 'running out of time'.

It would appear, therefore, that sufficient time ought to be left available for a concise summary to be made where the speaker considers it to be an important part of the interactive sequence.

Initiating or inviting questions

Drawing again from research into teaching it has been found that the use of oral feedback questions to assess understanding of material previously presented is positively related to pupil learning (Wright and Nuthall, 1970; Rothkopf, 1972; McKeown, 1977). This could be termed the evaluating aspect of factual closure. Evaluating is an essential part of closure where the focus is on what has been learned. Specific questions can be asked, designed to check for accuracy of facts or understanding, assimilate the logical sequence of ideas, or evaluate the comprehensiveness of a range of arguments. The responses can then serve as a basis for future courses of action such as to supply accurate information, consolidate ideas or provide information where omissions may occur.

While initiated questions are useful check-aids for teachers, lecturers, job trainers, coaches and demonstrators, they can be used at various times throughout a dyadic interview type situation as an alternative to the summary. Nelson-Jones (1988) noted this alternative strategy in a counselling context as a way of helping the client to consolidate learning. For example, if a client says that the sessions with the helper have been invaluable in helping to solve a set of problems, the helper could respond, 'What exactly have you learned that will help you to sort out your problems?' This conveys to the helper exactly what the client has gained from the interactive sessions. Alternatively, the interviewer can ask a candidate at the end of a selection interview, 'Is there anything you would like to ask me now?' All interviewers, suggest Stewart and Cash (1988), should initiate or invite questions in order to answer any queries or discrepancies which might have arisen during the interview. These authors also stress that the offer should be genuine and sincere rather than a mere formality.

Future links

Along with summarising and checking for accuracy of mutual understanding, closure may also draw attention to the work which will continue after the termination of the interview. At a simple level this may include making future organisational arrangements such as where and when to meet. At another level, it may involve mapping out, albeit loosely, the agenda for a future meeting. In other words, the summary states the position arrived at while the future link focuses on prospective tasks or decisions to be made. In this way, the chairperson of a committee meeting will usually recap the main points of the day's discussion but will also finish with a brief statement of what still has to be discussed at a future meeting. This has the express function of bringing together into a meaningful whole what may seem diverse elements simply because they have occurred over a period of time.

Identifying areas of future concern was considered by Schulman (1979) to be an important function of the counsellor's role. He stated that the helper's task is 'to create an agenda for future work, and to use their experience together to determine how the client can continue to work on these concerns' (p. 100). Knapp *et al.* (1973) referred to this aspect of leave-taking as a strategy of 'futurism', that is, an expressed desire on the part of the interviewer to continue the interaction at a later date. These authors claim this element has a strong supportive function and as such it will be dealt with more fully under social closure.

Motivational closure

Although it has been stated previously in this chapter that one of the main functions of the skill of closure is to focus on both the completion and consolidation of the main facets covered during interaction, there are times when to do so would be inappropriate. Instead, it would be more useful to motivate persons to explore and consider further some of the issues which have been revealed during the previous interactive sequence. Not all transactions can be accomplished in any one session and indeed it may be more expedient to employ a motivational type of closure when a series of sessions is required. By employing this type of closure, individuals can be directed to reflect more carefully, consider in greater depth, and relate any new insights gained from the present encounter to more general issues in a wider context. In essence, three principal methods can effectively be employed to bring about a motivational closure, the choice of any one being heavily dependent upon the social situation in which it is to be used.

Explicitly motivating statements

These are perhaps the most basic and obvious means of encouraging persons to relate experiences and insights gained to some future event. Final statements such as, 'Give it everything you've got', 'Let's show them what we can do', 'Go get 'em', are frequently used by sales promotion managers, sports coaches, entertainment promoters to name but a few in order to encourage greater effort following the 'pep' talk.

However, this type of statement is not only confined to the business of selling, the sports field or the entertainment business, it can also be used successfully by those in the helping professions, whereby clients can be motivated to put into practice some of the decisions that have been reached during the interview. Concluding statements such as 'You must try these out for yourself . . .', 'It's up to you to come to some agreement . . .',

'Only you can make the final decision . . .', are explicitly employed to facilitate future action.

Thought-provoking comments

The use of thought-provoking comments as well as being a useful device to encourage participation at the beginning of encounters can equally effectively be used at the end with the specific purpose of sending an individual or group away to consider the matter further. Teachers or lecturers often use this technique at the end of lessons in order to motivate their students to study further in their own time. By providing students with a problematic situation to finish, the teacher can effectively encourage students to explore the situation further so that there is a link between the present and the future lesson.

Some television and radio programmes also flourish using this technique. Thus a producer of a children's television drama series may close one programme with a number of intriguing questions such as 'What will happen to Mary?' or 'Will John escape from his captors?' coupled with short filmed sequences of the following week's production to accompany the thought-provoking questions. This is done with the express purpose of encouraging viewers to watch each episode from one week to the next.

Future orientation comments

The use of future orientation comments also allows individuals to give further consideration to issues long after the interaction sequence has ended. In addition, individuals are also given the opportunity to relate any new experience they have gained from the immediate encounter to a similar one in a wider environment or to relate knowledge gained in one context to another outside the present encounter.

Thus, teachers invite their pupils to relate knowledge gained in the classroom context to familiar situations they meet every day outside the school environment. For instance, a class teacher of 8- to 9-year-olds, helping children to grasp the concept of points on a compass, north, south, east and west, can finish her concept teaching by asking the children, when they go home, to find out which room gets the sun first thing in the morning and which room gets the sun before it disappears for the night. Alternatively, teachers often set children homework at the end of the lesson, specifically designed to consider an issue more deeply. Following a lesson which has concentrated on posing questions constructed to illuminate racial prejudice, pupils could be directed to ask the same questions of their parents, grandparents, brothers, sisters and friends to give them greater insights into attitude formation and attitude change.

These future orientation statements or questions are not the sole prerogative of those involved in the teaching profession. Trower *et al.* (1978) stressed the need for patients in a clinical context to be given 'between-session homework assignments' in social situations they have found difficult to master during practical skills training sessions. In addition, Ellis and Whittington (1981) suggested that the trainee, engaged in a variety of Social Skills Training (SST) programmes, should be 'asked to obtain feedback from real-life "others" for discussion when he returns to the [training] unit' (p. 74).

Apart from training situations, other professionals can use future orientation comments or questions. A nurse can motivate her patient to try new and more up-to-date techniques, even when she is not present, with a concluding statement such as 'The next time you need to inject you can use the method I've shown you this morning, can't you?' Similarly, counsellors can encourage their clients to examine their problems with new insights gained during the interview session.

In essence, therefore, in a situation where it is neither apt nor fitting to leave a person with a sense of finality or completion, it is more appropriate to use a type of motivational closure; which particular one to employ will depend upon the interactive situation, the nature of the task and the relationship between the interactors.

Social closure

In order to ensure that not only has an interaction been a fruitful one in the sense that substantive issues have been dealt with, but also that it has been an enjoyable experience for all parties, it is useful to employ a type of social closure. Support for the importance of this final leave-taking stage of the encounter also came from Benjamin (1974) who asserted, 'Closing is especially important because what occurs during this last state is likely to determine the interviewee's impression of the interview as a whole' (p. 34). In a recent study, designed to identify effective communication skills in pharmacist–patient consultations (Hargie et al., 1993), it was found that 'Expressing thanks to the patient and politeness were, however, considered crucial aspects of any closing sequence' (p. 31).

It is important to note, however, that this acknowledgement of 'pleasantries' should follow the factual closure with its emphasis on content, whereas in set induction, establishing a relationship precedes the factual or cognitive set. The main techniques which can be used in order to provide an effective social closure are as follows.

Task-related supportive statements

Administered immediately following the cognitive closure, these help to give participants a sense of satisfaction by drawing attention to that which has been achieved as a result of the encounter. Statements such as, 'That's good. You've helped me get things in perspective', 'Well done. We're beginning to get somewhere now', 'That's great. You've explained that to me so clearly

I've now got the picture', which follow a recap or summary of facts or ideas, convey to participants that the meeting has been worthwhile in that some kind of further understanding has been brought about.

Chairpersons, teachers and lecturers who are engaged in small group discussions or seminars, often employ this technique at the end of the discussion when they thank group members for their individual contributions to the overall discussion. Bales (1950), in his series of studies on group behaviour, noted that group leaders were more effective if they administered rewarding comments both to particular individuals who put forward interesting ideas or pertinent information, and to the group as a whole.

Although these statements are often made towards the end of an encounter it is also appropriate to use them at various points in any interaction where tasks have been partially completed. Thus it is quite common for two people who have been collaborating on the same task to say, 'I think we'll take a break now', or 'I think we've earned a rest because we are really getting somewhere.' This type of supportive comment provides participants with a feeling that something has been achieved and that even more can be accomplished in the future. Pope (1986) made the distinction between providing clients with subjective as opposed to objective feedback in a therapist–client interview situation. He claimed that subjective feedback can be given by the therapist without aiming to be scientific. On the other hand objective feedback is provided by the therapist being prepared to back up concluding statements (such as 'Well done! You are moving really well now') with supporting reasons. Comparing these two types of responses, Pope concluded that objective feedback 'is a stronger form of feedback than the subjective type, but is not necessarily more effective [since] the therapist has to be especially careful that he does not project his own opinions using this technique' (p. 174).

Non-task-related statements

Non-task-related statements are also frequently used when the main business of the interaction has been concluded satisfactorily. Knapp *et al.* (1973) referred to these statements as personal or welfare aspects of leave-taking. In other words, when decisions have been reached, solutions to the problems found or the general business has been concluded, participants recognise the 'human' aspect of leave-taking and invariably proceed to make statements or ask questions designed to show a warm, friendly disposition. Phrases such as, 'When are you going on holiday?', 'Now take it easy', 'I hope the weather stays fine until the weekend', can be used by a range of professionals.

Acknowledgement statements will often follow both task- and non-task-related supportive comments and are principally employed to indicate an appreciation of the opportunity to meet. Irrespective of the context, most professionals have the occasion, in a face-to-face situation, to say to their clients, 'It's been nice talking to you. I hope we'll meet again.' Alternatively, at the end of a telephone conversation, it is appropriate to conclude with, 'Thank you for talking to me. I look forward to our meeting next Tuesday.' All of these statements help to 'round off' the conversation and signal to the client that his presence has been appreciated. (See Chapter 4 for a fuller discussion on reinforcement.)

In addition, Shuy (1983) noted that non-task-related statements have a useful role to play when transferring from one topic to another. For example, if the dialogue has been serious and intense, there is often a recognised need to offer more light, social chit-chat as a transition to the next serious topic. Even in a medical interview, according to Shuy,

> the interview can become rather heavy unless there is some light talk
> occasionally. This is not to say that all medical interviews should be light and
> gay. But, if one goal of the interview is to make the patient comfortable . . .
> then some heed could be paid to learning how to create and use transitions
> between topics effectively as a means of putting the patient at ease.
>
> (p. 201)

Perceptual closure

In order to effectively terminate a discussion, conversation, talk or interview it is important to use specific closure markers, and so avoid embarrassing those who are not quite sure whether to carry on talking or rise and take leave. Goffman (1961) recognised the significance of 'terminal exchanges' by pinpointing a series of physical manoeuvres and positionings related to leave-taking. Schegloff and Sacks (1973) noted that what is perceived as the final closing acts can be achieved by verbal means alone (such as 'Bye', 'See you') but that they are usually accompanied by specific nonverbal behaviours (such as posture shifts, extended eye gaze, an increase in interpersonal distance, edging towards an exit). Knapp *et al.* (1973) found that leave-taking differed between formal and less formal situations. Whilst both types began the parting sequence with social reinforcers, the formal pairs followed up with rational-isations for the leave-taking ('I have an appointment with the dentist', 'The car is parked at a parking meter'), whereas the less formal pairs were making statements concerned with each other's welfare ('Take care now', 'Look after yourself'). Whichever strategy is used to terminate interaction, it is important that closure be accomplished between participants as sensitively and effec-tively as possible. The two main techniques available to achieve perceptual closure are verbal closure markers and nonverbal closure markers sometimes occurring separately but more often in tandem.

Verbal closure markers

Verbal closure markers are such an integral part of our everyday communi-cation network that to list them might almost seem superfluous. Such terms as

'Good-bye', 'Cheerio', 'Bye-bye', 'Cheers', 'Goodnight', 'See you' or 'All the best', are used interchangeably in a variety of social settings, yet even how we use them indicates our relationship with others. When we use the term 'good-bye' it often suggests either a more formal departure or that we may not see the other person again for at least some time. Most interviews terminate with a formal verbal closure remark. Television programmes, including news programmes and chat shows, leave the viewers usually with a 'Goodnight' closure. On the other hand, expressions such as 'See you', or 'All the best', have a more informal or casual flavour being used by close friends or work colleagues, and tend to indicate that the interactors will be meeting again in the near future. According to Berne (1964), 'an informal ritual, such as leave-taking may be subject to considerable local variations in details, but the basic form remains the same' (p. 36).

Laver (1981), on the other hand, has devised a flowchart for what he calls 'formulaic parting and greeting routines' based upon the relationship between the participants. The more formal parting ritual, according to Laver, is used between adults, with those who are not kin, with those of higher rank and with those who are considerably older. Thus the speaker's first task is to determine the status (e.g. adult versus child) of the interactor, so as to enable the appropriate verbal closure remark to be made.

Although these departure expressions which have been outlined are important in breaking any interactive sequence and so avoiding offending or snubbing another individual, there are other expressions perhaps more subtly employed which also indicate that some part of the interaction is coming to a close. Words such as 'OK', 'Well', 'Right', 'Now' by themselves do not denote a closing feature, but when accompanied by a downward intonation of the voice and appearing at a possible pre-closing stage of the discussion they effectively become verbal closure markers. It usually signals to participants that this is as far as the topic is to be explored and indeed to introduce new material at this stage would be unwelcome.

It is important to bear all of these aspects in mind when selecting the appropriate closure word or phrase since failure to do so could result in altering, albeit implicitly, the relationship previously set up in the encounter. Knapp et al. (1973) neatly encapsulated this as follows, 'Though minute and seemingful irrelevant on the surface, leave-taking behaviors do appear to be powerful interpersonal forces . . . [and] . . . the initiation and reception of leave-taking cues provides an offhand view of general interpersonal sensitivity' (p. 198).

Nonverbal closure markers

Nonverbal closure markers, which can be used to complement the verbal messages, are of two main types: first, the kind which has almost universal meaning, such as the handshake, a wave or a kiss which overtly signifies the departure of one person from another; second are more subtle cues which also signify that the interaction is drawing to a close. These are: a major change in body posture, hand leveraging (on the knees, legs or on the chair itself), breaking eye contact, explosive hand contacts (either on a part of the body such as the thighs, or an object such as a desk, files or books), orientation or movement towards an exit or looking at a watch or clock. These more subtle nonverbal cues have the distinct advantage of implicitly communicating closure to another person, thus avoiding the use of explicit, less effective verbal markers such as 'You may go now', or 'I've finished with you now.'

Bearing in mind that we are mostly concerned with terminating our interactions on the 'right note', that is on a note of mutual regard, it is important to combine these nonverbal behaviours with supportive verbal ones. According to Zaidel and Mehrabian (1969), verbal and nonverbal behaviours can be at variance, in which case more credence is apt to be placed on what we see rather than what we hear, although they also point out that this varies with age, children and young adolescents paying more attention to visual components than older adolescents and adults. This point was also borne out by Bugental *et al.* (1970). Since the support function is such a critical element in leave-taking, it is important to control the use of these nonverbal elements so that misinterpretations do not arise. For example, it is often difficult to break eye contact in situations where one wants to communicate support, but also wants to leave. The use of appropriate supportive verbal statements can help to reduce any potential ambiguity which may arise as to the nature of the relationship. Busy professionals, who work to a heavily burdened time schedule, should be aware of the importance of verbal and nonverbal leave-taking behaviours in bringing social encounters to a congenial and satisfactory conclusion.

Overview of closure

Although closure can be technically defined as directing attention to the completion of a task it can be analysed at four distinct levels: factual, motivational, social and perceptual.

Factual closure occurs not only at the end of the interaction but can also be used throughout, particularly when a 'topic shift' occurs. In an interview-type situation, for example, these segments are easily identifiable because they are separated by breaks in the smooth flow of communication where the participants are considering what to discuss next. One of the most common forms of factual closure is the summary. Summaries can include aspects of both feelings which have been expressed during interaction as well as information of a factual nature. In this respect a summarisation can draw diverse facts and feelings together to form some sort of meaningful whole. The final summary of any interaction, however, be it a class lesson, an interview, a sales promotion drive or a consultancy visit, will, of course, range over the entire spectrum and will conclude with the most important features, such as essential information covered, range of feelings expressed both positive and negative, problems explored or decisions reached.

When it is not appropriate to finalise or come to some conclusions about a problem, topic or event, a *motivational closure* can be employed in order to encourage participants to consider issues further long after the face-to-face discussion has taken place. This is an especially useful technique for teachers, lecturers and job trainers to use but can equally effectively be used by any professional helper whose main aim is to give clients the opportunity to help themselves.

A *social closure*, on the other hand, essentially is concerned with leaving participants feeling glad of the social interchange and at the same time feeling disposed to meet again when and if the situation arises. This serves to overcome any possible resentment which may arise if a client feels that he is being pushed out the door, just one of a number on a communication assembly line, or that he has imposed on the interviewer and her time. Such feelings may result in the client being less likely, first to implement any decisions which the interviewer has helped him arrive at, and, second, to return again at a future date.

Finally, a *perceptual closure* is instrumental in terminating any interaction be it formal, informal or conducted in a dyadic, small or large group context. Specific verbal closures varying from a single 'Goodbye' to phrases such as 'I must go now John or I'll be late for my next meeting' effectively terminate any interaction. These verbal markers are in most cases accompanied by nonverbal closures such as showing someone to the door, shaking hands, etc., and help to emphasise that the 'final exchange' has been reached.

These techniques can be operationalised singly or in combination depending upon the social context in which they are being employed. However, whichever techniques are used it is important to recognise that the 'closure' is that last point of contact between interactors and therefore is the one they are most likely to remember. Therefore, not enough emphasis can be put on employing the 'right' closure techniques on any given occasion in interpersonal interaction.

CONCLUSION

While no claim is made to suggest that this is an exhaustive analysis of the two skills of opening and closing, it is an attempt to add to the range of techniques currently available from which to choose. If our knowledge of these skills is to increase at all, more research is needed into the normative and specialised functions and strategies of these communicative acts. To gain insights into those relatively unexplored aspects of opening and closing, those little-noticed, seemingly irrelevant on the surface, verbal and nonverbal opening and closing behaviours, is to discover crucial information about the nature of social interaction itself.

Chapter 8

Explanation

INTRODUCTION

It is important at the outset to recognise that the term 'explain' has acquired a number of meanings in everyday usage. On the one hand, explaining can be used synonymously with describing, telling or instructing, where the explainer is mainly concerned with providing information of either a descriptive or prescriptive nature. On the other hand, 'to explain' goes beyond mere description to give reasons or reveal causes for the facts or events under discussion. In other words the key word 'why' is an implicit or explicit feature of this explanatory procedure

In addition, the term 'explain' has two further meanings. As Turney *et al.* (1983), in their review of the literature on explaining, pointed out, the verb 'to explain' has 'a meaning which emphasizes the intention of the explainer, and a meaning which emphasizes the success of the explanation' (p. 14). Thus it makes sense to say 'I explained it to him and it is not my fault if he did not understand it.' In professional usage, however, it has been pointed out that this sense of the verb 'to explain' is frequently not acceptable (Thyne, 1966; Martin, 1970). Rather, when it is said that something has been explained, we assume that it has been understood. Using this frame of reference, to explain is to give understanding to another. As a result, the skill of explaining contains, as an integral component, the use of feedback techniques to check the efficacy of the explanation. If the reader were to listen to a person's conversations during one single day it would usually be found that for much of the time that person was engaged in explaining; that is giving facts, information, directions, reasons, views or opinions. It would also be detected, upon listening to a number of different conversations, that some people are more effective at explaining than others. Gage *et al.* (1968) noted this difference in teachers' explanations when they pointed out that:

> Some people explain aptly, getting to the heart of the matter with just the
> right terminology, examples and organization of ideas. Other explainers,
> on the contrary, get us and themselves all mixed up, use terms beyond our

level of comprehension, draw inept analogies and even employ concepts and principles that cannot be understood without an understanding of the very thing being explained.

(p. 3)

The skill of explaining is one of the most important and widely used social skills and yet it is one of the most difficult to legislate for. This is because the perceived adequacy of an explanation is directly related to the recipient's age, background knowledge and mental ability. Imagine the following situation, so typical of classroom instruction: a social studies teacher is planning to teach a lesson, on the concept of 'status'. The problem is how to teach it, given the current level of understanding of the pupils and their perceived degree of interest in the topic. What words can the teacher use to introduce the concept? What activities can the pupils engage in? How thoroughly should the concept be explored? How can it be related to other lessons and other subjects? A plan of how to teach something to someone is faced by teachers on both an hourly and day-to-day basis. However, it would be erroneous to believe that only teachers are faced with such dilemmas, since they seem characteristic of any number of communicative activities. Indeed, McEwan (1992) has noted that the same problem arises in connection with any attempt to get one's meaning across. How should the psychologist present research results? How should the politician convey an agenda to the electorate? How should the chief commissioner of police brief the press after an explosion? Thus it would appear that far from being the prerogative of the teacher, the skill of explaining has a more general application.

The onus is on the explainer to ascertain at what level an explanation should be pitched in order to achieve a balance between being too complicated on the one hand and too patronising on the other. Gleason and Perlmann (1985), analysing the speech patterns and content of adults speaking to young children, found that adults simplify their speech in terms of pronunciation, grammar and vocabulary, as well as exaggerated intonations. Professionals should be aware when explaining to children and young adolescents that their cognitive development proceeds in a stage-like sequence from concrete to more abstract thinking (Bruner *et al.*, 1956). Concepts such as honesty, love, loyalty and fair play may need little explanation when dealing with adults, but with younger children they need to be spelled out in more detail and related where possible to everyday occurrences within the child's experience.

FUNCTIONS OF EXPLANATION

The main functions in utilising the skill of explaining in social encounters can be listed as follows:

1   to provide others with information to which they may otherwise not have access;
2   to share information with others in order to reach some common understanding;
3   to simplify for others more complex phenomena;
4   to clarify any uncertainties which have been revealed during social interaction;
5   to express opinions regarding a particular attitude, fact or value;
6   to illustrate the essential features of particular phenomena.
7   to demonstrate how to execute a specific skill or technique.

Although these are the principal general purposes of the skill of explaining, it is important to note that some purposes are more important than others, depending upon the context of the interaction. While a teacher may start off her lesson by explaining briefly what the lesson is about and what she hopes to achieve, this technique would be anathema to a non-directive counsellor who will usually only seek to direct a client towards a solution to his problem after first hearing the client's needs and ideas. While Ley (1988) and Dickson et al. (1989) have presented research reviews to demonstrate that patients positively value the presentation of information about their illness from their doctor or consultant, in an interesting study carried out by Wallen et al. (1979) it was found that less than 1 per cent of total time in information exchange between doctor and patient was spent on doctor explanations to patients. Further studies have shown that giving adequate and relevant information and explanation before operations or investigations can result in tangible benefits to patients in terms of reduced pain and discomfort, reduced anxiety and reduced stress (Boore, 1979; Wilson-Barnett, 1981). Although this evidence is apparent in medical contexts there is every reason to suppose that persons faced with other unknown situations, such as appearing in court as a witness or taking out a mortgage, would equally benefit from effective explanations.

TYPES OF EXPLANATION

Whilst there has been a proliferation of typologies of explanation from the 1960s onwards (Ennis, 1969; Hyman, 1974), one of the most pragmatic and robust set of categories has been provided by Brown and Armstrong (1984), these being termed the descriptive, the interpretive and the reason-giving. Descriptive explanations are provided in order to set out in detail specific procedures, structures or processes. Examples are: a midwife describing to a young mother how to bath her new baby, a careers officer outlining the function and format of a curriculum vitae to a school leaver, or a pharmacist instructing a customer on how to use an inhaler. Interpretive explanations define or clarify issues, procedures or statements. Thus, doctors may interpret for particular patients the results of an X-ray taken previously or inform others about the effects of a particular pill or treatment. Alternatively, TV presenters assist their audience's understanding of current affairs by, for instance, clarifying the effects of high inflation rates on job opportunities, or the effects of nuclear waste on the environment. Reason-giving explanations, according to Brown (1986), are produced in relation to questions beginning, 'Why?' Why is coronary thrombosis more prevalent in Western society? Why are some persons more susceptible to advertising than others? Why do birds migrate? Whilst a particular explanation may involve all three types of explanation, when to provide it is heavily dependent upon whether it is planned or unplanned. The unplanned explanation is frequently used in response to a specific question or problem posed by an individual seeking further clarification. The planned are prepared prior to the actual explaining episode and are the ones which we are concerned with in this text.

According to Brown and Hatton (1982), planning and presenting are the two essential broad features of explanation, although it must be noted that the two do not necessarily go hand in hand. In other words, it cannot be assumed that a well prepared and structured explanation inevitably results in an effectively presented one. Burns summed up this sentiment in the words, 'The best laid plans of mice and men gang aft aglay'. However, studies have shown that training in methods of planning and preparation is linked to clarity of explanations (Hiller, 1971; Brown and Armstrong, 1984).

PLANNING SKILLS

Much of the research on planning meaningful explanations focuses on how experts solve problems, make decisions or instruct clearly and the differences in how expert and novice teachers approach the act of instruction (Berliner, 1986; Livingstone and Borko, 1989; Huling-Austin, 1992). Carter (1990) noted that novices tend to jump in without giving adequate thought and planning to the task in hand. Experts on the other hand develop cognitive schemata which rely on the integration of specialised knowledge linked to specific situations; organisational knowledge in terms of how concepts are related and form a pattern; and tacit knowledge which is constructed or invented from repeated experiences over time. McLaughlin *et al.* (1992), however, suggest that the construction and success of explanatory accounts are daunting tasks since a considerable amount of information must be integrated and often require taking the others' perspective while doing so. Moreover, creating a successful explanation may take a reasonable length of time as alternatives are considered (see Chapter 2). Thus there are four specific components that are important to consider when planning an explanation. They are concerned with:

1 identifying the issue requiring explanation;
2 selecting the key elements in the problem or issue that is being explained;
3 determining the nature of the relationship between these key elements;
4 structuring and linking the explanation to the background knowledge and mental capacity of the recipient in order to promote maximum understanding.

There is ample evidence from research into teaching to suggest that the teacher's ability to prepare, structure, organise and sequence facts and ideas with the maximum of logical coherence is positively related to pupil achievement (Gage *et al.*, 1968; Nuthall, 1968; Wright and Nuthall, 1970; Hargie, 1980). Ivey and Gluckstern (1976) stressed the importance in interviewing of structuring explanations before presenting them to clients. More specifically in planning an interview, the interviewer should have a clear idea of the particular elements involved in the explanation and their relationship with each other. He should also consider the length of time he intends to spend on the explanation, since this will determine the amount of material he can cover in the time available. In addition, it is useful for the interviewer to consider at this stage what exactly he expects the client to know at the end of the explanation. Finally, as has been previously stated, when selecting, linking and structuring terms and ideas, the interviewer should take into account the age, sex, background, experience and mental ability of his client.

Although it is essential to pre-plan an explanation, it needs to be presented before its effectiveness can be judged. The remainder of this chapter, therefore, will look specifically at a number of skills which can be employed in order to present an explanation clearly and coherently.

PRESENTATION SKILLS

Prior to examining the essential presentation features of the skill of explaining it is important to note that there are three main techniques which can be identified and utilised within the overall skill of explanation. These are:

1 *Verbal explanation.* This usually takes place when no aids are available to facilitate explanation. Radio programmes, newspapers and books often rely solely on this type of explanation.
2 *Illustration.* Where audio-visual aids are available, such as charts, diagrams, films or hand-outs, these can be used to underline the more important aspects of the explanation, and so aid understanding.
3 *Demonstration.* This often occurs when a complex technique or skill is being explained and includes the demonstration by another person (or model) of the actual procedures involved in carrying out a practical task.

The effectiveness of an explanation is the result of including one or all of the above techniques into the flow of the discourse in order to enhance the overall clarity of the explanation. Each will be discussed more fully later in the chapter in the category relating to aids to explanation. Whilst few studies have been concerned with the identification of effective planning and structuring skills of explanation, a great deal of research attention has been focused on the subject of presentation skills (Rosenshine and Furst, 1973; Turney *et al.*, 1983; Land, 1985; Ley, 1988). An examination of these research findings has revealed a number of features and these are discussed and analysed in the remainder of this chapter.

Clarity

There is little doubt that clarity of speech is one of the most challenging features of effective explaining. Of course, clear explanations are highly dependent upon a thorough knowledge of what is to be explained. However, knowledge of a subject is only one part of the equation. This knowledge has to be communicated to an audience in a clear, unambiguous and structured way. Brown (1986), in a study of college lecturers' use of explanations, identified four structuring moves which were linked to clarity. These are as follows:

Signposts

These are statements which set out a structure for the presentation to come. Teachers will often signal the direction and structure of a lesson, likewise an interviewer may begin by stating the objectives of the interview or a nurse may outline the arrangements for a particular treatment to be carried out. Thus phrases such as, 'In the next half hour I would like to look at two approaches to treatment. First, what you yourself can do in terms of diet and life-style. And second, what we can do in terms of drugs and medicines.' In essence, these spoken statements are synonymous with what a writer would use in the introduction to a report or essay.

Frames

Frames are used to put parameters around specific topics or sub-topics contained in the explanation. They are words or phrases which circumscribe beginnings and endings of sections within the body of the talk. For example, phrases such as, 'Now that we have examined what you can do to help yourself, let us examine more closely what we can do in terms of. . . .'

Foci

Foci statements are concerned with highlighting or emphasising key features of the explanation in order to sift the essential from the inessential material covered. These phrases are particularly useful when giving information where safety matters are at a premium. Examples of foci statements as used in a health context would include: 'You must always remember to eat a balanced diet'; 'It is vital that you take one of these blue pills first thing in the morning.'

Links

Most talks or explanations cover a series of topics each designed to contribute to an audience's overall comprehensive knowledge of a subject. Clarity of comprehension is improved if the speaker links these topics into a meaningful whole. In this sense links are akin to frames. In addition, however, speakers should try to link their explanation to the experience, previously acquired knowledge and observations of the audience.

Brevity

Brevity is essential so that listeners can easily recall and therefore understand the explanation given. Verner and Dickinson (1967) found, from a comprehensive review of literature on purely verbal explanation, that recipients' 'learning begins to diminish seriously after fifteen minutes' (p. 90). Support for this finding has been noted by Stewart (1977), who stated that one of the barriers to effective listening is the long speech. Ley (1983), reviewing a number of studies related to patients' understanding and recall of information or instructions provided by the doctor, noted that 'Forgetting is associated with the amount of information presented. . .' (p. 94). In other words, the doctor frequently tells the patient more than she can possibly hope to remember.

Fluency

Verbal presentation should be as fluent as possible. It is not only annoying to listen to 'ums' and 'ers' or garbled, rambling sentences, but this annoyance can very quickly lead to inattention. Hiller *et al.* (1969) noted that verbal fluency, as measured by length of sentences, and hesitations such as 'uh', 'um', etc., differentiated between teachers who explained effectively to pupils and those who did not.

One of the causes of punctuating speech with sounds such as 'eh' or 'mm' is trying to put too many ideas or facts across in one sentence. It is better to use reasonably short crisp sentences, with pauses in between them, than long rambling ones full of subordinate clauses. This will generally tend to eliminate speech hesitancies. French (1983) asserted that 'Most of us do not notice the frequency with which we and others have these speech habits, until we focus on them' (p. 80). However, he advises that such habits should be minimised when they interfere unduly with the information being communicated so that comprehension of the listener is impaired. Another cause of dysfluency in speech is lack of adequate planning. The importance of the planning stage has already been outlined.

It is also fair to say that a speaker's lack of fluency in speech may be interpreted by his audience as a lack of knowledge. Hiller (1971), in a piece of classroom research, found that a teacher's knowledge of a subject area was directly linked to the amount of vague terms used in the explanation; the more knowledgeable the teacher was in the subject the less faltering his speech pattern. Unfortunately the results could not determine whether the lack of knowledge itself caused difficulty in finding precise definitions or whether the lack of knowledge produced stress in the teacher which resulted in vague and halting speech. Nevertheless, the results clearly indicate that knowledge of the topic to be explained is an important prerequisite to actually delivering the explanation.

While the evidence points overwhelmingly to the need for a verbal presentation to be as fluent as possible, one area in which dysfluency might be positively encouraged is outlined by Heath (1984). He noted that when doctors, in the medical interview, explain new technical terms they tend to adopt a speech hesitation or dysfluency which may actually gain the attention of the patient. In fact, doctors often combine an 'umm' or an 'ahh' with frame-devices such as, 'what we call' or 'it's something like' thereby helping the patient to locate and attend to the conversational moments in which they introduce medical terms.

Pausing

Pausing for a moment to collect and organise thought processes before embarking on the explanation can also lead to fluency in speech patterns. Added to that, pausing can also help to increase the understanding of the recipient of the explanation. Rosenshine (1968), in a research review of those behaviours which were related to teacher effectiveness, found that those teachers who used pauses following an explanation increased pupils' knowledge by ensuring that not too much material was covered too quickly.

Further support for use of pausing when presenting lengthy explanations was provided by Brown and Bakhtar (1983) in their study of lecturing styles. One of the five most common weaknesses reported by lecturers was 'saying too much too quickly'.

Appropriate language

Any explanation must contain language which is appropriate to the intellectual capacity of the listener. Professionals inevitably use technical terms (i.e. 'jargon') when they are conversing with other professionals in their field of work. A quick scan of the papers to be presented at an annual conference of the British Psychological Society or British Medical Association will surely leave the non-specialised reader nonplussed and bewildered. Yet these same professionals, in their everyday lives, communicate with persons who do not have access to this specialised language. For example, medical terminology describes medical content precisely and, therefore, provides relevant specificity in discourse between medical professionals. However, the same medical terms may create frustration and even confusion when medical professionals converse with their patients.

Hopper *et al.* (1992), in an interesting study of naturally occurring telephone conversations between specialists of the Cancer Information Service (CIS) in Houston, Texas, and callers seeking medical information, found that the specialists were encouraged to introduce terminology into the encounters in one of four ways: (1) to give a term and (as an aside) ask about the callers' familiarity with it; (2) to give a paraphrase with the term (see Chapter 6 for further details regarding the skill of paraphrasing); (3) to observe the callers' problems with terminology used and follow with a brief explanation; and (4) to apply a term to a condition that the caller describes. As Argyle (1991) put it, 'people say things quite differently depending on whether they are speaking to an expert or a lay-person . . . and depending on what they think the other person knows already and understands' (p. 181). Thus, lawyers use far less technical legal language when examining witnesses than when sparring with other lawyers in courtrooms; garage mechanics move rapidly down the technicality scale when answering a question about a car repair posed by somone with little technical knowledge; and accountants attempt to explain tax problems in simple terms to their non-expert clients. It is therefore important that 'jargon' or 'specialised' terms be translated into everyday words so that clients are not mystified or confused in their understanding of facts and events.

Of course, it is sometimes difficult for professionals to eliminate completely all technical terms, and to do so may gravely jeopardise the clients' full understanding of issues. To illustrate this, consider a careers officer, whose job is to convey accurate job descriptions to prospective employees. Often the actual title of the job is not an adequate description of what one actually does (e.g. Appraisal Adviser, Systems Analyst, Geophysicist) and a further, more comprehensive, explanation of what is involved in the job is required before understanding comes about. Thus careers officers spend a good deal of their time translating complex job specifications into simple everyday language for young job applicants. After the candidate has had a full explanation of the job the careers officer can on future occasions refer only to the title of the job and, indeed, can cross-refer from one situation to another where jobs are comparable.

Language also reflects the culture of the people who use it. In the USA, Canada, Australia and Britain, although we all speak the English language there are very definite cultural differences in the way language is used to express ideas and opinions (Becker, 1963; Barnes *et al.*, 1971; Bernstein, 1971, 1972). Listening to the language a middle-class mother uses with her child on the one hand, and a working-class mother on the other, reveals graphically that the middle-class child is usually provided with a greater range of vocabulary than the working-class counterpart. As these children grow into adulthood so the gap tends to increase.

There is evidence from work carried out by Pendleton and Bochner (1980) that many doctors volunteer fewer explanations to lower social class patients believing that they require and understand less. It is important, therefore, for all those involved in the business of communicating valid and relevant information to be sensitive to the amount and kind of words and phrases they use with people from different social class backgrounds in order to weaken any status differences there may be between them.

Reducing vagueness

An explanation which contains a number of vague, indeterminate words and expressions is not as clear as one which employs specific information. Research by Hiller *et al.* (1969) into teachers' explanations found that 'the greater the number of words and phrases expressing haziness, qualification and ambiguity ("some", "things", "a couple", "not necessarily", "kind of") the less clear the communication' (p. 674).

Land (1984) was interested to study the effect that teacher clarity, in particular vagueness of terms, had on student achievement and perception. From a cohort of eight-four undergraduate student lessons, he found that students could accurately distinguish teacher clarity on the basis of presence or absence of vague terms. In particular, he noted that high clarity lessons were significantly related to high student ratings on achievement tests along with high student ratings of perception of clarity.

Further evidence on the incidence of vagueness in explaining was provided by Gage *et al.* (1968) and Miltz (1972), who categorised some of these inexact expressions as follows:

1 Ambiguous designation – 'type of thing', 'all of this', 'stuff'.
2 Negative intensifiers – 'was not too', 'was not hardly', 'was not quite', 'not infrequently'.
3 Approximation – 'about as much as', 'almost every', 'kind of like', 'nearly'.
4 Bluffing and recovery – 'they say that', 'and so on', 'to make a long story short', 'somehow'.
5 Indeterminate numbers – 'a couple of', 'bunch', 'some'.
6 Groups of items – 'kinds', 'aspects', 'factors', 'things'.
7 Possibility and probability – 'are not necessarily', 'sometimes', 'often', 'it could be that', 'probably'.

It is fairly obvious that all imprecise expressions cannot be totally eliminated from verbal explanations. Most people will have experienced a situation when they have groped to find the exact term and, failing to find it, have uttered a less precise, more general term. It is when these vague expressions become habitual rather than occasional that interference with clarity occurs. Ivey and Gluckstern (1976) also stressed the importance of concrete, as opposed to vague, explanations in situations where a helper is giving directions to his client. They suggested that if directions are to be effective they must be specific and clear to the client. Consider the counsellor who gives her client the direction that she wants him to relax so that she can concentrate more fully on his problems. The counsellor could give the direction, 'Just relax', yet it is so general and vague that the client does not know what to do in order to bring about a state of relaxation in himself. However, if the counsellor enlarges upon her initial statement with further concrete directions, she could say 'Relax. Sit back in your chair. Let your arms and hands go limp. Feel heavy in your chair and breathe deeply and evenly.' The client now has been given the kind of information to enable him to begin to induce relaxation.

Emphasis

Another important feature which requires consideration when attempting to explain effectively is the need to provide emphasis. By providing points of emphasis the speaker can direct the listener's attention to the most important or essential information in the presentation, while 'playing down' the inessential information. In order to allow the listener to benefit from an explanation it is important that the speaker indicates those elements which are directly relevant to the problem or topic being explained.

Emphasis can be grouped into two categories, nonverbal and verbal. In the first, nonverbal, category, the speaker uses aspects of nonverbal behaviour (such as head-nodding, finger-pointing, loudness of voice), to indicate the salient features of an explanation. The second verbal category includes those aspects of language which the presenter uses to draw attention to important detailed information.

Nonverbal emphasis

Rosenshine (1971), reviewing research into variations in teacher manner, found that a 'dynamic' presentation was more effective than a 'static' one. In particular, he noted that nonverbal emphasis (voice variation, gestures and movement) resulted in gaining pupils' attention and in addition aided their recall of lesson material. Public speakers, politicians and television presenters, all versed in the skills of oratory, use purposeful variation in their voice to alert their audiences to key issues.

As well as the voice, effective speakers also employ appropriate focused gestures and movements to underline key features of their explanations. In particular, varied movements of the eyes, head, face, fingers, hands and whole body should be used purposefully and in a focused manner to suit the information that is being stressed.

Verbal emphasis

As well as using nonverbal behaviour to accentuate the essential parts of an explanation, the speaker can employ specific verbal techniques to achieve similar results. One technique which is very potent in highlighting specific aspects and also commonly used by a range of interactors is the technique known as verbal cueing.

Verbal cueing

This occurs when an individual employs specific verbal 'markers' which precede that part of the message that is being stressed as important to note or remember. These verbal markers could be individual words such as 'first', 'second', 'third', 'important', 'finally', 'major', 'fundamental', or they could be phrases or clauses such as 'listen carefully', 'the important point to remember is', 'take time before you answer this question'. Verbal cueing plays a significant part in helping many interpersonal professionals communicate to their clients what the essential features of any explanation are. It helps to differentiate between the relevant and the irrelevant, the more important and the less important and the specific detail from the general background information. Cues are often contained within *foci* statements.

Mnemonics

Perhaps not so common as verbal cueing but in a sense equally effective in acting as an *aide-mémoire* to the listener is the use of a type of mnemonic. An example of a mnemonic might be that the key words essential to the explanation all begin with the same letter of the alphabet, therefore it is easy to recall them when needed. An education lecturer, giving a lecture on practical teaching to first-year student teachers, may use the mnemonic '3Ps' 'Planning, Performance, Perception'. This would draw students' attention to the fact that there are three basic facets involved in teaching a lesson. They must *plan* what they intend to present to pupils, they must *perform* or implement the lesson in the classroom, and they must *perceive* the results of their teaching in order to diagnose any learning difficulties that may have been experienced by individual pupils. This simple device can be effective in helping the listener to classify the information being received.

Planned repetition

A third technique to employ is that of planned repetition of selected points during the presentation. This is especially useful if a great deal of new or unfamiliar material is being explained. Pinney (1969) found that periodic revision of material by the teacher throughout a lesson was positively related to the acquisition and retention of knowledge. Thus a careers officer may use this form of emphasis when giving a fourth-year pupil information regarding the subjects needed to pursue an advanced academic course on leaving school. He would supply a few pieces of information only and follow this with a short summary which reinforces in the pupil's mind the essential information.

Ley (1988), from a research review of patient compliance with doctors' prescriptions, suggested that one major way a doctor can increase patient compliance is to repeat the important points of the instructions. However, Maguire (1985), in an attempt to identify deficiencies in key interpersonal skills for nurses, warned that overuse of repetition can be wasteful and give insufficient time to assess patients properly. Nevertheless, structured summaries occurring at various points throughout a lengthy explanation appear to be beneficial to the recipient of information. (See Chapter 7 for a fuller discussion on summarisation.)

Aids to explanation

Where possible, the speaker should plan to include some kind of aid to facilitate the efficiency of an explanation. Such aids may be simple (such as examples, sketches, diagrams, charts, booklets and maps), or more elaborate (such as film, live demonstrations, excursions or placement visits). The use of a variety of different types of audio, visual and audio-visual material in teaching contexts has been widely researched and indeed in many modern classrooms a variety of aids can be found including books, wall charts, working models, animal cages, fish tanks and television monitors. Harris (1960), in his comprehensive review of research on the use of these audio-visual materials, found that the advantages of such aids in teaching were that they supplied students with a concrete basis for conceptual thinking, created interest, made learning more permanent, developed continuity of thought, and provided a variety of learning experiences. However, in an interesting study carried out by Togo and Hood (1992) it was suggested that there may be gender differences in the assimilation of information. One hundred and fourteen students with roughly equal numbers of males and females on a management accounting course were randomly assigned to either information conveyed using a graphic format or using a text and tabular format. Results significantly showed that women who received the graphics presentation did not perform as well as their male counterparts, or as well as other women and men who received the text and tabular format. These results showed that exclusive use of graphical material should be avoided and that in mixed gender groups a combination of textual and graphical presentations of information should be provided. Further evidence of integrating text and diagrams is available from a series of experiments designed to examine the consequences of combining these two formats in an instructional package on the learning outcome of students (Chandler and Sweller, 1992). These researchers found that where mental integration between diagrams and text is essential in order to make sense of the material, then integrated formats should be adopted.

Although these results have been obtained from 'educational contexts' there is no reason to suppose that similar results would not be obtained if research were to be carried out in other situations where information and understanding were being transmitted by means of textual or verbal explanation. Very few listeners of any age can master new material without the aid of examples. However, it is important to note that although the relationship between use of appropriate aids and understanding is a positive one, indiscriminate overuse of such aids for emphasis should be avoided since they can lead to confusion and eventually inattention (Rosenshine, 1968). It is advisable, therefore, to consider very carefully whether or not the illustrative material really does what it is designed to do: that is provide concrete examples to illuminate understanding.

Verbal examples

The most simple aid to use in an explanation is the verbal example, analogy or case study. In devising examples it is advisable to use concrete everyday situations whenever possible to make the subject 'come alive' for the listener. Rosenshine (1971) claimed that explanations were more effective if the opening statement was followed by an example or examples and then followed by a related statement. Thus a concept should be introduced as follows:

$$\text{Statement} \longrightarrow \text{Examples} \longrightarrow \text{Statement}$$

Let us illustrate this by taking the case of a sociology lecturer introducing the concept of 'role' to first-year sociology undergraduates. The lecturer may start by giving the definition (statement) that role is a pattern of behaviour associated with a position in society. She could either give or ask for *examples* of the roles persons perform (e.g. the role of student, teacher, father, mother, sister, brother, friend, etc.). Since a number of these roles will be common to one or other of the students in the lecture the examples are within the students' experience. The *statement* following the examples could be, 'You will note that individuals have many roles, thus a student may simultaneously play the roles of son, brother, friend and captain of the rugby team.'

However, Brown and Armstrong (1984), in an analysis of forty-eight video-recorded and transcribed lessons, found that the rule/example/rule model was more appropriate to an interpretive type of explanation on an unfamiliar topic than for other types of explanations aiming to restructure pupils' ideas. This suggests that the pattern of examples should be related both to the type of explanation given and to the listeners' previous knowledge.

Expressiveness

Listeners will pay more attention and learn more if they are highly motivated. Unfortunately, research is less than specific about how an audience's interest may be stimulated. Studies of expressiveness (Rosenshine, 1971) show that purposeful variations in voice, gesture, manner and use of teaching aids all contribute to the interest in an explanation. Brown (1986), in less specific terms, claimed that, 'Expressiveness, which includes enthusiasm, friendliness, humour, dynamism and even charisma, have long been regarded as essential ingredients of lecturing and explaining' (p. 211). However, research by Abrami *et al.* (1982) suggests that expressiveness is more likely to affect students' judgement of the lecturer and attitude to the subject, than to produce significant increases in achievement. Perhaps, in the long term though, favourable changes in attitude to subject matter may be the basis for further interest and eventual study of the subject in hand.

Not only is effective expressive behaviour advocated in a teaching context but there is evidence to suggest it is also highly valued in a medical context. Friedman (1979), examining the nonverbal behaviour between medical practitioners and patients, noted that expressions of care and concern were related to patient satisfaction with the consultation.

Finally, Knapper (1981) has recommended the introduction of appropriate humour into an explanation, including humour at the speaker's own expense, but warns that 'too much hilarity may pre-empt learning' (p. 168). The benefits of humour in public speaking are that 'Listeners like humour; often they expect it; they are relaxed by it and it captures their attention' (Foot, 1986, p. 374).

Feedback

It cannot be assumed that an explanation has been adequately understood by the listeners. Therefore, it is essential to find out if understanding has come about as a result of the explanation. Feedback is all important. A recent research report into the effects of different types of verbal feedback has shown that completeness of feedback significantly affects the speed at which complex concepts are initially acquired (Schroth, 1992). Subjects given verbal feedback after each response, irrespective of whether the response was correct or incorrect, did better than subjects receiving feedback signals only after correct responses or subjects receiving feedback only after incorrect responses.

There are several ways to check the efficacy of an explanation. An initial, and perhaps one of the simplest forms of check, is to note the nonverbal behaviour of the listener or listeners, since this is a rich source of evidence. Experienced and successful teachers and lecturers constantly scan the faces and movements of their audience, both during and after the explanation, to detect signs of puzzlement, confusion or uninterest. Established interviewers, too, are quick to note frowns, blushes, raised eyebrows or 'blank looks' when they are covering material which may be difficult for clients to comprehend. However, since individuals vary in the amount and kind of behaviour they overtly display it is not always easy, or even possible, to deduce the efficacy of explanations by nonverbal means alone.

Another method of obtaining knowledge of comprehension is to ask a series of general questions. Shutes (1969) found that teachers who asked recall questions at the conclusion of their lessons promoted higher pupil gains of achievement than teachers who did not question. Although this can be a direct measure of comprehension, there may, however, be areas of misunderstanding within the listener's mind which specific recall questions may overlook. For example, some minor detail may be troubling an interviewee which cannot be clarified by a series of global general questions posed by the interviewer.

In order to overcome this problem, another method of obtaining feedback is to invite listeners to ask questions on any aspect of an explanation which they feel requires further clarification. This would appear to be more valid in terms of 'real' problems encountered by listeners, yet there is a real danger that they may not respond for fear of seeming slow or stupid. In many situations, therefore, it is important to continually look out for nonverbal signs of discomfort or lack of confidence in a client in an attempt to detect underlying problems of miscomprehension.

It is also possible to ask the listener to summarise the explanation. Teachers can ask their pupils to summarise the lesson, and interviewers can ask their clients to sum up what they think the interview has achieved. Although this is often an effective technique with pupils in school it can sometimes be less effective in an interview situation, especially when the interview has been initiated by the client. The client may get the impression that she is being 'tested' and may therefore be anxious about articulating her understanding of what took place during the interview. If an interviewee does fail to sum up accurately it is better that the interviewer takes the blame for failing to explain clearly. This can be achieved quite simply and effectively by stating something like, 'I'm not sure I have explained that very well, could you tell me what you gathered from the discussion'. Ivey and Authier (1978), in their interpretation of the skill of 'direction', referred to the 'check-out' as being an important dimension of effective direction-giving for counsellors, stating that,

If a direction is to be effective, the helpee must be asked explicitly or implicitly if the direction was heard. 'Could you repeat what I just said?' or 'How does that come across to you?' are ways to check out the clarity of the direction.

(p. 100)

Demonstrations

An actual demonstration is another method of aiding an explanation, particularly when the type of information being conveyed is of a practical nature – such as the explanation of how to execute a new skill or technique. It would be unimaginable to listen to a golf expert explaining the rudiments of playing a tee shot to the beginner without actually seeing him demonstrate the swing itself. In addition, manufacturers of sophisticated machines such as dish-washers, rotary-irons, washing-machines, sewing-machines and new car models, usually arrange for first-time buyers to have a demonstration of the new models by an expert. These manufacturers are fully aware that such demonstrations can enthuse prospective buyers to purchase their machines, and at the same time give them confidence to operate the machine for themselves. There is much truth in the saying: 'A picture is worth a thousand words but a demonstration is worth a thousand pictures.' Basically, the main aims of accompanying an explanation with a live demonstration are to reveal the main features of the skill, to arouse and maintain the onlooker's interest, to learn about the techniques inherent in the skill and to inspire confidence in the viewer to try it out following the demonstration. If an explanation does require a demonstration there are several points which should be borne in mind in order to achieve effective results. They can be examined under three main headings: planning, presenting and obtaining feedback.

Planning

First, before proceeding with the demonstration, it is important to check that all items of equipment needed for the demonstration are prepared and available for use. In addition, the chief steps involved in the demonstration should be listed in the sequence in which they are to be presented.

Presenting

Having devised the procedures to be used in the demonstration the next step is to present it in action. Initially, observers must be alerted to the purpose of the demonstration and what they will be expected to accomplish once the demonstration has been completed. Once the viewers are prepared for the demonstration they should be guided step by step through the action with accompanying verbal descriptions of the essential features at each stage of the demonstration (e.g. 'The first point to remember is keep your feet shoulder-width apart . . .'). In addition, the linkage between one step and the next should be clearly illustrated so that observers can see how each step fits into the overall action.

Depending upon the complexity of the demonstration, it can be worked through completely, followed by a repeat demonstration emphasising the vital features at each stage. If, however, the skill or technique being explained is more complicated, the complete action can be broken down into coherent segments which the observer can practise in parts. Whichever format is adopted will be dependent upon both the task in hand and the knowledge and experience of the observer.

Obtaining feedback

Finally, it is important to assess whether or not the demonstration has been enacted effectively. Feedback can be obtained by a number of methods:

1 by having the observer or observers repeat the demonstration;
2 by repeating the demonstration slowly but requesting the onlookers to give the appropriate directions at each stage;
3 by requesting viewers to verbalise the salient features of the demon-stration following the initial enactment.

Whichever method is used to assess the effectiveness of the demonstration will depend again upon the experience of the observers and the complexity of the task.

OVERVIEW

In summary, research has shown that, in relation to the presentation of explanation, variations in the speaker's voice, gestures and movement, verbal cueing and an assortment of audio-visual aids (ranging from a simple verbal example to a complex demonstration linked to the explanation at appropriate points) can, at a simple level, attract attention. At another level they can help to convey meaning and, finally, can serve to emphasise the salient features in order to aid the acquisition and retention of information.

This chapter has explored the nature, functions and some of the techniques of explaining in a variety of professional and social contexts. It is purported that explaining is an attempt to give understanding to others, thus going beyond the mere reporting of facts to reveal causes, reasons, justification and motives underlying the problem or event being analysed. Whilst the bulk of research into the skill of explaining has its roots in educational settings it is by no means the sole prerogative of that profession. Indeed other professions, both on a group or one-to-one basis, are also involved in providing relevant and interesting explanations for their patients or clients. For example, in recent years the role of explanations in health care settings has attracted considerable research interest (Ley, 1988; Dickson *et al.*, 1989).

Research has uncovered that well planned or structured explanations result in greater understanding, that clear, unambiguous explanations are highly valued by listeners and that summaries or feedback checks are effective in aiding retention. Remember, the success of an explanation is indicated by the degree of understanding demonstrated by the listener. This is encapsulated in the maxim 'A little remembered is better than a lot forgotten!'

Chapter 9

Listening

INTRODUCTION

In interpersonal interaction the process of listening is of crucial importance. For communication to occur between individuals, there must be both the sending (encoding) and the receiving (decoding) of signals from one person to another (see Chapter 2 for further discussion of these processes). In order to respond appropriately to others, it is necessary to pay attention to the messages which they are sending and relate future responses to these messages.

The importance of listening is increasingly being recognised. Most texts on professional interaction devote at least a chapter to this skill, and several books have been written specifically on this topic (Burley-Allen, 1982; Steil *et al.*, 1983; Wolff *et al.*, 1983; Floyd, 1985; Wolvin and Coakley, 1988; Bostrom, 1990; Borisoff and Purdy, 1991a). In Chapter 3, it was pointed out that the average person does not actually speak for long periods in each day, and indeed several studies into the percentage of time spent in different forms of communication have found listening to be the predominant activity for most people. As Smith (1986) has illustrated, on average 45 per cent of communication time is spent listening, 30 per cent speaking, 16 per cent reading and 9 per cent writing.

Paradoxically, however, the skill of listening is still largely ignored in the school curriculum, with the emphasis being upon reading, writing and, to a lesser extent, speaking. Interestingly, Wolvin and Coakley (1982) discovered that: 'As a result of the schools' slight emphasis on the development of adequate listening skills, many leading corporations are recognizing the need to provide listening training for their employees so that costly communication barriers resulting from poor listening will be minimized' (p. 12). A postal survey of 500 major US corporations was carried out by the same authors (Wolvin and Coakley, 1991). This revealed that 59 per cent of the 248 companies which responded were providing training in listening skills for their workforce and viewed this as an important dimension of staff development.

Thus the importance of effective listening has been recognised in the business sphere. However, for professionals in most fields this is also a core skill, and knowledge and expertise in listening techniques are central to success in interactions with clients and other professionals. Indeed, for those professionals who play a counselling role, 'the capacity to be a good and understanding listener is perhaps the most fundamental skill of all' (Nelson-Jones, 1988, p. 17). At the same time, as Porritt (1984), in her discussion on nurse–patient communication, pointed out: 'Most life events, including admission to hospital, do not require highly skilled counselling but do require skilled listening' (p. 80).

Nevertheless, Armstrong (1991, p. 262) in his summative analysis of what patients seek from consultations with GPs concluded: 'though it would seem that listening is a medical skill more valued than previously, this does not necessarily mean that doctors have yet learnt always to hear what patients are saying'. Likewise, in a major survey of public perceptions of community pharmacists, Hargie *et al.* (1992) reported that over a third of respondents were not satisfied with the current listening approach of pharmacists during consultations. Yet there would, in fact, seem to be positive personal health benefits to be derived from adopting a listening approach, since: 'Not only is listening a valuable skill, it is also conducive to good health. Studies have shown that when we talk our blood pressure goes up; when we listen it goes down' (Borisoff and Purdy, 1991b, p. 5).

Listening is an important skill at the earliest stage of development. The infant begins to respond to a new world by hearing and listening. The child has to learn to listen before learning to speak, learns to speak before learning to read, and learns to read before learning to write. In this sense, listening is a fundamental skill and the foundation for other communication skills. But what exactly is meant by the term 'listening'? In their analysis, Wolff *et al.* (1983, p. 6) noted that: 'The word "listen" is derived from two Anglo-Saxon words: *hylstan*, meaning hearing and *hlosnian*, meaning to wait in suspense.' However, there is a lack of consensus in the literature with regard to the exact meaning of the term. Thus some theorists regard listening as a purely auditory activity, as a process that takes place 'when a human organism receives data aurally' (Weaver, 1972, p. 5). In terms of interpersonal interaction, the emphasis here is upon 'the process by which spoken language is converted to meaning in the mind' (Lundsteen, 1971, p. 1). More specifically 'Listening is the complex, learned human process of sensing, interpreting, evaluating, storing and responding to oral messages' (Steil, 1991, p. 203).

Such definitions make an important distinction between hearing and listening, in that hearing is regarded as a physical activity while listening is a mental process. Just as we see with our eyes but read with our brains, so we hear with our ears but listen with our brains. We do not need to learn to see but we need to learn to read. Similarly, we do not have to learn how to hear, but we have to learn how to listen. In this sense, listening is not something that happens physically in the ears, but rather happens mentally between the ears!

Aural definitions of listening ignore the nonverbal cues omitted by the speaker during social interaction. Yet such cues can have an important effect on the actual meaning of the communication being conveyed (see Chapter 3). As a result, listening is often conceived as encompassing both verbal and nonverbal messages. Wolff *et al.* (1983) defined listening as the 'process of hearing and selecting, assimilating and organizing, and retaining and covertly responding to aural and nonverbal stimuli' (p. 8). This is the perspective on listening which will be emphasised in this chapter, where listening will be regarded as the process whereby one person pays careful attention to, and attempts to understand, the verbal and nonverbal signals being emitted by another.

FUNCTIONS OF LISTENING

The skill of listening serves a number of purposes in social interaction. While these functions will vary depending upon the context, the main general functions are:

1   to focus specifically upon the messages being communicated by the other person;
2   to gain a full, accurate understanding of the other person's communication;
3   to convey interest, concern and attention;
4   to encourage full, open and honest expression;
5   to develop an 'other-centred' approach during interaction.

ACTIVE AND PASSIVE LISTENING

The term 'listening' has two main meanings in social encounters. The first sense in which this term is used emphasises the *overt* nature of listening, and is referred to as 'active listening'. Active listening occurs when an individual displays certain behaviours which indicate that he is overtly paying attention to another person. The second sense of listening emphasises the cognitive process of assimilating information. This second sense of the term 'listening' does not imply anything about the overt behaviour of the individual, but rather is concerned with the *covert* aspects. An individual may be listening covertly without displaying outward signs that he is so doing, and where this occurs the individual is said to be listening passively. Passive listening, therefore, occurs when an individual assimilates information without displaying behaviours to indicate to the other person that he is doing so. In terms of social skills, it is the former meaning of the term which is utilised, namely active listening, and it is therefore important to identify those verbal and nonverbal aspects of behaviour which convey the impression of listening.

At the same time, it is recognised that the processes of feedback, perception and cognition are important in relation to the utilisation of the skill of listening. As explained in Chapter 2, these processes are central to social action, wherein the individual receives responses from others, assimilates these responses and in turn responds to others. For an individual to demonstrate that she has been listening, she will have to pay attention to the responses of others and relate her future responses to those received.

In interpersonal interaction a constant stream of feedback impinges upon the individual, both from the stimuli received from other people involved in an interaction and from the physical environment. Not all of this feedback will be consciously perceived, since there is simply too much information for the organism to cope with adequately. As a result, only a certain amount of information is perceived and the individual will usually actively select information to filter into consciousness. Thus a *selective perception filter* (see Figure 9.1) is operative within the individual, and its main function is to filter only a limited amount of information into consciousness, while some of the remainder may be stored at a subconscious level (evidence that such subconscious storage does occur can be found in the field of hypnotism, wherein information which a person is not consciously aware of may be obtained from that person when he is under hypnosis).

As Figure 9.1 illustrates, from the large number of stimuli existing in the environment, a certain amount will be presented as feedback to the

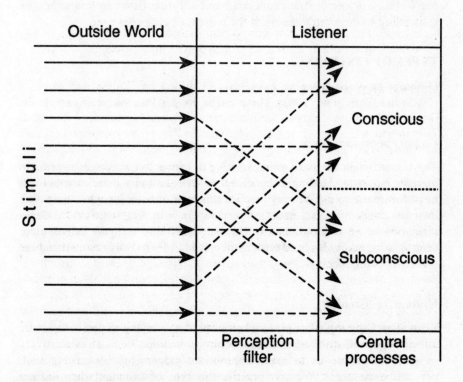

Figure 9.1 Selective perception process

individual. These stimuli are represented by the arrows on the extreme left of the diagram. A proportion of this feedback will either not be perceived at all, or will be filtered out at a very early stage. Of the remainder, a portion will be filtered into the individual's level of consciousness, while the rest will be filtered out of the conscious and stored in the subconscious.

Within the physical environment, the ticking of clocks, the hum of central-heating systems, the pressure of one's body on the chair, etc., are usually filtered into the subconscious during social encounters, if these encounters are interesting. If, however, one is bored during an encounter (e.g. sitting through a boring lecture) then these items may be consciously perceived, and the social 'noises' filtered into the subconscious! Unfortunately, in inter-personal interaction, vital information from another person may be filtered out, in that it is possible to be insensitive to the social cues emitted by others. Where this occurs, effective listening skills will not be displayed.

In social interaction, in order to listen effectively, it is necessary to be sensitive to the social cues emitted during interpersonal interaction, and to select the most relevant of these cues to focus upon. The cues received can be verbal or nonverbal, and both channels will convey vital information. By observing closely the actions and reactions of others, it is possible to improve one's ability to demonstrate concerted and accurate listening to another, by responding to the central theme of the message being conveyed.

TYPES OF LISTENING

Different types of listening have been identified by Wolvin and Coakley (1982) and Wolff *et al.* (1983). These can be divided into four main categories.

Comprehension listening

This occurs when we listen to informative or instructive messages in order to increase our understanding, enhance our experience and acquire data that will be of future use to us. We may practise this type of listening while attending lectures, conducting fact-finding interviews or watching radio or TV docu-mentaries or news programmes. The emphasis here is upon listening for central facts, main ideas and critical themes in order to fully comprehend the messages being received.

Evaluative listening

Evaluative listening takes place when a speaker is trying to persuade us, by attempting to influence our attitudes, beliefs or actions. We listen evaluatively in order to enable us to make appropriate judgements concerning such persuasive messages. We may practise this type of listening when dealing with sales people, negotiating at meetings, listening to party political speeches, watching TV adverts, or even when deciding with friends which pub to go to for the evening! In all of these instances we have to listen to the available evidence and the supporting arguments, weigh these up and evaluate them, before making a decision. The emphasis here is therefore upon listening for the central propositions being made by the speaker, and being able to determine the strengths and weaknesses of each.

Appreciative listening

We listen appreciatively when we seek out certain signals or messages in order to gain pleasure from their reception. We may listen appreciatively to relax and unwind, to enjoy ourselves, to gain inner peace, to increase emotional or cultural understanding, or to obtain spiritual satisfaction. This type of listening occurs when we play music which appeals to us, when we decide to attend a church service, when sitting in a park or walking in the country while assimilating the sounds of nature, and when we attend a public meeting in order to hear a particular speaker.

Empathic listening

Empathic listening occurs when we listen to someone who has a need to talk, and be understood by another person. Here the listener demonstrates a willingness to attend to and attempt to understand the thoughts, beliefs and feelings of the speaker. While the first three types of listening are intrinsic in that they are for the benefit of the listener, empathic listening is extrinsic in that the listener is seeking to help the speaker. This type of listening is common between close friends, spouses and in formal helping situations. As a result, many professionals will need to develop effective empathic listening skills. Depending upon the context, however, a knowledge of listening skills may be important for professionals in comprehension, evaluative and empathic situations. Indeed, many of the techniques covered in this chapter will be applicable to all three types of listening.

PROCESS OF LISTENING

As Rackham and Morgan (1977) illustrate, at first sight listening may be regarded as a simple process (Figure 9.2) in that each person takes turns to respond and listen, but in fact this perspective needs to be extended to take full account of the processes involved in listening (Figure 9.3). As we listen to others we evaluate them and what they are saying, we plan our response, rehearse this response and then execute it. While the processes of evaluation, planning and rehearsal usually occur subconsciously, they are important because they can interfere with the pure listening activity. Thus we may have decided what we are going to say before the other person has actually stopped

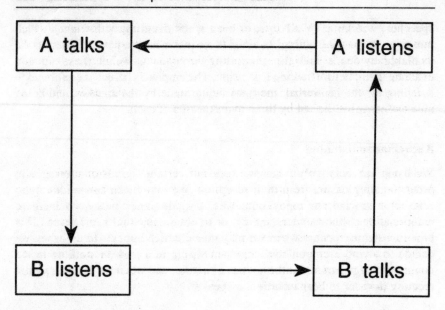

Figure 9.2 Basic model of listening

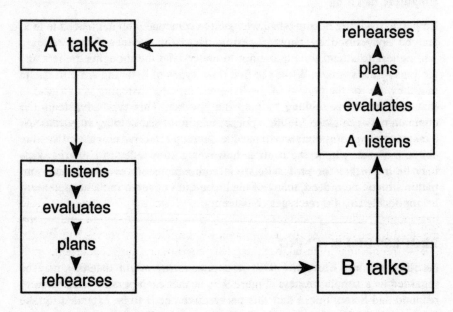

Figure 9.3 Extended model of listening

speaking, and as a result may not really be listening effectively. It is, therefore, important when listening to ensure that those activities which mediate between listening and speaking do not actually interfere with the listening process itself.

In terms of the verbal message being received, the assimilation of information is influenced by three main factors.

Reductionism

Since we can only retain a limited amount of verbal information at any particular time, if we are presented with a large amount of detail we must contract this in order to cope with it. Thus the message being received will be reduced, sometimes at the expense of vital information. For this reason it is important for the listener to attempt to ensure that the central information being conveyed is remembered. Several techniques have been put forward to facilitate the retention of information. These include: recording, note-taking, memory devices and organisation.

Recording

Obviously, where it is possible to audio-record the interaction this will provide verbatim recall. However, this is not always feasible.

Note-taking

Retention can be facilitated by noting the main points emanating from the interaction. As Bostrom (1990, p. 29) pointed out: 'Notetaking may enhance memory by enabling the receiver to transform the message so that it corresponds more closely with his or her own cognitive structure.' Such transformation involves several subprocesses, including: repetition of the core features being presented; selection and reduction of material; and adaptation or translation of the message into personally meaningful and accessible terminology. These processes involved in note-taking should enable the message to be more readily assimilated by the listener. Watson and Barker (1984) report that note-taking interchanged, rather than concurrent, with listening is more effective in terms of remembering what has been said. It is also socially more appropriate if note-taking does not dominate the interaction, but is rather something which occurs sporadically, and is explained to the speaker ('Can I just note down some details before I forget them?').

Memory devices

A range of techniques have been proposed as aids to memory. Smith (1986) highlighted a number of these mnemonics, including: the use of *acronyms*, such as PAIL for the four types of skin cuts Puncture, Abrasion, Incision, Laceration; the use of *rhymes* to remember names, such as Big Bobby Miles hardly ever smiles; and *visualisation* whereby the listener creates a mental 'picture' of what the speaker is saying – for example a counsellor may actually try to visualise a client's home environment and relationships as they are being described. While there is some research evidence to vindicate the use of these memory aids (Gregg, 1986), it would appear that their success is dependent both on the ability of the listener to use them, and upon the nature of the message being communicated.

Organising material

Material should be organised into main themes, ideas and categories, and into a chronological sequence where possible. Such organisation must not, of course, interfere with the act of listening, but where time is available during interaction (as is usually the case), then this type of 'conceptual filing' can facilitate later recall.

Rationalisation

As we listen, we assimilate information in such a way as to make it fit with our own situation and experience. If it does not fit immediately we may rationalise what we hear in order to make it more acceptable, but by so doing distort the facts. This can occur in a number of ways. First, we may attribute different causes to those presented. Thus a patient may attribute a troublesome cough to the weather, or argue that it 'runs in the family', rather than accept a doctor's explanation that it is due to heavy smoking. Second, transformation of language is a common form of rationalisation. This is often due to what Gregg (1986) referred to as *acoustic confusions*, caused by close similarity in the sounds of certain words. In the medical field products with similar-sounding names can be mixed up by doctors, nurses and pharmacists, with potentially tragic consequences (for example, in one recent case a Belgian patient died after being given the diuretic Lasix® instead of the anti-ulcer drug Losec®). Third, and perhaps paradoxically given the aforementioned reductionism, there may be the addition of material. A classical instance of this occurs in everyday gossip, whereby a basic story is enlarged and embroidered upon during each re-telling, until it eventually becomes a sensational story! Care needs to be taken in professional situations to avoid 'reading too much into' what the client has said.

Change in the order of events

This is a common occurrence in the assimilation of information, whereby data become jumbled and remembered in the wrong order. Thus 'take two tablets three times daily after meals' is remembered as 'take three tablets twice daily before meals'; or 'he lost his job and then started to drink heavily' becomes 'he started to drink heavily and then lost his job as a result'. Such mistakes can be avoided by the careful conceptual organisation of material being received.

FACETS OF LISTENING

There are four main facets which need to be taken into consideration in relation to the process of listening. These are the characteristics associated with the listener, the speaker, the message and the environment. From the available evidence, the following conclusions can be reached (for fuller reviews, see Wolff *et al.*, 1983; Wolvin and Coakley, 1988; Borisoff and Purdy, 1991a).

The listener

Several positive correlations have been found between characteristics of the listener and ability to listen effectively.

Linguistic aptitude

Those with a wider vocabulary are better listeners, since they can more readily understand and assimilate a greater range of concepts. Academic achievement has also been shown to be associated with listening ability (although as might be expected academic achievement is also usually highly correlated with linguistic aptitude).

Motivation

If the listener is highly motivated she will remember more of the information presented. Such motivation can be caused by a variety of factors, ranging from a school pupil's fear of retribution from a harsh teacher, to the desire of a caring professional to help a particular client.

Organisational ability

As mentioned earlier, the ability to organise incoming information into appropriate categories facilitates learning. Good listeners can identify the key elements of the messages received, and can store these in appropriate conceptual compartments.

Use of special concentration techniques

There are several such techniques employed by effective listeners. One of these is for the listener to attempt to put herself in the speaker's position and try to see the world through his eyes. The listener can also employ some of the memory aids mentioned previously. A final approach is the use of intrapersonal dialogue related to listening, wherein the listener covertly talks to herself to heighten receptivity. This may involve the use of covert coaching ('I'm not paying enough attention. I need to listen more carefully'), self-reinforcement ('I'm listening well and understanding what he is saying') or asking covert questions ('Why is he telling me this now?'). There is some evidence that when listening to lectures, the latter technique of self-questioning may be most effective. King (1992) carried out a study in which she found that undergraduates trained to use self-questions (asking themselves questions during the lecture such as 'What is the main idea of...?', 'How is this related to what we studied earlier...?') remembered more about the lecture content one week later than either those taught to summarise the lecture in writing or those who simply took notes.

Gender

There is now a substantial body of research to substantiate the view that females are more perceptive at recognising and interpreting nonverbal messages. Borisoff and Merrill (1991, p. 65), after reviewing the available evidence, concluded: 'Numerous studies have established women's superior abilities as both decoders and encoders of nonverbal messages when compared with men.' They suggest that part of the reason for these differences may be attributable to a status factor, in that lower status people spend more time listening to higher status people than vice versa and males may therefore conceptualise the listening role as being of lower status. One early study found that males scored higher than females on oral tests of listening comprehension (Brimer, 1971), but this must remain a tentative finding pending further investigation of this area. Much more research is required in order to chart the precise nature and extent of gender influence on listening ability.

Physical condition

Physical condition is important, in that listening ability deteriorates as fatigue increases. Thus someone who is extremely tired will not be capable of displaying prolonged listening. Professionals with a heavy case-load need to attempt to ensure that they do not have to handle their most demanding cases at the end of a tiring day.

Disposition

Introverts are usually better listeners than extroverts, since they are content to sit back and let the other person be the centre of attention. Furthermore, highly anxious individuals will not usually make good listeners, since they tend to be too worried about factors apart from the speaker to listen carefully to what is being said. Also, people who are more susceptible to distractions will not be good listeners, an extreme example being the hyperactive child.

The speaker

A number of aspects pertaining to the speaker will influence the listening process.

Speech rate

While the average rate of speech is between 125 and 175 words per minute, the average 'thought rate' at which information is cognitively processed is between 400 and 800 words per minute. The differential between speech rate and thought rate gives the listener an opportunity to assimilate, organise, retain and covertly respond to the speaker. However, this differential may also encourage the listener to fill up the spare time with other unrelated mental processes (such as daydreaming). Listening can be improved by using this spare thought time positively, by, for example, asking covert questions such as: 'What are the main points being made?', 'What reasons are being given?', 'In what frame of reference should this be viewed?', and 'What further information is necessary?'

Where a speaker drops below the 125 words per minute rate, or far exceeds 300 words per minute, listening can become much more difficult. In the former case, it becomes very difficult to listen to a very slow speaker. Professionals who have to deal with depressed clients will be aware of the problems involved in maintaining concentration with someone who says very little. At the other extreme, it can also be difficult to listen effectively to a very rapid speaker, since we cannot handle the volume of information being received. Wolff *et al.* (1983), in reviewing the literature on speech rate, however, pointed out that listeners:

> prefer to listen, can comprehend better, and are more likely to believe a message that is presented at the rate of 190 words or more per minute. . . . They demonstrate marked efficiency when listening to a speaker talking at 280 words per minute – twice the rate of normal speech.
>
> (p. 155)

Interestingly, as a result of such findings, television advertisers speeded up the rate of verbal presentation in their adverts, with positive results in terms of viewer comprehension and recall. These findings would also suggest that most professionals will have problems paying attention for lengthy periods to clients who talk at, or below, the normal rate of speech.

However, the topic of conversation and its degree of difficulty need to be taken into consideration in relation to speech rate. A slow speech rate may be appropriate with a complex issue whereas with more basic material a faster rate is usually the norm. As Dabbs (1985) observed: 'Long pauses are accepted by the participants in intellectual conversation as a normal result of trying to "figure things out", while long pauses in social conversation indicate things are not going well and will tend to be avoided' (p. 191). Similarly, in various professional settings long pauses and a slow speech rate by the client may be displayed, and will necessitate concentrated listening by the professional.

Speech delivery

The clarity, fluency and audibility of the speaker all have an influence on listening comprehension. Thus it is difficult to listen to, and comprehend, someone who speaks English with a pronounced foreign accent, or who has a strong regional dialect unfamiliar to the listener. It is also difficult to listen to someone with a severe speech stammer, or other marked speech dysfluency, both because the message being delivered is disjointed, and because the listener is preoccupied thinking about how to respond to the dysfluency. Finally, it is difficult to pay attention to an individual who speaks in a dull monotone (as most students will testify!), or who mumbles and does not have good voice projection.

Emotionality

If the speaker displays high levels of emotion, the listener may be distracted by this and cease to listen accurately to the verbal message. In situations where individuals are in extreme emotional states, their communication is inevitably highly charged with this message emotion. It is often necessary to sustain an interaction in these circumstances. Sustaining can be defined as the process whereby someone experiencing an extreme emotional state is encouraged to ventilate, talk about and understand, their emotions.

When faced with someone who is experiencing extreme emotions (e.g. of depression or aggression) it is often not advisable either to reinforce positively or to rebuke him for his behaviour, since such reactions may well be counterproductive. For example, by rebuking an individual who is displaying aggressive behaviour, it is likely that this will only serve to heighten the aggression (Owens, 1986). A more reasoned response is to react in a calm fashion, demonstrating an interest in the emotional person without overtly reinforcing him, but also showing a willingness to listen and to attempt to understand what exactly has caused the emotional state to occur.

Only when strong emotional feelings begin to decrease can a more rational discussion take place. If someone is 'too emotional about something', it is likely that he will be 'too worked up about it' to listen to reasoned arguments. When listening to an individual who is displaying high levels of emotion, it may be necessary to be prepared to wait for a considerable period of time before the emotion is ventilated. During this period the anxiety of the listener may interfere with his ability to listen carefully, and this can become a serious obstacle to effective listening. The listener may pay too much attention to the emotional message being conveyed by the speaker, and as a result may not assimilate important information of a more factual nature (Montgomery, 1981). Conversely, the listener may concentrate only on the factual content and attempt to ignore the emotional message. In both of these cases, message distortion will occur, in that the listener is not perceiving the total message being conveyed by the speaker.

Status

If the speaker is regarded as an important person, listening comprehension is increased. Thus if the speaker is a recognised authority then more credence will be attached to what she has to say. Also, more attention will be given if the speaker is in a position of superiority over the listener. Listening is therefore facilitated if the listener has admiration and respect for the speaker, and if the speaker has high credibility in terms of the topic.

The message

The nature of the message itself can influence the process of listening, in terms of the following.

Structure

If the message is unclear and lacking in any coherent structure it will be more difficult to listen to and comprehend. Quite often the speaker may be consciously or unconsciously distracting or misleading. He might not be saying anything important, could be emphasising the trivial, being deliberately vague and evasive or speaking for a long time without a break. Thus it is sometimes the goal of the speaker to confuse the listener by distorting the message being conveyed (many politicians are quite adept in this field!), or the speaker may be incapable of expressing himself clearly. In both of these cases, it is often necessary to interrupt the speaker, by asking questions in an attempt to understand what is being said.

Significance

If the message is of particular interest, or of special significance to the listener, comprehension and recall are heightened. When the message conveys similar values, attitudes or viewpoints to those held by the listener, listening is facilitated. In this sense, most people like to have their beliefs and expectations confirmed. Paradoxically, however, it has also been found that if a message contains a disconfirmation of listener expectations, listening is also heightened since presumably the listener is motivated to evaluate the unexpected message. Frick (1992) in an investigation of the concept of 'interestingness' carried out a study in an attempt to ascertain those factors which make statements interesting. It was found that people find most interesting those statements which change, or challenge confidence in, their existing beliefs. Results also suggested that statements which advance our understanding are attended to with particular interest. An example given by Frick is that: 'a clinician would find most interesting those statements by a client that further the clinician's understanding of the client' (p. 126). In similar vein, a social worker who suspects a parent of child abuse is likely to pay concerted attention to both the parent and the child when they are discussing parent–child relationships.

Complexity

The difficulty of the material being delivered by the speaker will also affect listening. As discussed in relation to speech rate, the listener can cope more effectively with basic material delivered at a fast rate, but with complex information a slower rate of speech is required in order to allow the listener time to assimilate such information fully.

The environment

The final facet of listening which needs to be considered is the environment in which the interaction is taking place. In particular, three elements of the environment are important, as follows.

Ventilation and temperature

Listening is impaired if the environment is either unpleasantly warm or cold, and optimum listening occurs when the room temperature is at a comfortable level. Likewise, ventilation is important, especially where individuals are smoking cigarettes in the room, since it has been found that such smoke adversely affects the performance of non-smokers.

Noise

Listening comprehension deteriorates when there is intrusive noise entering the room (such as a pneumatic drill outside the window). Non-intrusive background noise does not have an adverse effect on listening. Indeed most pubs, restaurants and hotel lounges will play some form of background music to encourage conversation. Thus the level of noise is important, since background noise can easily be filtered out whereas intrusive noise cannot (see Figure 9.1). However, the nature of the interaction is also important, so that a lecturer would not encourage even background noise, since she wants total concentration from students. Dentists, on the other hand, often play background music to encourage patients to relax while in the surgery.

Seating

It is important for the listener to have a comfortable chair if he has to listen for a prolonged period. Yet most schools provide hard, uncomfortable chairs for pupils and expect sustained, concerted attention from them throughout the school day! In group contexts, a compact seating arrangement is more effective than a scattered one. People pay more attention and recall more when they are brought close together physically, as opposed to when they are spread out around the room.

OBSTACLES TO EFFECTIVE LISTENING

In addition to some of the above factors, other factors which may be operative within a social encounter can militate against effective listening, and have therefore to be overcome by the listener. As Egan (1977) pointed out 'the good listener is an active listener, one truly engaged in the communication process, one who goes out of himself in search of significant cues emitted by others' (p. 229). Thus the good listener is aware of the selective nature of listening and of the following possible obstacles to effective listening.

Dichotomous listening

Dichotomous listening occurs when an individual attempts to assimilate information simultaneously from two different sources. This may occur when the listener attempts to listen to two people in a group who are speaking at the same time, when the listener attempts to conduct a telephone conversation while carrying on a face-to-face interaction with another person, or when the listener is distracted by some form of extraneous 'noise'. In all of these instances it is likely that the dichotomous nature of the listening will interfere with the ability of the listener to interact effectively, since messages may be either received inaccurately or not received at all. Effective listening is encouraged by paying attention to only one person at a time, and by manipulating the environment in order to ensure that extraneous distractions are minimised (e.g. by closing doors, switching off television or having telephone calls intercepted).

Inattentiveness

Inattentiveness is another obstacle to effective listening, where the listener for some reason may not be giving full attention to the speaker. If the listener is self-conscious, and concerned with the impression he is conveying, he is unlikely to be listening closely to others. Similarly, if the listener has an important engagement looming ahead, his preoccupation with this may militate against the present situation, whereby the listener is thinking more about how he will handle the future encounter than about what the speaker is currently saying. A parallel case occurs where the listener has had an important meeting in the recent past, and is still pondering the ramifications of this, at the expense of listening to the speaker in the present interaction. Such situations were aptly summarised by 'Neil' in the lines from the song 'Everybody's Talkin'', recorded by Nilsson:

> Everybody's talkin' at me,
> I don't hear a word they're saying,
> Only the echoes of my mind.

Individual bias

Individual bias can be an obstacle to effective listening, wherein an individual may, because of personal circumstances, distort the message being conveyed by the speaker. This can occur in a number of contexts. If the listener has a limited period of time, he may not wish to get involved in lengthy dialogue with the speaker and therefore may choose to 'hear' only the less provocative or less difficult messages. Similarly, someone who does not want to recognise difficult realities, may refuse to accept these when expressed by another – either by distorting the message or by refusing to listen to the speaker altogether (a common example where this occurs is in bereavement where the bereaved may initially not accept the fact that a person close to them is actually dead – this is referred to as the 'denial stage' of bereavement).

At another level, people may not respond accurately to questions or statements, simply because they wish to make a separate point when given the floor. One example of this is the politician who wants to ensure, at all costs, that he gets his message across, and when asked questions in public meetings frequently does not answer these questions accurately, but rather takes the opportunity to state his own point of view. These examples of individual bias are neatly encapsulated in the lyrics of the song 'The Boxer' written by Paul Simon: 'a man hears what he wants to hear and disregards the rest'.

Mental set

The mental set of the listener may be an obstacle to effective, objective listening. The listener will be affected by previous experiences, attitudes, values and feelings, and these in turn will influence the way she is mentally set in any given situation. The listener will make judgements about the speaker based on his dress and appearance, initial statements, or what was said during previous encounters. These judgements can influence the way the speaker is heard by the listener, in that his statements may be filtered and only those aspects which fit with specific expectations be perceived.

By ascribing a stereotype to the speaker (e.g. racist, communist, delinquent or hypochondriac) there is a danger that the listener will become less objective in judging what is being said. Judgements will tend to be based on who is speaking, rather than on what is being said. While it is often important to attempt to evaluate the motives and goals of the speaker, this can only be achieved by a reasoned, rational process, rather than by an irrational or emotional reaction to a particular stereotype. It is, therefore, important to listen carefully and as objectively as possible to everything that is being said, in order to be an effective listener.

Blocking

The process of blocking occurs when an individual does not wish to pursue a certain line of communication, and so various techniques are employed to end or divert the conversation. These blocking techniques are presented in Figure 9.4. On occasions, some of these techniques are quite legitimate. For example, a pharmacist would be expected to advise a patient to see the doctor immediately if a serious illness was suspected. However, it is where blocking is used negatively that it becomes a serious obstacle to effective listening.

ACTIVE LISTENING

In social interaction a number of behaviours can be employed in order to demonstrate effective listening. Although verbal responses are the main indicators of successful listening, wherein person A responds in an appropriate verbal manner to person B to indicate that he has heard B's message, there are related nonverbal behaviours associated with the skill of listening. If these nonverbal behaviours are not displayed, it is usually assumed that an individual is not paying attention, and *ipso facto* not listening to what is being said. Thus while these nonverbal behaviours are not crucial to the assimilation of verbal messages, they are expected by others. Furthermore Harrigan (1985) found that there are clear nonverbal signals emitted by listeners, in terms of changes in posture, eye gaze and gestures, which serve to signal that they wish to move from listening to speaking. It should also be recognised that the nonverbal information conveyed by the speaker can often add to, and provide emphasis for, the verbal message (see Chapter 3). An example of this was shown in a study by Strong *et al.* (1971) who asked eighty-six college students to listen only, or both view and listen, to tapes of counsellors, and

—	Rejecting involvement	'I don't wish to discuss this with you' 'That has nothing to do with me'
—	Denial of feelings	'You've nothing to worry about' 'You'll be all right'
—	Selective responding	Focusing only on specific aspects of the speaker's message, while ignoring others
—	Admitting insufficient knowledge	'I'm not really qualified to say' 'I'm only vaguely familiar with that subject'
—	Topic shift	Changing the topic away from that expressed by the speaker
—	Referring	'You should consult your doctor about that' 'Your course tutor will help you on that matter'
—	Deferring	'Come back and see me if the pain persists' 'We'll discuss that next week'
—	Pre-empting any communication	'I'm in a terrible rush. See you later' 'I can't talk now. I'm late for a meeting'

Figure 9.4 Blocking tactics to listening

rate these counsellors on a 100-item checklist. Results indicated that when the counsellors in this study were both seen and heard they were described as more cold, bored, awkward, unreasonable and uninterested, than when they were heard only. This study highlighted the importance of attending to both verbal and non-verbal information in judging social responses.

Verbal responses which are indicators of listening, have already been discussed to some extent in many of the social skills previously reviewed in this book. Within the skill of reinforcement, for example, *verbal reinforcers* are often regarded as being associated with attending and listening (see Chapter 4). In terms of listening, however, caution is needed when employing verbal reinforcement. Rosenshine (1971), for example, found that the curve of the relationship between amount of verbal reinforcement by teachers and degree of pupil participation in classroom lessons took the form of an inverted U-shape. While verbal reinforcers (e.g. 'very good', 'yes') initially had the effect of increasing pupil participation, if this reinforcement was continued in its basic form, pupils began to regard it with indifference. Rosenshine pointed out that it is simple to administer positive reinforcers without much thought, but in order to demonstrate genuine listening some reasons have to be given for the use of the reinforcers. Pupils need to be told why their responses are good, for the reinforcement to be regarded as genuine. In other words, there must be response development (see Chapter 4).

One aspect of reinforcement which is a potent indicator of effective listening is *reference to past statements* made by another person, and especially to the use of such statements in conversation. This can range from simply remembering someone's name, to remembering other details about facts, feelings or ideas they may have expressed in the past. By focusing on these aspects it is possible to convey interest in another person, by showing an ability to listen and pay attention to what they have talked about previously. This is likely to encourage the person to participate more fully in the present interaction.

Another aspect of verbal responses which is indicative of careful listening is *verbal following*. This refers to the process whereby the listener matches his verbal comments closely to the responses of the speaker, so that they 'follow-on' in a coherent fashion from what the speaker has said. If the listener follows the comments of the speaker, by asking related questions, or making related statements which use the ideas expressed by the speaker, this is usually taken as an indication of attentiveness and interest. The ability to utilise verbal following to a high degree is vital in many contexts, such as interviewing, teaching and counselling, where it is important to follow certain lines of debate, discussion or guidance with other people, and demonstrate a willingness to listen to their points of view.

Adelman *et al.* (1992), in a study of topic initiation between physicians and patients, found that the doctors raised almost two-thirds of all topics discussed, although patients raised 55 per cent of psychosocial matters and were more likely to discuss the physician–patient relationship. In this study sixty-six routine general medical visits between doctors and elderly patients (65 years and above) were audio-recorded. It was also found that doctors paid significantly more attention to topics they themselves raised as opposed to patient initiated topics. They point out that this result confirms previous research findings that 'older patients may have difficulty getting their concerns addressed by physicians' (p. 38), which in turn may discourage them from attempting to initiate further topics.

In discussing the issue of topic shifts, Crow (1983) distinguished between *coherent topic shifts* which occur once the previous topic has been exhausted, and *noncoherent topic shifts* which are abrupt changes of conversation which are not explained. As Crow pointed out, we often use *disjunct markers* to signal a change of topic ('Incidentally', 'Can I ask you a different question?' 'Before I forget'). In the early stages of a relationship, individuals usually ensure that a disjunct marker is used before making a noncoherent topic shift, whereas once a relationship has been developed the need for such disjunct markers recedes. Thus Crow found that married couples used unmarked noncoherent topic shifts during conversation without this unduly affecting their interactions.

In most professional interactions disjunct markers will be required where verbal following does not take place. However, research by Ainsworth-Vaughan (1992) suggests that there may be a gender difference in the use of topic shifts. In her study she examined the way topic transitions were made in physician–patient encounters in terms of topic shifts which were either unilateral (one person just switches topic) or reciprocal (where overt agreement is secured from both sides about the decision to move on to a new topic). She found differences between male and female doctors, in that females used many more reciprocal topic shifts than males who in turn used many more unilateral shifts. For females the ratio of reciprocal to unilateral topic shifts was 5:1, for males it was 1.4:1. She argued that this difference may be because females are more willing than males to envisage the consultation as an activity in which power is shared between doctor and patient, whereas male doctors may be more likely to perceive themselves as being the dominant partner.

Within the skill of questioning (see Chapter 5) the use of *probing questions* is a direct form of listening, wherein the questioner follows up the responses of the respondent by asking related questions. Similarly, the skill of *reflecting* (see Chapter 6) represents a powerful form of response development. In order to reflect accurately the feeling, or the content, of what someone has said, it is necessary to listen carefully before formulating a succinct reflecting statement. Reflection of feeling, therefore, demands a much higher level of listening than does minimal verbal reinforcement, and it may be for this reason that it has been found to be more effective in increasing the participation of clients in interview situations.

Zuker (1983) argued that individuals have different dominant sensory channels, in that people are either predominantly visual, auditory or kinesthetic. A visual person will use expressions such as 'I see what you mean' or 'It's all become clear to me now'; an auditory person 'It doesn't sound quite right' or 'That rings a bell'; and a kinesthetic person 'It still doesn't feel right' or 'I've got to grips with it now'. Zuker suggests that we can facilitate the listening process by *using similar language to the speaker* when providing feedback, such as 'I've got the picture now' (visual), 'I hear what you're saying' (auditory), or 'I'm in touch with you now' (kinesthetic). While it is true that good listeners adjust their use of language to accommodate the speaker, research evidence linking this to the notion of predominant sensory channels is as yet lacking.

The use of *summarisation* during periods of closure is also evidence of prolonged listening throughout an interaction sequence (see Chapter 7). By using summarisation of the main points arising from the thoughts, ideas, facts and feelings expressed by the other person during an encounter, the impression conveyed is usually one of overall attentiveness and careful listening to what has been said.

Nonverbal responses are also important during listening. As Burley-Allen (1982) pointed out 'one of the most important skills of effective listening is listening to nonverbals . . . [and] to the pitch, rate, timbre and subtle variations that the tone of voice is communicating' (p. 56). In addition, certain nonverbal behaviours on the part of the listener are usually associated with attending, while other nonverbal behaviours are associated with lack of listening. Rosenfeld and Hancks (1980) found that head-nods, forward leaning posture, visual attention and eyebrow raises were all associated with positive ratings of listening responsiveness. They also reported that the most prevalent nonverbal listening indicator is the head-nod, and the most frequent vocalisation is 'mm hmm'.

Thus several nonverbal responses are important, including:

1 *Smiles* used appropriately as indicators of willingness to follow the conversation or pleasure at what the speaker is saying.
2 *Direct eye contact*, again to indicate interest in listening to what is being said. In Western society, the listener will usually look more at the speaker than vice versa.
3 Indicating enthusiasm for the speaker's thoughts and ideas, by using appropriate *paralanguage* when responding (e.g. tone of voice, emphasis on certain words, lack of interruption of speaker).
4 Mirroring the facial *expressions* of the speaker, in order to reflect and express sympathy with the emotional message being conveyed.
5 Adopting an attentive *posture*, such as a forward or sideways lean on a chair. This is taken as a sign of listening. Similarly a sideways tilt of the head (often with the head resting on one hand), is usually taken as an indicator of listening. In many situations, 'sympathetic communication' will involve the mirroring of overall posture, as well as facial expressions, and indeed where problems arise in communication such mirroring usually ceases to occur.
6 *Nods* of the head to indicate readiness to listen to what the speaker is saying.
7 Refraining from distracting mannerisms, such as doodling with a pen, fidgeting or looking at a watch. This is also important in conveying an impression of attention and desire to listen.

While these nonverbal behaviours are usually regarded as signs of listening, there are parallel nonverbal cues which are taken as signs of inattentiveness or lack of listening. These negative behaviours are the opposite of the behaviours employed to signal positive listening. Nonverbal signs of non-listening include absence of head-nods, lack of eye contact, no smiles or appropriate facial expressions, poor use of paralanguage (e.g. flat tone of voice, interrupting the speaker, no emphasis), slouched posture and the use of distracting behaviours such as rubbing the eyes, writing or reading while the speaker is talking, or yawning. (In fact, an effective technique to induce someone to stop talking is to use these indicators of non-listening.) It should be realised, however, that these nonverbal signals can be deceiving, in that someone may not appear to be listening as judged nonverbally, while in fact they are listening closely. In this respect the only true measure of listening is in terms of verbal responses. Most teachers will have experienced the situation where a pupil appears to be inattentive and not listening, and yet when asked a question is able to give an appropriate response.

Although it is quite possible to listen to another person without overtly indicating that listening is taking place, in most social settings it is desirable not only to listen but also to demonstrate such attentiveness. Thus both the verbal and nonverbal determinants of effective active listening are of importance in social interaction. In fact, the verbal and nonverbal signs of listening are integrated in such a fashion that, in most cases, if either channel of communication signals lack of attention, this will be taken as an indication of lack of listening.

OVERVIEW

Listening is a fundamental component of interpersonal communication, since in its absence communication will either be superficial or will break down completely. It is important to realise that listening is not something that just happens, but rather is an active process in which the listener decides to pay careful attention to the speaker. As Rogers and Farson (1973) iterated, 'the listener has a very definite responsibility. He does not passively absorb the words which are spoken to him. He actively tries to grasp the facts and the feelings in what he hears' (p. 541). Listening involves focusing upon both the verbal and nonverbal messages being emitted by the speaker, while at the same time actively demonstrating both verbal and nonverbal signs of listening.

In professional contexts, the ability to listen effectively is of paramount importance. The following basic guidelines need to be borne in mind in order to ensure successful listening:

1   Get physically prepared to listen. If the interaction is taking place in your own environment, ensure that it is conducive to effective listening, by providing an appropriate physical layout of furniture, ensuring adequate

temperature and ventilation, and keeping intrusive noise and other distractions to a minimum.

2   Be mentally prepared to listen objectively. Try to remove all other thoughts from your mind, and concentrate fully on the speaker. Be aware of your own biases, avoid preconceptions and don't stereotype the speaker.

3   Use spare thought time positively. Keep your thoughts entirely on the speaker and the message being delivered, by asking covert questions, constructing mental images of what is being said, or employing other concentration techniques.

4   Avoid interrupting the speaker where possible. Develop a system of mental 'banking', where ideas you wish to pursue can be cognitively 'deposited' and 'withdrawn' later. This allows the speaker to have a continuous flow, and the fact that you can later refer back to what has been said is a potent indicator of active listening.

5   Organise the speaker's messages into appropriate categories and, where possible, into chronological order. Identify the main thrust and any supporting arguments. This process facilitates comprehension and recall of what has been said.

6   Don't overuse blocking tactics. These are often used subconsciously to prevent the speaker from controlling an interaction. On occasions blocking is a legitimate option. For example, at the end of a counselling encounter a client may raise an important issue which the counsellor does not have time to deal with, and so may use the tactic of deferring discussion until the next session. However, the overuse of such tactics is indicative of a lack of desire to listen.

7   Remember that listening is hard work. It takes energy to listen actively and demands a firm initial commitment to listen. Professionals who spend their working day listening, will testify that it is an exhausting activity, and one which requires discipline and determination.

Listening is therefore a core skill for professionals, and one that should be emphasised during training programmes. Professional educators have a particular responsibility in this respect, both to develop listening skills in trainees and to act as listening models since, as Conine (1976), in a discussion of the role of listening in physical therapy, remarked: 'In the course of their education many physical therapy students have had little experience of being listened to, a factor contributing to a lack of appreciation for listening to others' (p. 160). The same criticism could apply to a number of professions, and where this is the case it is the responsibility of educators to rectify such a state of affairs.

Likewise, it is clear that more research is required into the field of listening in general. The present state of affairs was summed up by Bostrom (1990, p. 2), who concluded that: 'In spite of the obvious importance of listening, researchers in communication have not paid as much attention to it as [to] other aspects of the process'. Hopefully, this dearth of research activity will be rectified in the next few years. Finally, in concluding this chapter, many would do well to follow one of the precepts proffered by Polonius to his son Laertes in Shakespeare's *Hamlet, Prince of Denmark*: 'Give every man thine ear, but few thy voice.'

Chapter 10

Self-disclosure

INTRODUCTION

A great deal of social interaction consists of participants making statements, or disclosures, about a wide variety of issues. These disclosures may relate either to objective statements about other people, places or events, or they may be subjective disclosures about the speaker. This latter type of disclosure is referred to as self-disclosure, whereby the speaker reveals some personal information to others.

However, there is some disagreement about the exact meaning of the term 'self-disclosure'. In discussing the problems associated with its delineation and definition, Tardy (1988, p. 323) highlighted the fact that: 'Self-disclosure has been conceptualised many different ways during the last 20 years.' Some definitions restrict the field of study to verbal disclosures only, for example: 'self-disclosure may be defined as any information about himself which Person A communicates verbally to Person B' (Cozby, 1973, p. 73). But this approach excludes the study of nonverbal self-disclosures, which can be an important channel for communicating personal information, especially about feelings and emotions. Thus Stewart (1977, p. 172) defined self-disclosure as: 'the act of verbally and non-verbally sharing with another some aspects of what makes you a person, aspects the other individual would not be likely to recognize or understand without your help.'

Other definitions highlight the importance of intentionality on the part of the discloser, such as the definition given by Worthy et al. (1969, p. 59): 'that which occurs when A knowingly communicates to B information about A which is not generally known'. A similar viewpoint has been expressed by Fisher (1984) who argued that information disclosed unintentionally, or by mistake, is a self-revelation rather than a self-disclosure. Allen (1974, p. 198) limited the scope even further by defining self-disclosure as the 'uncoerced exchange of personal information in a positive relationship', thereby excluding, for example, disclosures made under interrogation.

In this chapter, however, a wider perspective is held and self-disclosure is defined as the process whereby person A verbally and/or nonverbally communicates to person B some item of personal information which was previously unknown to B. In this sense, telling a close friend your name would not be a self-disclosure since this information would be already known, whereas telling a complete stranger your name would be a self-disclosure. Likewise, nonverbal disclosures, whether intentional or not, are included since these are the main means whereby we provide information about our emotional state (see Chapter 3). One important difference between verbal and nonverbal self-disclosure is that we have greater control over the former than the latter. For this reason, the nonverbal channel provides important information regarding the detection of deceptive communication from others (Zuckerman *et al.*, 1982).

The importance of self-disclosure, as a social skill, is usually associated with the work of Sidney Jourard (1964, 1971), who stressed the need for a high degree of openness between individuals in many contexts, and illustrated the potency of self-disclosure as a technique for encouraging deep levels of interpersonal sharing. An enormous amount of interest has been generated in the field of self-disclosure, leading to a proliferation of research studies. Several books have been devoted to this topic (e.g. Derlega and Chaikin, 1975; Weiner, 1978; Chelune, 1979; Derlega and Berg, 1987; Stricker and Fisher, 1990; Derlega *et al.*, 1993), together with numerous book chapters and journal articles.

A knowledge of the nuances of self-disclosure is important to most professionals, for two main reasons. First, it is vital for professionals to be aware of contexts in which it is appropriate for them to self-disclose to clients. Second, professionals also need to be aware of the benefits which accrue from, and the methods whereby they can encourage, full, open and honest self-disclosures from clients.

FEATURES OF SELF-DISCLOSURE

In interpersonal encounters a number of features of self-disclosure will influence the nature of the interaction that is taking place. Ivey and Authier (1978) highlighted four of the main features of self-disclosure.

First, verbal self-disclosures involve the use of the personal pronoun 'I', or some other personal self-reference pronoun such as 'my', 'mine', or 'I'm'. While these words may be implied from the context of the speaker's utterances, their presence serves to remove any ambiguity about whether or not the statement being made is a self-disclosure. For this reason, the basic reference point for all self-disclosures should be a personal pronoun. Compare, for example, the statements:

A: Selection interviews can create a great amount of stress.
B: I find selection interviews very stressful.

In statement A it is not immediately clear whether the speaker is referring to selection interviews in general or to his feelings about attending selection interviews. The use of the personal pronoun 'I' in statement B, however, serves to clarify the nature of the statement as a self-disclosure.

The use of a personal self-reference pronoun as evidence of a disclosure is often the criterion used in research investigations. Chelune (1979), however, identified three methods which are used to measure disclosure. These are: observer or recipient ratings or estimates of disclosure; self-report measures such as inventories, self-ratings or sentence completion tasks; and objective measurements of actual disclosures made during interaction. One problem here is that different research studies use different methods, which may not always be comparable. Even studies which use an 'objective' approach may not be directly comparable owing to differing definitions about what exactly constitutes a self-disclosure. While the counting of self-reference pronouns is one measurement criterion, another definition of self-disclosure used in research studies is: 'a verbal response (thought unit) which describes the subject in some way, tells something about the subject, or refers to some affect the subject experiences' (Tardy, 1988, p. 331). This definition obviously requires detailed training on the part of observers to ensure accuracy and agreement about instances of disclosure. Such differences need to be borne in mind when evaluating research findings in this field.

Second, self-disclosures can be about either facts or feelings. When two people meet for the first time, it is more likely that they will focus upon factual disclosures (name, occupation, place of residence) while keeping any feeling disclosures at a fairly superficial level ('I hate crowded parties'; 'I like rock music'). This is largely because the expression of personal feelings involves more risk and places the discloser in a more vulnerable position. At the same time, however, deep levels of disclosure may be made to a complete stranger providing we feel sure that we will never meet the person again (Chaikin and Derlega, 1974). Thus two strangers sitting beside one another on a long-haul plane journey who discover that their encounter is likely to be 'one-off' may reveal personal information and feelings, which they would not do if they were planning to meet one another on a regular basis.

Falk and Wagner (1985) found that a gradual progression from low to high levels of self-disclosure leads to better relationship development. In this way the expression of deep feeling or of high levels of factual disclosure (e.g. 'I was in prison for five years') will increase as a relationship develops. For this reason, professionals should expect clients to experience difficulties in self-disclosing at any depth at the early stage of an encounter. Even if the client has a deep-rooted need to 'tell someone', such an experience will inevitably be embarrassing, or at least awkward, where the disclosures relate to very personal details. The skilled helper will be aware of this and employ techniques which help the client to overcome such initial feelings of embarrassment.

Factual and feeling disclosures at a deeper level can be regarded as a sign of commitment to a relationship. Two people who are in love will usually expect to give and receive disclosures about their feelings – especially towards one another. They will also want to know everything about one another. In such a relationship there will be a high level of trust, just as there will be in the confession box, a doctor's surgery or a counsellor's office (areas where disclosures will also be high).

The third aspect of self-disclosure relates to the object of the statement. A self-disclosure can be about one's own personal experience, or it can be about one's personal reaction to the experiences being related by another person. Ivey and Authier contend that the latter type of reactive self-disclosure is more likely to enhance the development of interpersonal relationships. Consider the following interaction:

John: I haven't been sleeping too well recently. I work from early morning until after midnight every day, and yet nothing seems to sink in. I'm really worried about these exams. What would I do if I failed them?

Mary: You know John, I am very concerned about you. It seems to me that you are working too much, and not getting enough rest.

This is an example of a self-disclosure as a personal reaction to the experiences of another person, in which one individual is expressing concern and giving an opinion about the statements made by the other. In the example given, Mary could have chosen to give a parallel self-disclosure about her own personal experience by saying something like 'I remember when I was sitting my final exams. I was worried about them too. What I did was to make sure I stopped working in time to get out of the house and meet other people. This took my mind off the exams. . . .' In this case, while Mary is reciprocating by self-disclosing she is taking the focus away from John and on to herself. Danish *et al.* (1976), however, argued that technically the former approach is an example of *self-involving* oneself in the affairs of another person, whereas the latter is an actual instance of self-disclosure in that the speaker is providing new information about herself. Others would purport that both are examples of self-disclosure, albeit of different types (Hargie and Morrow, 1991).

Regardless of such semantic disputes, both of these types of approach are appropriate in different contexts, depending upon the nature of the interaction which is taking place and the goals of the interactors. If it is desirable to give concerted attention to an individual and encourage him to disclose fully, then concentrating upon one's reactions to the feelings or thoughts of the other person would probably be most successful. If, however, the intention is to demonstrate to someone that he is not alone in feeling as he does, then the use of a parallel self-disclosure relating one's own experience may be more effective.

Fourth, self-disclosure can be about the past ('I was born in 1950'; 'I was really grief-stricken when my father died'), the present ('I am a vegetarian';

'I am very happy'), or the future ('I hope to get promotion'; 'I want to get married and have a family'). One situation in which people are expected to self-disclose in terms of facts and feelings about the past, present and future, is in the selection interview. Candidates will be asked to talk about their previous experience or education, to say why they have applied for the job and to outline their aspirations. Not only will candidates be expected to give factual details about themselves, they will more often than not be expected to relate their attitudes and feelings towards these factual experiences. The depth of self-disclosure required will, of course, vary from one interview to another. In selection interviews at an executive level, for example, the candidate may be asked to answer a question such as 'What type of person would you say you are?'

ELEMENTS OF SELF-DISCLOSURE

Several important elements of self-disclosure have been identified by Derlega and Grzelak (1979) and these need to be taken into consideration in any evaluation of the effectiveness of self-disclosure.

Valence

This is the degree to which the disclosure is positive or negative for both the discloser and the listener. In the early stages of relationship development, disclosures will be mainly positive and negative self-disclosures will usually only emerge once a relationship has developed. This is another reason why some clients will find difficulty in disclosing negative information to an unfamiliar professional.

There is some research evidence to confirm that negative disclosures can be disadvantageous. Lazowski and Andersen (1991) carried out a study in which they had university undergraduates watch video-tapes of an individual self-disclosing to someone off-camera. They found that the use of negative disclosures (e.g. 'I felt like telling him that I practically hated him, that I disliked him more than anyone I'd met in a long time'), when compared to positive disclosures (e.g. 'I felt like telling him that he was really a pretty nice guy'), led both male and female viewers to like the male speaker significantly less and to expect to be less comfortable when interacting with him.

In another study, Miller et al. (1992) contrasted the relative effects of negative, positive and bragging disclosures. The last contained more superlatives (e.g. 'best' rather than 'good'); reference to doing better than others or having power over them; less emphasis on working hard and more on being a 'wonderful' person; and less credit given to group efforts and more to personal achievements. Examples of each of the three categories used in this study were as follows.

Positive: 'I even got the most valuable player award. Boy, was I surprised. . . . I was pleased to get the award and the recognition. I
was glad to help my team finish the season so well.'
Negative: 'I didn't play well this season. I was embarrassed. . . . I tried to
look like I was having fun but I kept thinking how lousy I played
and that I shouldn't have come.'
Bragging: 'I was the leading player all summer. Actually, I'm the best all-
round player this league has ever seen. I could have my choice to
play in any team I want next year.'

The results from this study indicated that, to be rated as competent and
successful, the use of bragging disclosures was a better strategy than negative
disclosures, whereas the latter were seen as being more socially sensitive.
However, the highest overall evaluations were given for positive disclosures
which were viewed as being both successful and socially sensitive. Thus the
optimum approach to self-disclosure would seem to be a mid-point between
being self-deprecating at one extreme and boastful at the other.

An interesting dimension of valence is highlighted by Emler (1992). In his
analysis of gossip as a phenomenon worthy of social scientific study, he
argues that: 'We self-disclose, particularly about our own doings, to modify
the gossip about us and to moderate its effects' (p. 33). In other words, we
select our disclosures carefully in an attempt to influence and guide what the
recipient in turn will then say about us to others. Thus, we are aware of the
wider implications, regarding the valence of our disclosures, beyond the
immediate encounter.

Informativeness

This relates to the amount of information being provided by the discloser.
Self-disclosures can be assessed along two dimensions, namely breadth and
depth. The relationship between these two dimensions is such that as the
depth (or intimacy) of disclosures increases, the breadth (or total number)
decreases. The Derlega and Chaikin (1975) questionnaire was designed to
measure both breadth and depth of disclosures. Examples of shallow levels
of disclosure given in this questionnaire include: 'How often my aunts and
uncles and family get together', 'Whether or not I have ever gone to a
church other than my own', and deeper levels such as 'Times that I have lied
to my girlfriend (boyfriend)', 'The kinds of things I do that I don't want
people to watch.'

In the Lazowski and Andersen (1991) study mentioned earlier, it was found
that negative disclosures were seen as more informative than positive ones.
They postulated one reason for this finding as being that, since it is less
acceptable for people to disclose negative information, such disclosures are
likely to be more heartfelt and revealing. Their study also revealed that

disclosures about thoughts and feelings were viewed as deeper and more informative than those concerned with actions and they surmise that this is because: 'it is access to otherwise hidden cognitions and affects that gives listeners the feeling that they have heard something significant about the speaker' (p. 146).

Appropriateness

This is perhaps the most crucial aspect of self-disclosure. Each disclosure needs to be evaluated in the light of the context in which it occurs. While there are no hard and fast rules about the exact appropriateness of self-disclosure in every situation, there are some general indicators. Self-disclosures are more appropriate:

1   From low status to high status individuals but not vice versa. Thus workers may disclose personal problems to their supervisors, but the reverse does not usually happen. This is because for a supervisor to disclose personal information to a subordinate would cause a 'loss of face' which would affect the status relationship. Research findings tend to suggest, however, that self-disclosures are most often employed between people of equal status (Slobin *et al.*, 1968). While some self-disclosure from the professional to a client can be very appropriate, in most contexts clients will expect only minimal disclosures from professionals. Woolfolk (1979), for example, in a study of the use of self-disclosure by teachers, found that 'intimate teacher self-disclosure was viewed negatively by adult students and that superficial self-disclosure elicited a greater response' (p. 138).
2   When the listener is not flooded with them. There would seem to be a relationship between psychological adjustment and self-disclosure in that individuals who are extremely high or low disclosers will be regarded as less socially skilled.
3   Depending upon the roles of the interactors. For example, we may disclose information to our spouses which we would not disclose to our children. Similarly, clients will often discuss a problem with a 'neutral' counsellor, that they would not wish to discuss with their spouses or with close friends.
4   Depending upon the setting. Thus we would not normally discuss bowel problems during an intimate dinner with a member of the opposite sex on a first date, but we would do so in a doctor's surgery!

Flexibility

Self-disclosure flexibility refers to the ability of an individual to vary the breadth and depth of disclosures across situations. Highly flexible disclosers are able to modify the nature and level of their self-disclosures whereas less flexible disclosers tend to disclose at the same level regardless of context. Fong *et al.* (1986) found that counsellors with high self-disclosure flexibility provided more effective counsellor responses. Furthermore, as Miller and Kenny (1986) pointed out, 'individuals who disclose across-the-board (not differentially) are not the recipients of disclosure across-the-board from others' (p. 718). They termed this the 'blabber-mouth' effect, wherein an individual reveals all kinds of information readily, as opposed to the person who discloses discreetly and will as a result tend to receive more disclosures from others.

Accessibility

This refers to the ease with which self-disclosures can be obtained from an individual. Some people will disclose freely while others will be much more reluctant to reveal personal information. This may be due to personality, for example extroverts will talk more and therefore tend to disclose more than introverts; upbringing and culture, where the child may have grown up in a context where the norm is not to disclose too much; or lack of learning about how and what to disclose during social encounters. Quite often clients will disclose a 'presenting' problem and only after they have established confidence in the professional will they reveal the real problem. This is particularly true where the problem is of an intimate or embarrassing nature.

Honesty

Self-disclosures can be true or false. As mentioned earlier, an awareness of some of the nonverbal indicators of deception is important when considering the truth of self-disclosures. Rozelle *et al.* (1986) summarised the main deception indicators as including: speech errors, tone of voice, fidgeting with objects, less time spent looking at the other person, rocking, more leg movements, self-fidgeting and frequent head movements. However, it is necessary to be aware of the normal, or 'baseline', behaviour of the individual in order to judge whether or not these nonverbal behaviours are in fact deviations from the individual's normal pattern.

FUNCTIONS OF SELF-DISCLOSURE

The goals of the discloser appear to be of paramount importance in determining the amount, content and intimacy of disclosure in different contexts (Oguchi, 1991). The skilled use of self-disclosure can therefore facilitate goal achievement both for the professional and the client. The main functions of self-disclosure by the professional are as follows.

To overcome fear

Many people have a fear of disclosing too much about their thoughts and feelings, since they feel they may not be understood or will be subjected to ridicule. Indeed in many sub-cultures self-disclosure will be actively discouraged with the child being told 'Whatever you say, say nothing' or 'Tell people only what they need to know'. This attitude then persists into later life where respect is often given to the person who 'plays his cards close to his chest'. While in a game of poker it is wise not to disclose too much, either verbally or nonverbally, the attitude of avoiding self-disclosure can cause problems for people when they may have a need to talk about personal matters. However, the initial dangers of self-disclosure are such that we expect an equal commitment to this process from people with whom we may wish to develop a relationship. For this reason, reciprocation is expected in the early stages of everyday interaction. In relation to the poker analogy it is a case of the individual wanting to see all of the cards on the table! The fear of self-disclosure can sometimes be overcome partially by a self-disclosure from the professional to the effect that she has often dealt with this type of problem, or that she feels it is quite acceptable for the client to have the problem. This form of 'reassuring' self-disclosure will usually be appreciated by clients.

To encourage reciprocation

In everyday interaction, reciprocation of self-disclosures will usually occur in that if one person is prepared to reveal personal details about herself, this usually results in the listener also revealing personal details (Tubbs and Baird, 1976). In professional situations, clients can often be encouraged to 'open up' by receiving a self-disclosure from the professional. Such a disclosure can have a very potent effect on the client, who will then be more likely to begin to self-disclose more freely. As Stricker (1990, p. 289) noted, in the field of psychotherapy: 'The self-disclosure of the therapist serves as a model for the patient and also provides information that encourages further disclosures and recognitions.'

O'Neill and O'Neill (1977) concluded that where reciprocation of self-disclosures does not occur, one of three types of situations will usually prevail.

First, the person making the disclosures is not really interested in the listener. This type of person's need is so great that he wants to tell all, without worrying about the effect this may have upon the listener. The speaker is simply using the listener as a receptacle into which he pours his disclosures. This is quite common when someone is undergoing some form of inner turmoil, and needs a friendly ear to encourage the ventilation of fears and emotions. To use another analogy, the listener becomes a 'wailing wall' for the speaker! In professional contexts this is often acceptable, as in counselling and therapy.

Second, the person who is receiving the disclosures does not care about the speaker. In this case the speaker is foolish to continue disclosing, since it is possible that the listene may use the disclosures against the speaker, either at the time of the disclosure or later.

Third, neither one cares about the disclosures of the other. In this case there is no real relationship. If one person discloses, it is a monologue; if both disclose it is a dialogue in which exchanges are superficial. A great deal of everyday, fleeting conversation falls into the latter category.

In many fields there is a need for more self-disclosure from the professional. For example, Hargie *et al.* (1993) found that self-disclosure was recognised by pharmacists as a core skill, but in their study, which involved video-recording community pharmacist–patient interactions, few pharmacist disclosures actually occurred. Likewise, Fisher and Groce (1990) analysed forty-three medical interviews and found that: 'it was a rare occurrence in our data for doctors to disclose even the obvious about themselves' (p. 233). Yet, the use of some disclosures, however shallow, would help practitioners to present a more 'human' face to patients. Self-disclosure by the professional can be advantageous in other contexts. Gallagher (1987) in her review of research into self-disclosure in counselling, presented a considerable body of research evidence to indicate that appropriate counsellor self-disclosures do encourage client disclosures.

To open conversations

When two people meet for the first time they will give and receive self-disclosures. Chaikin and Derlega (1976) identified three main stages or levels of relationship development. The first of these is *awareness* when two people have not actually interacted but are becoming aware of the presence of one another. At this stage, for example, a female may stand close to, or walk slowly past, a male whom she is interested in. The second stage is that of *surface contact*, when individuals give superficial information about themselves, and make judgements about whether or not to pursue the relationship. The final stage is *mutuality*, where the two people begin to disclose personal feelings and engage in more intimate self-disclosures. Many professionals will use self-disclosure to open interactions and establish surface contact. Thus a social worker visiting a family for the first time will usually begin by saying something like 'Hello. My name is John Whiteside. I'm a social worker from the . . .'. Such disclosures will be directly related to the job role.

To search for commonalities

At the surface contact stage of a relationship, people give self-disclosures in the hope that the other person may be able to identify with them. At this stage they search for shared interests or experiences in order to identify some common ground on which to build a conversation. This would usually occur in informal meetings between professionals and clients. It is also important in certain business contexts, such as selling, where the professional salesman may want to establish a common frame of reference with his client, in order to facilitate the development of a relationship (and the likelihood of a successful outcome in terms of sales!). On occasion, the professional may want to highlight commonalities. Thus a health visitor visiting a young mother who has just had her first child may say 'I know the problems associated with motherhood since I have three children myself', thereby establishing a common bond, and providing a good foundation for a discussion of the particular problems faced by this mother.

To express concern for the other person

This is the type of self-disclosure in which the professional expresses her feelings about the other person. Such self-disclosure can serve as a potent form of reinforcement for the client (see Chapter 4). Rackham and Carlisle (1978), however, also found that self-disclosure was a skill employed by effective negotiators. By making disclosures such as 'I am worried that we are so far apart on this', the negotiator gives an impression of openness and honest concern for the other side, which in turn is usually reciprocated.

To share experiences

In certain instances, the professional will have had similar experiences to the client, and can share these to underline the fact that there is a depth of understanding between the two. This helps to underline the fact that the professional is 'human'. For example, one situation where this can be of immense benefit is where a client has recently been bereaved, and the professional has also faced the pain of bereavement. The use of a self-disclosure here can be a valuable reassurance to the client that the pain will pass (e.g. 'I remember when my mother died I thought I would never get over it . . .'). However, obviously this approach needs to be used appropriately and should not be taken to the extreme of what Yager and Beck (1985) termed the 'We could have been twins' level!

To express one's point of view

In many contexts, such as at staff meetings, interviews, case conferences, the professional will be expected to put forward her thoughts, ideas and opinions. The ability to do so confidently and competently is therefore important.

These are the main functions of professional self-disclosure. However, self-disclosure by clients also serves a number of important functions.

To facilitate self-expression

It can become a burden not being able to tell others about personal matters, and having to keep things 'bottled up'. Self-disclosure can have a therapeutic effect, by enabling us to 'get it off our chest', which is why counselling, the confessional or discussing something with a close friend can all make us feel better (Weiner, 1978). The importance of self-expression was recognised by Shakespeare in *Macbeth* when he had Malcolm speak the following lines:

> Give sorrow words; the grief that does not speak,
> Whispers the o'er fraught heart, and bids it break.

It is interesting to note that, when people may not be able to utilise interpersonal channels for disclosure, they often use substitutes such as keeping a personal diary, talking to a pet or conversing with God. Thus most of us have a strong need to express ourselves, and professionals should be aware both of the existence of this need and of ways to allow clients to satisfy it. (This need can be observed at an early stage in young children who often disclose to a teddy bear or doll.)

There is evidence that written disclosures can also be beneficial. Greenberg and Stone (1992) carried out a study in which sixty undergraduates (36F; 24M) were requested to write about the most traumatic and upsetting experience of their lives which they had not previously discussed in any depth with other people. They were also instructed to write down their deepest thoughts and feelings relating to this traumatic event, and were assured that the written accounts would be treated in strictest confidence with each student given a code number and no names required on the accounts. It was found that students who disclosed more severe traumas reported fewer physical symptoms on a health questionnaire in the months following the study than either those who described low-severity traumas, or a control group not involved in the written exercise. Greenberg and Stone conclude that the written expression of feelings had a definite therapeutic effect and argue that on occasions this may even be superior to oral disclosures, since the recipient of interpersonal disclosures may respond inappropriately. As an example of this, they cite research evidence to show that when incest victims tell their mothers about the event, a high proportion of mothers respond by disbelieving or blaming the victim.

These findings are interesting for the process of therapy. It would appear that writing about trauma may contribute to the healing process because the written task necessitates the person having to work through the event and come to terms with thoughts and feelings about it. For this reason, in clinical contexts, victims of rape, child abuse or assault are sometimes encouraged to write down their deepest feelings about the experience as part of the process of coping with the trauma. A recent well publicised example of this process was that of the singer Eric Clapton, who disclosed that writing songs (including 'Tears in Heaven') about the tragic death of his 4-year-old son had helped him to cope with the loss.

To heighten personal knowledge

This is exemplified by the saying 'How do I know what I think until I hear what I say?' As DeVito (1986, p. 105) put it: 'while the individual is self-disclosing, she or he recognizes some facet of behaviour or some relationship that was not known before'. The value of the 'talking cure' (Levin, 1977) in therapy is a good example of how the process of allowing someone freely to express their thoughts, ideas, fears, problems, etc., actually facilitates the individual's self-awareness. The importance of self-disclosure in therapy has been aptly summarised by Stricker (1990, p. 289) as follows:

> It is through the self-disclosure of the patient to the therapist that he can begin to recognize previously hidden and unacceptable aspects of himself, to recognize the acceptability of what had been experienced as forbidden secrets, and to grow in a healthier fashion.

Thus self-disclosure can help people to understand their feelings and the reasons for them; in other words it encourages them to know themselves more fully. This view was confirmed in a study by Franzoi and Davis (1985) where it was found that individuals who had a more accurate and detailed self-understanding engaged in more self-disclosure.

To promote social comparison

People who do not have access to a good listener may not only be denied the opportunity to heighten their self-awareness, they are also denied valuable feedback as to the validity and acceptability of their inner thoughts and feelings. By discussing such inner thoughts and feelings with others, we receive feedback as to whether these are experiences which others have as well, or whether they may be less common. Furthermore, by gauging the reactions of others to our self-disclosures, we learn what types of disclosures are acceptable or unacceptable with particular people and in specific situations. On occasions it is the fear that certain types of self-disclosure may be unacceptable to family or friends which motivates an individual to seek professional help. Counsellors will be familiar with client statements such as: 'I just couldn't talk about this to my husband'; 'I really can't let my mother know my true feelings.'

To develop relationships

The appropriate use of self-disclosure is crucial to the development and maintenance of long-term relationships. People who either disclose too much, or too little, will tend to have problems in establishing and sustaining relationships with others. Even in close relationships there can be dangers with deep disclosures. The novelist Andrea Newman in a feature article about the dangers of deep disclosure in relationships concluded that:

> we're all divided to some extent between the longing to be wholly known and the need to keep something in reserve. The thing to remember is that you can always reveal more later, whereas a secret once told cannot be taken back.
>
> *(Sunday Express,* 27 December 1992)

Similarly, individuals who disclose at a deep level to relative strangers, or who make only negative disclosures, will find it difficult to make friends. By encouraging clients to self-disclose, and giving sensitive feedback, professionals can provide such clients with a valuable learning experience about how to use the skill of self-disclosure.

To ingratiate and manipulate

Some clients will use self-disclosures in an attempt to ingratiate themselves with the professional, for whatever reason. This type of client will tend to disclose quite a lot, and will say more positive things about the professional ('You are the only person who understands me'; 'I don't know what I would do without you'). In a sense, the client is 'coming on too strong', and this can be very difficult to deal with. It may be a technique used by the client to manipulate the professional for some form of personal gain. On the other hand, if this type of revelation is genuine, it can be a signal that the client is becoming over-dependent on the professional. Either way, it is advisable to be aware of this function of client self-disclosure.

An interesting instance of self-disclosure occurred in November 1992 when Queen Elizabeth declared publicly that she was glad the year was coming to an end and that it had been for her an *annus horribilis*. However, this disclosure occurred following a fire at Windsor Castle when there was a great deal of public debate about whether the Queen or the tax-payer should pay the multi-million pound bill for repairs and, indeed, whether she should not also pay income tax like all other UK citizens. At a time of recession, high unemployment and increasing house repossessions many people regarded this disclosure as self-centred, inappropriate and perhaps even ingratiating or manipulative. The Queen does not normally make personal disclosures and certainly not ones intended to evoke sympathy. It prompted one tabloid newspaper, the *Daily Star*, to retort with the headline 'What about our Annus, Ma'am?'! This example also illustrates how people of high status need to be careful about their disclosures to those of lower status.

These, then, are the main functions of self-disclosure by both the professional and the client. A number of these functions can be illustrated with reference to the Johari Window (Luft, 1970) developed by two psychologists, Joseph Luft and Harry Ingram (and named after the initial letters of both Christian names). As depicted in Figure 10.1 this indicates four dimensions of the self. There are aspects which are known both by the self and by others (A); aspects unknown by the self but known to others (B), including personal mannerisms, annoying habits and so on; aspects known by the self but not revealed to others (C), such as embarrassing personal details, thoughts or feelings; and aspects which are unknown both to the self and others (D). One of the effects of self-disclosing is that the size of segment A is increased and the size of the segments B, C and D reduced. In other words by encouraging clients to self-disclose, not only will they find out more about themselves, but the professional will also gain valuable knowledge about them, and thereby perhaps understand them more fully.

FACTORS INFLUENCING SELF-DISCLOSURE

A number of factors, pertaining to the nature of the discloser, the recipient, the relationship and the context, will influence the extent to which self-disclosure will be employed.

	Known to self	Unknown to self
Known to others	A	B
Unknown to others	C	D

Figure 10.1 The Johari Window

The discloser

The following characteristics of the discloser are related to self-disclosure.

Age

First-born children tend to disclose less than later-born children. This difference has been attributed by Dimond and Hellkamp (1969) to the possibility that later-borns are more socially skilled, because their parents have more experience of child-rearing, and they have older siblings to interact with.

Disclosure also seems to increase with age. As Archer (1979) pointed out, this finding has been reported in studies of children between the ages of 6 and 12 years, and in college students between the ages of 17 and 55 years. However, Sinha (1972), in a study of adolescent females, found that 12- to 14-year-old girls disclosed most, followed by 17- to 18-year-olds, with 15- to 16-year-olds disclosing least. Sinha argued that at this latter stage the adolescent is at a stage of transition, from girl to woman, and may need more time to 'find herself'.

In a study of 174 adolescents in the USA, Papini *et al.* (1990) found that self-disclosures about emotional matters to best friends increased from 12 to 15 years of age. They also found that at the age of 12 years adolescents preferred to emotionally disclose to parents, but by the age of 15 years they preferred to disclose to friends. It was further discovered that adolescents with high self-esteem and the esteem of peers were more likely to disclose their emotional concerns to friends, whereas those who felt 'psychosocially adrift' did not communicate such worries to friends. The adolescents in this study disclosed more about their concerns to parents who were perceived to be open to discussion, warm and caring. The above findings have obvious implications for professionals dealing with mid-adolescent individuals.

Coupland *et al.* (1991) conducted a series of studies on 'painful self-disclosure' (PSD) in interactions between women aged 70 to 87 years and women in their mid-30s. PSD refers to the revelation of intimate information on ill-health, bereavement, immobility, loneliness, etc. They found that the older women revealed more PSDs, initiated more of them and were less likely to close such disclosing sequences. Since older women will usually have experienced more painful events simply by virtue of longevity, it is perhaps not surprising that they disclose more of them than younger women. However, Coupland *et al.* suggest that PSDs can have positive effects for older women in terms of earning credit for having coped successfully with difficult life events, and speculate that such PSDs can help them to 'locate oneself in relation to past experiences, to one's own state of health, to chronological age and perhaps to projectable future decrement and death'

(p. 191). Many older people clearly enjoy, and benefit from, talking about their past and indeed reminiscence is now used as a positive method of therapy for this age group (Gibson, 1989).

Gender

Dindia and Allen (1992) conducted a meta-analysis of 205 studies involving a total of 23,702 subjects in an attempt to determine whether there were gender differences in self-disclosure. They found that women did tend to disclose more than men. In numerical terms the results of their meta-analysis indicated a 10 per cent increase in self-disclosure for females in com-parison with males. In other words, if 45 per cent of men would disclose about a particular topic some 55 per cent of women would disclose the same information.

There are several impinging variables which interact with gender to determine disclosure levels. Hill and Stull (1987) identified the following variables.

1 *Situational factors* such as the topic of disclosure, gender of recipient and relationship between discloser and recipient.
2 *Gender role identity.* This refers to how strongly a person feels male or female. It would seem that individuals, either male or female, who regard themselves as possessing female attributes will disclose more. Shaffer *et al.* (1992) ascertained that measures of sex role identity were better predictors of self-disclosure to same-sex strangers than was gender *per se* (which failed to predict willingness to disclose). Both males and females high in femininity (as measured by the Personal Attributes Questionnaire – Spence and Helmreich, 1978) self-disclosed more. Masculinity had no effect upon disclosure levels, while androgynous subjects (those high in both male and female traits) demonstrated high levels of intimacy and flexibility in their disclosures across various contexts.
3 *Gender role attitudes.* This refers to how one believes a male or female should behave. We all learn to display what we feel are the appropriate behaviours for our gender role. These will have been influenced by same-sex parent and significant others. Thus, if a male believes his role to be the solid, strong, silent type he is unlikely to be a high discloser.
4 *Gender role norms* of the culture or sub-culture. Grigsby and Weatherley (1983) found that women were significantly more intimate in their disclosures than men. It would seem that it is more acceptable in Western society for females to discuss personal problems and feelings. Males disclose more about their traits, work and personal opinions while females disclose more about their tastes, interests and relationships. Males also disclose less negative personal information than females (Naifeh and Smith, 1984). It is therefore important to be aware that males

may find difficulty in discussing personal matters, and may need more help, support and encouragement to do so.

Ethnic group

Research evidence indicates that in the USA, whites disclose more than blacks, who in turn disclose more than hispanics. Americans have been found to be more disclosing generally than similar groups in Germany, Great Britain and the Middle East. Yet Wheeless *et al.* (1986), in a study of 360 students, found no difference in disclosure levels between American students and students of non-Western cultural origin studying in the USA. However, since the latter group of students had been studying in the USA for an average of 19 months, Wheeless *et al.* suggest that they may have learned to adapt their patterns of self-disclosure to the US cultural norm.

Religion

There is little evidence regarding the effects of religious affiliation upon disclosure levels. One early study was conducted by Jourard (1961) at the University of Florida, in which he investigated differences between affiliates of the Baptist, Methodist, Catholic and Jewish faiths in relation to level of disclosures to parents and closest friends of both genders. No significant differences were found between denominations for females, although Jewish males were significantly higher disclosers than members of the other denominations, none of whom differed from one another. Jourard speculated that this difference may have been due to closer family ties in the Jewish community and therefore could have been a factor of sub-culture rather than religion *per se*.

In another American study, Long and Long (1976) found that attire (presence or absence of a habit) but not religious status (nun versus non-nun) produced significant differences in interviewee responses. Males were more open in the presence of an interviewer not in habit, whereas the opposite was true for females. Thus, religious dedication appeared to be less important than the impact of clothing whereby such dedication is usually signalled.

A similar 'identification' effect was reported by Chesner and Beaumeister (1985), in a study of disclosures by clients to counsellors who identified themselves as devout Christians or Jews compared with counsellors who did not disclose religious convictions. It was found that Jewish subjects disclosed significantly less to the counsellor who declared himself a devout Christian. Chesner and Beaumeister conclude that counsellor disclosure of religion does not facilitate client disclosure and may in fact reduce it.

In the Northern Ireland context, a study of Protestant (P) and Catholic (C) female undergraduates revealed that although C had higher overall levels of disclosure than P, as measured by the Derlega and Chaikin (1975) Inventory, the difference level was not significant (Hargie and McNeill, 1993). One interesting finding in this investigation was that there was a significant difference in disclosure levels once strength of religious affiliation was accounted for. Thus, females with a strong sense of C identity disclosed at a significantly higher level to another C female when compared with disclosure levels from C to P, P to P or P to C. More research is needed, however, in order to chart the role of religion in determining self-disclosure patterns.

Personality

Introverts disclose less than extroverts. Also those with an external locus of control (who believe their destiny is shaped by events 'outside' themselves over which they have no control) disclose less than those with an internal locus of control (who believe they can largely shape their own destiny). Anxious people also tend to disclose more. It has further been found that neurotics tend to have low self-disclosure flexibility, in that they disclose the same amount, regardless of the situation.

Another aspect of personality has been explored by Reno and Kenny (1992). They investigated the relationship between self-disclosure and level of private consciousness as measured by the Self-Consciousness Scale (Scheier and Carver, 1985), which examines awareness of the covert aspects of self, such as attitudes, moods and traits. In this study, 102 unacquainted female undergraduates were required to engage in 10-minute dyadic interactions following which they estimated their own and their partner's levels of self-disclosure. The results showed a significant correlation between the subjects' self-reported levels of disclosure and private self-consciousness. However, no such correlation was found between the partners' assessment of the individual's disclosure and her level of self-consciousness. Unfortunately, no actual counts of disclosure were obtained in this investigation. As Reno and Kenny point out, it has been argued that people high in self-consciousness are likely to be higher disclosers since they have greater self-knowledge and therefore more to disclose about themselves. Such an intuitive belief needs to be tested by future research.

Finally, there is evidence that machiavellianism may be related to disclosure. O'Connor and Simms (1990) carried out an investigation in which subjects (29M; 27F) were set the task of securing the participation of another person of the same gender in an experiment. The challenging nature of the task was underlined and subjects were encouraged to be successful in their endeavours. The results showed a significant and positive correlation between machiavellianism and disclosure for females but not for males. O'Connor and Simms concluded that 'female manipulators may use self-revelation as a means of influencing the structure and outcomes of interpersonal control attempts' (p. 98).

The recipient

A number of characteristics of the listener will influence the amount of self-disclosure received.

Acceptance/empathy

Accepting/empathic people receive more disclosures. Miller *et al.* (1983) found that certain individuals, whom they term 'openers', are able to elicit intimate disclosures from others. They found particularly that those who demonstrated *perspective-taking* ability received more self-disclosures. In other words, those who could demonstrate to the discloser that they could understand his perspective, thereby encouraged further self-disclosures to be made. Also, listeners who are accepting and supportive will receive more self-disclosures, since this acts as a form of reinforcement to the discloser. Thus Purvis *et al.* (1984) found that individuals who used appropriate visual display and speech behaviour promoted more self-disclosure from others. In particular 'the appearance of comfort, interest, enjoyment and an attentive facial expression' (p. 65) is the visual display used by high openers, who also employ brief responsive utterances ('mm hmm', 'yeah', etc.). Furthermore, Yeschke (1987) illustrated how acceptance is important in encouraging self-disclosure in the often stressful context of interrogations, giving the following advice to interrogators: 'Even if dealing with so called rag bottom, puke, scum bag type interviewees, select a positive accepting attitude' (p. 41).

Gender

From their comprehensive meta-analysis of the effects of gender on self-disclosure, Dindia and Allen (1992, p. 106) summarise the main findings as follows:

Sex differences in self-disclosure were significantly greater to female and same-sex partners than to opposite-sex or male partners. When the target had a relationship with the discloser (i.e. friend, parent, or spouse), women disclosed more than men regardless of whether self-disclosure was measured by self-report or by observation.

Thus, it would seem that females in general tend to receive more disclosures than males. However, this depends upon the context. For example, a male may prefer to discuss embarrassing personal health problems with a male, rather than a female, doctor.

Status

Generally, individuals disclose more to those of the same status than to people of higher status, and disclose least to lower status individuals (Burger and Vartabedian, 1985).

Attractiveness

The attractiveness of the listener is another important element in encouraging self-disclosures. Brundage *et al.* (1977) reported findings to suggest that individuals will disclose more to a physically attractive, as opposed to an unattractive, recipient, irrespective of the sex of discloser and recipient. Similarly, there is evidence to indicate that more disclosures are made to individuals who are liked by the discloser. Interestingly, it has also been found that we tend to like people who disclose more to us. As Taylor (1979, p. 122) put it, 'self-disclosure leads to liking and liking leads to self-disclosure'. Not surprisingly, therefore, more self-disclosures tend to be made to individuals who are perceived as being similar (in attitudes, values, beliefs, etc.) to the discloser, since such individuals will usually be better liked.

Wetzel and Wright-Buckley (1988) carried out a study in which thirty-six black undergraduate females at the University of Mississippi were told that they were participating as a control group in a study of racial difference on nonverbal behaviour in therapy. They were then requested to communicate with a white or black therapist through an intercom system without seeing this person, but they were given a photograph of either a black or white woman and told this was the therapist. All interviews were conducted by a black woman who spoke in a 'racially ambiguous dialect' and who was unaware of the real purpose of the study. It was found that race had a significant impact at high levels of disclosure but not at low levels. At high levels, the black therapist's disclosures were reciprocated but those of the white therapist were not; also, the black therapist was rated as being significantly more trustworthy. Indeed the white therapist received more disclosures when she herself used low as opposed to high levels and at the lower level she actually received more disclosures than the black therapist. Wetzel and Wright-Buckley explain these findings in terms of trust, arguing that the subjects were likely to be suspicious of a high disclosing white therapist perhaps seeing her as condescending or ingratiating. Given the artificial nature of the design of this study the results need to be treated with caution. However, they do raise the important issue of the effects of race on disclosure.

The relationship

The following features of the relationship between discloser and recipient will influence the amount of self-disclosure used.

Trust

There is a well established positive relationship between trust and self-disclosure (Steel, 1991). As the following well-known rhyme illustrates, if the discloser trusts the recipient to keep his disclosures in confidence, and not use them against him in any way, then he will use more self-disclosure; this is the reason that deep disclosures tend to be given only when a relationship has been firmly established.

> The wise old owl he sat on an oak
> The more he heard the less he spoke
> The less he spoke the more he heard
> Why can't we all be like that bird?

In certain contexts the professional can be faced with an ethical dilemma when receiving self-disclosures. For example, if a client discloses that he has committed a crime of some sort, there may be a legal requirement for the professional to inform the police, yet to do so could well destroy the relationship of trust which has been developed. How such ethical dilemmas are resolved will, of course, depend upon the particular circumstances involved.

There is some evidence to suggest that people regard trust as a relative dimension in relation to self-disclosure. Petronio and Bantz (1991) investigated the use of prior restraint phrases (PRPs) such as 'Don't tell anyone'; 'This is only between ourselves'; 'Please treat this as strictly confidential' on disclosures. Their study of 400 undergraduates revealed that: 'a substantial percentage of both disclosers and receivers of private information expect recipients to pass on that information' (p. 266). Petronio and Bantz argue that by using PRPs the discloser is engaging in 'boundary management' by attempting to *limit* the number of people the recipient will tell, but is aware that the information is likely to be revealed to one or more others. They point out that when one self-discloses information of a highly private nature there is both the possibility and temptation of betrayal by the recipient, while for the discloser there is the external danger of being discovered and the internal danger of giving oneself away. This makes such disclosures particularly fascinating elements of interpersonal encounters.

Interestingly, a gender difference emerged in the Petronio and Bantz study, in that males were more likely to expect subsequent disclosure when a PRP was not used, whereas females were more likely to expect subsequent disclosure when a PRP was used! It was also found that the five types of people most likely to receive disclosures were (in order and for both genders) best female friend; non-marital significant other; best male friend; mutual friend; and spouse. Those most unlikely to be told were strangers and the recipient's father. This latter finding is compatible with other research findings which show that fathers do not tend to receive high levels of disclosure.

Reciprocation

As Archer (1979, p. 47) pointed out, 'the most frequently demonstrated determinant of disclosure is disclosure itself'. Thus those who reciprocate with self-disclosures will receive further self-disclosures. Also, in everyday interaction if person A makes an intimate self-disclosure, this will influence the depth of disclosure reciprocated by person B. Fisher (1984) identified three main theories which have been proposed to explain this reciprocation effect.

1 *Trust/attraction.* The argument here is that when A discloses, B perceives this as conveying trust. As a result, B is likely to be more attracted to A and this increased liking will in turn lead B to disclose to A.
2 *Social exchange.* Interpersonal encounters have been conceptualised as a form of joint economic activity or social exchange in which both sides seek rewards and try to minimise costs, which may be in the form of money, services, goods, status, love or affection (Kelley and Thibaut, 1978). Thus, when A discloses, this is a form of investment in the relationship and a reciprocal return will be expected. There also tends to be a norm of equity between people which means that we do not like to feel in debt or beholden to others and so B will feel under pressure to reciprocate the initial disclosure at a similar level of intimacy in order to return the investment.
3 *Modelling.* This approach purports that, by disclosing, A is providing B with a model of appropriate and perhaps expected behaviour in that context. B then follows the model as provided and so reciprocates the disclosure.

There is no firm evidence to support one of these theories over the other two and different studies have lent support to one or other (Wetzel and Wright-Buckley, 1988; Cline, 1989). Indeed it is likely that all three explanations can partially account for reciprocation and that the relative importance of each will vary across situations.

Role relationships

In certain relationships it is the norm that one person will demonstrate most, if not all, of the disclosures made. At a selection interview the candidate will be the discloser, and in most professional contexts the client will be the main discloser.

Anticipated length and commitment

As previously indicated, an awareness of the 'one-off' nature of an interaction can encourage self-disclosure in certain situations. This was termed by Thibaut and Kelley (1959) the 'stranger-on-the-train phenomenon' and, perhaps in the light of a more recent form of transport, has been referred to as an example of 'in-flight intimacy' (DeVito, 1993). Another example of this is discussed by the journalist Byron Rogers who, in an article about hitch-hiking, described one of the car drivers who gave him a lift as having:

> talked about himself, his mileages, his mortgage (currently £650 a month), his vasectomy. . . . I had forgotten just how much people confide when no names are exchanged and they know they will never see you again. Hitch-hiking is the nearest lay equivalent to a confessional.
>
> (*Sunday Telegraph*, 15 July 1990)

This phenomenon can also apply to some professional situations. For example, a client may be reluctant to return to a counsellor, following an initial session in which deep self-disclosures may have been made to the counsellor, who is usually in effect a complete stranger. Counsellors should therefore employ appropriate closure skills in order to help overcome this problem (see Chapter 7).

Physical proximity

Johnson and Dabbs (1976) found that there was less intimate disclosure at close interpersonal distances (18 inches), and more tension felt by the discloser, than at a medium distance (36 inches). However, there is some evidence to suggest that it is males, but not females, who find close interpersonal distance a barrier to disclosure (Archer, 1979).

Gaze

Direct gaze from a stranger has been shown to decrease the intimacy of male disclosures, but to increase the intimacy of female disclosures.

Voluntary involvement

There is more self-disclosure in relationships where the client has volunteered to talk about some issue. An extreme example of the negative effects of coercion upon self-disclosure is the individual who is 'helping police with their enquiries'. However, this can also be a problem where a client has been referred to the professional and is present under some degree of duress. In such a relationship greater efforts need to be made to encourage self-disclosure.

The situation

Finally, the following aspects of the situation in which the interaction is taking place will influence the degree of self-disclosure which will occur.

Warmth

A 'warm' environment has been found to encourage more self-disclosures, in that if there are soft seats, gentle lighting, pleasant decor and potted plants in an office a client will be more likely to 'open-up' (Chaikin *et al.*, 1976). This finding is interesting, since interrogation sessions normally take place in 'cold' environments (bare walls, bright lights, etc.). Presumably, the willingness of the person to self-disclose will be an important factor in determining the type of environment for the interaction.

Privacy

Solano and Dunnam (1985) found that self-disclosure was greater in dyads than in triads, which in turn was greater than in a four-person group. They further found that this reduction applied regardless of the gender of the interactors and concluded that 'there may be a general linear decrease in self-disclosure as the size of the group increases' (p. 186).

In an experimental study, Derlega *et al.* (1973) found that when student subjects were informed that their interaction with another subject (a confederate of the experimenter) was being video-recorded for later showing to an introductory psychology class, their depth of self-disclosures stayed at a superficial level, regardless of the intimacy of disclosures of the confederate subject. However, when no mention was made of being video-taped, the level of intimacy of disclosure from the confederate subject was reciprocated by the 'true' subject. This study highlights the importance of privacy for encouraging self-disclosure.

Crisis

People are more likely to self-disclose in situations where they are undergoing some form of crisis, especially if this stress is shared by both participants. Thus patients in a hospital ward who are awaiting operations will generally disclose quite a lot to one another.

Isolation

If individuals are 'cut off' from the rest of society they tend to engage in more self-disclosure. For example, two prisoners sharing a cell will often share a great deal of personal information. Indeed, for this reason the police will sometimes place a 'stooge' in a cell along with a prisoner from whom they want some information.

These, then, are the main findings relating to the influence which the characteristics of the discloser, the recipient, the relationship and the situation have upon the extent to which self-disclosure will be employed during interpersonal interaction. From this brief review of research findings, it is obvious that self-disclosure is affected by a wide range of variables, many of which will be operative in any particular social encounter. It is important for professionals to be aware of the effects of these variables when making decisions about giving and receiving self-disclosures.

OVERVIEW

From this analysis of self-disclosure, it will be clear that this is an important skill for professionals to be aware of, from two perspectives. First, professionals need to be aware of the likely effects of any self-disclosures they may make upon the clients with whom they come into contact. Second, many professionals operate in contexts wherein it is vital that they are able to encourage clients to self-disclose freely, and so a knowledge of some of the factors which facilitate self-disclosure is very useful. Our impressions of other people can be totally wrong in many cases since we do not know what is 'going on inside them'. As Jourard (1964, p. 4) pointed out, 'Man, perhaps alone of all living forms, is capable of *being* one thing and *seeming* from his actions and talk to be something else.' The only method of attempting to overcome this problem of finding out what people are 'really like', is to encourage them to talk about themselves openly and honestly. If we cannot facilitate others to self-disclose freely, then we will never really get to know them.

When giving and receiving self-disclosures the following factors need to be considered:

- the total number of disclosures made;
- the depth of these disclosures;
- the nonverbal, as well as verbal, disclosures;
- the physical environment;
- the age, gender and personality of the interactors;
- the status and role relationships between the interactors;
- the timing of the disclosures;
- how best to respond to client disclosures.

The general importance of self-disclosure in everyday interaction reflects the fundamental value of this skill in many professional contexts. It is therefore useful to conclude with a quote from Chaikin and Derlega (1976, p. 178), which neatly encapsulates the central role which this aspect has to play:

The nature of the decisions concerning self-disclosure that a person makes will have great bearing on his life. They will help determine the number of friends he has and what they are like: they will influence whether he is regarded as emotionally stable or maladjusted by others: they will affect his happiness and the satisfaction he gets out of life. To a large extent, a person's decisions regarding the amount, the type, and the timing of his self-disclosures to others will even affect the degree of his own self-knowledge and awareness.

Chapter 11

Influencing

INTRODUCTION

Since the early 1960s a great deal has been written and said about social influence and persuasion. However, much of the literature has centred on the effects of persuasion on attitude and attitude change (Beisecker and Parson, 1972), mass media effects of social influence (Corner, 1979) and persuasive techniques in public communication – that is a one-to-many context (Miller and Burgoon, 1978). This continuing interest in matters of persuasion stems partly from its potential social significance. Those who occupy positions of power in our society have an almost abiding fascination with the diverse ways that persuasive communication can be used to ensure their continued privileged positions. Thus a great deal of research has been aimed at improving the persuasive effectiveness of messages emanating from commercial conglomerates selling anything from soap to holidays. Conversely, until relatively recently there has been a dearth of literature related to the skills and techniques inherent in interpersonal influence and persuasion settings. However, in the last ten years this situation has been reversed and a number of communication researchers have underscored the importance of persuasion and social influence to interpersonal communication (Miller *et al.* 1984; Seibold *et al.* 1985). A number of books have been written solely on the topic (e.g. Turner, 1982; O'Keefe, 1990; Reardon, 1991) together with journal articles, and book chapters (Miller, 1987; Burgoon, 1989).

This is a particularly important skill for professionals to acquire since at some point in the relationship with their clients they will be influencing them to follow a recommended course of action. Thus, a health professional may need to employ persuasion techniques in order to ensure that a recalcitrant patient employs the proposed treatment (Hargie and Morrow, 1987), or a manager, if she is to manage her workforce effectively, needs to be persuasive rather than coercive (Bies *et al.*, 1988).

To date, in this chapter, the terms social influence and persuasion have been used synonymously. Before proceeding, however, it is important to define these terms more precisely in order to avoid conceptual confusion since some textbooks treat them differently. A useful and common way to clarify a concept is to provide a definition of it since a definition encapsulates specific features to which the concept applies.

Reardon (1991) defines *persuasion* as a process of 'guiding people toward the adoption of some behavior, belief or attitude preferred by the persuader through reasoning or emotional appeals' (p. 2). Raven and Haley (1982) define *social influence* as 'a change in the cognitions, attitudes or behaviours of a person (or persons) which is attributable to the actions of another person (influencer)' (p. 427). Note that these two authors are virtually using the terms interchangeably. Thus when we say that one person persuaded another we are implying that there has been a successful attempt to influence that person. The notion of success is central to the concept of persuasion and influence. So, it is meaningless to state 'I persuaded her but failed'. One can say 'I *tried* to persuade her, but failed', but to simply say 'I persuaded her' is to imply a successful attempt to influence.

However, some authors, notably Stang and Wrightsman (1981), define social influence as 'direct or indirect effects of one person on another' (p. 47). This definition brings in the notion of intentionality on the part of the influencer. In other words, one person may influence another intentionally whilst on other occasions it may be totally unintentional. For instance, film idols and pop stars may influence teenagers to dress in a distinctive manner and adopt a particular lifestyle without ever intending this to be the outcome. This definition of social influence is broader in nature, bringing out the direct or intentional feature of the skill as well as the indirect or unintentional aim. However, from the definitions of persuasion and influence previously cited the aims of the persuader and the influencer are deliberate and intentional. For the purposes of this chapter, we will be concerned with this type of direct, intentional interpersonal influence as a social strategy, rather than with an impromptu or unwitting influence which may accrue.

Now that we have advocated the position that people can unintentionally influence but that it is impossible to unintentionally persuade it is important to look at a second characteristic of persuasion (or intentional influence), that of the existence of some criterion or goal and the presence of some intent to reach that goal. We cannot assume that the goals of the persuader and persuadee will automatically be similar or complementary. Indeed, they may be conflicting and so present a problematic situation for the persuader (for further information on goals of interaction see Chapter 2). Thus it is important to take account of the recipients' goals, motivation and commitments when implementing persuasive strategies.

As well as featuring the goal-oriented nature of persuasion, the definition also implies that persuasive effects are achieved through communication, notably though not solely through the medium of language. According to Miller (1983, p. 124) 'Persuasive (compliance-gaining) strategies constitute the symbolic inducements of persuasive messages: they are the linguistic communication communicators use to accomplish their persuasive missions'.

A knowledge of the range of compliance-gaining tactics which can be used to increase client or patient compliance is clearly of benefit and importance for professionals. Indeed, given the wealth of research evidence currently available that patients do not always comply with instructions given for taking medication (Brigham, 1986) it is fundamental that health professionals acquire this skill. However, teachers, social workers, community workers and others aiming to change, shape or reform the attitudes, values or behaviour of others should place this skill at the centre of their repertoire.

One remaining aspect of Reardon's definition of persuasion needs to be clarified: that of persuading through reasoning or emotional appeals. Literature suggests that there is a range of persuasive source variables which effect attitude change ranging from the rational (logos) to the emotional (pathos) (Cialdini, 1987). Therefore, it is at times more effective to apply rational argument and logic to ensure compliance (appealing to the cognitive aspect of attitudinal change) and at others it is more appropriate to adopt friendly, rewarding tactics (appealing to the predispositional aspect of attitudinal change). However, as advertisers know only too well, emotions can often stand in the way of reasoned arguments by distracting the persuadee. Given the complexity involved in gaining compliance, the remainder of this chapter will delineate a number of factors which should be considered when utilising influencing strategies.

ATTITUDE AND SOCIAL INFLUENCE

One of the main functions of utilising the skill of social influence or persuasion is to induce people to change their attitudes. In order to appreciate more extensively the significance of attitude change in social communication it is important to have some knowledge of its theoretical background. Psychologists have long been concerned with the concept of attitude particularly in defining it, examining its structure and coming to terms with what determines it. As early as 1935 Allport, drawing upon earlier reviews of the theoretical status of attitude defined it as:

> a mental and neural state of readiness, organised through experience, exerting a directive or dynamic influence upon the individual's response to all objects (where object is understood in a broad sense to mean persons, events, products, policies, institutions and so on) and situations with which it is revealed.
>
> (pp. 40–41)

This definition implies that attitudes represent what an individual knows about and how he feels and intends to act towards an object or situation. These three components of knowing, feeling and acting are referred to as the cognitive, affective and conative components of attitude.

The cognitive component of attitude refers to what a person knows about or how he perceives an object or situation. For example, it would be very hard to have an attitude on Chinese culture without any knowledge whatsoever of the subject. Anti-smoking campaigners, on the other hand, have capitalised on this aspect of attitude by issuing detailed medical information regarding what happens to the lungs as a result of persistent smoking.

The affective component of attitude deals with the person's feelings of liking and disliking about the object of the attitude. Some psychologists would contend that of the three components this one is more potent and at the very core of attitude formation. Referring again to the anti-smoking lobby, campaigners often have great difficulty persuading long-term smokers to 'kick' the smoking habit, despite issuing them with information regarding the harmful effects of cigarette smoking. The affective component can have more influence than the cognitive component in attitude to smoking. In addition, much research on attitude formation and attitude change, using questionnaires designed to measure the 'intensity' of attitude and the related dimension of 'extremity' of attitude are more likely to measure the affective component.

The conative component of attitude refers to what a person is likely to do as a result of a distinct attitude towards an object or situation. That is, it is the action or behavioural aspect of attitude. It would appear that this component is the most directly measurable of the three, and hence the most useful as the criterion component of attitude. However, closer examination of the research (Festinger, 1964; Larson and Sanders, 1975; Berger and Bradac, 1982) shows that it tends to be measured, as the cognitive and affective components often are, by paper and pencil questionnaires, which indicate how the person says she would behave rather than by observation of how she actually behaves. It has long been recognised by planners of social, commercial and recreation facilities that there is often a mismatch between what individuals want in the way of facilities and how they actually use them when they are provided. In the area of leisure facility provision, it is well documented that large urban recreation centres are underused by the vast majority of the population yet surveys carried out prior to building have indicated that the majority of the population have a positive attitude to recreational leisure and would welcome such provision.

Some everyday instances of influence involve a change in the mental state of the persuadee (mainly as a forerunner to an actual behavioural change). In this way, a health professional may persuade a patient to adopt a healthier lifestyle by pointing out the advantages to be gained from eating a high fibre diet and taking regular and sustained exercise. Thus, when a persuader's eventual aim is to influence what people do (e.g. buy a specific product, vote for a particular political party or take regular exercise), that aim is seen to be accomplished by changing what people think (e.g. of the product, the political candidates or the effects of exercise). That is, social influence is conceived of as changing people's perceptions rather than by somehow influencing their behaviour directly.

Of course, those who wish to influence others may not necessarily be concerned solely with attempting to change the attitudes of others. In addition, it may be the aim of the persuader to shape the attitudes of others. Thus it may be more appropriate on some occasions to develop rather than to change attitudes. Teachers, parents, community workers, doctors, dentists, all have a role in shaping children's attitudes in order that they grow up to be enlightened adults. Finally, the goals of the influencer may be to reinforce the existing attitudes of individuals. (See Chapter 4 for those techniques of reinforcement which the influencer can adopt.)

Attitudes, therefore, are the cornerstone on which influencing techniques are based – whether we want to develop, modify, radically change or even reinforce existing ones. The attitude determinant, therefore, which will be stressed throughout the remainder of this chapter will be that of social influence in particular verbal messages which contain information that induces respondents to change their attitude but also nonverbal communication (e.g. paralanguage, appearance, facial expression) designed to encourage interpersonal influence.

SOURCE FACTORS OF INFLUENCE

What are the source characteristics which people of influence have when delivering impactual persuasive messages? At present, it is thought that three main components contribute to social influence, namely power, credibility and attractiveness (Lindzey and Aronson, 1985).

Influence and power

Much of the evidence revealing power as a source of influence has emanated from research conducted into the role of leadership in particular contexts. Indeed theories of leadership often conceptualise leadership as the exercise of influence by superiors over subordinates (House and Baetz, 1979; Bass, 1984). (For further information on leadership see Chapter 13.) Six types of social power have been identified as contributing to a leader's overall effectiveness (Raven and Rubin, 1983). Since a range of professionals adopt at times a leading or influencing role in order to gain the compliance of their target audience, it would be useful to examine these power bases.

Legitimate power

Here, persons retain power because the role they occupy demands the respect of others. On the whole, in Western cultures, people have been socialised to have a high regard for authority and so revere people in high positions. Thus children are taught to acknowledge parents' and teachers' authority whilst as adults authority is associated with employers, judges, police officers and the like. Dickson *et al.* (1989) note that an authority structure operates within the health service (e.g. ward sister will have power over nurses) but that patients can have legitimate power over health practitioners, in that a doctor or para-medical will be expected to assist a patient in distress. Linked to legitimate power is the impact of authority (real and symbolic). For instance, Bickman (1974a) found that when wearing a security guard's uniform, a requester could produce more compliance with requests (e.g. to pick up sweet papers in the street, or asking a motorist to move his car) even though they were outside a security guard's remit. Con artists frequently make use of the influence inherent in authority attire (further information on the effects of appearance can be found in Chapters 3 and 7).

Expert power

While legitimate power is essentially given to a person, expert power has to be earned. Here the influencer's power is based upon the merit of what she says or does. So, accountants have 'power' over their clients in relation to tax matters, lawyers have power regarding legal implications and doctors have power when it comes to medical decisions. In other words, persons are prepared to be influenced by 'experts' in the belief that they know best about such matters. Advertisers have not been slow at exploiting this facet of influencing when the audiences are informed of the level of expertise of product manufacturers (e.g. products carrying the Royal 'By appointment' symbol; 'Tailor's Outfitters since 1879' or 'Babies are our business, our only business').

Expert power is underscored by two main elements. First, the use of titles such as Head, Doctor or Professor are enough to trigger the mechanism that governs expert influence. Cialdini (1987) claims that at times this type of power can have worrying or even devastating consequences and cites an experiment carried out by Hofling *et al.* (1966) in which 95 per cent of hospital nurses followed the commands of an individual whom they had never met, but who had claimed in a phone call to be a doctor. Second, artefacts can convey expertise such as certificates or diplomas displayed on walls, bookshelves containing seminal texts or names and credentials writ large on office doors or wall plaques.

Reward power

One powerful source of persuasion maintenance is reward. The power derives from being in a position to administer the rewards the persuadees desire. People do not comply easily on all occasions and indeed may even be sceptical regarding any adjustments or changes they may be asked to make, particularly in their working environment. Most businessmen will testify that there is something almost as powerful as gravity about the status quo. We cling to what we know even if it is not particularly beneficial for us to do so. Here is where reward comes in, since people usually need visible signs if they comply with requests to progress or change. Teachers have long recognised the need for rewarding good pupil activities by administering pats on the back, words of encouragement and approval, etc. (Wheldall and Glynn, 1989). Managers wishing to offer inducements to employees to execute new work patterns use feedback on performance, social recognition and praise for contributions (Komaki, 1982).

Of course the complexity of the reward process will be apparent from reading Chapter 4 ('Reinforcement'). Thus the influencer needs to be aware of what makes persons feel good about their changed behaviour, when and how often rewards need to be administered in order to maintain such changes. For some people, a simple remark such as 'That's a good job' is all that is needed to motivate them to greater efforts. For others, the demands may be greater such as reduced work time, longer holidays, etc.

Coercive power

This is the converse of reward power, where it is believed that some persons are in a position to administer punishments for transgressions. Coercion can involve some kind of physical force or some form of threat. Children are often coerced into behaving as their parents wish them to behave. However, while there are times when reasoning with children would not be as appropriate as removing them from a dangerous or hazardous situation, coercion as a practice in childrearing does not teach children to reason on their own. Since much childhood learning occurs by example, or modelling, parents who do not reason with children are less likely to encourage these children to reason on their own (Bandura, 1977). When parents use coercive power it may occasionally appear expedient, but in the majority of cases the result is compliance for the moment. Once coerced persons are no longer under surveillance, they are likely to revert to behaving as they prefer. Coercive influence, therefore, is less likely than reward influence to lead to long-term changes in behaviour since the persuadee has not chosen to adopt the new behaviour and thus is not committed to retaining it.

Referent power

Most people like to interact with individuals whom they admire and find attractive and this desire for acceptance induces people to give them referent power. Cialdini (1988) refers to this phenomenon as the principle of social proof or social validation which states that one important means that people use to decide what to believe in or how to act in a particular situation is to observe and examine what significant others are believing or doing. Craig and Prkachin (1978), in a series of experiments, demonstrated how the experience of pain could be affected by the principle of social proof. These researchers found that subjects who received a series of electric shocks felt less pain (as indicated by self-reports and such physiological responses as heart rate and skin conductivity) when they were in the presence of another subject who was tolerating the shocks as if they were not painful. Powerful modelling effects of others have also been found in such diverse areas as phobia remission (Bandura and Menlove, 1968), accidents (Phillips, 1980) and suicides (Phillips and Cartensen, 1986).

This principle of social validation can, in addition, be adopted to induce a person's compliance with a request by informing the person that many other individuals (either important in status or in sheer numbers) are or have been complying with it. Sales persons may attempt to use referent power to influence customers to buy the 'latest' model by making a statement such as 'This is what the well dressed person is wearing this season!' On the other hand, parents and teachers can often be powerless against advertisers who use famous people to sell to teenagers products which are expensive and transient.

Information power

John Stuart Mill, a British political thinker and philosopher who died just over a hundred years ago was reputed by some to be the last man to know everything there was to know in the world. Today such a notion would be thought absurd and even laughable since we now live in a world where most of the information which abounds is less than fifteen years old (West, 1981). Having access to that information particularly when it is not available or is denied to others is a strong basis for power over others. McCall *et al.* (1988), in an examination of leadership style within large organisations, found that some of the toughest leadership situations were those requiring subordinates to do things when they did not have to and in addition had no desire to do them. Successful chief executives were those who provided subordinates with technical and functional information and who issued reasonable and credible accounts in an attempt to gain compliance from the employees. In addition, Bies *et al.* (1988) found that the boss's sincerity in communicating a reasoned and rational account influenced the emotional responses of employees in that they showed a greater desire to adopt new work patterns.

Another variable important to this type of power is evidence; that is, proof offered by communicators to support their claim. Research indicates that statistical evidence alone, without arguments that make the message come alive, are not as persuasive as when the statistics are reported together with a description of the research from which it resulted (Petty and Cacioppo, 1984). Even greater influencing results are obtained when statistical evidence is explained in terms of audience experiences (Clark, 1984). A police officer might more readily convince a young audience of the importance of wearing helmets when riding motorcycles by explaining that 80 per cent of motorcycle fatalities involve people under 25 years of age. Health promotion experts can perhaps encourage audience members to change their diets by mentioning that one out of every two people in the room will die of heart disease unless current trends are reversed. However, Petty and Cacioppo (1981) warn that if the audience is not concerned with the topic or is unable to comprehend the message, this form of influence will not work.

Influence and credibility

Credibility refers to the inferences made by an observer concerning the believability of the speaker. It is noted, therefore, that credibility is not totally under the control of the speaker since a message may be thought highly credible by one listener and not at all credible by another. Most writers (Miller and Burgoon, 1982; Bell et al., 1984; O'Keefe, 1990) would agree that two broad dimensions make up perceived speaker credibility. These are variously labelled in the literature but generally the terms used are 'competence' and 'trustworthiness'.

When speakers attempt to influence us with their knowledge of a subject or subjects we can judge their credibility in terms of the competence dimension sometimes called expertise, authoritativeness or qualification. When it is felt a speaker's credibility is low we often say they are unqualified, uninformed or inexpert. The trustworthiness dimension of credibility usually refers to a person's integrity, honesty and fairness or whether the speaker will likely be inclined to tell the truth. Eagly and Chaiken (1984), in describing how messages may be received, referred to a 'knowledge' dimension and a 'reporting' dimension as twin aspects of influential and credible communications. However, the two aspects may not always go hand in hand. Thus we can conceive of a situation in which the speaker gives us a great deal of sound information (judged competent) but at the same time be seen to be withholding or distorting that information as they report it (untrustworthiness) and so messages are produced which are unreliable guides of credibility. On the other hand, sincere (trustworthy) but uninformed (incompetent) speakers may produce the same result, notably lacking credibility. In order to increase the credibility factor, therefore, in influential messages, speakers must give attention to both the information contained in the message and the way the message is delivered. Salespersons, when persuading customers to buy an advanced technological product, need to have all the relevant facts and information concerning the advantages to be gained from that product but at the same time be aware that the style of their verbal delivery is a potent feature of credible persuasion. In the next section four features, which tend to promote the effectiveness of credibility in persuasive communication, will be outlined.

Occupation

Judgements of a speaker's credibility both in terms of trustworthiness and expertise have been found to be significantly influenced by knowledge of the speaker's occupation and background training (Swenson *et al.*, 1984). A number of experimental studies (Hewgill and Miller, 1965; Ostermeier, 1967) have compared the effects of a highly credible source with those of a low credibility source on the listener's perceptions of a communicator's message, by varying the information given regarding the communicator's education, occupation, experience and the like. As predicted, those who are introduced to the listener as an expert or authority in the field do generally lead respondents to perceive the speaker as more trustworthy and particularly more competent than do those given low credibility introductions. Thus, a person introduced as a Professor of Nuclear Research, and recognised as a national authority on the biological effects of radioactivity, will persuade an audience of the dangers of nuclear warfare more than a university student whose arguments are based upon a term paper prepared for a Social Studies Seminar.

Evidence

Influencers very commonly include precise evidence in their persuasive explanations; the relevant facts, opinions, information and so on intended to support their claims. By citing the sources of such evidence (e.g. 'Miller *et al.*, 1992 noted that' or 'Studies by Jones, 1993. . .') as opposed to providing only vague documentation (using phrases such as 'It has been found that. . .', 'Studies show that. . .') or no documentation at all, a speaker can enhance his competence and trustworthiness. However, Reinard (1988) noted that these effects are more commonly found with communicators who are initially low or moderate in credibility than with communicators initially high in credibility, but this may reflect a ceiling effect. In other words, those already perceived as highly credible may not be able to improve others' perceptions of these qualities very much. These results suggest that a speaker's credibility can be greatly enhanced by the citation of competent and trustworthy sources of evidence; the high credibility of the cited source appears to transmit to the speaker. Further evidence of this phenomenon is provided by Cantor *et al.* (1976) who compared the influencing success of experts (medical student or nurse) and non-experts (music student or teacher) using messages concerning intra-uterine birth control devices (IUDs) and found no differences between the influencing powers of the experts *vis-à-vis* the non-experts. These authors go on to suggest that the citation of credible evidence sources by the 'non-experts' may have minimised differences in the perceived expertise of the 'experts' to the point that expertise manipulation made no difference in influence outcome. This surely must reinforce the need for professionals to keep up to date with literature sources in the field and not rely solely on personal knowledge and experience if they are to convince others of their credibility.

Message delivery

As stated earlier, the delivery of messages can influence the credibility judgements made of the speaker. One delivery characteristic, notably speech dysfluencies, which include vocalized pauses ('uh, uh' or 'um'), the super-fluous repetition of words or sounds, using incorrect words and articulation difficulties, have a significant effect upon the believability of the speaker. Those who include a number of dysfluencies in their speech are rated significantly lower on competence, with judgements of trustworthiness unaffected (Norton, 1983; Giles and Street, 1985). (Further information regarding this behaviour can be found in Chapter 8.)

Another delivery characteristic whose effect on credibility perception has been investigated is rate of speech. In an early study by Miller et al. (1977) it was noted that increasing speaking rates led to significantly greater perceived knowledgeability, intelligence and objectivity. However, more recent studies (Woodall and Burgoon, 1983; Hausknecht and Moore, 1986) have testified that effect of speaking rate on credibility is not a straight-forward correlation, since with natural speech, as speaking rate increases, there are also changes in other vocal characteristics such as pitch, intonation and fluency. Therefore, it is very difficult to attribute speaker's credibility to the cue characteristic, rate of speech. Using mechanical means, it is possible to alter rate without those other changes, although more research needs to be conducted in this area before reliable results can be produced.

Liking the speaker

There is indirect evidence indicating that the receiver's liking for a speaker can influence estimates of the speaker's trustworthiness or morals but not competence or abilities. The evidence emanates mainly from studies on attraction and influence which will be discussed more fully in the next section. Basically, factor-analytical studies of general liking have revealed high loadings on components of friendliness, pleasantness, worthiness, honesty and trustworthiness (Applbaum and Anatol, 1973; Falcione, 1974). This suggests that liking for a person is much more likely to influence one's judgements about that person's dispositional trustworthiness. Thus all professional interactors need to develop and maintain positive warm relationships with their clients in order to gain their trust, a precursor to influencing them.

Humour has been found to directly involve the enhancement of the audience's liking for the presenter, and thus the trustworthiness of the presenter since liking and trustworthiness are associated (Chang and Gruner, 1981). However, the use of humour in a presentation can also decrease the audience's liking for the presenter, particularly when the humour is perceived as excessive or inappropriate for the context (Munn and Gruner, 1981). Lecturers, politicians and other groups of public speakers must note this finding by including small amounts of relevant humour at appropriate junctures in their presentations if they wish to gain the trust of their audience. As Foot (1986) states, 'Humour is valued as a social asset and, exercised judiciously, confers upon its encoder the animated interest and welcoming approval of others' (p. 361).

Influence and attractiveness

It comes as no surprise to learn that as a general principle we tend to be influenced by those persons whom we know and like. One of the main factors which contributes to the liking bond between individuals is the 'attractiveness' factor. Thus if professionals can increase their overall atractiveness to clients, they are in a more eminent position to be liked and so enhance their overall effectiveness to gain compliance. There are several factors which contribute to a person's overall attractiveness and these will be discussed in the following section.

Physical attractiveness

Although it is widely acknowledged in our society that physically attractive individuals are at an advantage, Cialdini (1988) believes that 'We may have sorely underestimated the size and reach of that advantage' (p. 161). Chaiken (1986, p. 150), reviewing studies of attractiveness as one of the main features of persuasion, found that 'Existing research does indicate that heightened physical attractiveness generally enhances one's effectiveness as a social influence agent.'

The general point to be underscored is this: the evidence is clear that good-looking people can be a powerful source of influence in our society. Therefore, it is hardly any wonder that sales training programmes include grooming classes, shop assistants are expected to dress well and fashionably and that con men are usually handsome and con women pretty. De Bono (1992) set up an interesting experiment in which participants observed a perfume advertisement in which either a physically attractive or relatively unattractive spokesperson promoted a new perfume using relatively strong or weak arguments. As expected, those participants who sampled and subsequently purchased the perfume were influenced more by the spokesperson's attractiveness than by the strength of the arguments.

What accounts for the observed effects of physical attractiveness on persuasive success? A plausible starting point for an explanation is that a communicator's physical attractiveness influences the listener's liking for the communicator, which in turn influences persuasive success (Berscheid and Walster, 1974; Chaiken, 1986). One recent study corroborates this supposition. Wright et al. (1992) conducted an experiment in which female undergraduates were asked to rate the relative attractiveness of two males after being variously influenced by the experimenter in terms of putting 'no pressure' on an individual (simply left the room) to complete the ratings to 'high pressure' (experimenter said 'I don't see that there is any choice but to choose A' and left the room). Results showed that high pressure subjects made rating judgements contrary to the experimenter's not because of reactance but rather because they wished to dissociate themselves from an individual they deemed unfriendly and did not like.

The second noteworthy point which needs to be made regarding physical attractiveness is what social psychologists call the 'halo effect'. A halo effect occurs when one positive characteristic of a person dominates the way that person is perceived by others. There is ample evidence to suggest that physical attractiveness is one such characteristic (Efran and Patterson, 1976; Adams, 1977). When a person is perceived as being attractive there are many other attributes which are automatically assigned to that person such as friendly, competent, trustworthy, talented, sensitive, sociable and altruistic. Thus research results confirm that attractive people are more likely to obtain help when needed (Benson et al., 1976), be persuasive in changing the opinion of others (Chaiken, 1979), receive lighter jail sentences (Solomon and Schopler, 1978), influence clients to disclose major problems in their lives (Vargas and Borkowski, 1982) and obtain higher ratings on teaching performance (Hore, 1971).

Similarity

While it has previously been shown that physical attractiveness has obvious implications for professionals who are invariably expecting their clients to accept and carry out their professional advice, it has also been found that people are more influenced by those whose clothing, attitudes, tastes and beliefs are similar to their own (Hensley, 1981). Indeed the notion that, aside from appearance, similar attitudes and personalities are instrumental in making us attracted and attractive to other people, has been persuasively argued by Byrne (1971) and other psychologists, notably Clore (1977). There is ample evidence in the literature to substantiate this claim. Byrne (1971) found that bank managers were persuaded to give bigger loans to people with similar attitudes to themselves and Tajfel (1981) noted that we are more likely to come to the assistance of those who are similarly dressed to ourselves. It is invariably the method used by dating agencies who match partners according to similar attitudes, values and beliefs. In addition, car salespeople are trained to look for evidence of backgrounds and interests similar to their own when negotiating a sale. If there are golf clubs in a customer's trade-in vehicle they might remark that they hope the weather will remain fine until the weekend when they have a scheduled golf tournament. Thus perhaps we should exercise caution when dealing with similar negotiators since the degree to which similarity affects our liking for one another is, according to Gonzales *et al.* (1983), extremely powerful.

While these results show that similarity can be a potent feature of influencing, Lea and Duck (1982) have added to our knowledge by suggesting that uncommon similarity or similarity on attitudes that are not regarded as widely held generally is particularly influential. This is perhaps the basis for the powerful influence cult groups have initially in recruiting new members to their sect.

Familiarity

It is worth pointing out that, in addition to physical attractiveness and similarity of attitudes and values, an individual becoming familiar to us over time will have a strong effect upon our liking for that person which in turn can facilitate the effects of influencing. Thus a teacher who has been regarded by a generation of pupils as warm, caring and good at her job may compensate for her less than glamorous appearance.

Duck (1986) postulates that long-term attraction may depend more upon the selection and communication of information about ourselves so that we can create a relationship which will endure. Thus a range of social skills such as the use of self-disclosures and overt listening behaviours to denote interest; head-nodding and paralanguage to encourage others; the correct postural and gestural cues to denote warmth and empathy and smiling and touch to show support and praise can be regarded as the sources of ongoing attraction towards others as the relationship develops. We can be greatly influenced, therefore, by those we most commonly come into contact with. Professionals, taking note of this point, ought to be concerned with the need to develop, maintain and extend relationships with clients if they wish to have an influence on them.

Scarcity

Scarcity is a potent weapon of influence since objects, services or opportunities which become more scarce are perceived as more valuable. Why should this be so? There are two principal reasons why scarcity increases attractiveness. The first, according to Brehm and Brehm (1981) is that when opportunities become less available to us we lose freedom and largely we hate to lose those freedoms we already have. Psychologists have termed this phenomenon *reactance theory*. Thus when we deem that an object or opportunity is about to become rare we will react against this state of affairs by having a greater desire to possess the item than we did previously. In other words, our loss of free access to an item increases the drive to have it. A number of tactics can be employed to heighten the scarcity value of an item or service, such as the rare value tactic (e.g. ancient art treasures); the limited number tactic (e.g. limited editions of books and prints); and the time limit tactic (e.g. an offer ends on a particular day).

The second reason why scarcity increases attractiveness, according to Worchel *et al.* (1975), is that what is less available is more valuable. Thus, when we are told of an item's exclusivity it becomes more appealing for us to purchase it. Or when we are told, for example, that the information we are about to receive is confidential or rather secret in nature, the message itself assumes increased importance. A range of professionals can and do use the scarcity principle to encourage and influence their clients to follow a certain course of action.

Praise

Reinforcers such as praise, encouragement, support and admiration can, if used appropriately, be instrumental in the process of persuasion. Thus, for example, a doctor who has, during the previous four weeks, been attempting to wean a patient off sleeping pills and finds since the last visit that she has drastically reduced her weekly intake may respond 'Well done, Mrs White, you are doing really well.' By dint of praising Mrs White, the doctor is attempting to influence her to keep on with her efforts in order to eliminate her dependence on the sleeping draught. This technique can be employed by a range of professionals in education, health care, social and public services, and management settings (Miller *et al.*, 1992).

However, the reinforcing effects of influencing are not straightforward, neither are they guaranteed. The reader is encouraged to turn to Chapter 4, where the complex nature of praise is discussed more fully. Before leaving this section, though, it is important to take note of the claim by Byrne *et al.* (1974) that we tend, as a rule, to believe praise and to like those who provide it, often when it is probably untrue. Drachman *et al.* (1978) conducted a series of experiments in which a group of men received comments about themselves from another person who needed a favour from them. One-third of the group received only positive comments, one-third got negative comments and one-third got a mixture of positive and negative comments. The research showed that the evaluator who provided positive comments (praise) was liked best even though the men fully realised that the evaluator stood to gain from their liking of him. However, more worrying was the fact that praise did not have to be accurate to work. Praise comments produced just as much liking for the evaluator when they were untrue as when they were true. Flattery is a potent force.

Reciprocation

The decision to comply with another's request is frequently influenced by the reciprocity rule which is to *give* something before *asking* for something in return. In other words, as Cialdini (1987, p. 172) states 'One should be more willing to comply with a request to the extent that the compliance constitutes a reciprocation of behavior.'

The business world has been more than ready and willing to embrace this principle by, for example, sending free gifts or samples through the post, or allowing customers to try and test new products in order to persuade future customers to purchase them. Charity organisations, too, have successfully employed the reciprocation tactic by perhaps sending targeted persons a package of Christmas cards or calendars. Those who receive the charity cards feel obligated to keep the cards and send the appropriate recompense in return. So powerful is this sense of obligation engendered by the need to reciprocate that it pervades our everyday behaviour. If we are invited to a dinner party, we feel under pressure to invite our hosts to one of ours; if someone gives us a gift, we need to return it in kind; if someone offers to buy us a drink, we need to return the offer, and so on. Professionals also can employ the strategy of reciprocation by reminding clients of the work and effort they have put in on their behalf, before requesting compliance to a prescribed course of action.

One variation of the reciprocation principle is known as reciprocation of concessions, or door-in-the-face technique. By starting with an extreme request which is almost certain to be rejected at the outset, a requester can then profitably retreat to a second smaller request (the one that was intended) which is more than likely to be accepted since it seems to be a concession. Cialdini and Ascani (1976) used this technique to recruit blood donors. When a request for a person's long-term commitment to a blood-donor programme was refused, a smaller request for a one-time donation was made. This pattern of a large request that is refused followed by a smaller request significantly increased compliance with the smaller request. Again, a range of professionals can adopt this strategy in order to influence their client group to perform in a particular way. For instance, a teacher could ask a pupil who is falling behind in his work to stay behind every day after school. This request could then be scaled down to attending for only one afternoon after school.

A second variation of the reciprocation concession principle has been defined as the foot-in-the-door tactic in which an initial small request is gradually increased to larger requests if the initial request is agreed to. While this tactic has been found to work reasonably well, if later requests are too high or too remote from the original request compliance may not be guaranteed (Feldman, 1985). Most professionals use this reciprocation tactic to cajole and encourage their respected clients to make more effort or try out new practices or set new targets or goals for their eventual benefit.

INFLUENCE OF THE MESSAGE

McGuire (1989) suggests that of the two routes information may take in influencing persuasion outcomes, the message (arguments and language) takes the direct route while the more indirect route includes elements which support the message such as, you may recall, power, credibility and attractiveness. Petty and Cacioppo (1981) argued that preference for one line of communication *vis-à-vis* the other is largely dependent on the message receiver's commitment to and knowledge of the information being presented. A receiver who has little knowledge of the area is more likely to be influenced by indirect cues than the arguments contained in the message. So it follows that the content of the message has greatest influence when the receiver is concerned with the topic and understands the message. This section will examine briefly some of the effects that selected message variations have on influencing. The message factors discussed are grouped into two broad categories: message content and message structure.

Message content

Evidence

While it was shown earlier in the chapter that statistical evidence has a strong influence in persuading others, the use of an example (or case history) has an equally and sometimes more compelling persuasive impact. Several researchers have compared the information about the experience of one or a few individuals (case history) with the summarised statistical information about the experiences of many. Results have revealed that examples or case histories are more influential than statistical information or other data summaries (for a review, see Taylor and Thompson, 1982). Koballa (1986) confirmed this finding in research which provided secondary teachers with favourable information regarding a specific type of science curriculum. In one condition the information was presented as a report from a single teacher who had tried out the new curriculum and in the other condition, teachers were presented with a statistical summary of the findings of a large number of teachers who had adopted the new curriculum. It was found that the case study report was significantly more persuasive than the statistical summary report, even although the evidence from the latter report came from the experiences of a large number of teachers rather than one. Doctors and health clinicians can capitalise on this aspect of message persuasion by drawing attention to well-publicised or famous individual cases of early detected breast cancers, for instance, in order to increase substantially the numbers coming forward for breast-screening, as opposed to providing a ream of statistics denoting cure rates with early detection.

Fear appeals

The use of fear as an influencing tactic is all told fairly common and can be summed up in phrases such as 'If you don't do what I recommend then those terrible things will happen to you' or 'You are warned that if you continue to take these pills you will irrevocably damage your health.' So, for example, police officers may show video-tapes depicting gruesome traffic accidents in an effort to discourage dangerous driving; stop smoking posters display the horrors of lung cancer; dental hygiene wall charts may depict the ravages of gum disease and so on.

A number of researchers have studied the effectiveness of such 'fear appeal' messages in terms of the strength of the appeal (Sutton, 1982; Boster and Mongeau, 1984). Are stronger fear messages more effective than weaker ones and vice versa or are there no apparent differences? The research to date suggests two general conclusions. The first is that it is not easy to manipulate the level of fear experienced by an audience. In other words, a presenter may compose a message that is very carefully designed to arouse fear and anxiety – a message containing all sorts of gruesome details intended to create fear – and yet that message may fail to do so.

The second important finding is that message materials which do produce greater fear and anxiety are more persuasive in nature as reported by persuadees. In summary, therefore, it is important to note that not all explicit, fear-laden, vividly depicted images or messages will be effective in influencing or persuading. But messages that do successfully arouse relatively greater fear are likely to be more influential than those that arouse less fear. Why should this happen? One explanation put forward by a number of researchers (Leventhal *et al.*, 1983; Chaiken and Stangor, 1987) is that it should not be assumed that messages are linked only to emotional responses (fear): instead a cognitive reaction may be evoked. A given message which could initially induce fear and anxiety may also lead individuals to believe that the fearful consequences are more severe (more harmful, more noxious, more disadvantageous) than had been previously thought. Therefore, it may be that the real force at work behind the message's influential effectiveness is the change in those beliefs, not the arousal of fear. Fear might arise as a by-product of the influencing process. A driver may believe the consequences of fast and dangerous driving are much more severe than hitherto thought and, therefore, be more anxious now than he was before. It is the cognitive changes not the emotional ones which might actually explain the message's effectiveness.

One final point, however, suggests that subjects themselves may have greater or lesser tendencies to process fear-arousing persuasive messages (Jepson and Chaiken, 1991; Dillard and Harkness, 1992). Some persons are more motivated to react to fear than others. Perhaps this is because the ways individuals handle fear vary across situations or that what causes fear in one person may be ignored by another. More research is needed into these and other related issues on the processing of fear messages.

Appeal to the self-image

Most of us at some time or another have been at the receiving end of phrases such as 'You will feel better if you finish your work on time' or 'You'll feel ashamed if you don't try to do better.' Such statements are designed to inform us that we are morally obligated to carry out a particular course of action and if we do not comply we will have negative feelings such as shame, guilt, lack of pride.

An early taxonomy of compliance-gaining techniques, developed by Marwell and Schmitt (1967) and later extended by Miller *et al.* (1977) identified a category of compliance strategies which would appeal to a person's self-image in either a positive way ('You will feel good if you comply') or in a negative way ('You will feel ashamed of yourself if you do not comply'). The Miller *et al.* study went on to determine if this strategy of activating self-feeling was used more typically in interpersonal or non-interpersonal situations with long- or short-term consequences. Interestingly, their findings indicate that appeal to positive and negative self-feelings are more likely to be used in interpersonal settings. In addition, these appeals are more likely to be found in long-term consequence situations. Parents, teachers, church leaders, youth workers, etc., who have a distinct mandate for developing the moral value system of our young people, often employ moral appeals by reminding youngsters that they have a duty to help others in society, particularly those less fortunate than themselves (e.g. flag selling, sponsored runs, telethons, etc. for charity).

Message structure

Burgoon (1989) in a review of the persuasive effects of messages suggests that '[no] one organizational pattern is inherently superior to any other. However, an abundance of evidence suggests that some organizational structure is superior to none' (p. 139). The remainder of this chapter will examine four variables: namely, number of arguments, opposing arguments, argument order and repetition of arguments which can enhance the influencing effects of interpersonal communication.

Number of arguments

The number of arguments contained in a message can have a degree of influence on how the message is received but there are several factors to be considered when considering this strategy (Stone, 1983). For example, Petty and Cacioppo (1984) noted that those persons who are not centrally involved or committed to a particular topic are more likely to be influenced by a greater number of arguments than those persons who are highly involved. This supports the notion that the quality of the argument is more persuasive with an already knowledgeable audience while the reverse is the case with a lay audience where quantity of arguments may be more appropriate. In addition, Norman (1976) found that when so-called 'experts' in a subject used a large number of arguments they were more likely to produce attitude change in their audience. Perhaps the reason for this is that expert sources are expected to provide adequate arguments and evidence to support their claim, so that any omission of such arguments can undermine their influencing effects.

Opposing arguments

How should an influencer handle opposing arguments? Summarising research in this area to date, Jackson and Allen (1987) show that, as a general rule, two-sided arguments are more influential than providing one side of an argument only. However, Bettinghaus and Cody (1987) suggested that two-sided messages tend to be more effective with those persons who have had more formal education. One reason for this finding may be that, through formal or higher education, the individual has been exposed to this strategy and, therefore, can handle the data in a more facilitative way than those who have not had this experience. Brown and Atkins (1988) make this point when they state that 'one of the most relevant [persuasive techniques] to lecturing is the use of pairs of contrasting statements' (p. 25).

Thus, when there are arguments in favour of and against a procedure, the college lecturer can have more influence if both sides of the argument are presented. Atkinson (1984) also provides evidence of this by suggesting that politicians are most persuasive when they provide the electorate with those arguments in favour of a particular policy decision and those against.

Argument order

Where should the strongest influential argument be placed in a message? Here, when we turn to research we find the evidence is equivocal (Bettinghaus and Cody, 1987) as to whether one believes the main argument will be remembered best if presented at the outset (primacy effect) or the most important arguments will be remembered best if included in a build-up towards the end (recency effect). Lind (1982), on the other hand, demonstrated that a primacy effect is likely to obtain when a person is attempting to influence others' judgements regarding a particular person. This is consistent with those views put forward in Chapter 3 which indicated that impressions of others are formed within the first few minutes of meeting and are usually based upon limited information.

While research is ambivalent on this aspect of message influence, it might be appropriate to use the strategy of important arguments first when time is at a premium (e.g. at a case conference where you are given a few minutes to argue your case) or when there is a more than likely chance that you may be interrupted before you can complete your argument (e.g. during a lively debate where there is a range of opposing views).

Repetition of arguments

There is some evidence to suggest that repetition adds to the persuasive impact of a message (Gorn and Goldberg, 1980) but at some point (around five repetitions) a satiation point is reached beyond which nothing more can be gained from further repetition (McGuire, 1973). With few exceptions, the majority of the research into this aspect of message appeals has been conducted in the area of advertising and marketing, where the goal is to influence customers to purchase specific brands of goods. However, Burgoon (1989) warns that this influencing technique may not be appropriate to use in other contexts. One recent finding by Barry and Bateman (1992), who examined the influence tactics used by managers, suggests that perceivers of repeated arguments can interpret messages as insistent (making repeated requests) or persistent (pestering requests). Insistent messages were associated with perceptions of higher levels of influence than persistent messages which were perceived as aggressive in nature and so working against the influencer. Much more research is needed to recommend the optimal number of repeated messages.

OVERVIEW

This chapter has focused upon the characteristics and message variations of the communicator and the effects she has in influencing the receiver during interpersonal communication. However, it must be borne in mind that some persons are more easily influenced than others (e.g. personality and gender differences) while context has a strong bearing on the influencing outcome. Therefore, receiver and contextual factors need to be considered before deciding upon a relevant influencing strategy (O'Keefe, 1990; Reardon, 1991).

Influencing is a particularly important skill for professionals to acquire since, at some time in their dealings with clients, they will be attempting to gain their compliance to perhaps adopt a distinctive point of view or follow a prescribed course of action. As Dickson *et al.* (1993) pointed out 'Social influence can be said to exist when the actions of one individual have a causal effect on the outcomes or life events of another' (p. 144).

Sometimes the terms 'social influence' and 'persuasion' have been used interchangeably, but a subtle difference can be found between the two concepts in terms of the intentionality of the influencer. One can influence another intentionally or unintentionally but only persuasion subsumes the notion of intentionality.

One of the main functions of employing the skill of social influence or persuasion is to induce individuals to adopt, maintain or even change their attitudes. Bearing in mind that attitudes refer to what a person knows about (cognitive aspect), feels about (affective aspect) and how he intends to act towards an object or situation (conative aspect), the influencer can target the influencee's perceptions, emotions or actions.

There are three major characteristics which people of influence have when delivering impactual highly influential messages; namely, power, credibility and attractiveness. Thus individuals who possess one or many of a range of power bases are in a strong position to manipulate the attitudes and beliefs of others often without them even being aware of it. Credibility refers to the inferences being made by an observer concerning the competence and trustworthiness of the speaker. The more credible the speaker the more influence she will have over an audience. Also, it is not surprising to learn that, as a general rule, we are more influenced by those we like and find 'attractive' than those we dislike and find 'unattractive'. Aside from appearance, there are several factors which enhance our attractiveness and therefore, provide us with an advantage to persuade. These are: holding similar view or opinions; becoming known and familiar to others over a period of time; limiting the availability of knowledge or goods and so increasing their scarcity value; reinforcing, encouraging and supporting others' views and behaviour; and reciprocating, that is giving something before asking for something in return.

While the characteristics previously cited are more indirectly involved in influencing outcomes, the message or words themselves present a more direct approach when attempting to persuade. In terms of message content, several factors contribute to overall influencing effectiveness. These are; providing concrete evidence in the form of statistical results or case histories of events or situations; including 'fear appeal' messages to lead individuals to follow a course of action; and appealing to positive and negative self-feelings (although these appeals are more likely to be effective in long-term consequence situations).

In addition to the content of the message, the way the message is structured (such as the number of arguments put forward, citing opposing arguments), which arguments should be presented at the outset or used to build up to a climax, and the repetition of arguments in order to be more influential, can all enhance the influencing effects of interpersonal communication. It is important to remember that some people are more susceptible to the powers of persuasion than others and the situation itself can exert a strong influence on the outcome. However, this chapter has provided a range of tactics and strategies which the professional can employ to be reasonably assured of a successful influencing conclusion.

Chapter 12

Assertiveness

INTRODUCTION

Assertiveness is an area of study which has a long history within the field of behaviour therapy, dating back to the pioneering work of Salter (1949) and Wolpe (1958), who recognised that certain individuals in society had specific problems in standing up for their rights. As a result the skill of assertiveness was introduced during therapy, in an attempt to help such individuals function more effectively in their everyday lives.

During the last twenty years the skill of assertiveness has attracted enormous interest, reflecting the importance of this aspect of social interaction across many areas. Numerous books have been published on this topic (e.g. Alberti and Emmons, 1986; Phelps and Austin, 1987; Canter and Canter, 1988; Rakos, 1991; Wilson and Gallois, 1993). A large volume of research has also been conducted and assertion training (AT) programmes introduced in many settings. It has increasingly been recognised that most groups of professionals can benefit from becoming more assertive, and so programmes of AT are now employed in the training of many such professionals.

While a knowledge of assertiveness will be of benefit to most professionals, for some it would seem to be of particular importance. In an investigation into core skills in pharmacy practice, Morrow and Hargie (1987) found that pharmacists rated assertiveness as being both the most important skill needed when dealing with other professionals and ancillary staff, and also the most difficult skill to put into practice. Likewise, there is evidence that social workers find assertion a difficult skill in the context of their job role (Pardeck et al., 1991). Nurses apparently represent another profession with reported problems in being assertive (Porritt, 1984; McCartan and Hargie, 1990). In discussing this issue, McIntyre et al. (1984) attributed these problems to many of the values associated with nurses, in that they are expected to 'think of others first (even if they are tired or hurting), they should be humble, they should always listen and be understanding and they should never complain or confront' (p. 312). In a study of twenty-six nurses, McIntyre et al. found that, based upon a number of measures, nurses were clearly nonassertive (submissive) when compared with other professional groups. However, following an AT programme, the nurses demonstrated significant increases in assertiveness, which were maintained at a 2-month follow-up period. AT is also one of the most prevalent topics for training in business and industrial contexts (Whetten and Cameron, 1984) and such AT programmes have indeed been shown to be effective with business studies students (Baldwin, 1992).

Thus assertiveness is an aspect of interpersonal communication which can be developed and improved. It is a skill which is of importance when dealing with peers, superiors and subordinates. It is also pertinent to interactions between different groups of professionals, especially where differences of power and status exist (such as between nurses and doctors), and it is of relevance to interactions between professionals and clients.

Early definitions of assertiveness were fairly all-embracing in terms of interactional skills. Lazarus (1971), for example, regarded assertiveness as comprising four main components, namely the ability to:

1 refuse requests;
2 ask for favours and make requests;
3 express positive and negative feelings; and
4 initiate, continue and terminate general conversations.

It is obvious that this conceptualisation of assertiveness is very wide, encompassing almost all forms of human interaction. Indeed, in the USA, as Kelly (1982) pointed out: 'Until somewhat recently, the terms "assertion training" and "social skills training" were often used in an interchangeable fashion; it was not recognized that assertiveness represents one specific kind of interpersonal competency' (p. 172). It would seem that training in this field was introduced and found to be beneficial before the concept of assertiveness was defined with any precision. Dissatisfaction with this state of affairs has led to a more focused study of assertion, based specifically upon the theme of standing up for one's rights in a sensitive, competent manner. This latter interpretation is the one given by most dictionaries and the perspective held by most lay people, and it is the view adopted in this chapter.

While differing definitions of assertion proliferate within the literature (St Lawrence, 1987), useful definitions of assertive behaviour can be found in two of the central texts in this area of study. Thus Lange and Jakubowski (1976) stated that 'assertion involves standing up for personal rights and expressing thoughts, feelings and beliefs in direct, honest, and appropriate ways which respect the rights of other people' (p. 38). In like vein, Alberti and Emmons (1982) defined assertion as behaviour which 'enables a person to act in his or her own best interests, to stand up for herself or himself without undue anxiety, to express honest feelings comfortably, or to exercise personal rights without denying the rights of others' (p. 13). Both of these definitions emphasise an important component of assertion, namely respect for the rights of other people, and the skilled individual should be able to achieve a balance between ensuring personal rights and not infringing the rights of others.

Assertiveness can be conceptualised as comprising seven response classes. Three of these are negative: expressing unpopular or different opinions; requesting behaviour change from others; and refusing unreasonable requests. The remaining four are positive: admitting personal shortcomings; giving and receiving compliments; initiating and maintaining interactions; and expressing positive feelings. However, most research and training efforts have been devoted to the negative, or conflict, components, since this is the aspect of assertion many people find particularly difficult.

STYLES OF RESPONDING

In order to fully understand the concept of assertiveness, it is necessary to distinguish this style of responding from other approaches. Alberti and Emmons (1975) distinguished between three such styles, namely nonassertion, assertion and aggression, as follows.

Nonassertive responses involve expressing oneself in such a self-effacing, apologetic manner that one's thoughts, feelings and rights can easily be ignored. In this 'cap in hand' style, the person hesitates, speaks softly, looks away, tends to fidget nervously, avoids issues, agrees regardless of his own feelings, does not express opinions, values himself 'below' others, lacks confidence and hurts himself to avoid any chance of hurting others. The objective here is to appease others and avoid conflict at any cost. Hargie and Morrow (1988) termed this the 'Uriah Heep' style, as epitomised in Charles Dickens' *David Copperfield* in which Uriah explains how he was brought up: 'to be 'umble to this person, and 'umble to that; and to pull our caps off here, and to make bows there; and always to know our place, and abase ourselves before our betters'.

Assertive responses involve standing up for oneself, yet taking the other person into consideration. The assertive style involves answering spontaneously, speaking with a conversational yet firm tone and volume, looking at the other person, addressing the main issue, openly expressing personal feelings and opinions, valuing oneself equal to others, and hurting neither oneself nor others. The objective here is to try to ensure fair play for everyone.

Aggressive responses involve threatening or violating the rights of the other person. Here the person answers before the other is finished speaking, talks loudly and abusively, glares at the other person, speaks 'past' the issue (accusing, blaming, demeaning), vehemently states feelings and opinions in a dogmatic fashion, values himself above others, and hurts others to avoid hurting himself. The objective here is to win, regardless of the other person.

These three styles can be exemplified in relation to a situation in which someone is asked for the loan of a book which she does not wish to lend:

1 'Um . . . How long would you need it for? It's just that . . . ah . . . I might need it for an assignment. But . . . if it wasn't for long . . .' (Nonassertion)
2 'I'm sorry. I'd like to help you out, but I bought this book so I would always have it to refer to, so I never loan it to anyone.' (Assertion)
3 'No. Why don't you buy your own damn books!?' (Aggression)

From these examples, it can be seen that these three styles of responding form a continuum of:

Nonassertion   Assertion   Aggression
|_____|_____|

Assertiveness forms the mid-point of this continuum, and is usually the most appropriate response. Aggressive individuals tend to be viewed as intransigent, coercive, overbearing and lacking in self-control. They may initially get their own way by browbeating and creating fear in others, but they will often be disliked and avoided. Alternatively, this style may provoke a similar response from others, with the danger that the verbal aggression may escalate and eventually lead to overt physical aggression. Nonassertive individuals, on the other hand, will often be viewed by others as weak, 'mealymouthed' creatures who can be easily manipulated, and as a result nonassertive people will frequently express dissatisfaction with their lives, owing to a failure to attain personal goals. They may be less likely to inspire confidence in others or may even be seen as incompetent. Assertive individuals, however, tend to feel more in control of their lives, derive more satisfaction from their relationships and achieve their goals more often. They also will obtain more respect from, and inspire confidence in, those with whom they interact since they tend to be viewed as strong characters who will not be easily swayed.

Several research studies have verified the behavioural responses associated with these three styles. Rose and Tryon (1979) carried out a systematic, carefully controlled study, in which they found that assertive behaviour was clearly associated with louder voice (68 decibel (dB) level was viewed as nonassertive; 76dB level was the assertive ideal; 84dB level was towards the aggressive end of the continuum); reduced response latency (pauses of 16 seconds before responding were seen as nonassertive, whereas pauses of 3–4 seconds were viewed as assertive); increased use of gestures (although increased gestures coupled with approach behaviour were seen as aggressive); and increased vocal inflection. Similarly McFall et al. (1982), in a detailed research investigation, identified what they termed 'assertive body movements' the most salient being hands, arms and overall body cues. Assertive individuals used 'controlled, smooth, steady, and purposive movement as opposed to shifty, shaky, fidgety extraneous body activity' for nonassertive people (p. 137). Furthermore, Kolotkin *et al.* (1983) found that duration of eye contact was greater for assertive, as opposed to nonassertive individuals. They also found that the use of smiles can help to convey that a response is meant to be assertive rather than aggressive.

Types of aggression

Although most texts on assertion differentiate between three styles of responding, some theorists have made a distinction between different types of aggression. Buss and Perry (1992) have developed an Aggression Inventory which contains four factors, or subdivisions, of aggression. These are outlined below, with examples of actual items from the Inventory.

1 *Physical aggression.* 'Given enough provocation, I may hit another person.' 'If I have to resort to violence to protect my rights, I will.'
2 *Verbal aggression.* 'I tell my friends openly when I disagree with them.' 'When people annoy me I may tell them what I think of them.'
3 *Anger.* 'I sometimes feel like a powder keg ready to explode.' 'Sometimes I fly off the handle for no good reason.'
4 *Hostility.* 'I am sometimes eaten up with jealousy.' 'When people are especially nice, I wonder what they want.'

The relationship between these elements is that they each represent different dimensions of aggression: physical and verbal responses represent the instrumental or behavioural components; anger is the emotional or affective aspect; and hostility the cognitive element.

Another common distinction is that which is made between open, direct aggression and passive, indirect aggression (Phelps and Austin, 1975; De Giovanni, 1979). Del Greco (1983) has argued that these two types of aggression can be combined with nonassertion and assertion to form two continua, rather than one. As depicted in Figure 12.1, these two continua are coerciveness and directness.

The passive, or indirect, aggressive style of responding seems to embrace a range of behaviours including sulking, using emotional blackmail (such as crying in order to get your own way), pouting and being subtly manipulative. Del Greco (1983) has developed an Inventory to measure all four response styles. Indirect, or passive, aggressive items include 'When I am asked for my preference I pretend I don't have one, but then I convince my friends of the advantages of my hidden preferences'; and 'When my friend asks me for my opinion I state that I have none, then I proceed to make my true preference seem the most attractive.' This type of machiavellian approach is one clear example of indirect aggression. Another example would be where a person slams drawers and doors shut while refusing to discuss the reason for so doing.

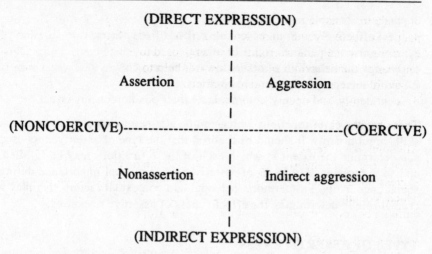

(DIRECT EXPRESSION)

Assertion | Aggression

(NONCOERCIVE)---(COERCIVE)

Nonassertion | Indirect aggression

(INDIRECT EXPRESSION)

Figure 12.1 Four styles of responding

The four response styles can be illustrated with reference to alternative ways of responding to someone smoking in a 'no smoking' area:

1 'Hey, you, there's no smoking allowed in this area. Either put out or get out!' (Aggressive)
2 'Excuse me, but do you realise that this is a "no smoking" area? Cigarette smoke affects me quite badly, so I'd be grateful if you would not smoke here.' (Assertive)
3 Not mentioning your discomfort, and hoping that someone else will confront the smoker. (Nonassertive)
4 Coughing loudly and vigorously waving a hand towards the smoker as if to fan the smoke away. (Indirectly aggressive)

Once again, assertiveness is regarded as the optimum approach. While it is possible to be skilfully manipulative, there is always the danger of being found out, with resulting negative consequences. Similarly in the case of passive aggression, as in the fourth example above, this can lead to a negative evaluation, and may simply be ignored by the other person.

FUNCTIONS OF ASSERTIVENESS

The skill of assertion serves a number of purposes, depending upon the situation in which one has to assert oneself. Generally, however, the skilled use of assertive responses will help individuals to:

1 ensure that their personal rights are not violated;
2 withstand unreasonable requests from others;

3   make reasonable requests of others;
4   deal effectively with unreasonable refusals from others;
5   recognise the personal rights of others;
6   change the behaviour of others towards them;
7   avoid unnecessary aggressive conflicts;
8   confidently, and openly, communicate their position on any issue.

These are the chief functions which can be attained by employing assertion skills appropriately. It should be realised that the type of assertiveness used can determine the extent to which each of these functions may be fulfilled, and so a knowledge of types of assertiveness is of vital importance during social encounters. Furthermore, personal and contextual factors also play a crucial role in determining the effectiveness of assertive responses.

TYPES OF ASSERTIVENESS

A number of different types of assertive behaviour can be employed. Lange and Jakubowski (1976) identified five types of assertiveness as follows.

Basic assertion

This involves a simple expression of standing up for personal rights, beliefs, feelings or opinions. For example, when interrupted, a basic assertive expression would be: 'Excuse me, I would like to finish what I was saying.'

Empathic assertion

This type of assertion conveys some sensitivity to the other person, by making a statement that conveys some recognition of the other person's situation or feelings before making the assertive statement. Thus an empathic assertion to an interruption might be: 'I know you are keen to get your views across, but I would like to finish what I was saying'.

Escalating assertion

Here the individual begins by making a minimal assertive response, and, if the other person fails to respond to this, gradually increases or escalates the degree of assertiveness employed. An example of escalating assertiveness may occur where a professional in her office is being pressurised by a very determined salesperson, and the escalation may proceed as follows:

1   'No, I've decided that I don't wish to purchase any of these products.'
2   'No, as I've already said, I'm not buying any of them.'
3   'Look, I've told you twice that the answer is no. I'm going to have to ask you to leave now.'

Confrontive assertion

This is used when someone's words contradict his actions, and involves clearly telling the person what he said he would do, and what he actually did. The speaker then expresses what he now wants. An example would be: 'You said you would have the report typed by Tuesday. It is now Thursday and you still haven't typed it. I would like you to type it for me now please.'

I-language assertion

Here the speaker objectively describes the behaviour of the other person, how this affects the speaker's life or feelings and why the other person should change his behaviour. In the case of being interrupted, an I-language assertive response would be: 'This is the fourth time you've interrupted me in the past few minutes. This makes me feel that you aren't interested in what I am saying, and I feel a bit hurt and annoyed. I would like you to let me finish what I want to say.'

'You-language' tends to be perceived as blaming or accusing the other person and can result in defensive reactions. Compare the following two statements.

1 'You are annoying me because you never pay for your fair share of these expenses.'
2 'I feel annoyed because I believe that I am paying more than my fair share of these expenses.'

Statement 2 is much less accusatory than the first and therefore is less likely to provoke a hostile response. However, there may be a danger with I-language, especially if overused, being perceived as selfish, self-centred and unconcerned with the other person. Indeed, I-language statements do not seem to be characteristic of most everyday conversations (Gervasio, 1987). For these reasons, the use of 'We-language' can be an effective alternative to a heavy reliance upon I-language. Continuing with the above exemplar, the We-language response would be 'We need to talk about how we are both contributing to the payment of these expenses. It is important that neither of us feels annoyed about the present arrangement.' The use of We-language helps to convey the impression of partnership in, and joint responsibility for, any problems to be discussed.

Direct and indirect assertion

Linehan and Egan (1979) distinguished between a direct and an indirect style of assertiveness. They argued that a direct, unambiguous assertive style may not always be most effective, especially for those individuals for whom it is important to be liked and regarded positively by others. Rather, a more ambiguous, indirect style of response seems more appropriate in some instances (despite the fact that most texts recommend a direct style). An example of these two styles can be seen in relation to the following question:

Q: 'Could you loan me that tape you bought yesterday?'
Direct: 'No, I never loan my tapes to anyone.'
Indirect: 'Oh, you mean The Oceans – You know, I'm still trying to get a chance to sit down and listen to it myself. I usually take ages listening to a new tape.'

Here the direct approach may be seen as brusque or even offensive. In the indirect approach, however, there has been no refusal and so the other person may reply by attempting to obtain a commitment about borrowing the tape at a later time.

There is consistent research evidence to show that standard, direct assertion is viewed as being as effective as, and more socially desirable than, aggressive behaviour, and more socially competent but distinctly less likeable than nonassertion (Wilson and Gallois, 1993). However, Linehan and Egan pointed out that the direct style can be less abrasive if turned into a complex-direct style. Thus it is better to use what Woolfolk and Dever (1979) termed 'extra considerations' to soften the impact of direct assertion. This latter approach would involve the use of an embellishment associated with a refusal. Linehan and Egan identified five main embellishments which can be employed, namely, empathy, helplessness, apology, flattery and outright lying (although this one would need to be used with caution). The idea here is to lessen the impact of the refusal and so maintain the relationship. Thus, using this style a response to the above question might be:

Complex-Direct: 'I know you would look after it really well, but I've recently had two tapes that I loaned damaged, so I've just had to make the general decision never to loan my tapes to anyone again. That way I hope no one will feel personally offended.'

Protective assertion

Fry (1983) identified three types of assertiveness which she referred to as 'protective skills', and which are a form of verbal defence commonly used against manipulation, nagging or rudeness. The first of these skills is the *broken record* where the person simply makes an assertive statement and keeps repeating this statement (as if the 'needle had stuck') until it is accepted by the other person. For example, to repeated pleas for a loan the individual may just keep saying 'No, I'm not going to give you any money.' The second protective skill is known as *fogging*, wherein the person appears to accept negative criticism without changing his behaviour. An example of a fogging sequence would be:

A: 'You always look down in the dumps.'
B: 'Yes, I probably do.'
A: 'Could you not try to look a bit happier?'
B: 'I suppose I could.'
A: 'If you did, you would be a bit more pleasant to work with.'
B: 'Yes, you're probably right.'

The idea here is that eventually the other person will become tired getting no real response to the criticisms and will eventually give up.

It should be realised that these two skills are basic forms of assertion which should really only be used as a form of protection from prolonged or unwarranted criticism. They are not intended as general methods for expressing one's rights. The third type of skill listed by Fry is that of *meta-level* assertion whereby someone, who realises that a solution is unlikely, suggests that wider perspectives should be considered rather than specific issues. One example of this approach, of moving from the particular to the general, would be where someone involved in an argument with a colleague says 'We obviously are not going to agree about this, and I think this is typical of what is happening to our whole working relationship.'

COMPONENTS OF ASSERTIVENESS

In order to execute assertiveness skills effectively, a number of central components need to be mastered. There are four main components of assertion.

Content

The actual content of an assertive response should include both an expression of rights, and a statement placing this expression of rights within the context of socially responsible and appropriate behaviour. Rakos (1986) identified five possible accompanying statements. We will illustrate in relation to a refusal to a request from a colleague to go to the bar at lunchtime:

1 An explanation for the necessity to assert oneself – 'I can't go today because I have some work to finish off during the lunch break.'
2 An empathic statement recognising the other person's situation – 'I can't go today. I know you are disappointed . . .'
3 Praise for the other person – 'It's very nice of you to ask, but I can't go today . . .'
4 An apology for any resulting consequence – 'I can't go today. I'm sorry if you are on your own over lunch.'
5 An attempt to identify a mutually acceptable compromise – 'I haven't time to go out to the bar today. How about just having a quick snack in the canteen?'

These content statements, which are similar to the embellishments recommended by Linehan and Egan, could obviously be combined to soften the assertion, and distinguish the response from aggression.

One situation which can be difficult to cope with assertively is that of embarrassment. In their discussion of strategies for handling embarrassing predicaments, Cupach and Metts (1990) identified four main types of content responses.

1   *Apology*. This can range from a basic statement ('I'm sorry') to elaborate expressions of remorse and attempts at remediation or restitution (e.g. offering to replace a spilled drink).
2   *Accounts*. These can be either in the form of an *excuse* which expresses denial of responsibility for an untoward act without denying its severity ('That's a terrible mess, but it was an accident'); or a *justification* which expresses responsibility for the untoward act but denies the pejorative nature of the consequences ('OK I did spill it, but there's no real harm done').
3   *Humour*. A joke can be one of the most effective methods for dealing with embarrassment, since it can convert a potential loss of social approval into a positive gain. In this sense 'a well formed joke, especially one reflecting on the unintentional incompetence of the transgressor, can express remorse, guilt, and embarrassment as an apology would without unduly lowering the individual's status *vis-à-vis* others who are present' (Cupach and Metts, 1990, p. 329).
4   *Avoidance*. This strategy would include not mentioning sensitive topics to particular people, quickly changing an embarrassing topic, staying silent or simply leaving the room.

Obviously, two or more of these can be used at the same time. Thus an assertive response might involve giving an excuse, apologising and offering restitution, while at the same time employing appropriate humour. Cupach and Metts, however, point out that aggression towards the person who may have partially caused the embarrassment (e.g. 'If you had not bloody well been standing there it wouldn't have happened!') is not an appropriate response.

Rose and Tryon (1979) made a distinction between three general types of assertion content, which can be exemplified in relation to complaining about a meal in a restaurant, as follows:

1   Description of the behaviour – 'Excuse me, this meal is cold.'
2   Description of behaviour plus indication of your noncompliance – 'Excuse me, this meal is cold. I couldn't eat it.'
3   Description, noncompliance, plus request for behaviour change – 'Excuse me, this meal is cold. I couldn't eat it. Could you please replace it?'

Rose and Tryon found that ratings of assertiveness increased as individuals moved from simply giving a description, through to using all the above three types of content.

Kolotkin *et al.* (1983) also found that assertiveness was associated with requests for behaviour change. In addition, they found that it was associated with use of 'I' statements, whereas use of 'you' statements (which imply accusatory content) were associated with aggression. They identified other important aspects of assertion as including: cognitive statements (what the person thought about the situation), orienting statements (indicating the topic or issue that is going to be raised) and statements of feeling. Galassi *et al.* (1981) emphasised the importance of recognising the separate sub-elements of assertion, which they summarised as: statement of rights, refusal behaviour, request for behaviour change, empathy statement, threat or conflict statement, and giving reasons for behaviour.

Covert elements

This refers to the influence of thoughts, ideas and feelings upon the ability to be assertive. The importance of the role of covert responses in assertion has been increasingly recognised. Rakos (1991, p. 26) in his text on assertion found that in recent years: 'An exhaustive literature search of approximately 1800 journal articles and dissertations confirmed that assertiveness investigators have turned their attention from overt behaviors to either covert responses or contextual issues.' He identified the following covert elements.

Knowledge

In order to be assertive it is necessary to know both what one's rights are, and how to enforce them. It is not always clear in many situations exactly what one's rights are, and it is therefore sometimes necessary to consult with others in order to gauge their views about whether personal rights have been infringed. This process of consultation is termed *reality testing* (Dawley and Wenrich, 1976), which may involve asking other people either for advice about what exactly your rights are (e.g. 'Has he the right to ask me to do that?') or about their perceptions of your behaviour (e.g. 'Have I upset you in some way?', 'Do you mind doing this?'). There is evidence to indicate that assertive individuals may have a greater awareness of what their job role actually entails. In a study of eighty-seven social workers in Israel, Rabin and Zelner (1992) found that assertiveness in the work setting was significantly and positively correlated to both role clarity and job satisfaction. Knowing the parameters of one's job would therefore seem to facilitate the protection of personal rights, which may in turn contribute to increased happiness in the work environment.

In terms of actual rights, Zuker (1983) produced a general Assertive Bill of Rights for individuals which includes the right to:

- be treated with respect;
- have and express personal feelings and opinions;
- be listened to and taken seriously;
- set one's own priorities;
- say no without feeling guilty;
- ask for what one wants;
- get what one pays for;
- make mistakes;
- assert oneself even though it may inconvenience others;
- choose not to assert oneself.

Beliefs

Submissiveness can result from mistaken beliefs. For example, someone may believe that they should always do what their superiors tell them to do or negative consequences may accrue. Before such a person could effectively be assertive, he would have to replace this belief with a new one, for example that it is always valid to ask for a good reason if requested to do anything that seems unreasonable. Kuperminc and Heimberg (1983) found that submissive individuals expected negative consequences to follow from noncompliance, and positive consequences from compliance, with unreasonable requests, whereas assertive individuals expected positive outcomes from noncompliance and negative consequences from compliance. This research finding lends further support to the view that changes in beliefs and expectations may well be a prerequisite for changes in assertive behaviour.

Dawley and Wenrich (1976) referred to this as a process of *cognitive restructuring* for people with inappropriate beliefs. Such restructuring would include changes in self-instructions, those covert behaviour-guiding self-statements we employ when making decisions about which responses to carry out. Kern (1982) found that nonassertive individuals have 'a high frequency of negative self-statements and expectations that their behaviour will yield a relatively large number of negative consequences' (p. 496). Thus submissive individuals would use self-statements such as 'She will not like me if I refuse', rather than 'I have the right to refuse.' In terms of intrapersonal dialogue, there would also seem to be a difference in the use of self-reinforcements, with nonassertive people again being more negative in their self-evaluations of performance. Thus, submissive people are more likely to think 'I sounded terrible, stuttering and stammering. She is probably laughing at me now', whereas assertive individuals tend to be more positive (e.g. 'I'm glad I said "no". He is not likely to bother me again.').

In reviewing research in this field, Rakos (1991) illustrated how nonassertive individuals emit roughly equal numbers of positive and negative self-statements in conflict situations whereas assertive people generate about twice as many positive as negative self-statements. He concluded that 'direct training in autonomous self-instruction, apart from any other intervention, has resulted in significant gains in assertiveness' (p. 53).

Social perception

Nonassertive people are more likely to perceive the behaviour of others inaccurately by, for example, perceiving unreasonable requests as being reasonable. Such people will be viewed by others as 'easy touches' in terms of borrowing items, doing extra work, etc., since they are always ready to be helpful. There comes a time when being helpful develops into being used, and people need to learn not only to be able to draw the line between these two, but also to actually learn to perceive the behaviour of others more accurately, in order to distinguish reasonable and unreasonable requests.

Process

The way in which assertive responses are carried out can be crucial to their success. Thus the correct timing of vocalisations and nonverbal responses is vital. As mentioned earlier, assertive responses should be given without undue delay or hesitation. On occasions, we may have our rights infringed because we are unsure about whether they actually have been violated. If we later discover this to be the case then it is necessary to reconstruct the situation in which the infringement occurred ('Yesterday you asked me to do X. I have since discovered that it is not my job to do X. I would therefore be grateful if you would not ask me to do this again.').

Stimulus control skills are also important. These refer to manipulations of the environment, or other people, to make the assertive response more successful. For example, asking someone to come to your room (where you will feel more in charge) rather than discussing an issue in the corridor; requesting that the opinion of another person be sought to help settle the matter (where you already know the views of this third person); or simply asking for time to think over a request (which allows you to think through the ramifications thereof).

The use of reinforcement (see Chapter 4) is also important, for two reasons. First, rewarding another person is a positive use of assertion. Someone who has performed a task well has the right to expect reward. Second, the use of reward for a person who has complied with an assertive response can help to minimise any negative feelings resulting from the assertion, and it can encourage the person to behave more appropriately in the future.

Nonverbal responses

The final component of assertiveness relates to the nonverbal behaviour of the asserter. This includes: medium levels of eye contact; avoidance of inappropriate facial expressions; smooth use of gestures while speaking, yet inconspicuous while listening; upright posture; direct body orientation; appropriate paralinguistics (short response latency, medium response length, good fluency, medium volume and inflection, increased firmness).

PERSONAL AND CONTEXTUAL FACTORS

There are several factors which influence the degree, nature and effectiveness of assertion.

Gender

The skill of assertiveness has attracted a great deal of interest within the feminist movement, so that the training programmes of many women's groups include AT as one of their core themes. Likewise, several assertiveness books have been written specifically for women, which is not surprising given that females consistently report difficulties in being assertive (Butler, 1976; Linehan and Egan, 1979; Phelps and Austin, 1987). Indeed, the plethora of written material and self-help texts specifically designed for women and the popularity of women's AT programmes is in itself a form of evidence that females feel they need more help in this field. Kahn (1981) suggested that this is because:

> People expect women to behave unassertively. Women may not only accept this judgement of others and behave so as to fulfil prophecies based on stereotyped beliefs, but ... may avoid behaviors that do not fit 'the feminine role' and when they do engage in 'masculine assertiveness', they are likely to encounter disbelief or even hostility from others.... A common attack against females is the labeling of women who assert themselves as aggressive.
>
> (p. 349)

In the Buss and Perry (1992) aggression inventory mentioned earlier it was found that males scored significantly higher than females on physical aggression, verbal aggression and hostility but there was no gender difference for anger. The most marked difference was for scores of physical aggression. Thus, it would seem that at the extreme end of the aggression continuum there are clear gender differences in approaches to conflict.

At the mid-point of this continuum, Kern *et al.* (1985) found that, in a review of fourteen studies comparing the reactions to male and female assertiveness, ten found no significant difference, three found male assertions to be more favourably evaluated and one found female assertions more favourably evaluated. In their ensuing study, Kern *et al.* also discovered that how female assertion was evaluated was a function of the individual's attitude towards females. Males or females holding a conservative, low attitude towards women (LATW) devalued females' assertions, whereas those with a liberal, high attitude towards women (HATW) were not influenced by the gender of the asserter. However, although a study by Wilson and Gallois (1985) supported this finding, subsequent studies by St Lawrence et al. (1985) and Levin and Gross (1987) have failed to substantiate this result for sex-role orientation.

Lewis and Gallois (1984) found that both males and females were more assertive towards those of the same gender; that expression of negative feeling was more acceptable from a member of the opposite sex; and that aggressive encounters were more prevalent in same-sex dyads. In another study, Nix et al. (1983) concluded that assertiveness is a masculine sex-role characteristic. They found that females achieving high masculinity scores in the Bem Sex Role Inventory scored significantly higher on measures of assertiveness than those high in femininity. This finding is consistent with general trends wherein masculine sex-role characteristics tend to be attributed to assertive individuals; masculine or androgynous females are more likely to be assertive than feminine women; masculinity and conflict assertiveness are positively correlated; and direct assertiveness tends to be viewed as masculine (Rakos, 1991).

The situation in which assertion occurs may also be important. In the professional context there is research evidence to suggest that male and female assertiveness is valued equally when employed by businesspersons (Mullinix and Galassi, 1981), corporate managers (Solomon et al., 1982) and lawyers (Sigal et al., 1985). Yet a conflict assertive response by a female police officer confronting someone on the street has been shown to be less positively rated than the same response by a male officer (Sterling and Owen, 1982). This latter finding may be explained by the stereotypical view that it is acceptable for females to be empathically assertive but not confrontative.

Overall, however, there is no clear picture as to the exact nature of the relationship between the effects of different types of assertiveness, the situations in which they are employed and the gender of asserter and assertee. One problem here, as with all studies in the field of assertion, is that different investigators use differing measurements and methodologies. For example, subjects may be asked to evaluate written, audio or video vignettes of assertiveness, to engage in role-plays, or they may be confronted with an experimentally contrived assertive encounter they believe to be real. This makes comparisons between studies very difficult. Interestingly, there is some evidence that assertiveness is evaluated more positively in the 'theoretical' episodes, whereas when the subject engages in practical situations assertion is rated less favourably than nonassertion (Gormally, 1982). This suggests that assertiveness is a respected style, but not one we like to have to deal with.

In relation to gender, however, when females are making decisions about being assertive, Rakos (1991, p. 74) recommended that:

each circumstance must be carefully assessed, and women must learn to attend to the relevant situational cues (e.g. gender of recipient, degree of sex typing) so that the risk is accurately predicted. Then the woman can make her decision whether to assert herself or whether to select another response option.

The final factor here is that the role of women in society has changed rapidly in recent years. It may therefore be that as females increasingly undertake occupations which were previously the primary preserve of males, perceptions of the acceptability of female assertiveness will undergo corresponding changes.

Situation

The situation in which assertiveness is required is another important factor. Following a detailed research investigation, Eisler *et al.* (1975) concluded that

an individual who is assertive in one interpersonal context may not be assertive in a different interpersonal environment. Furthermore, some individuals may have no difficulty responding with negative assertions but may be unable to respond when the situation requires positive expressions.
(p. 339)

Thus some people may find it easy to be assertive at home, but difficult to be assertive at work, or vice versa. In such instances, attention needs to be devoted to the difficult situation, and strategies evolved to overcome particular difficulties.

In the context of the work environment, Bryan and Gallois (1992) carried out a study in which sixty-four people (27M; 37F), who were all in employment in a variety of occupations ranging from professionals to unskilled labourers, judged written vignettes of supervisors, subordinates and co-workers sending either positive or negative assertive messages to one another. Results indicated that positive messages were more favourably rated than negative ones, especially in relation to judgements concerning the likely outcome of the interaction and the probable effects on the relationship. The expression of a personal limitation was rated least favourably of the positive messages, while expressing displeasure was rated as the most negative message. The only difference which emerged between the status groupings was that subordinates were rated more favourably than supervisors or co-workers when using negative assertions. The judges in this study were also asked to generate rules which would apply to, or govern, these assertive interactions. The most common rules identified, in order of frequency, were maintaining eye contact, being polite, being friendly and being pleasant. These findings suggest the importance of using relationship maintenance skills when being assertive.

Certain types of assertiveness may well be more appropriate in some settings than in others. Cianni-Surridge and Horan (1983) found this to be the case in the job interview. They had 276 employers rate the efficacy of six-teen 'frequently advocated assertive job-seeking behaviours' in terms of whether or not each would enhance the applicant's chances of being offered employment. They found that some behaviours were advantageous and some disadvantageous. Thus, for example: 'Following an interview, an applicant writes you a letter thanking you for interviewing him/her and expressing his/her continued interest in the position' was regarded by 54 employers as greatly enhancing, by 176 as enhancing, by 46 as having no effect and by none as diminishing or greatly diminishing job prospects. On the other hand: 'An applicant feels his/her interview with you went poorly. He/she requests a second interview with another interviewer' was regarded by 44 employers as greatly diminishing, by 100 as diminishing, by 119 as having no effect, by 10 as enhancing and by 3 as greatly enhancing job prospects.

Cultural background

The cultural context within which assertive responses are employed is also important. For example, a sub-culture of people with certain strong religious beliefs may actually eschew assertiveness as a valid *modus operandi* and be guided by biblical maxims of submissiveness such as the following from Matthew 5: 'Blessed are the meek: for they shall inherit the earth'; 'whosoever shall smite thee on thy right cheek, turn to him the other also'; and 'Give to him that asketh thee, and from him that would borrow of thee turn not thou away.' For such groups, obviously AT would not be either relevant or appropriate.

The following are some of the differences identified by Thomlinson (1991) between the prevailing cultural values in the USA and those of some other countries:

USA values	Values in other countries
Personal control over environment	Fate
Change	Tradition
Equality/egalitarianism	Hierarchy/rank/status
Individualism/privacy	Group's welfare
Self-help	Birthright/inheritance
Competition	Cooperation
Action/work orientation	'Being' orientation
Informality	Formality
Directness/openness/honesty	Indirectness/ritual/face

In Western Europe the values are often similar to those of the USA, although again there are differences both between Europe and the USA and between European countries themselves. These differences make any attempts to employ assertive behaviour in other countries or with people from different sub-cultures fraught with difficulty. As Furnham (1979) pointed out, the concept of assertiveness tends to be culture-bound, so that assertive responses which may be appropriate in Europe or the USA may not be so appropriate in other countries where values of humility, tolerance or subservience may be prevalent. Conversely, Margalit and Mauger (1985) found that Israelis generally responded more aggressively than Americans. Israelis were found to express anger more readily and more frequently ignored the rights of others, while Americans were more ready to give and accept praise.

Most of the studies on the cultural effects of assertiveness have been carried out in the USA, where 'studies with diverse cultural groups generally find the normative level of self-reported assertive behavior generally approaches that of white Americans as the group's sociocultural similarity to mainstream American norms and values increases' (Rakos, 1991, p. 13). Minorities and sub-cultures in the USA with a strong sense of separate identity, such as the Mexican, Japanese and Chinese communities, tend to report being less assertive than whites. These sub-cultures also emphasise respect for and obedience to elders and in particular parents, so that any form of assertion from child to parent is likely to be frowned upon. This again is different from the norm for Caucasians, where open disagreement and negotiated decisions are acceptable between parents and children. In similar vein, in some sub-cultures assertion may be associated with a 'macho' male role model, with females being expected to play an acquiescent or sub-servient role.

There is increasing evidence to indicate that cultural differences in assertion may be cognitively based, emanating from cultural values and norms rather than from assertive behaviour deficits, since in role-play situations people from these cultures are able to behave as assertively as whites. For example, Sue *et al.* (1990) found that second generation Chinese-American female undergraduates were as assertive as Caucasian females on scores on the Rathus Assertiveness Scale and on role-play tests with either an Asian or a Caucasian experimenter. The only significant difference between the groups was that the Chinese-Americans scored higher on the Fear of Negative Evaluation Scale. It could therefore be the case that in real-life encounters such apprehension of disapproval from others may result in Chinese-American females being less assertive. As Sue *et al.* put it 'Chinese-Americans are able to demonstrate assertiveness in laboratory settings, but do they inhibit this response in other situations?' (p. 161).

There is a need for more multivariate research to identify which factors contribute most to assertiveness, with which groups and in what contexts. In one of the few such studies, Nettles and Bayton (1988) investigated the relationship between race, gender, assertive behavioural intentions (BIs) and subjective expected utilities (SEUs) or outcome benefits. They found that black undergraduates (in the USA) displayed a higher level of BIs towards white than black targets and also indicated higher SEUs from such assertiveness towards whites. One gender difference was that black males expected a greater pay-off in terms of the desirability of the consequences if they were assertive to whites in "nice" situations (such as giving compliments) whereas black females expected a greater pay-off in conflict situations (such as expressing annoyance). These findings remain tentative pending the results of further studies, but they do illustrate the need for more fine-grained research in this area. As Nettles and Bayton concluded: 'One contribution of this research is the demonstration that generalizations about the responses of broadly defined groups of people (blacks, whites, men, women, etc.) in basic social interactions are highly untenable' (p. 171).

Other factors

The day of the week may also be of importance in making decisions about when to employ assertiveness, since there is evidence from a study in the USA to suggest that there is a marked and significant tendency for greater conflict to occur in personal relationships on Wednesdays (Duck *et al.*, 1991). More investigation is required before any definite conclusions can be made about such temporal effects upon behaviour. As Duck *et al.* put it: 'there is a need for thorough exploration of the nature of, and reasons for, daily variation in communications, particularly as they influence relationship experiences and dynamics' (p. 258). However, the results from this initial study would suggest that, where possible, it may be advisable to avoid confrontations with close friends on Wednesdays!

Age may be another important factor in assertiveness. Pardeck *et al.* (1991), in a study of postgraduate students in the USA, found a significant and positive correlation between age and assertiveness. It may be that older people are more confident about standing up for their rights, or that they have gained more experience in the practice of assertion. However, more research is needed in order to ascertain the exact nature of the relationship between assertiveness and maturation.

From our own evaluation of a range of professional groups, we have ascertained a number of situations in which it can be more difficult to be assertive. These include: when interacting in someone else's home or office; when in a strange country or sub-culture; when alone as opposed to when with friends or colleagues; when dealing with superiors at work; when promoted to a position of authority over those who were formerly friends and colleagues; when dealing with elderly people; when interacting with those who are seriously or terminally ill and with their relatives; when dealing with people who are in poverty or in severe social deprivation; when interacting with other professionals of higher status and power; with friends or close work colleagues; with members of the opposite sex; and when dealing with those who are disabled.

In relation to the latter group, AT has in fact been shown to be of benefit to physically disabled individuals. Glueckauf and Quittner (1992), in a Canadian study, found that people confined to wheelchairs who received AT made significant increases in the number of assertive responses and concomitant decreases in passive responses during a role-play test as compared to a control group who received no AT. The AT group also reported significantly higher increases in assertiveness in both general and disability related situations. This result is of particular interest since previous research has shown that people in wheelchairs often experience discomfort in situations which involve refusing help, managing patronising remarks and giving directives. Furthermore, it has also been shown that nondisabled individuals experience difficulties (e.g. show more motoric inhibition, end interactions sooner and are more likely to express attitudes inconsistent with true beliefs) in interactions with the wheelchair-bound (Glueckauf and Quittner, 1992). There is clearly a need for more research into the possible inhibiting effects of wheelchairs during interpersonal encounters and to ways in which such effects can be overcome.

The assertee

Gormally (1982) found that assertive behaviour was rated more favourably by individuals who were assertive themselves, while Kern (1982) discovered that low assertive subjects reacted negatively to assertive behaviour whereas high assertive subjects generally devalued nonassertive behaviour. These findings suggest that decisions about when and how to apply assertion should be moderated by the assertive nature of the other person.

Thus the relationship with the other person is of vital import in deciding how to be assertive. An interesting dimension of relationships has been explored by Alberts (1992) in relation to teasing behaviour (banter). Alberts illustrated how teasing can be interpreted as either playfulness/joking or as derogation/aggression since it usually has both friendly and hostile components. Between friends it is normally the former purpose that is served by banter and the humour is therefore two-way. In other contexts there would seem to be a dominance or control function prevalent, since high status people can tease low status people but not usually vice versa. Alberts points out that decisions about how to react to teasing behaviour are made on the basis of four main elements: the perceived goal of the teaser; background knowledge of and relationship with this person; the context in which the tease is employed; and the paralinguistic tone with which it is delivered. Where banter is used as a form of sarcasm, or 'put down', it is necessary to assertively indicate that such behaviour is unacceptable. This needs to be done skilfully to avoid accusations of not being able to take a joke.

Lewis and Gallois (1984) investigated the influence of friendship on assertiveness. They found that certain types of negative assertions (expression of anger, or difference of opinion) were more acceptable when made by friends as opposed to strangers. However, refusal of a request from a friend was perceived to be less socially skilled and more hurtful than refusal from a stranger. As a result, they recommend that with strangers it is 'wise to refrain from assertively expressing a difference of opinion or negative feelings, at least until the relationship is well established' (p. 366).

Finally, as mentioned earlier, the gender of the assertee is also an important factor. There is evidence to indicate that empathic assertions are more likely to produce immediate positive benefits when the recipient is female (Zollo *et al.*, 1985). However, as discussed in the section on gender, the sex-role orientation of the individual is also important, since conservative males or females are less likely to react favourably to assertive responses from females.

OVERVIEW

Assertiveness is a very important social skill both in professional contexts and in everyday interactions. We feel hurt, aggrieved and upset if our rights have been violated. Some individuals find it difficult to be assertive. This is often related to upbringing in that they may have been raised under a very strict regime by parents in which as children they were 'seen and not heard', and learned in school that the quiet child who did as it was told was most approved of by the teacher. It can then be difficult in later life to overcome this residue of parental and educational upbringing. However, research evidence clearly indicates that it is possible to improve assertion skills.

Where such changes in assertiveness occur, it is useful to be aware of some possible reactions of other people to new-found assertiveness. Alberti and Emmons (1975) identified four such reactions:

1 *Backbiting*. Making statements behind the person's back, which they ensure are overheard ('Who does she think she is?', 'All of a sudden he's a big fellow').
2 *Aggression*. Others may try to negate the assertion by using threatening or aggressive behaviour in an attempt to regain dominance.
3 *Over-apologising*. Some people may feel they have caused offence and as a result will apologise profusely.
4 *Revenge-seeking*. The assertion may be accepted but the person will retain hidden resentment and hold a desire to 'get their own back'.

It is important to be alert to such possible consequences of changing from nonassertion to assertion, and to help reduce any negative outcomes by ensuring skilful use of assertiveness. It should also be realised that assertion may not always be the most appropriate response in every situation. There are at least three contexts in which it may be more skilled to be non-assertive:

1 *Seeing that someone is in a difficult situation.* If you are in a busy restaurant and know that a new waitress has just been employed, you are more likely to overlook certain issues, such as someone who came in later being served before you. Here it is appropriate to be nonassertive, since personal rights are not deliberately being denied, and to be assertive may cause undue stress to the other person.
2 *Interacting with a highly sensitive individual.* If by being assertive someone is liable to burst into floods of tears, or physically attack you, it may be wise to be nonassertive, especially if the encounter is 'one off'.
3 *Manipulating others.* Some females will deliberately employ a helpless style in order to achieve their goals, for example to encourage a male to change a flat tyre on their car. Equally, males may do likewise. For example, if stopped by police following a minor traffic misdemeanour it may be wise to be nonassertive ('I'm terribly sorry officer, but I've just bought this car. . .'). Such behaviour is more likely to achieve positive benefits.

Nevertheless, a pattern of continued nonassertion will not be the most productive approach for the majority of people. Quite often what happens is that individuals will move from prolonged nonassertion straight into aggression, feeling they can no longer put up with being used, taken for granted or having their rights ignored. It is therefore more appropriate to employ assertiveness at an early stage during social interaction. The advantages of so doing have been underlined by Zuker (1983) who pointed out that assertiveness is:

> not a mysterious, mystical gift that some have and others don't. Rather it's a series of skills that anyone can master with a little practice. The exciting thing about acquiring these skills is that you will suddenly find yourself being able to say no without guilt, to ask for what you want directly, and in general to communicate more clearly and openly in all your relationships. Most important, your self-confidence will improve dramatically.
>
> (p. 12)

Chapter 13

Group interaction and leadership

INTRODUCTION

This book is about people and how they behave when interrelating and communicating. This can take place either in dyadic interactions or alternatively in larger gatherings. The various social skills which have occupied the preceding chapters, questioning, nonverbal communication, reinforcing, reflecting, listening and so on, are broadly applicable regardless of the number of individuals involved, although nuances of deployment will obviously differ depending upon the context. Some skills, however, e.g. reflecting and self-disclosure, are more likely to be made use of in smaller, more intimate encounters. Consequently, much of this book, including various examples of skill utilisation, has concentrated, at least implicitly, upon what happens when two people communicate. Interaction in the group context has not been directly considered. While many of the communication skills which form part of dyadic interaction can also be used when people get together in groups, there are added complexities associated with the latter which must be appreciated. As Applbaum *et al.* (1973, p. 63) pointed out:

> Research has shown that communication patterns between two people are different from those that occur with three or more people in face-to-face interaction. The difference is not just a matter of size. . . . Many of the principles of intrapersonal and interpersonal communication apply as well to group communication, but some new factors affect the communication between individual members.

It is with such factors that the first half of this chapter is concerned. The remainder concentrates upon the characteristics and skills associated with a rather special and particularly important position within the group – that of leader.

Before progressing, however, it may be a useful and interesting exercise to pause momentarily, to reflect upon the ubiquity of the group in social life. The individual is born into a social group and, as he develops, comes to play a more active part in an increasing range of them. Apart from the family he may be a member of a staff group, a sports team, study group, choir, appreciation society, yoga class, trade union committee, parent–teacher association, amateur photographic club, political party executive, to mention but a very few of the possibilities. (It may be worthwhile and illuminating for the reader, at this point, to list the various groups to which he or she belongs, to reflect upon the amount of time spent actively involved in each and the extent to which, collectively, they account for the various social activities engaged in. The outcome will probably be quite surprising! Does it concur with the observation by Simpson and Wood (1992, p. 1) that, 'Most of our waking hours are spent in, and the bulk of our work-related productivity occurs within, settings consisting of [groups]'?)

Argyle (1983a) suggested that the three most important types of group in terms of everyday interaction are family, friendship and work groups. Other types of small group activity identified by Argyle include committee, problem-solving and creative groups and, second, T-groups and therapy groups. Each category could, of course, be further differentiated. Dealing solely with groups in the therapeutic context, Massarik (1972), for instance, listed no fewer than thirty-nine identifiable variants. Since it is highly unlikely that being involved in this particular type will feature prominently in the daily routine of the typical individual, this figure serves to underscore the plethora of groups which abound and their pervasion in social life.

Focusing upon work groups it is evident that an important part of the service provided by such interpersonal professionals as doctors, nurses, social workers, teachers, etc., entails group involvement. Indeed, it would seem that there is a growing trend towards an even greater use of groups among health professionals for the delivery of care (Northouse and Northouse, 1992). In addition to the many types of practitioner-led group presently serving to maintain health and prevent illness, Naisbitt (1982) estimated some half a million self-help varieties in the USA alone! Commenting upon the group with which the social worker is involved, Brown (1979) made an initial distinction between direct work with clients and indirect work for clients. The former may include dealing with natural groups, such as the family, as the target of intervention rather than an individual member of that family; second, institutionalised groups in, for example, psychiatric hospitals, prisons or residential centres; third, community groups such as self-help, pressure or action groups. The second dimension of group involvement, while not directly encompassing the client, nevertheless plays an important part in enabling professional duties to be discharged effectively. Here can be listed meetings: with colleagues; in association with further training; during inter-professional case conferences; with voluntary groups; and in connection with professional associations. Such a system of classification could, no doubt, be applied with varying degrees of flexibility to other professions apart from that of social work and again serves to emphasise the range of group contexts within which the professional is called upon to operate.

A more general system of classification, however, has been proposed by Northouse and Northouse (1992). Drawing upon the essential nature of activities engaged in, they identified a continuum of involvement with process groups at one end and content groups located at the other. The latter are primarily concerned with substantive issues, quality of decisions reached, amount of output, etc. Process groups, by contrast, devote more of their attention and energies to the internal workings of the group and the well-being of its members. (This distinction is an echo of an earlier one encountered in Chapter 2 when the multi-dimensionality of communication was discussed. It will also re-appear shortly.) All groups share elements of both concerns, Northouse and Northouse (1992) believe; it is the balance which serves to locate them at some point on this continuum and provides a distinct identity.

WHAT IS A GROUP?

The word 'group' has occurred several times in the preceding pages without, presumably, causing undue confusion. It is highly unlikely, however, that each reader will have attached the same meaning to it. If asked to attempt to produce a formal definition, many would probably find the task more difficult than it might have seemed at first blush. (You can test this for yourself by closing the book at this point and committing your deliberations on the issue to paper.) Most would probably agree that a group necessarily involves a plurality of individuals – but how many? While four or five people would probably be acceptable would forty or fifty – and what about 4000 or 5000?

A common distinction is that between small groups and larger aggregations with the lower limits of the former being in the region of two to five and the upper limits fifteen to twenty. However, there is little agreement on precise numbers (Bormann, 1990), leading many to agree with Hare (1976) that attempts to define small groups purely in terms of size are fruitless. Size *per se* is not the key factor but rather availability for face-to-face interaction. This characteristic also forms the basis of the distinction between 'primary' and 'secondary' groups, first drawn by Cooley (1929). Primary groups are typified by the potential for close and frequent face-to-face association. It is with groups of this type that this chapter will be concerned to the exclusion of larger assemblies.

This notion of face-to-face contact has been extended by a number of authors who stress the importance of interaction and interpersonal influence among members in defining group existence (Saks and Krupat, 1988). A small group was regarded by Bales (1950), for instance, as 'any number of persons engaged in interaction with one another in a single face-to-face meeting or series of such meetings, in which each member receives some impression or perception of each other member' (p. 33). In a similar vein, Shaw (1981, p. 8), wrote that 'two or more persons who are interacting with one another in such a manner that each person influences and is influenced by each other person', constitutes a group and that small groups, for practical reasons, tend to have an upper limit of about twenty members.

In addition to interacting with and influencing each other, the interdependence of group members has been noted (Zander, 1982; Brown, 1988). Thus events that affect one person will have a bearing on the rest of the group and group outcomes will affect each individual member.

The fact that groups are typically formed for some identifiable purpose and that those who belong share at least one common goal, has been regarded as an essential characteristic by many authors (Hare, 1976). In the case of a formal group, this goal is often reflected in its name (e.g. Eastham Branch of the Animal Rights Movement; Eastham F.C. Supporters Club; Eastham Brass Band). Interestingly, when a group's goal has been attained or rendered obsolete, members may channel their energies in other directions, thus ensuring the continued existence of the group. Eastham F.C. Supporters Club may still meet to have a drink and play snooker even though Eastham F.C. has long since ceased to exist! New goals have come to dominate group activities. This does not always happen, of course. In many cases the achievement of the group goal or goals results in its disbandment.

Apart from acting to maintain the group and directing its activities, goals also influence the development of particular structures and procedures within the group. Such considerations will be dealt with more fully in a later section of the chapter.

While interaction and interpersonal influence, interdependence and the pursuit of a common goal or goals are commonly accepted as the quintessence of the concept, various other defining features of groups can be found in the literature. Campbell (1958), for example, pointed out that groups are reasonably enduring units and that any aggregate, in order to be so regarded, must have a certain permanency. But how long must it last? As with questions of size, no easy, absolute or commonly accepted answer can be given. Perhaps one way around this problem is to invoke members' perceptions of their 'groupness'. Thus, in order to merit the label 'group', members must see themselves as forming a group. This type of more subjective criterion has been advocated by, amongst others, Turner *et al.* (1987), invoking the concept of people's self-categorisations. As such, a group exists to the extent that two or more individuals consider themselves as belonging to the same social category. The corresponding perceptions of non-group members have also been held to be important (Feldman, 1985). Individuals must be seen by outsiders to belong to this type of collective.

WHY DO PEOPLE JOIN GROUPS?

Accepting the universality of group involvement, the next question to tackle is why should this be so? Why should this prevalence to associate closely with others in social units exist? One reasonable attempt at explanation suggests that individuals rely upon group membership in order to achieve goals and satisfy certain felt needs (Brigham, 1991). These needs may be interpersonal, informational or material and, in some cases, by their nature, may only be capable of being met in a social context. While we may not have to join a group in order to gain knowledge of our physical environment it is only through association with others that we come to an understanding of the social world which we inhabit and, indeed, of ourselves. Festinger (1954) proposed that individuals engage in a process of social comparison in order to establish where they stand in certain respects. For example, it is only possible to decide if you are a good, average or poor student by comparing your marks with those of others on your course. By so doing you gradually create an impression of yourself, including your strengths and weaknesses.

When it comes to satisfying interpersonal needs, the necessity to establish some form of group contact is obvious. These particular needs, according to Schutz (1955), may be for varying degrees of, first, inclusion – to want to belong or feel part of a social entity; second, control – to dominate or be controlled; and third, affection – at the extremes, to love or hate. Argyle (1983b) also proposed that much of interpersonal behaviour is in response to social drives for affiliation, dominance, dependency or aggression. But, of course, being able to, for example, dominate depends upon one or more others who are prepared to be submissive. There is some evidence that groups composed of members whose needs are complementary rather than conflicting tend to be more satisfying and enduring. In a study involving student nurses, Bermann and Miller (1967) reported that those who complemented each other in terms of dominance formed more stable and satisfying associations.

Groups may also be established for material reasons. It may be to their mutual benefit for a number of individuals to pool their various resources in order to complete some task. Trade union and cooperative movements are some of the more contemporary examples of collectives being formed to further the material well-being of members. Indeed the gregarious nature of *Homo sapiens* is thought to have stemmed from the advantages of hunting in groups and sharing the kill.

HOW ARE GROUPS ORDERED AND REGULATED?

Given that groups are made up of individuals, each with particular, and perhaps contrasting, personalities, opinions and preferences, it seems reasonable to ask how they manage to become sufficiently organised and ordered for goals to be pursued efficiently. The emergence of group *norms* is of crucial importance in this respect. As groups evolve, regularities of operation begin to emerge reflecting the creation of expectations on the part of members. Such norms can be thought of as, 'those behaviours, attitudes, and perceptions that are approved of by the group and expected (and, in fact, often demanded) of its members. Such norms will generally have powerful effects on the thoughts and actions of group members' (Baron *et al.*, 1992, p. 11). It should be noted that it is not only overt behaviour which is subject to a normative influence but also the characteristic perceptions, thoughts and feelings which members entertain. Not all aspects of group life are governed to the same extent by norms (Northouse and Northouse, 1992). Those most stringently subjected to this type of influence include activities: directly concerned with the achievement of group goals and the satisfaction of members' needs, especially the needs of the most powerful in the group; commonly associated with group membership both by those within and outwith the group; and amenable to public scrutiny. Thus strict norms govern the examination of patients but not the colour of underwear that the doctor should use! Secord and Backman (1974) pointed out that behaviours which have a strong physiological basis and those which could only be performed at considerable personal cost to the individual are less likely to come under normative control.

Apart from facilitating goal achievement, norms serve to increase regularity and predictability in the operation of the group (Brown, 1988). Members can determine, with reasonable accuracy, what is likely to happen in most situations. This also means that they have certain guidelines as to the nature and extent of their own involvement. Personal needs for status and esteem can also be satisfied through the operation of norms. Thus many of the tacit rules of everyday conversation are intended to avoid causing offence or embarrassment in public. A further advantage of having certain actions norm-governed is that it obviates the necessity of frequently having to rely upon personal influence (Secord and Backman, 1974). It can be pointed out, for example, that student nurses are expected to behave in a deferential manner to *all* ward sisters. Again the fact that certain norms have to do with the maintenance and integrity of the group must not be overlooked. Their importance is reflected in the level of disapprobation associated with terms such as traitor, scab, etc.

Norms may be implicit and only realised upon their contravention, or explicit and laid down in a set of formal prescriptions. The latter are often communicated directly to those in the group (Wilke and van Knippenberg, 1988). A case in point would be giving a new club member a set of formal rules and regulations governing club activities or a landlady informing a new lodger, in no uncertain terms, what he can and cannot do. More often, however, implicit normative expectations are made known more discreetly by, perhaps, watching what established members do and following their example. It is sometimes only when a violation occurs that one realises the existence of the norm. This information is often conveyed by subtle verbal and nonverbal cues.

Regardless of how they are communicated, norms are prescriptive. They must, to a greater or lesser extent, be complied with – members, to varying degrees, must conform. The origins of these pressures to conform to the expectations of the group may be internal. Feelings of shame or guilt may be sufficient to force the errant member to mend his ways. If not, external pressures in the form of positive and negative group sanctions may be brought to bear. In extreme cases, recalcitrance may result in boycott or indeed expulsion from the group.

Conformity to the commonly held views and practices of the majority has a number of advantages for the group. It tends to increase efficiency and facilitate group maintenance as well as reduce uncertainty and confusion among members and project a strong group image to the rest of society. Intense pressures to conform can, however, result in less desirable outcomes. One of these was identified by Janis (1972) and labelled 'Groupthink' which was defined as the 'deterioration of mental efficiency, reality testing, and moral judgement that results from in-group pressures' (p. 9). More recently, Janis has defined it in simpler terms as a tendency to seek concurrence (Deaux and Wrightsman, 1988). Groupthink tends to be fostered under conditions which stifle minority dissent from accepted points of view expressed and decisions arrived at. When group pressures to conform militate against the reasoned and objective consideration of a range of available options and discourage exploration of individual opinions, the decision reached by the group is frequently seriously flawed.

Norms, as we have seen, apply to all group members. In any group, however, it would be highly undesirable for everyone to act in exactly the same way. Specific sets of expectations concerning the behaviour of those in particular positions in the group are referred to as *roles*. Bormann (1990, p. 161), puts it as follows, 'Role, in the small group, is defined as that set of perceptions and expectations shared by the members about the behaviour of an individual in both the task and social dimension of group interaction.' Thus we would expect, even demand, a committee secretary to behave differently from the chairperson, and the smooth operation of a committee meeting, leading to a fruitful outcome, would depend upon this being the case.

Roles, in part, reflect status differences which exist between various positions in the group. *Status* represents the evaluation of a position in terms of the importance, prestige, etc., associated with it. Most groups are hier-archically structured in this respect with high-status positions affording greater opportunities to exercise social power and influence. Although status and power are usually closely associated, this need not necessarily be the case. Baron *et al.* (1992) cite the example of the British monarchy as having, 'exceptional status but relatively little power' (p. 7). As shall be seen in the following section, one facet of intra-group communication has to do with the acknowledgement and confirmation of status differences. This frequently operates at a covert level; for example, the chairperson *directs* the secretary while the secretary *advises* the chairperson. Further ramifications of status and the role of the group leader will be detailed later in the chapter.

Roles which evolve are a function of a number of determinants, including the nature of the specific group and its tasks. Nevertheless it would seem that there are certain roles which typify small group interaction and some of these have been identified and labelled by Benne and Sheats (1948), in a seminal work which still has considerable currency. They distinguished three categories of role. First, group task roles, second, those to do with group-building and maintenance, and third, individual roles. Examples of group task roles include information giver, information seeker, opinion giver, opinion seeker, evaluator-critic, and energiser, all of which contribute to the ability of the group to successfully accomplish its objective. Group building and maintenance roles promote good internal relations and a strong sense of solidarity. They encompass those of encourager, harmoniser, compromiser and gatekeeper. Finally individual roles such as aggressor, blocker, playboy/playgirl, and dominator may be played out. Unlike the previous two categories these tend to be dysfunctional to the smooth and successful operation of the group.

Some groups have a member who tends to be much more reticent than the rest, who interacts minimally with others and fails to participate fully in group activities. This individual is commonly labelled the isolate and, indeed, in larger groups may, for the most part, go unnoticed. The fact that this individual does not become fully involved does not mean that he has nothing to offer as tactful handling by an adroit leader can often demonstrate. When a group is beset by setback and failure it is not uncommon for some member to be singled out as the cause and accused of not 'pulling his weight' or letting the group down. By 'identifying' the source of failure members can have their flagging beliefs in the worth of the group reaffirmed and redouble their efforts to achieve the goal. The projection of unacceptable personal feelings or tendencies upon the scapegoat can also assuage feelings of guilt among the others.

Through the establishment and operation of norms and roles, therefore, regular and predictable patterns of activity come to characterise much of group life. Communication between members is a necessary prerequisite for the emergence and perpetuation of such norms and roles. At the same time, the communication process is heavily influenced by them as will be seen in the next section.

INTRA-GROUP COMMUNICATION

The essential part which communication among members plays in the group is widely acknowledged. Applbaum et al. (1973, p. 61) made this point forcefully when they wrote,

The importance of communication in the group cannot be overestimated. Initially communication unites the collection of individuals when they interact to fulfil some common purpose. The pressures to communicate are induced by the need to resolve internal and external problems that arise when the group tries to meet that goal.

Thus communication makes it possible for those belonging to the group to organise themselves, pool resources and, through co-operative action, solve some common difficulty or reach a desired goal (Wilke and Meertens, 1994). But, in addition, the resolution of interpersonal and indeed personal difficulties within the group and the creation and maintenance of harmonious relationships relies upon effective communication. These two types of communication should, by now, be familiar. In relation to groups, they have been referred to as *content* and *process* dimensions, or alternatively, as *task* and *socio-emotional* or *psyche* communication (Luft, 1984; Littlejohn, 1989). Task communication, as the name suggests, concerns substantive group activities and typically operates in accordance with reason and logic. Psyche communication, on the other hand, 'refers to feelings and attitudes of people who are interacting, to how people relate to one another' (Luft, 1984, p. 126). This does not necessarily mean, as will be recalled from earlier in the book, that each communicative act must either be task or psyche in function. While ostensibly discussing how to solve a task issue, members may, contemporaneously, be forming impressions of where they stand in relation to the others in terms of status, positive regard, etc. Such judgements are often heavily influenced by nonverbal as well as verbal communication. (The reader may wish to turn back to Chapter 2 to reconsider some of the general features of communication and to Chapter 3 on the functions of NVC.)

Task and socio-emotional (roughly comparable to psyche communication) aspects of group communication have also been identified by Bales (1950, 1970). Using a system which he developed known as Interaction Process Analysis, Bales found that interpersonal behaviour during small group interaction could be located in some one of twelve distinct categories. Six of these were concerned with task functions. Of these, two involved the asking or giving of opinions, evaluations, etc.; another two, the asking or giving of information, repetition or clarification; and the final two the asking or giving of suggestions or directions. A further three categories related to positive socio-emotional reactions. These were, first, showing solidarity, helping or rewarding; second, showing tension release (e.g. joking, laughing) or satisfaction; and third, showing agreement, acceptance, understanding, etc. The final three categories were also in the socio-emotional area but were negative in character. They were, first, showing antagonism; second, showing tension, withdrawing or asking for help; and, third, disagreeing or rejecting. By analysing the communication between members in this way a number of interesting discoveries can be made. It can be established, for example, whether most of what takes place is concerned with task or socio-emotional issues, and, if the latter, the types of relationship which seem to predominate in the group. Different types of difficulty in group operation can also be detected. At the level of the individual, the extent and nature of the contribution of each member can also be ascertained.

A common finding to emerge from this sort of detailed analysis is that some members participate markedly more than others in group discussion. This seems to be a function of several factors including: (1) position in the group and status – high-status members, particularly group leaders, tend to contribute extensively. (2) Knowledge – those with relevant information are frequently vociferous and indeed may be encouraged to be so by other group members. (3) Personality – extroverts, almost by definition, are more communicative than their more introverted colleagues. There is some evidence to suggest that individuals have their characteristic levels of participation across groups, although these are not immutable. (4) Physical location – those centrally located in the group frequently take a more active part. (5) Group size – it has been found that differences between members in the amount of contribution to group interaction increase in relation to increases in overall group size (Bormann, 1990).

As well as quantitative differences existing between high and low participants, disparities in the typical form of their communications have also been identified (Bales, 1970). While high participators tend to provide information, give opinions and make suggestions, low participators, when they do contribute, do so by asking questions or expressing agreement. Again the target of such communication is frequently different. While low contributors, for the most part, direct contributions to individual members, high contributors are more inclined to address their remarks to the group. This is frequently associated with attempts to exert influence and exercise power. (This will be dealt with further, in the second part of the chapter, in relation to group leadership.) Those who contribute most are also likely to be the recipients of frequent messages from others.

Alternative systems for conducting fine-grained analysis of the sorts of communicative acts carried out by group members have been formulated. While Interpersonal Process Analysis is one of the most frequently cited, Honey (1988) produced interesting findings using procedures similar to, but more simple than, those used of Bales (1970). The nine possibilities for categorising behaviour identified by Honey (1988) are (a) Seeking Ideas (b) Proposing (c) Suggesting (d) Building (e) Disagreeing (f) Supporting (g) Seeking Clarification (h) Clarifying/Explaining/Informing and (i) Difficulty Stating. A number of fascinating outcomes have emerged from sequential analyses of the interaction of a range of groups. If we take the categories of Suggesting and Proposing, which are quite similar apart from the fact that the former is a more tentative expression of a possible course of action often couched in the form of a question (e.g. Could we see how everyone has gone about tackling the question before discussing reasons why?), the most probable response to instances of each was markedly different. Thus Proposing was most likely to evoke a statement by another member outlining difficulties associated with the advocated course of action. The most probable reaction to Suggesting, by contrast, was an expression of support for the procedure or course of action intimated!

As those forming groups commence to interact with one another, regularities begin to emerge in the form of identifiable patterns of communication. Restrictions on access which may develop as group structures emerge, help shape such networks (Baron *et al.*, 1992). The effects of these patterns, or communication networks, on a number of variables, including group efficiency and member satisfaction, has been investigated by researchers. As initially described by Bavelas (1950), five subjects were each given a number of cards, each containing several symbols. Their task was to identify the symbol common to each member's card. Since the subjects were located in separate booths, channels of communication between them could be carefully controlled by the experimenter, creating the four networks outlined in Figure 13.1.

In each of the four diagrams in Figure 13.1, the circles represent particular group members and the adjoining lines are available channels of communication. Thus in the Circle arrangement, for example, (a) and (b) could communicate but not (a) and (e) – at least not directly. It should also be appreciated that members do not necessarily have to bear the particular spatial relationships to each other depicted in each of the diagrams in order for those networks to pertain. It is rather the communication channels in each case which is the telling feature.

Networks differ in two important respects. The first is in terms of *connectivity*; the second, *centrality*. Connectivity refers to the number of channels available to members, in the network. The Circle in Figure 13.1 contains five channels and is therefore a more highly connected structure than any of the others. Centrality is defined as a function of the number of channels from a given position to each other's position (Raven and Rubin, 1983). Thus, of the four alternatives in Figure 13.1, the Circle, although the most highly connected, is the least centralised structure, followed by the Chain, Y and Wheel, in order. With the Wheel it can be seen that one person (c) can communicate directly with a total of four others.

Results from a number of research studies suggest that these networks have a significant impact on group efficiency and member satisfaction. Group productivity in terms of the number of tasks completed, and efficiency measured by time taken to complete each together with the number of messages needed, were found to increase with increases in group centrality. The Wheel was, therefore, more productive and efficient followed by the Y, the Chain and the Circle. The likelihood of emerging as group leader was also found to be directly related to the centrality of that person's position in the arrangement. Such findings led Guetzkow and Simon (1955) to propose organisational development as an explanatory concept. The increased productivity and efficiency of more centralised structures was regarded as a consequence of the greater opportunities which they afford for groups to organise themselves. Upon reviewing some of the research, Shaw (1981) concluded, however, that it was not entirely in keeping with this hypothesis. Rather, the concept of saturation would seem to have greater explanatory

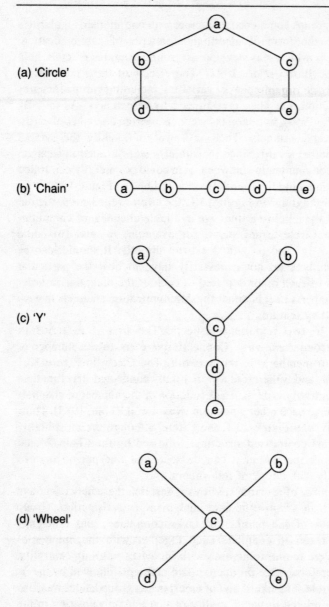

(a) 'Circle'

(b) 'Chain'

(c) 'Y'

(d) 'Wheel'

Figure 13.1 Communication networks

power. In this sense, with tasks which are much more complex than those investigated by Bavelas, highly centralised networks may be less, rather than more, effective due to the unreasonable demands placed upon the individual in the most central position – this position becomes saturated.

While more centrally organised groups tend to be more productive and efficient (especially when dealing with simple problems), members frequently manifest low morale and express little satisfaction with group activities. Subjects operating in the Circle typically express much greater satisfaction with their involvement in the group than those in the Wheel, in spite of the fact that they may not, collectively, achieve as much. Shaw (1981) proposed that this is most likely a result of the greater independence of action which members enjoy in the former.

In naturally operating groups though, the communication channels between members are not limited in the contrived fashion described by Bavelas. Networks are completely connected, in principle, with each individual free to communicate with each other. In practice, however, it has been found that those which actually emerge frequently resemble one of the more restricted configurations (Secord and Backman, 1974). A range of factors (including the roles being played by different individuals) may serve to reduce the number and sequence of channels typically used. Physical arrangement determining visual accessibility of certain members to others may also play a part. Cary (1978) demonstrated that likelihood of initiation of conversation was dependent upon the prior engagement, by those individuals, in eye contact.

Having considered the defining characteristics of groups, some of the reasons for their existence, the mechanisms by which they become ordered and regulated, and the types and patterns of communication between members, the next step is to examine a particularly influential position within the group – that of leader – and the characteristics and skills associated with leadership.

LEADERS AND LEADERSHIP

What is a leader? What is leadership? Are leaders born to or are they created by the society in which they live? The concepts 'leader' and 'leadership' have been examined and defined in more different ways than almost any other concept associated with group dynamics. Preoccupation with the role of leader has not merely been confined to the investigations of social scientists. Although not studied extensively and scientifically until the last three or four decades, leadership has intrigued philosophers and historians for centuries. Such famous leaders as Benjamin Franklin, Disraeli, George Washington, Gandhi and Hitler, have intrigued and tested the ability of historians to clarify the qualities and behaviours of these people. Despite the fact that so many people have studied this phenomenon there is still no precise or commonly agreed definition of leadership. Instead there is a range of definitions which have a fair degree of concordance.

DEFINITION OF LEADERSHIP

One of the earliest definitions of leadership was provided by Stogdill (1950) who claimed that, 'Leadership may be considered as the process (act) of influencing the activities of an organized group in its efforts toward goal setting and goal achievement' (p. 3). Stogdill spent the next twenty years or so attempting to identify, analyse and develop the concept of leadership using a range of perspectives, such as leadership as a focus of group dynamics, a feature of personality, the art of inducing compliance, a function of the situation, to name but a few. In other words, many of the diverse definitions were a result of the researcher's a priori selection of one perspective rather than another (Stogdill, 1974).

Nevertheless, subsequent authors appear to endorse Stogdill's original claim that leadership is concerned with the act of influencing others, whether the influence is strong or overt as in the case of a supervisor or teacher, or more facilitating or subtle, as in the case of a moderator or counsellor. Hollander (1978), for example, maintained that 'leadership is a process of influence between a leader and those who are followers' (p. 1). Rauch and Behling (1984) defined leadership as 'the process of influencing the activities of an organized group toward goal achievement' (p. 46). Continuing this theme of 'influencing', Hosking and Morley (1986) defined leaders as 'those who are both perceived, and expected, to make consistent, influential contributions to decision-making processes' (p. 11). The common elements in these definitions imply that leadership involves a process of social influence in which a person guides group members towards a goal. (Further consideration of the features and effects of social influence can be found in Chapter 11.)

But how does one person influence others in a group context? According to Anthony (1988), a leader invests considerable attention, practice, energy and time in learning to manage the impression he makes on others. Even by appearance alone, stated Stone (1962), 'a person [leader] announces his identity, shows its value, expresses his mood or proposes his attitude' (p. 101). More recently, Meindl et al. (1985) and Shamir (1992) have experimentally demonstrated that performance outcomes, leadership style and leader behaviours are instrumental in accounting for the degree of influence which the leader has on group members. The latter part of this chapter will examine in more detail how leadership can influence the decision-making process in groups.

Using the context of a discussion group, it is fair to say that each statement or question put forward by an individual group member could be identified as an act of leadership. However, some individuals appear to be more effective than others at directing a group toward the attainment of its goals. These persons can be described as focal persons or leaders since their contributions to the accomplishment of group goals are significantly greater than any other member's contribution. Although a leader may be appointed either formally or informally to lead a group, seldom does that person completely dominate the group's procedures. Instead, in most discussion or decision-making groups, other members can be called upon occasionally to perform certain acts of leadership. Thus, although certain individuals are elected to provide group leadership, acts of leadership can be exhibited by any other group member.

THEORIES OF LEADERSHIP

Whilst most researchers have been centrally concerned with the problems of why or how leaders emerge, their investigations have been conducted using a range of perspectives. As a result, several theories have emerged which attempt to provide a better understanding about the character of leadership or about the effects of different styles of leadership in different situations. What follows is a brief outline of three of the most notable of these theories, namely trait, situation and need theory.

Trait theory

Throughout history many people have believed that leaders are born, not made, and that truly great leaders are discovered, not developed. The assumption underlying this belief is that a leader is a unique person possessing some innate ability which allows him or her to assume a leadership position no matter the social situation. Thus the trait approach attempted to distinguish leaders from non-leaders on the basis of how they differ on personal characteristics.

Since the early twentieth century, hundreds of research studies have been conducted to identify the personal attributes of leaders, such as physical factors (height, weight, physique, appearance and age), ability characteristics (intelligence, fluency of speech, scholarship and knowledge) and personality features (conservatism, introversion–extroversion, dominance, emotional control, etc.). The most influential review of literature on leadership 'traits' (Stogdill, 1948) came to the conclusion that general qualities or abilities could not be discerned. Instead, the qualities and skills which leaders require were largely determined by the demands of the situation in which the leader is to function. Since these early reviews were generally pessimistic about this line of research, many researchers abandoned the search for innate characteristics of leaders. Despite a number of later studies (England, 1975; Bass, 1981; Yukl, 1981) aimed at identifying 'traits' in relation to managerial ability, no single trait has been consistently associated with leadership. To date, the traits approach has failed to provide a coherent set of personal characteristics which differentiates between effective and ineffective leaders. While the personality approach to leadership did provide interesting data, situational factors seemed to be more important in determining who would become a leader.

Situation theory

Researchers, therefore, began to turn from studying traits of leaders to studying the situation in which leadership was located. In other words, it was assumed that as situations varied, so did the amount and type of leadership required. Thus the traits or skills which constituted an effective leader in one group did not necessarily transfer to another. The situationally contingent approach explicitly claims there are no universally appropriate styles of leadership; rather the leader's behaviour is contingent upon the demands of the situation.

In the work of Fiedler (see especially 1978 and 1986) can be found the earliest systematic attempt to develop a contingency approach to the study of leadership style. Using a variety of group situations, ranging from sports groups through to military and industrial settings, Fiedler's starting point was that some leaders were more committed to the nature or structure of the task whilst others were more oriented to achieving good personal relationships within the group. He concluded that it was unusual to find individuals who were equally oriented to both group needs and task completion. (This aspect will be dealt with more fully later in the chapter.)

Very briefly, Fiedler, using a questionnaire technique as opposed to direct observation, examined the attitudes of the leader towards co-workers. A scale, known as the least preferred co-worker (LPC) and comprising eighteen pairs of adjectives (e.g. cold–warm, boring–interesting, kind–unkind), enabled researchers to distinguish between leaders who provided favourable depictions ('high LPC' leaders) and those whose descriptions were unfavourable ('low LPC' leaders). On the basis of his own and other research evidence, Fiedler maintained that high LPC leaders extract superior performances from their subordinates in some situations whilst, in other contexts, low LPC leaders do better.

For instance, task-oriented leaders appear to be most effective when they are on very good terms with group members, the task is clearly structured and they are held in high esteem within the group Alternatively, task-oriented leaders are still effective when they are on poor terms with group members, the task is ambiguous and they are held in low esteem. However, it would appear that when moderate relationships exist between leader and group members, when the task is moderately clear and when the leader has a moderate position of esteem, the leader who emphasises good relationships within the group is the most effective at achieving member participation in the problem-solving or decision-making process. In other words, Fiedler maintained that the type of leader required in order for group performance to be enhanced, is situationally contingent.

One major criticism of this approach is that group performance is measured in terms of its task or goal completion. Output is only one measure of a group's value, however. Individual group members' satisfaction may be equally important yet not contribute to the achievement of the extrinsic goal. It will be recalled from earlier in the chapter that the most satisfied members don't necessarily belong to the most productive groups. Fiedler's model leaves questions relating to group relationships unresolved. Overall, therefore, while Fiedler's contingency model has its supporters (Chemers, 1983), it also has its critics (Hosking and Morley, 1986). However, both groups are of the opinion that considerably more research needs to be conducted on the relationship between leadership style and situational control (Fiedler and Garcia, 1987).

Need theory

According to need theory, leadership arises out of the necessity for the group to perform certain functions or roles in order that its goals be achieved. The leader who emerges has the skills and ability to ascertain what the group needs are and is most capable at providing the means for their achievement. Groups have at least two basic objectives: to complete a task and to maintain effective social relationships among the members.

The work of Hollander is most closely associated with this idea, which he tends to refer to as a 'transactional approach'. According to Hollander and Offerman (1990), in order for a leader to continue his position of leadership he must be responsive to the needs of the group members. That is, leaders must pay attention to maintaining good working relationships while at the same time moving the group towards successful task completion. In other words, it does no good to complete a task if the manner of doing so alienates most of the group members. Thus if some group members refuse to come to the next meeting, the group has not been successful.

Hollander (1985) claimed that this theoretical approach to understanding leadership effectiveness includes two basic ideas. First, any member of a group may become a leader by taking actions that assist the group to *complete its task* and *maintain effective relationships*. Second, any leadership function may be fulfilled by different members performing a variety of relevant behaviours such as suggesting how the group's work can be improved, relieving tension when it gets too high, listening carefully and respecting other people's views and facilitating interaction between group members by asking questions and reinforcing responses.

A further theory of leadership, linked to Hollander's need theory, has been forwarded by Blake and Mouton (1982), based largely on the answers to two basic questions: how *strong* is the leader's concern for task completion or production (i.e. group performance) and how *strong* is the leader's concern for the feelings of group members? Thus the ideal leader is one who values both personal relationships and effective task completion highly. However, there is some concern that this potent combination of high production coupled with high care for people may not be pertinent to all situations (Quinn and McGrath, 1982).

According to Hersey and Blanchard (1982) the maturity of the group (i.e. whether newly formed or existing) can have a major influence on optimal leadership style. These authors contend that the best leadership style for a newly formed group is one in which there is a *high* task concern and *low* concern for group members. Only as the group matures can the leader adopt an "ideal" style, as described by Blake and Mouton, which involves high task output and strong concern for people.

Another factor which impinges greatly on the style of the leader is that of gender. Eagly and Koran (1991), in a review of studies of leadership in small groups, noted that males emerged as leaders significantly more often than females. They postulated that there were two principal reasons for this finding. First, leadership is largely perceived as linked to task competence and, in experimental studies, mixed gender groups are often requested to complete a specific task or reach a satisfactory decision. Second, males tend to specialise more in task behaviours (Stasser, 1992) and since prominent contributions to task completion lead to the attribution of leadership qualities, men are invariably perceived as leaders. However, it was also noted from Eagly and Koran that when groups were asked to perform more complex tasks over a longer period of time, men fared less well than women in the leadership stakes. Women emerged significantly more than men as socio-emotional leaders, that is catering for the emotional needs of the group. In summary, it would appear that complementary roles for both genders is the most effective strategy, depending upon the composition of the group and the tasks which confront group members.

This need approach to leadership is one of the most concrete and direct approaches available for improving a person's leadership skills and so improving the effectiveness of a group. However, it must be noted that this approach is not without its critics, who claim that there are so many diverse and varied actions that individual members can make when trying to accomplish task completion and group maintenance that defining specific skills for every situation is hard to achieve. Morley and Hosking (1985) recognised that 'the literature on leadership has not been informed by attempts systematically to articulate the nature of the skills which make leaders effective' (p. 2). Despite an absence of empirical research into leadership skills *per se*, insights can be gained from an analysis of studies in allied areas such as teaching, industry, military and management, which have drawn their inspiration from and added to interaction theory. Some of these skills will be identified and examined later in the chapter.

LEADER PERFORMANCE

The performance of the leader can be examined at two different but related levels. First, at the macro level, observing leaders in action has revealed that leadership style can affect group productivity and the attitudes of group members. Second, at the micro level, specific skills can be identified as depicting a particular leadership style.

Leadership styles

In what is now considered a classical study, Lewin, Lippitt and White (1939) distinguished three different group climates produced by these distinct styles of leadership: the autocratic (authoritarian), democratic and the laissez-faire (lax). Briefly, the researchers requested three adult leaders to adopt an autocratic (dictating orders and determining all policy), democratic (encouraging and helping group members to interact) or laissez-faire (no participation in the group's decision-making process) style with groups of 10- and 11-year-old boys in a recreational youth centre. The results revealed that when the groups were led by an autocratic leader, they were more dependent on the leader and did not cooperate freely with their peers. When the leaders adopted a democratic approach, the same boys showed more initiative and responsibility for the progress of the group and were more friendly towards each other, even when the leader left the room. In the laissez-faire or leaderless group, the boys lacked interest in their tasks and failed to complete successfully any of the tasks they had been set. Aggressive acts were more frequent under autocratic and laissez-faire leaders than they were under a democratic leader. There was more scapegoating in the autocratic group, in the form of boys occasionally being made a target of hostility until they eventually left the group. This hostility among the boys was three times as great in the autocratic group as it was in the democratic group. Finally, when a measure of 'liking' the leader was collected it was found that the most liked was the democratic leader, the least liked being the autocratic leader.

Building upon the original research and results of Lewin *et al.* (1939), Likert (1977) conceived of three categories of leadership, namely: exploitative/autocratic, benevolent/autocratic, and democratic/consultative. The distinctions drawn in the two autocratic categories are that the exploitative/autocratic emphasises threats, fear and punishment with little praise or reward while the benevolent/autocratic stresses more positive and less negative reinforcement. However, both use top-down communication patterns, with group members having little influence on goal-setting, methods adopted and decisions reached. The leadership processes in the consultative/democratic category are such that leaders and group members trust each other a great deal, leaders are supportive, easy to talk to, constantly asking for and using the group's ideas and praising and encouraging all-round participation. A bottom-up communication is adopted so allowing members to determine goals, tasks and methods. Decisions and controls are decentralised. Using these three scales in over 500 surveys, involving 20,000 managers in a wide range of organisations (banking, government, military, voluntary, business and health to name a few), Likert reported that the most effective leaders were located in the consultative/democratic category described above.

Since this study, a number of researchers have investigated the relative impact of leadership styles on group functioning (Martinko and Gardner, 1984; Miller and Monge, 1986; Wilke, 1991). From their findings it can be concluded that different styles are effective under different conditions. For example, autocratic leadership appears to be more effective when an urgent decision has to be made (a pilot giving orders to his crew to avert an air disaster, or a surgeon ordering his medical team to carry out specific procedures to save a patient's life). In such crucial circumstances, leaders would be ill advised to stop and take a vote. On the other hand, when formal groups are meeting to establish or perhaps change certain operational rules or procedures (e.g. a school principal meeting with her staff to decide on school rules) it would be more appropriate to adopt a democratic approach, since there is then a greater chance of group members complying with the group findings.

Since we live in a democratic society, we would like to believe that all decisions should be made democratically and that the autocratic leader should not be acknowledged. However, this belief would be erroneous. A more constructive means of describing leadership styles is to suggest that a leader's behaviour ranges from autocratic to democratic to laissez-faire on different occasions (Bass, 1990).

Leadership skills

There are several behaviours which can be employed in order to be an effective leader in contexts ranging from the captaincy of a sporting group to the chairmanship of an organisation. These behaviours can be related to the task function of the leader or the maintenance function. Cartwright and Zander (1968) noted that this kind of division can be problematic, in that

> a member who helps a group to work co-operatively on a difficult problem may inadvertently help it to develop solidarity. . . [alternatively] an eager member may spur the group on in such a way that friction develops among the members, and even though the goal is achieved efficiently, the continued existence of the group is seriously endangered.
>
> (pp. 306–7)

However, Harnack et al. (1977) suggested that it matters little how these functions are labelled; what is important is the understanding that both these functions need to be performed if the group is to succeed.

Task skills

In this section it has been necessary to be selective given the range of literature available on leadership behaviour (Zander, 1982; Bryman 1986;

Anthony, 1988). What follows is a checklist of four basic task skills, gathered from a variety of sources, which a leader can use to produce effective group functioning.

Initiating/focusing

From the outset, it is important that the leader establishes aims for the group, proposes tasks or goals for its members and suggests procedures or ideas for the group's functioning. Halpin and Winer (1957) conducted a factor analysis of the results of 300 aircrewmen's descriptions of leadership behaviour and found that 'consideration and initiating structure' were central ingredients of the measurement of leader behaviour. This factor contained statements such as 'emphasizing the mission or job to be done', 'assigns crew members to particular tasks' and 'talks about how much should be done'. Tjosvold (1984) found that leader directiveness and warmth (corresponding to Halpin and Winer's consideration and initiating structure) had a pronounced impact on group performance. Whittington (1986) advocated that chairpersons, at the beginning of a meeting, should 'clarify the objectives of the meeting, deal with any procedural matters and introduce the main business' (p. 299). In addition, it is useful for the leader or chairperson to provide transitional summaries at the end of each phase of the meeting or discussion before introducing the next issue as this alerts the group to where they have been, where they are now and where they are going. (See Chapter 7 for further information on closure.)

Clarifying/elaborating

Once a meeting is under way or discussion of a topic begun, it is important that the group leader interprets or reflects ideas or suggestions by 'clearing-up' confusion which may have arisen, indicating alternatives which may be considered or by giving appropriate examples so that the group gains a clearer understanding. Turney et al. (1983) suggested that there are three separate but interrelated skills that are important in keeping a discussion full and to the point. The first is paraphrasing or summarising a member's contribution which has been rather involved or lengthy so that it is clearer both to him or herself and to the group (see Chapter 6 for more information on this skill). A good example of this skill in practice can be found in some TV programmes set up with a panel of academic experts to discuss profound philosophical problems related to modern-day living. Often the chairperson of such a programme will clarify or simplify the contributions of such academics for the understanding of a lay audience. Second, leaders who use probing questions will help the group clarify, support or develop an idea (see Chapter 5 on 'Questioning'). Finally, leaders should elaborate on contributions, by providing further information or appropriate examples, when the group has reached an impasse (see Chapter 8 on 'Explanation').

Promoting contributions

Most of us have at some time had the experience of engaging in animated conversation after the conclusion of a meeting with people who hardly spoke at all during the meeting. When asked why they kept interesting or perhaps novel ideas or suggestions to themselves they are apt to say, 'I couldn't get a word in edgeways', or 'I wasn't sure whether my idea was appropriate or not.' If one of the main purposes of a leader is to encourage maximum participation in the decision-making or problem-solving process, it is imperative that all members have an equal chance of contributing regularly in the group's proceedings. The leader can achieve this in a number of ways. If a member has appeared to be interested but has not made many contributions, the leader may be able to secure participation by tactfully asking for an opinion. However, emphasis must be placed on tact. It is more useful to say 'Before we go on, I would like to make sure that we have heard everyone's views or opinions', than bluntly asking, 'What do you think Harry?' where nothing is received at all because Harry has been caught off his guard. By warning everyone that their opinions are going to be solicited, there is a better chance of securing a response when attending to the non-participant.

The opposite of a 'non-talker', of course, is an 'over-talker'. Often one or two discussants monopolise proceedings, and leaders are sorely tempted to rebuke them. Instead, the leader should sensitively discourage such monopolisation by using phrases such as 'John, if we're not careful, this will end up as a two-person conversation' or words to that effect. It is important to be aware that while John's participation needs to be curtailed in no way should it be nullified.

Abercrombie (1974) and Turney *et al.* (1983) emphasised the point that members should be encouraged to comment on each other's contribution and suggested that one of the best ways this can be achieved is for the leader to remain silent and curb her nonverbal behaviour such as withdrawal of eye contact. There may be times when individual contributions are not being made as readily. In such circumstances, it is important that the leader remains quietly waiting and expectant rather than filling in periods of silence with talk.

Finally, the use of controversial or provocative questions or comments can, on occasions, help to revive a 'flagging' discussion.

Summarising

Several studies have been set up to investigate the specific communicative behaviours which leaders use to achieve their desired goals (Cartwright and Zander, 1968; Rackham and Morgan, 1977). One category which emerges from these research findings is that of 'integrating and summarising group activity'. This ability to summarise clearly and briefly the main group findings can differentiate effective from non-effective leaders. Rackham and Morgan (1977), comparing chairman behaviour with that of other group members, found that the difference on this summarising category between the two groups was significantly greater than on any other category, emphasising how strongly associated summarisation is with the role of chairman. These same authors go on to suggest that, 'the association is so strong that if another member of the meeting attempts to summarise, this is frequently seen as a personal challenge to the chairman and his authority' (p. 273).

In addition to the summary, it can be advantageous for the group to be encouraged to think further about some of the issues or ideas which have been explored during a meeting. The leader can achieve this by relating these issues to other areas not previously covered.

Finally, having the group evaluate how it functioned and what it has achieved is an appropriate way of checking the efficiency of the original goals which were set. In the light of this evaluation, goals can be maintained, extended or refined in order to enhance their realism.

Maintenance skills

There is some evidence to suggest that while formal leaders are the most sensitive to the task needs of the group, maintenance needs are more likely to be accurately perceived by ordinary group members (Katz and Kahn, 1976). If groups are to function effectively and with commitment, it is important that the leader is sensitive to maintaining good interpersonal relations within the group. Two basic skills can be applied to achieve this.

Relieving group tension

There are occasions when individuals within a group have ideologically opposing views regarding a particular issue, resulting in a tense situation, particularly when both participants are putting forward their views forcefully. There are two techniques which the leader can apply in such a situation. First, the leader may alleviate the situation by perhaps focusing on the ideas and away from personalities, with a view to draining off negative feelings between the two main protagonists and so putting a tense situation into a wider context.

Alternatively, the leader can introduce humour into the situation. Foot (1986) advocated the use of humour to

defuse a tense or hostile situation prevailing between two other interactants, thus enabling the contesting parties to back off from the confrontation without loss of face. . . . The humour serves not only as a corrective to restore the normal boundaries of social etiquette, but as an admonition that the argument has gone quite far enough.

(p. 362)

Supporting or encouraging

If members are to become totally involved in the group's activity, they must feel that any contribution they make will be accepted. Nothing will cool the eagerness of a discussant more quickly than having a contribution ignored or summarily dismissed. While it is apparent that not all contributions are equally valuable, the leader must administer supportive, encouraging statements appropriate to the individual (see Chapter 4 on 'Reinforcement'). Wilke (1991) carried out a series of experimental studies of leaders in informal groups and came to the conclusion that group members will support their leader when he is achieving group success and when he behaves in an equitable and fair way to all group members' contributions.

On the other hand, not only can rewards help an individual member to participate more willingly if encouraged to do so by the leader, they can also enhance the leader's control over the group. Bass (1981) suggested that those leaders who employed rewards as a way of influencing people felt they had a great deal of social control in the group situation. Alternatively, leaders who were more coercive and threatening in their approach felt they were a product of forces over which they had no control. In other words, the leaders' administration of rewards and punishments appeared to influence their social control.

OVERVIEW

This chapter has been concerned with small groups, how they operate and the manner in which leaders emerge and leadership is exercised within them. Groups, in this sense, can be thought of as involving a plurality of individuals who influence each other in the course of interaction and share a relationship of interdependence in pursuit of some common goal or goals. Members also characteristically develop a sense of belonging to this particular social entity. People come together to form groups to satisfy needs which may be interpersonal, informational or material. In so doing they become part of an ordered and regulated system which evolves through the establishment of, for example, norms, or commonly expected and accepted ways of perceiving, thinking, feeling and acting; the enactment of roles including that of leader; and the creation of identifiable forms and patterns of communication between members.

Additionally, an attempt has been made to show leadership as virtually synonymous with the act of influencing others in a range of group contexts. However, it is important to bear in mind the distinction between leadership and leader. While specific individuals are elected leaders, acts of leadership can be manifested by any group member.

Recent theories of leadership, notably situation and need theories, offer some scope in attempting to explain the emergence of leaders and their functioning. These theories suggest that leaders display specific skills and abilities in order to help the group achieve its goals; the skills and abilities exhibited being dependent upon the demands of the situation. Focusing on the actual performance of leaders, their behaviour can be examined on two levels: leadership styles at the macro level and leadership skills at the micro level. While at least three styles have emerged, notably autocratic, democratic and laissez-faire, it is important to note that a leader's behaviour can be exemplified using all three styles either at different points on the same occasion or on distinctly different occasions.

Six basic skills were identified, examined and defined and it was propounded that leaders who execute these skills can increase the productivity of the group and at the same time ensure the longevity of the group's life. As Zander (1982) succinctly writes, 'We are not directly interested in changing individuals except where changes in their information, skill, experience or confidence may help them to be more effective on behalf of their group' (p. xiii).

Chapter 14

Concluding comments

This book has been concerned with an examination of the central components of interpersonal com. unication, namely the social skills which individuals employ in order to achieve their goals in social encounters. The skills approach to the study of interpersonal behaviour, as outlined in Chapters 1 and 2, has provided a most productive and useful conceptual framework. As Buck (1991, pp. 87–8) pointed out:

> The notion of social skills has proved to be remarkably useful in many ways: It is a flexible concept that can be applied in a wide variety of situations; it has both theoretical and practical implications; it has led to a great volume of research in recent years, and there is evidence that social skills training is effective.

Thus, there is a solid theoretical base underpinning the skills perspective. The skills themselves obviously have direct application to interpersonal encounters and, when individuals receive tuition in these skills, their social performance tends to improve. It is not surprising, therefore, that the past twenty years have witnessed an explosion of publications pertaining to social skills, across a wide variety of contexts.

In this text the focus has been upon professional communication. The skills selected for inclusion were: nonverbal communication, reinforcement, questioning, reflecting, set induction, closure, explanation, listening, self-disclosure, influencing, assertiveness and group interaction. It is recognised that this selection is not exhaustive, since other specialised skills may be employed in particular settings. However, we believe that the skills included do represent the core behavioural elements of interpersonal communication and, for this reason, the practising professional needs to have a sound working knowledge of them.

It has not been our intention, however, to offer a cook-book approach to the study of interpersonal interaction. There are no 'right' or 'wrong' ways to communicate with others. Rather, there are alternative approaches which can be employed in any particular interactive episode to achieve a desired outcome, and it is up to the individual to select what is deemed to be the most appropriate. Such selection, however, demands an extensive knowledge of the range of alternatives available and their likely effects in any given context. It is at this level that the present book has been geared. The model of the interpersonal process outlined in Chapter 2 provides a conceptual framework which can be used as a basis for making such strategic decisions. An awareness of the skills covered and of their behavioural determinants, as presented in the remaining chapters, will contribute to the increased understanding of the process of interpersonal communication. It provides the reader with a language which can be used to study and interpret this process more fully.

In the final analysis, however, improvements in skilled performance necessitate practical action. In other words, it is only by converting knowledge of skills into skilled behaviour that improvements in social competence can occur. Thus we would encourage the reader to experiment with various social techniques in order to develop, refine, maintain or extend their existing repertoire of social skills. Once a wide repertoire has been developed, the individual thereby becomes a more effective communicator with the ability to adjust and adapt to varying social situations. For most professionals, this is an essential prerequisite to effective functioning.

Bibliography

Abele, A. (1986) 'Function of gaze in social interaction: communication and monitoring', *Journal of Nonverbal Behavior*, 10, 83–101.

Abelson, R. (1981) 'Psychological status of the script concept', *American Psychologist*, 36, 715–29.

Abercrombie, M.L.J. (1974) 'Aims and techniques of group teaching', Society for Research in Higher Education, London.

Abrami, P., Leenthal, L. and Perry, R. (1982) 'Educational seduction', *Review of Educational Research*, 52, 446–64.

Adams, C. (1977) 'Physical attractiveness research: toward a developmental social psychology of beauty', *Human Development*, 20, 217–39.

Adelman, R. D., Greene, M.G., Charon, R. and Friedmann, E. (1992) 'The content of physician and elderly patient interaction in the medical primary care encounter', *Communication Research*, 19, 370–80.

Adler, R. and Towne, N. (1975) *Looking out, looking in*, Reinhart Press, San Francisco.

Agar, M. (1985) 'Institutional discourse', *Text*, 5, 147–68.

Ainsworth-Vaughan, N. (1992) 'Topic transitions in physician–patient interviews: power, gender and discourse change', *Language in Society*, 21, 409–26.

Alberti, R. and Emmons, M. (1975) *Stand up, speak out, talk back: the key to assertive behavior*, Impact, San Luis Obispo, California.

—— (1982) *Your perfect right: a guide for assertive living* (4th edition), Impact, San Luis Obispo, California.

—— (1986) *Your perfect right: a guide for assertive living* (5th edition), Impact, San Luis Obispo, California.

Alberts, J.K. (1992) 'An inferential/strategic explanation for the social organisation of teases', *Journal of Language and Social Psychology*, 11, 153–78.

Allen, J.G. (1974) 'When does exchanging personal information constitute self-disclosure?' *Psychological Reports*, 35, 195–8.

Allen, K. and Stokes, T. (1987) 'Use of escape and reward in the management of young children during dental treatment', *Journal of Applied Behavior Analysis*, 20, 381–9.

Allport, G. (1935) 'Attitudes', in C. Murchison (ed.), *A handbook of social psychology*, Clark University Press, Worcester, Mass.

Allwinn, S. (1991) 'Seeking information: contextual influences on question formulation', *Journal of Language and Social Interaction*, 10, 169–84.

Altman, I. (1977) 'The communication of interpersonal attitudes: an ecological approach', in T.L. Houston (ed.), *Foundations of interpersonal attraction*, Academic Press, London.

Anderson, N. and Shackleton, V. (1990) 'Decision making in the graduate selection interview: a field study', *Journal of Occupational Psychology*, 63, 63–76.

Anthony, R.N. (1988) *The management control function*, Harvard Business School Press, Boston, Mass.

Applbaum, R. and Anatol, K. (1973) 'Dimensions of source credibility: a test for reproducibility', *Speech Monographs*, 40, 231–7.

—— Anatol, K., Hays, E.R., Jenson, O.O., Porter, R.E. and Handel, J.E. (1973) *Fundamental concepts in human communication*, Cranfield Press, New York.

Archer, R. (1979) 'Role of personality and the social situation', in G. Chelune (ed.), *Self-disclosure*, Jossey-Bass, San Francisco.

Argyle, M. (1975) *Bodily communication*, Methuen, London.

—— (1981) *Social skills and health*, Methuen, London.

—— (1983a) 'Five kinds of small social group', in H.H. Blumberg, A.P. Hare, V. Kent and M.F. Davies (eds), *Small groups and social interaction, Vol. 1*, Wiley, Chichester.

—— (1983b) *The psychology of interpersonal behaviour*, Penguin, Harmondsworth, Middlesex.

—— (1988) *Bodily communication* (2nd edition), Methuen, London.

—— (1991) *Co-operation: the basis of sociability*, Routledge, London.

—— and Cook, M. (1976) *Gaze and mutual gaze*, Cambridge University Press, Cambridge.

—— Furnham, A. and Graham, J. (1981) *Social situations*, Cambridge University Press, Cambridge.

—— and McHenry, R. (1971) 'Do spectacles really increase judgements of intelligence?' *British Journal of Social and Clinical Psychology*, 10, 27–9.

Armstrong, D. (1991) 'What do patients want?' *British Medical Journal*, 303, 261–2.

Aronson, E. (1969) 'The theory of cognitive dissonance: a current perspective', in. L. Berkowitz (ed.), *Advances in experimental social psychology, Vol. 4*, Academic Press, New York.

—— (1984) *The social animal*, W.H. Freeman and Co., New York.

Arvey, R. and Campion, J. (1984) 'Person perception in the employment interview', in M. Cook (ed.), *Issues in person perception*, Methuen, London.

'At Emery Air Freight: Positive Reinforcement Boosts Performance' (1973) *Organisational Dynamics*, 1, 41–50.

Atkinson, J. and Raynor, J. (1974) *Motivation and achievement*, Winston, Washington, DC.

Atkinson, M. (1984) *Our master's voice*, Methuen, London.

Aubertine, H.E. (1968) 'The set induction process and its application to teaching', *Journal of Educational Research*, 61, 363–7.

Auerswald, M.C. (1974) 'Differential reinforcing power of restatement and interpretation on client production of affect', *Journal of Counseling Psychology*, 21, 9–14.

Backman, C. (1988) 'The self: a dialectical approach', in L. Berkowitz (ed.), *Advances in experimental social psychology, Vol. 21*, Academic Press, NY.

Bakken, D. (1977) 'Saying goodbye: an observational study of parting rituals', *Man–Environment Systems*, 7, 95–100.

Baldock, J. and Prior, D. (1981) 'Social workers talking to clients: a study of verbal behaviour', *British Journal of Social Work*, 11, 19–38.

Baldwin, J.D. and Baldwin, J.I. (1981) *Behavior principles in everyday life*, Prentice-Hall, Englewood Cliffs, NJ.

Baldwin, T. (1992) 'Effects of alternative modeling strategies on outcomes of interpersonal-skills training', *Journal of Applied Psychology*, 77, 147–54.

Bales, R.F. (1950) *Interaction process analysis: a method for the study of small groups*, Addison-Wesley, Cambridge, Mass.

—— (1970) *Personality and interpersonal behavior*, Holt, Rinehart and Winston, New York.

Balsam, P.D. and Bondy, A.S. (1983) 'The negative side-effects of reward', *Journal of Applied Behavior Analysis* 16, 283–96.

Bandura, A. (1977) *Social learning theory*, Prentice-Hall, Englewood Cliffs, NJ.

—— (1986) *Social foundations of thought and action: a social cognitive theory*, Prentice-Hall, Englewood Cliffs, NJ.

—— (1989) 'Self-regulation of motivation and action through internal standards and goal systems', in L. Pervin (ed.), *Goal concepts in personality and social psychology*, Lawrence Erlbaum, Hillsdale, NJ.

—— and Menlove, F. (1986) 'Factors determining vicarious extinction of avoidance behaviour through symbolic modeling', *Journal of Personality and Social Psychology*, 8, 99–108.

Banks, D.L. (1972) 'A comparative study of the reinforcing potential of verbal and non-verbal cues in a verbal conditioning paradigm', Unpublished doctoral dissertation, University of Massachusetts.

Bardovi-Harlig, K. and Hartford, B. (1990) 'Congruence in native and normative conversations: status balance in the academic advising session', *Language Learning*, 40, 467–501.

Barnabei, F., Cormier, W.H. and Nye, L.S. (1974) 'Determining the effects of three counselor verbal responses on client verbal behavior', *Journal of Counseling Psychology*, 21, 355–9.

Barnes, D., Britton, J. and Rosen, H. (1971) *Language, the learner and the school*, Penguin, Harmondsworth.

—— and Rosenthal, R. (1985) 'Interpersonal effects of experimenter attractiveness, attire and gender, *Journal of Personality and Social Psychology*, 48, 435–46.

Barnlund, D. (1976) 'The mystification of meaning: doctor–patient encounters', *Journal of Medical Education*, 51, 716–25.

Baron, R., Cowan, G., Ganz, R. and McDonald, M. (1974) 'Interaction of locus of control and type of reinforcement feedback: considerations of external validity', *Journal of Personality and Social Psychology*, 30, 285–92.

—— Kerr, N. and Miller, N. (1992) *Group process, group decision and group action*, Open University Press, Buckingham.

Barry, B. and Bateman, T. (1992) 'Perceptions of influence in managerial dyads: the role of hierarchy, media and tactics', *Human Relations*, 45, 555–74.

Bass, B.M. (1981) *Stogdill's handbook of leadership*, Free Press, New York.

—— (1984) *Stogdill's handbook of leadership* (2nd edition), Free Press, New York.

—— (1990) *Handbook of leadership: theory, research and managerial applications* (3rd edition), Collier-Macmillan, London.

Baumeister, R., Hutton, D. and Cairns, K. (1990) 'Negative effects of praise on skilled performance', *Basic and Applied Social Psychology*, 11, 131–48.

Bavelas, A. (1950) 'Communication patterns in task-oriented groups', *Journal of the Acoustical Society of America*, 22, 725–30.

Baxter, J. and Rozelle, R. (1975) 'Nonverbal expression as a function of crowding during a simulated police–citizen encounter', *Journal of Personality and Social Psychology*, 32, 40–54.

Beattie, G. (1979) 'Contextual constraints on the floor-apportionment function of speaker-gaze in dyadic conversations', *British Journal of Social and Clinical Psychology*, 18, 390–2.

—— (1981) 'A further investigation of the cognitive interference hypothesis of gaze patterns during conversation', *British Journal of Social Psychology*, 20, 243–8.

Becker, F.D. (1973) 'Study of spatial markers', *Journal of Personality and Social Psychology*, 26, 439–45.

Becker, H.S. (1963) *Outsiders*, Collier-Macmillan, New York.

Beezer, R. (1956) 'Research on methods of interviewing foreign informants', George Washington University, Hum RRO Technical Reports, No. 30.

Beharry, E.A. (1976) 'The effect of interviewing style upon self-disclosure in a dyadic interaction', *Dissertation Abstracts International*, 36, 4677B.

Beisecker, T. and Parson, D. (eds) (1972) *The process of social influence*, Prentice-Hall, Englewood Cliffs, NJ.

Bell, R., Zahn, C. and Hopper, R. (1984) 'Disclaiming: a test of two competing views', *Communication Quarterly*, 32, 28–36.

Bellack, A.S. and Hersen, M. (eds) (1979) *Research and practice in social skills training*, Plenum, New York.

Benjamin, A. (1974) *The helping interview*, Houghton Mifflin, Boston.

—— (1981) *The helping interview* (2nd edition), Houghton Mifflin, Boston.

—— (1987) *The helping interview with case illustrations*, Houghton Mifflin, Boston.

Benne, K.D. and Sheats, P. (1948) 'Functional roles of group members', *Journal of Social Issues*, 4, 41–9.

Benson, P., Karabenic, S. and Lerner, R. (1976) 'Pretty pleases: the effects of physical attractiveness on race, sex and receiving help', *Journal of Experimental Social Psychology*, 24, 73–83.

Berger, C. (1985) 'Social power and interpersonal communication', in M. Knapp and G. Miller (eds), *Handbook of interpersonal communication*, Sage, Beverly Hills.

—— (1989) 'Goals, plans and discourse comprehension', in J. Bradac (ed.), *Message effects in communication science*, Sage, Newbury Park.

Berger, C.R. and Bradac, J.J. (1982) *Language and social knowledge*, Edward Arnold, London.

Berliner, D.C. (1986) 'In pursuit of the expert pedagogue', *Educational Research*, 15, 3–13.

Bermann, E. and Miller, D.R. (1967) 'The matching of mates', in R. Jessor and S. Feshback (eds), *Cognition, personality and clinical psychology*, Jossey-Bass, San Francisco.

Berne, E. (1964) *Games people play*, Grove Press, New York.

Bernstein, B. (1971, 1972) *Class codes and control*, Vols. 1 and 2, Routledge and Kegan Paul, London.

Berscheid, E. (1983) 'Emotion', in H. Kelley, E. Berscheid, A. Christensen *et al.* (eds), *Close relationships*, W.H. Freeman, New York.

—— and Walster, E. (1974) 'Physical attractiveness', in L. Berkowitz (ed.), *Advances in experimental social psychology*, Random House, New York.

—— and Walster, E. (1978) *Interpersonal attraction*, Addison Wesley, Reading, Mass.

Bettinghaus, E. and Cody, M. (1987) *Persuasive communication*, Holt, Rinehart and Winston, New York.

Bickman, L. (1974a) 'Social roles and uniforms: clothes make the person', *Psychology Today*, 7, 48–51.

—— (1974b) 'The social power of a uniform', *Journal of Applied Psychology*, 4, 47–61.

Bies, R., Shapiro, D. and Cummings, L. (1988) 'Causal accounts and managing organizational conflict: is it enough to say it's not my fault?' *Communication Research*, 15, 381–99.

Birdwhistell, R.L. (1970) *Kinesics and context*, University of Pennsylvania Press, Philadelphia.

Blackman, D., Howe, M. and Pinkston, E. (1976) 'Increasing participation in the social interaction of the institutionalized elderly', *The Gerontologist*, 16, 69–76.

Blake, B.R. and Mouton, J.S. (1982) 'How to choose a leadership style', *Training and Development Journal*, 36, 39–46.

Bless, H., Bohner, G., Hild, T. and Schwarz, N. (1992) 'Asking difficult questions: task complexity increases the impact of response', *European Journal of Social Psychology*, 22, 309–12.

Bligh, D. (1971) *What's the use of lectures?* Penguin, Harmondsworth.

Boddy, J., Carvier, A. and Rowley, K. (1986) 'Effects of positive and negative verbal reinforcement on performance as a function of extroversion–introversion: some tests of Gray's theory', *Personality and Individual Differences*, 7, 81–8.

Bond, M. and Ho, H. (1978) 'The effect of relative status and the sex composition of a dyad on cognitive responses and non-verbal behaviour of Japanese interviewees', *Psychologia*, 21, 128–36.

Boore, J. (1979) *Prescription for recovery*, RCN, London.

Borden, M. (1972) *Purposive explanation in psychology*, Harvard University Press, Cambridge.

Borisoff, D. and Merrill, L. (1991) 'Gender issues and listening', in D. Borisoff and M. Purdy (eds), *Listening in everyday life*, University of America Press, Maryland.

—— and Purdy, M. (eds) (1991a) *Listening in everyday life*, University of America Press, Maryland.

—— and Purdy, M. (1991b) 'What is listening?', in D. Borisoff and M. Purdy (eds), *Listening in everyday life*, University of America Press, Maryland.

Bormann, E. (1990) *Small group communication: theory and practice*, Harper and Row, New York.

Boster, F. and Mongeau, P. (1984) 'Fear arousing persuasive messages', in R. Bostrom (ed.), *Communication yearbook. Vol. 8*, Sage, Beverly Hills.

Bostrom, R.N. (1990) *Listening behavior*, Guilford Press, New York.

Bower, G. and Hilgard, E. (1981) *Theories of learning*, Prentice-Hall, Englewood Cliffs, NJ.

Bowers, J., Metts, S. and Duncanson, W. (1985) 'Emotion and interpersonal communication', in M. Knapp and G. Miller (eds), *Handbook of interpersonal communication*, Sage, Beverly Hills.

Boy, A.V. and Pine, G.J. (1963) *Client-centered counseling in the secondary school*, Houghton Mifflin, Boston.

Bradburn, N. and Sudman, S. (1980) *Improving interview method and questionnaire design: response effects to threatening questions in survey research*, Aldine, Chicago.

Brammer, L. (1988) *The helping relationship: process and skills*, Prentice-Hall, Englewood Cliffs, NJ.

—— Shostrom, E. and Abrego, P. (1989) *Therapeutic psychology: fundamentals of counseling and psychotherapy*, Prentice-Hall, Englewood Cliffs, NJ.

Brehm, S. and Brehm, J. (1981) *Psychological reactance*, Academic Press, New York.

Brigham, J. (1986) *Social psychology*, Little, Brown and Co., Boston.

—— (1991) *Social psychology* (2nd edition), HarperCollins, New York.

Brimer, M. (1971) 'Sex differences in listening comprehension', in S. Duker (ed.), *Listening: readings*, Scarecrow Press, Metuchen, NJ.

Brokaw, D.W. and McLemore, C.W. (1983) 'Toward a more rigorous definition of social reinforcement: some interpersonal clarifications', *Journal of Personality and Social Psychology*, 44, 1014–20.

Brooks, W. and Heath, R. (1985) *Speech communication*, W.C. Brown, Dubuque, Iowa.

Brophy, J. (1981) 'Teacher praise: a functional analysis', *Review of Educational Research*, 51, 5–32.

Brown, A. (1979) *Groupwork*, Heinemann, London.

Brown, G. (1982) 'Two days on explaining and lecturing', *Studies in Higher Education*, 2, 93–104.

—— (1986) 'Explaining', in O. Hargie (ed.), *A handbook of communication skills*, Croom Helm, London/New York University Press, NY.

—— and Armstrong, S. (1984) 'On explaining', in E. C. Wragg (ed.), *Classroom teaching skills*, Croom Helm, London/Nichols, New York

—— and Atkins, M. (1988) *Effective teaching in higher education*, Wellnen and Co., London.

—— and Bakhtar, M. (eds) (1983) *Styles of lecturing*, Loughborough University Press, Loughborough.

—— and Hatton, N. (1982) *Explaining and explanations*, Macmillan, London.

Brown, P. and Levinson, S. (1978) 'Universals in language usage: politeness phenomena', in E. Goody (ed.), *Questions and politeness: strategies in social interaction*, Cambridge University Press, Cambridge.

Brown, R. (1988) *Group processes: dynamics within and between groups*, Basil Blackwell, Oxford.

Brundage, L., Derlega, V. and Cash, T. (1977) 'The effects of physical attractiveness and need for approval on self-disclosure', *Personality and Social Psychology Bulletin*, 3, 63–6.

Bruner, J. and Taguiri, R. (1954) 'The perception of people', in G. Lindzey (ed.), *Handbook of social psychology*, Addison-Wesley, Reading, Mass.

Bruner, J.S. Goodnow, J.J. and Austin, G.A. (1956) *A study of thinking*, Wiley, New York.

Bryan, A. and Gallois, C. (1992) 'Rules about assertion in the workplace: effects of status and message type', *Australian Journal of Psychology*, 44, 51–9.

Bryman, A. (1986) *Leadership and organizations*, Routledge and Kegan Paul, London and New York.

Buck, R. (1989) 'Emotional communication in personal relationships: a developmental interactionist view', in C.D. Hendrick (ed.), *Close relationships*, Sage, Newbury Park.

—— (1991) 'Temperament, social skills and the communication of emotion: a developmental-interactionist view', in D.J. Gilbert and J.J. Connolly (eds), *Personality, social skills, and psychopathology*, Plenum, New York.

Buckwalter, A. (1983) *Interviews and interrogations*, Butterworth, Stoneham, USA.

Bugental, D., Kaswan, J.W., Love, L.R. and Fox, M.N. (1970) 'Child versus adult perception of evaluative messages in verbal, vocal and visual channels', *Development Psychology*, 2, 267–75.

Bull, P. (1983) *Body movement and interpersonal communication*, Wiley and Sons, Chichester.

Burger, J. and Vartabedian, R. (1985) 'Public self-disclosure and speaker persuasiveness', *Journal of Applied Social Psychology*, 15, 153–65.

Burgoon, M. (1989) 'Message and persuasive effects', in J. Bradac (ed.), *Message effects in communication science*, Sage, Newbury Park.

Burley-Allen, M. (1982) *Listening: the forgotten skill*, Wiley, New York.

Burton, M. (1985) 'The environment, good interactions and interpersonal skills in nursing', in C. Kagan (ed.), *Interpersonal skills in nursing: research and applications*, Croom Helm, London.

Busch, P. and Wilson, D. (1976) 'An experimental analysis of a salesman's expert and referent bases of social power in the buyer–seller dyad', *Journal of Market Research*, 13, 3–11.

Buss, A. (1983) 'Social rewards and personality', *Journal of Personality and Social Psychology*, 44, 553–63.

—— and Perry, M. (1992) 'The aggression questionnaire', *Journal of Personality and Social Psychology*, 63, 452–9.

Butler, P.E. (1976) *Self-assertion for women*, Canfield Press, San Francisco.

Button, G. (1987) 'Moving out of closings', in G. Button and J. Lee (eds), *Talk and social organisation*, Multilingual Matters, Clevedon, England.

Byrne, D. (1971) *The attraction paradigm*, Academic Press, New York.

Byrne, P. and Long, B. (1976) *Doctors talking to patients*, HMSO, London.

—— Rasche, L. and Kelley, K. (1974) 'When "I like you" indicates disagreement', *Journal of Research in Personality* , 8, 207–17.

Cairns, L. (1986) 'Reinforcement', in O. Hargie (ed.), *A handbook of communication skills*, Croom Helm, London/New York University Press, NY.

Cameron, G.T., Schleuder, J. and Thorson, E. (1991) 'The role of news teasers in processing TV news and commercials', *Communication Research*, 18, 667–84.

Campbell, D.T. (1958) 'Common fate, similarity and other indices of the status of aggregates of persons as social entities', *Behavioural Science*, 3, 14–25.

Cannell, C.F., Oksenberg, L. and Converse, J.M. (1977) 'Striving for response accuracy; experiments in new interviewing techniques', *Journal of Marketing Research*, 14, 306–21.

Canter, D. and Wools, R. (1970) 'A technique for the subjective appraisal of buildings', *Building Science*, 5, 187–98.

Canter, L. and Canter, M. (1988) *Assertive discipline for parents*, Harper and Row, New York.

Cantor, J., Alfonso, H. and Zillmann, D. (1976) 'The persuasive effectiveness of the peer appeal and a communicator's first-hand experience', *Communication Research*, 3, 293–310.

Cantor, N. (1981) 'A cognitive-social approach to personality', in N. Cantor and J. Kihlstrom (eds), *Personality, cognition and social interaction*, Erlbaum, Hillsdale, NJ.

Cappella, J.N. (1985) 'Controlling the flow in conversation', in A.W. Siegman and S. Feldstein (eds), *Multi-channel integrations of nonverbal behavior*, Erlbaum, Hillsdale, NJ.

Carkhuff, R.R. (1973) *The art of helping: an introduction to life skills*, Human Resource Development Press, Amherst, Mass.

Carson, R. (1969) *Interaction concepts of personality*, Allen and Unwin, London.

Carter, K. (1990) 'Teacher's knowledge and learning to teach', in W.R. Houston (ed.), *Handbook of research on teacher education*, Macmillan, New York.

Cartwright, D. and Zander, A. (1968) *Group dynamics* (3rd edition), Harper and Row, New York.

Cary, M. (1978) 'The role of gaze in the initiation of conversation', *Social Psychology*, 41, 269–71.

Catano, V. (1976) 'Effectiveness of verbal praise as a function of expertise of its source', *Perceputal and Motor Skills*, 42, 1283–6.

Chaiken, S. (1979) 'Communicator physical attractiveness and persuasion', *Journal of Personality and Social Psychology*, 37, 1387–97.

—— (1986) 'Physical appearance and social influence', in C. Herman, M. Zanna and E. Higgins (eds), *Physical appearance, stigma and social behavior: the Ontario Symposium*, Lawrence Erlbaum, Hillsdale, NJ.

—— and Stangor, C. (1987) 'Attitudes and attitude change', *Annual Review of Psychology*, 38, 575–630.

Chaikin, A. and Derlega, V. (1974) *Self-disclosure*, General Learning Press, New Jersey.

—— and Derlega, V. (1976) 'Self-disclosure', in J. Thibaut, J. Spence and R. Carson (eds), *Contemporary topics in social psychology*, General Learning Press, New Jersey.

—— Derlega, V. and Miller, S. (1976) 'Effects of room environment on self-disclosure in a counseling analogue', *Journal of Counseling Psychology*, 23, 479–81.

Chandler, P. and Sweller, J. (1992) 'The split-attention effect as a factor in the design of instruction', *British Journal of Educational Psychology*, 62, 233–46.

Chang, M. and Gruner, C. (1981) 'Audience reaction to self-disparaging humor', *Southern Speech Communication Journal*, 46, 419–26.

Chelune, G. (ed.) (1979) *Self-disclosure*, Jossey-Bass, San Francisco.

Chemers, M. (1983) 'Leadership theory and research: a systems process integration', in P.B. Paulus (ed.), *Basic group processes*, Springer-Verlag, New York.

Chesner, S. and Beaumeister, R. (1985) 'Effects of therapist's disclosure of religious beliefs on the intimacy of client self-disclosure', *Journal of Social and Clinical Psychology*, 3, 97–105.

Cialdini, R. (1987) 'Compliance principles of compliance professionals: psychologists of necessity', in M. Zanna, *et al.* (eds), *Social influence: the Ontario Symposium Vol. 5*, Lawrence Erlbaum, Hillsdale, New Jersey.

—— (1988) *Influence: science and practice* (2nd edition), Scott, Foresman and Co., Illinois.

—— and Ascani, K. (1976) 'Test of a concession procedure for inducing verbal, behavioral and further compliance with a request to give blood', *Journal of Applied Psychology*, 61, 295–300.

—— Vincent, J., Lewis, S., Catalan, J., Wheeler, D. and Darby, B. (1975) 'Reciprocal concessions procedure for inducing compliance: the door-in-the-face technique', *Journal of Personality and Social Psychology*, 31, 206–15.

Cianni-Surridge, M. and Horan, J. (1983) 'On the wisdom of assertive jobseeking behavior', *Journal of Counseling Psychology*, 30, 209–14.

Cipani, E. (1990) 'The communicative function hypothesis: an operant behavior perspective', *Journal of Behavior Therapy and Experimental Psychiatry*, 21, 239–74.

Citkowitz, R.D. (1975) 'The effects of three interview techniques – paraphrasing, modelling, and cues – in facilitating self-referent affect statements in chronic schizophrenics', *Dissertation Abstracts International*, 36, 2462B.

Clark, R.A. (1984) *Persuasive messages*, Harper and Row, New York.

Cline, R.J. (1989) 'The politics of intimacy: costs and benefits determining disclosure intimacy in male–female dyads', *Journal of Social and Personal Relationships*, 6, 5–20.

Cline, V.B., Mejia, J., Coles, J., Klein, N. and Cline, R.A. (1984) 'The relationship between therapist behaviors and outcome for middle and lower class couples in marital therapy', *Journal of Clinical Psychology*, 40, 691–704.

Clore, G. (1977) 'Reinforcement and affect in attraction', in S. Duck (ed.), *Theory and practice in interpersonal attraction*, Academic Press, London.

—— and Byrne, D. (1974) 'A reinforcement–affect model of attraction', in T.S. Huston (ed.), *Perspectives on interpersonal attraction*, Academic Press, New York and London.

Cody, M. and McLaughlin, M. (1985) 'The situation as a construct in interpersonal communication research', in M. Knapp and G. Miller (eds), *Handbook of interpersonal research*, Sage, Beverly Hills.

Cohen-Cole, S.A. (ed.) (1991) *The medical interview: the three-function approach*, Mosby Year Book, St Louis.

—— and Bird, J. (1991) 'Function 1: gathering data to understand the patient', in S.A. Cohen-Cole (ed.), *The medical interview: the three-function approach*, Mosby Year Book, St Louis.

Collins, J. and Collins, M. (1992) *Social skills training and the professional helper*, Wiley, Chichester.

Conine, N. (1976) 'Listening in the helping relationship', *Physical Therapy*, 56, 159–62.

Cook, M. (1970) 'Experiments on orientation and proxemics', *Human Relations*, 23, 61–76.
—— (1977) 'The social skill model and interpersonal attraction', in S. Duck (ed.), *Theory and practice in interpersonal attraction*, Academic Press, London.
Cooley, C.H. (1929) *Social organization*, Scribner, New York.
Corey, S. (1940) 'The teachers out-talk the pupils', *School Review*, 48, 745–52.
Corner, J. (1979) 'Mass in communication research', *Journal of Communication*, 29, 26–32.
Coupland, J., Coupland, N. and Grainger, K. (1991) 'Integrational discourse: contextual variations of age and elderliness', *Ageing and Society*, 11, 189–208.
—— Coupland, N. and Robinson, J. (1992) 'How are you? Negotiating phatic communion', *Language in Society*, 21, 207–30.
Cozby, P. (1973) 'Self-disclosure: a literature review', *Psychological Bulletin*, 79, 73–91.
Craig, K.D. and Prkachin, K.M. (1978) 'Social modelling influences on sensory decision theory and psychophysiological indexes of pain', *Journal of Personality and Social Psychology*, 36, 805–15.
Cramer, R., Lutz, D., Bartell, P., Dragna, M. and Helzer, K. (1989) 'Motivating and reinforcing functions of the male sex role: social analogues of partial reinforcement, delay of reinforcement and intermittent shock', *Sex Roles*, 20, 551–73.
Crow, B. (1983) 'Topic shifts in couple's conversations', in B. Craig and K. Tracy (eds), *Conversational coherence: form, structure and strategy*, Sage, Beverly Hills, California.
Crowne, D. and Marlowe, D. (1964) *The approval motive*, Wiley, New York.
Culley, S. (1991) *Integrative counselling skills in action*, Sage, London.
Cupach, W. and Metts, S. (1990) 'Remedial processes in embarrassing predicaments', in J. Anderson (ed.), *Communication yearbook, Vol. 13*, Sage, Newbury Park.
Dabbs, J. (1985) 'Temporal patterns of speech and gaze in social and intellectual conversation', in H. Giles and R. St Clair (eds), *Recent advances in language, communication and social psychology*, Lawrence Erlbaum Associates, London.
Danish, S., D'Augelli, A. and Brock, G. (1976) 'An evaluation of helping skills training: effects of helper's verbal responses', *Journal of Counseling Psychology*, 9, 119–23.
—— and Hauer, A.L. (1973) *Helping skills: a basic training program*, Behavioral Publications, New York.
Davey, G. (1981) 'Behaviour modification in organisations', in G. Davey (ed.), *Applications of conditioning theory*, Methuen, London.
—— (1988) 'Trends in human operant theory', in G. Davey and C. Cullen (eds), *Human operant conditioning and behaviour modification*, Wiley, Chichester.
Davidhizor, R. (1992) 'Interpersonal communication: a review of eye contact', *Infection Control and Hospital Epidemiology*, 13, 222–5.
Davitz, J.R. (1964) *The communication of emotional meaning*, McGraw-Hill, New York.
Dawes, R.M. and Smith, T.L. (1985) 'Attitude and opinion measurement', in G. Lindzey and E. Aronson (eds), *Handbook of social psychology* (3rd edition), Random House, New York.
Dawley, H. and Wenrich, W. (1976) *Achieving assertive behavior: a guide to assertive training*, Brooks/Cole, Monterey, California.
Deaux, K. and Wrightsman, L. (1988) *Social psychology*, Brooks/Cole, Pacific Grove, California.
De Bono, D. (1992) 'Pleasant scents and persuasion: an information processing approach', *Journal of Applied Social Psychology*, 22, 910–19.
Deci, E. (1992) 'On the nature and functions of motivation theories', *Psychological Science*, 3, 167–71.

—— and Porac, J. (1978) 'Cognitive evaluation theory and the study of human motivation', in M. Lepper and D. Greene (eds), *The hidden costs of rewards: new perspectives on the psychology of human motivation*, Lawrence Erlbaum, Hillsdale, NJ.

—— and Ryan, R. (1985) *Intrinsic motication and self-determination in human behavior*, Plenum Press, New York.

De Giovanni, I. (1979) 'Development and validation of an assertiveness scale for couples', *Dissertation Abstracts International*, 39 (9-B), 4573.

Del Greco, L. (1983) 'The Del Greco assertive behavior inventory', *Journal of Behavioral Assessment*, 5, 49–63.

Dell, D.M. and Schmidt, L.D. (1976) 'Behavioral cues to counselor expertness', *Journal of Counseling Psychology*, 23, 197–201.

Derlega, V. and Berg, J. (eds) (1987) *Self-disclosure; theory, research and therapy*, Plenum Press, New York.

—— and Chaikin, A. (1975) *Sharing intimacy: what we reveal to others and why*, Prentice-Hall, Englewood Cliffs, NJ.

—— Chaikin, A., Easterling, R. and Furman, G. (1973) 'Potential consequences and self-disclosure reciprocity', unpublished mimeo, Old Dominion University, Norfolk, Virginia.

—— and Grzelak, J. (1979) 'Appropriateness of self-disclosure', in G. Chelune (ed.), *Self-disclosure*, Jossey-Bass, San Francisco.

—— Metts, S., Petronio, S. and Margulis, S. (1993) *Self-disclosure*, Sage, Newbury Park.

De Paulo, B.M. (1992) 'Nonverbal behavior and self-presentation', *Psychological Bulletin*, 111, 203–43.

DeVito, J.A. (1986) *The interpersonal communication book* (4th edition), Harper and Row, New York.

—— (1993) *Essentials of human communication*, Harper Collins, New York.

Dickson, D.A. (1981) 'Microcounselling: an evaluative study of a programme', unpublished PhD thesis, Ulster Polytechnic.

—— (1986) 'Reflecting', in O. Hargie (ed.), *A handbook of communication skills*, Croom Helm, London/New York University Press, NY.

—— Hargie, O.D.W. and Morrow, N.C. (1989) *Communication skills training for health professionals: an instructor's handbook*, Chapman and Hall, London.

—— Saunders, C. and Stringer, M. (1993) *Rewarding people: the skill of responding positively*, Routledge, London.

Dillard, J. (1990) 'The nature and substance of goals in tactical communication', in M. Cody and M. McLaughlin (eds), *The psychology of tactical communication*, Multilingual Matters, Clevedon, England.

—— and Harkness, C. (1992) 'Exploring the affective impact of interpersonal influence messages', *Journal of Language and Social Psychology*, 11, 179–91.

Dillon, J.T. (1982) 'The multidisciplinary study of questioning', *Journal of Educational Psychology*, 74, 147–65.

—— (1986) 'Questioning', in O. Hargie (ed.), *A handbook of communication skills*, Croom Helm, London/New York University Press, NY.

—— (1988a) *Questioning and teaching*, Croom Helm, London/New York.

—— (1988b) 'The remedial status of student questioning', *Journal of Curriculum Studies*, 20, 197–210.

—— (1990) *The practice of questioning*, Routledge, London/New York.

DiMatteo, M. and DiNicola, D. (1982) *Achieving patient compliance: the psychology of the medical practitioner's role*, Pergamon, New York.

Dimond, R. and Hellkamp, D. (1969) 'Race, sex, ordinal position of birth, and self-disclosure in high school students', *Psychological Reports*, 25, 235–8.

Dindia, K. and Allen, M. (1992) 'Sex differences in self-disclosure: a meta-analysis', *Psychological Bulletin*, 112, 106–24.

Dinkmeyer, D. (1971) 'Contributions to teleoanalytic theory and techniques to school counseling', in C. Beck (ed.), *Philosophical guidelines for counseling*, W.S. Brown, Dubuque, Iowa.

Dittmar, H. (1992) 'Perceived material wealth and first impressions', *British Journal of Social Psychology*, 31, 379–92.

Dohrenwend, B. (1965) 'Some effects of open and closed questions on respondents' answers', *Human Organization*, 24, 175–84.

—— and Richardson, S. (1964) 'A use for leading questions in research interviewing', *Human Organization*, 3, 76–7.

Domjan, M. and Burkhard, B. (1986) *The principles of learning and behavior*, Brooks Cole, Monterey.

Dovidio, J.F., Ellyson, S.L., Keating, C.F., Heltman, K. and Brown, C. (1988) 'The relationship of social power to visual displays of dominance between men and women', *Journal of Personality and Social Psychology*, 54, 233–42.

Drachman, D., De Carufel, A. and Insko, C. (1978) 'The extra credit effect in interpersonal attraction', *Journal of Experimental Social Psychology*, 14, 458–67.

Duck, S. (ed.) (1977) *Theory and practice in interpersonal attraction*, Academic Press, London.

—— (1986) *Human relations: an introduction to social psychology*, Sage, London.

—— Rutt, D.J., Hurst, M.H. and Strejc, H. (1991) 'Some evident truths about conversations in everyday relationships', *Human Communication Research*, 18, 228–67.

Dulany, D. (1968) 'Awareness, rules and propositional control: a confrontation with S-R behavior theory', in T. Dixon and D. Horton (eds), *Verbal behavior and general behavior theory*, Prentice-Hall, Englewood Cliffs, NJ.

Duncan, S. (1972) 'Some signals and rules for taking speaking turns in conversations', *Journal of Personality and Social Psychology*, 23, 283–92.

—— and Fiske, D.W. (1977) *Face-to-face interaction: research, methods and theory*, Lawrence Erlbaum Associates, Hillsdale, NJ.

Eagly, A. and Chaiken, S. (1984) 'Cognitive theories of persuasion', in L. Berkowitz (ed.), *Advances in experimental social psychology, Vol. 17*, Academic Press, New York.

—— and Koran, S.J. (1991) 'Gender and the emergence of leaders: a meta-analysis', *Journal of Personality and Social Psychology*, 60, 685–710.

Eder, R.W., Kacmar, K.M. and Ferris, G.R. (1989) 'Employment history research: history and synthesis', in R.W. Eder and G.R. Ferris (eds), *The employment interview: theory, research and practice*, Sage, Newbury Park.

Efran, M. and Patterson, E. (1976) 'The politics of appearance', unpublished PhD Thesis, University of Toronto.

Egan, G. (1977) 'Listening as empathic support', in J. Stewart (ed.), *Bridges not walls*, Addison-Wesley, Reading, Mass.

—— (1982) *The skilled helper*, Brooks/Cole, Monterey, California.

—— (1986) *The skilled helper* (3rd edition). Brooks/Cole, Monterey, California.

—— (1990) *The skilled helper* (4th edition). Brooks/Cole, Monterey, California.

Ehrlich, R.P., D'Augelli, A.R. and Danish, S.J. (1979) 'Comparative effectiveness of six counselor verbal responses', *Journal of Counseling Psychology*, 26, 390–8.

Eisler, R., Hersen, M., Miller, P. and Blanchard, D. (1975) 'Situational determinants of assertive behavior', *Journal of Consulting and Clinical Psychology*, 43, 330–40.

—— and Frederiksen, L.W. (1980) *Perfecting social skills: a guide to interpersonal behavior development*, Plenum Press, New York.

Ekman, P (ed.) (1982) *Emotion in the human face* (2nd edition), Cambridge University Press, Cambridge.

—— (1985) *Telling lies*, Norton, New York.

—— and Friesen, W.V. (1969) 'The repertoire of non-verbal behaviour: categories, origins, usage and coding', *Semiotica*, 1, 49–98.

—— and Friesen, W.V. (1975) *Unmasking the face: a guide to recognising emotions from facial cues*, Prentice-Hall, Englewood Cliffs, NJ.

—— and Friesen, W. (1986) 'A new pan-cultural expression of emotion', *Motivation and Emotion*, 10, 159–68.

—— Friesen, W.V. and Tomkins, S.S. (1971) 'Facial affect scoring technique: a first validity study', *Semiotica*, 3, 49–98.

—— and Oster, H. (1979) 'Facial expressions of emotion', *Annual Review of Psychology*, 30, 527–55.

—— and O'Sullivan, M. (1991) 'Facial expression: methods, means and mouses', in R. Feldman and B. Rime (eds), *Fundamentals of nonverbal behaviour*, Cambridge University Press, Cambridge.

—— O'Sullivan, M., Friesen, W. and Scherer, K. (1991) 'Invited article: face, voice and body in detecting deceit', *Journal of Nonverbal Behavior*, 15, 125–35.

Ellis, A. and Beattie, G. (1986) *The psychology of language and communication*, Weidenfeld and Nicolson, London.

Ellis, R. and Whittington, D. (1981) *A guide to social skill training*, Croom Helm, London.

—— and Whittington, D. (eds) (1983) *New directions in social skill training*, Croom Helm, London.

Ellison, C.W. and Firestone, I.J. (1974) 'Development of interpersonal trust as a function of self-esteem, target status and target style', *Journal of Personality and Social Psychology*, 29, 655–63.

Emler, N. (1992) 'The truth about gossip', *BPS Social Psychology Section Newsletter*, 27, 23–37.

Emmons, R. (1989) 'The personal striving approach to personality', in L. Pervin (ed.), *Goal concepts in personality and social psychology*, Lawrence Erlbaum, Hillsdale, NJ.

England, G.W. (1975) *The manager and his values: an international perspective*, Ballinger, Cambridge, Mass.

Ennis, R. (1969) *Logic in teaching*, Prentice-Hall, New York.

Epling, W. and Pierce, W. (1988) 'Applied behavior analysis: new directions from the laboratory', in D. Davey and C. Cullen (eds), *Human operant conditioning and behavior modification*, Wiley, Chichester.

Eysenck, H. and Eysenck, S. (1963) *The Eysenck personality inventory*, University of London Press, London.

Falcione, R. (1974) 'The factor structure of source credibility scales for immediate superiors in the organisational context', *Central States Speech Journal*, 25, 63–6.

Falk, D. and Wagner, P. (1985) 'Intimacy of self-disclosure and response processes as factors affecting the development of interpersonal relationships', *Journal of Social Psychology*, 125, 557–70.

Fantino, E. (1977) 'Conditioned reinforcement: choice and information', in W. Honig and J. Staddon (eds), *Handbook of operant behavior*, Prentice-Hall, Englewood Cliffs, NJ.

Faraone, S. and Hurtig, R. (1985) 'An examination of social skill, verbal productivity, and Gottman's model of interaction using observational methods and sequential analyses', *Behavioural Assessment*, 7, 349–66.

Feigenbaum, W.M. (1977) 'Reciprocity in self-disclosure within the psychological interview', *Psychological Reports*, 40, 15–26.

Feldman, R.S. (1985) *Social psychology: theories, research and applications*, McGraw-Hill, New York.

—— Philippot, P. and Custrini, R. (1991) 'Social skills, psychopathology, and nonverbal behavior', in R.S. Feldman and B. Rime (eds), *Fundamentals of nonverbal behaviour*, Cambridge University Press, Cambridge.

—— and Rime, B. (eds) (1991) *Fundamentals of nonverbal behaviour*, Cambridge University Press, Cambridge.

Festinger, L. (1954) 'A theory of social comparison processes', *Human Relations*, 7, 117–40.

—— (ed.) (1964) *Conflict, decision and dissonance*, Stanford University Press, California.

Fiedler, F.E. (1978) 'Recent developments in research on the contingency model', in L. Berkowitz (ed.), *Group processes*, Academic Press, New York.

—— (1986) 'The contribution of cognitive resources and leader behavior to organizational performance', *Journal of Applied Social Psychology*, 16, 532–48.

—— and Garcia, J.E. (1987) *New approaches to effective leadership: cognitive resources and organizational performance*, Wiley, New York.

Field, S., Draper, J., Kerr, M. and Hare, M. (1982) 'A consumer view of the health visiting service', *Health Visitor*, 55, 299–301.

Fillmore, C. (1979) 'On fluency', in C. Fillmore, D. Kemper and W. Wang (eds), *Individual differences in language ability and language behavior*, Academic Press, New York.

Fisch, H., Frey, S. and Hirsbrunner, H. (1983) 'Analyzing nonverbal behavior in depression', *Journal of Abnormal Psychology*, 92, 307–18.

Fisher, B. (1987) *Interpersonal communication: pragmatics of human relationships*, Random House, New York.

Fisher, D. (1984) 'A conceptual analysis of self-disclosure', *Journal for the Theory of Social Behaviour*, 14, 277–96.

Fisher, J., Rytting, M. and Heslin, R. (1975) 'Hands touching hands: affective and evaluative effects of interpersonal touch', *Sociometry*, 39, 416–21.

Fisher, S. and Groce, S. (1990) 'Accounting practices in medical interviews', *Language in Society*, 19, 225–50.

Fiske, J. (1982) *Introduction to communication studies*, Methuen, London.

Fitts, P. and Posner, M. (1973) *Human performance*, Prentice-Hall, London.

Floyd, J. (1985) *Listening: a practical approach*, Foresman, Glenview, Illinois.

Fong, M., Borders, L. and Neimeyer, G. (1986) 'Sex role orientation and self-disclosure flexibility in counselor training', *Counselor Education and Supervision*, 25, 210–21.

Foot, H. (1986) 'Humour and laughter', in O. Hargie (ed.), *A handbook of communication skills*, Croom Helm, London/New York University Press, NY.

Forbes, R.J. and Jackson, P.R. (1980) 'Nonverbal behaviour and the outcome of selection interviews', *Journal of Occupational Psychology*, 53, 65–72.

Forgas, J. (1985) *Interpersonal behaviour*, Pergamon, Oxford.

Forsythe, S.M. (1990) 'Effect of applicant's clothing on interviewer's decision to hire', *Journal of Applied Social Psychology*, 20, 1579–95.

Fowler, F.J. and Mangione, T.W. (1990) *Standardised survey interviewing: minimising interviewer-related error*, Sage, Newbury Park.

Foxman, R., Moss, P., Boland, G. and Owen, C. (1982) 'A consumer view of the health visitor at six weeks post practicum', *Health Visitor*, 55, 302–8.

Franzoi, S. and Davis, M. (1985) 'Adolescent self-disclosure and loneliness: private self-consciousness and parental influences', *Journal of Personality and Social Psychology*, 48, 768–80.

French, P. (1983) *Social skills for nursing practice*, Croom Helm, London.

Fretz, B.R., Corn, R., Tuemmler, J. and Bellet, W. (1979) 'Counselor nonverbal behaviors and client evaluations', *Journal of Counseling Psychology*, 26, 304–11.

Frick, R. (1992) 'Interestingness', *British Journal of Psychology*, 83, 113–28.

Friedman, H. (1979) 'Nonverbal communications between patients and medical practitioners', *Journal of Social Issues*, 35, 82–99.

Friesen, W., Ekman, P. and Wallblatt, H. (1980) 'Measuring hand movements', *Journal of Nonverbal Behavior*, 4, 97–113.

Fry, L. (1983) 'Women in society', in S. Spence and G. Shepherd (eds), *Developments in social skills training*, Academic Press, London.

Furnham, A. (1979) 'Assertiveness in three cultures: multidimensionality and cultural differences', *Journal of Clinical Psychology*, 35, 522–7.

Gage, N.L., Belgard, M., Dell, D., Hiller, J.E., Rosenshine, B. and Unruh, W.R. (1968) 'Explorations of the teachers' effectiveness in explaining', *Technical Report 4*, Stanford University Center for Research and Development in Teaching, Stanford.

Galassi, J., Galassi, M. and Vedder, M. (1981) 'Perspectives on assertion as a social skills model', in J. Wine and M. Smye (eds), *Social competence*, Guilford Press, New York.

Gall, M. (1970) 'The use of questions in teaching', *Review of Educational Research*, 40, 709–21.

Gallagher, M. (1987) 'The microskills approach to counsellor training: a study of counsellor personality, attitudes and skills', Unpublished DPhil thesis, University of Ulster at Jordanstown, N. Ireland.

—— and Hargie, O. (1992) 'The relationship between counsellor interpersonal skills and core conditions of client-centred counselling', *Counselling Psychology Quarterly*, 5, 3–16.

Garramone, G. (1984) 'Audience motivation effects', *Communication Research*, 11, 79–96.

Gatewood, J.B. and Rosenwein, R. (1981) 'Interactional synchrony: genuine or spurious? A critique of recent research', *Journal of Nonverbal Behavior*, 6, 12–29.

Gervasio, A.H. (1987) 'Assertiveness techniques as speech acts', *Clinical Psychology Review*, 7, 105–19.

Giacolone, R. and Rosenfeld, P. (1987) 'Impression management concerns and reinforcement interventions', *Group and Organizational Studies*, 12, 445–53.

Gibson, F. (1989) *Using reminiscence: a training pack*, Help the Aged Education Department, London.

Giles, H. and St Clair, R. (1985) *Recent advances in language, communication and social psychology*, Lawrence Erlbaum, Hillsdale, NJ.

—— and Street, R. (1985) 'Communicator characteristics and behavior', in M. Knapp and G. Miller (eds), *Handbook of interpersonal communication*, Sage, Newbury Park.

Glass, D. and Singer, J. (1972) *Urban stress*, Academic Press, New York.

Gleason, J. and Perlmann, R. (1985) 'Acquiring social variation in speech', in H. Giles and R. St Clair (eds), *Recent advances in language, communication and social psychology*, Lawrence Erlbaum, London.

Glueckauf, R.L. and Quittner, A.L. (1992) 'Assertiveness training for disabled adults in wheelchairs: self-report, role-play, and activity pattern outcomes', *Journal of Consulting and Clinical Psychology*, 60, 419–25.

Goffman, E. (1959) *The presentation of self in everyday life*, Doubleday, Garden City, New York.

—— (1961) *Encounters*, Bobbs-Merrill, Indianapolis.

—— (1972) *Relations in public: micro-studies of the public order*, Penguin, Harmondsworth.

Goldfried, M.R. and Davison, G.C. (1976) *Clinical behavior therapy*, Holt, Rinehart and Winston, New York.

Goldman, M. (1980) 'Effect of eye-contact and distance on the verbal reinforcement of attitude', *Journal of Social Psychology*, 111, 73–8.

Gonzales, M., Davis, J., Loney G., Lukens, C. and Junghans, C. (1983) 'Interactional approach to interpersonal attraction', *Journal of Personality and Social Psychology*, 44, 1192–7.

Gormally, J. (1982) 'Evaluation of assertiveness: effects of gender, rater involvement and level of assertiveness', *Behavior Therapy*, 13, 219–25.

Gorn, G. and Goldberg, M. (1980) 'Children's responses to television commercials', *Journal of Consumer Research*, 6, 421–4.

Gouran, D. (1990) 'Introduction: speech communication after seventy-five years, issues and prospects', in G. Phillips and J. Wood (eds), *Speech communication: essays to commemorate the 75th anniversary of the Speech Communication Association*, Southern Illinois University Press, Carbondale and Edwardsville, Illinois.

Graesser, A. and Black, J. (1985) *The psychology of questions*, Lawrence Erlbaum Associates, Hillsdale, NJ.

Graham, J. and Heywood, S. (1976) 'The effects of elimination of hand gestures and of verbal codability on speech performance', *European Journal of Social Psychology*, 5, 189–95.

Green, R.T. (1977) 'Negative reinforcement as an unrewarding concept – a plea for consistency', *Bulletin of the British Psychological Society*, 30, 19–22.

Greenbaum, P. and Rosenfeld, H. (1980) 'Varieties of touching in greetings: sequential structure and sex-related differences', *Journal of Nonverbal Behavior*, 5, 13–25.

Greenberg, M.A. and Stone, A.A. (1992) 'Emotional disclosure about traumas and its relation to health: effects of previous disclosure and trauma severity', *Journal of Personality and Social Psychology*, 63, 75–84.

Greenspoon, J. (1955) 'The reinforcing effect of two spoken sounds on the frequency of two responses', *American Journal of Psychology*, 68, 409–16.

Gregg, V. (1986) *Introduction to human memory*, Routledge and Kegan Paul, London and New York.

Grigsby, J. and Weatherley, D. (1983) 'Gender and sex-role differences in intimacy of self-disclosure', *Psychological Reports*, 53, 891–7.

Gudjonnson, G. (1992) *The psychology of interrogation, confessions and testimony*, Wiley, Chichester.

Gudykunst, W. (1991) *Bridging differences: effective intergroup communication*, Sage, Newbury Park.

Guetzkow, H. and Simon, H.A. (1955) 'The impact of certain communication acts upon organization and performance in task-oriented groups', *Management Science*, 1, 233–50.

Guirdham, M. (1990) *Interpersonal skills at work*, Prentice-Hall, New York.

Gupta, S. and Shukla, A. (1989) 'Verbal operant conditioning as a function of extroversion and reinforcement', *British Journal of Psychology*, 80, 39–44.

Gupton, T. and LeBow, M. (1971) 'Behavior management in a large industrial firm', *Behavioral Therapy*, 2, 78–82.

Haase, R.F. and Di Mattia, D.J. (1976) 'Spatial environment and verbal conditioning in a quasi-counseling interview', *Journal of Counseling Psychology*, 23, 414–21.

Haines, J. (1975) *Skills and methods in social work*, Constable, London.

Halberstadt, A.G., Hayes, C.W. and Pike, K.M. (1988) 'Gender and gender role differences in smiling and communication consistency', *Sex Roles*, 19, 589–604.

Hall, E.T. (1959) *The silent language*, Doubleday, Garden City, New York.

—— (1966) *The hidden dimension*, Doubleday, Garden City, New York.

Hall, J.A. (1984) *Nonverbal sex differences: communication accuracy and expressive style*, John Hopkins University, Baltimore.

Halpin, A.W. and Winer, B.J. (1957) 'A factorial study of the leader behavior descriptions', in R.M. Stogdill and A.E. Coons (eds), *Leader behavior: its description and measurement*, Bureau of Business Research, Ohio State University, Ohio.

Hare, A.P. (1976) *Handbook of small group research*, Free Press, New York.

Hargie, O. (1980) 'An evaluation of a microteaching programme', unpublished doctoral dissertation, University of Ulster, Northern Ireland.

—— (1983) 'The importance of teacher questions in the classroom', in M. Stubbs and H. Hiller (eds), *Readings on language, schools and classrooms*, Methuen, London.

—— (1984) 'Training teachers in counselling skills: the effects of microcounselling', *British Journal of Educational Psychology*, 54, 214–20.

—— (1986) 'Communication as skilled behaviour', in O. Hargie (ed.), *A handbook of communication skills*, Croom Helm, London/New York University Press, NY.

—— (1988) 'From teaching to counselling: an evaluation of the role of microcounselling in the training of school counsellors', *Counselling Psychology Quarterly*, 1, 75–83.

—— and Dickson, D. (1991) 'Video-mediated judgements of personal characteristics based upon nonverbal cues', *Journal of Educational Television*, 17, 31–43.

—— and Marshall, P. (1986) 'Interpersonal communication: a theoretical framework', in O. Hargie (ed.), *A handbook of communication skills*, Croom Helm, London.

—— and McCartan, P. (1986) *Social skills training and psychiatric nursing*, Croom Helm, London.

—— and McNeill, A. (1993) 'Self-disclosure and religious affiliation in Northern Ireland', Department of Communication Paper, University of Ulster, Jordanstown.

—— and Morrow, N.C. (1987) Interpersonal communication: the sales approach, *Pharmacy Update*, 3, 320–4.

—— and Morrow, N.C. (1988) 'Interpersonal communication: assertiveness skills', *Pharmacy Update*, 4, 243–7.

—— and Morrow, N.C. (1990) 'Counselling and health care: a perspective from pharmacy', *International Pharmacy Journal*, 4, 255–9.

—— and Morrow, N.C. (1991) 'The skill of self-disclosure', *Chemist and Druggist: Parts 1 and 2*, 235, 343–4 and 769–70.

—— Morrow, N.C. and Woodman C. (1992) 'Consumer perceptions of and attitudes to community pharmacy services', *Pharmaceutical Journal*, 249, 688–91.

—— Morrow, N.C. and Woodman C. (1993) 'Looking into community pharmacy: identifying effective communication skills in pharmacist–patient consultations', University of Ulster, Jordanstown.

—— Saunders, C. amd Dickson, D. (1981) *Social skills in interpersonal communication* (1st edition), Croom Helm, London.

Harnack, R.V., Fest, T.B. and Jones, B.S. (1977) *Group discussion: theory and technique* (2nd edition), Prentice-Hall, Englewood Cliffs, NJ.

Harper, R., Wiens, A. and Matarrazo, J. (1978) *Nonverbal communication: the state of the art*, Wiley, Chichester

Harré, R. (1979) *Social being*, Basil Blackwell, Oxford.

—— and Lamb, R. (eds) (1986) *The dictionary of personality and social psychology*, Basil Blackwell, Oxford.

Harrigan, J. (1985) 'Listeners' body movements and speaking turns', *Communication Research*, 12, 233–50.

Harris, C.W. (ed.) (1960) *Encyclopedia of educational research* (3rd edition), Macmillan, New York.

Harris, J. (1973) 'Answering questions containing marked and unmarked adjectives and adverbs', *Journal of Experimental Psychology*, 97, 399–401.

Harris, M.B. (1991) 'Sex differences in stereotypes of spectacles', *Journal of Applied Social Psychology*, 21, 1659–80.

Hartford, B. and Bardovi-Harlig, K. (1992) 'Closing the conversation: evidence from the academic advising session', *Discourse Analysis*, 11, 93–116.

Haslett, B. and Ogilvie, J. (1988) 'Feedback processes in small groups', in R. Cathcart and L, Samovar (eds), *Small group communication*, W.C. Brown, Dubuque, Iowa.

Hausknecht, D. and Moore, D. (1986) 'The effects of time-compressed advertising on brand attitude judgements', in R. Lutz (ed.), *Advances in consumer research*, Assoc. for Consumer Research, Provo, Utah.

Heath, C. (1984) 'Talk and recipiency: sequential organization in speech and body movement', in J.M.Atkinson, and J. Heritage (eds), *Structures of social actions*, Cambridge University Press, Cambridge.

Heider, F. (1958) *The psychology of interpersonal relations*, Wiley, New York.

Henley, N.M. (1977) *Body politics: power, sex and nonverbal communication*, Prentice-Hall, Englewood Cliffs, NJ.

Henry, S.E., Medway, F.J. and Scarbo, H.A. (1979) 'Sex and locus of control as determinants of children's responses to peer versus adult praise', *Journal of Educational Psychology*, 71, 604–12.

Hensley, W. (1981) 'The effects of attire, location and sex on aiding behavior: a similarity explanation', *Journal of Nonverbal Behavior*, 6, 3–11.

—— and Cooper, R. (1987) 'Height and occupational success: a review and critique', *Psychological Reports*, 60, 843–9.

Hersey, P. and Blanchard, K.H. (1982) *Management of organizational behavior* (4th edition), Prentice-Hall, Englewood Cliffs, NJ.

Heslin, R. (1974) 'Steps toward a taxonomy of touching', Paper presented at the Convention of the Midwestern Psychological Association, Chicago, May.

—— and Alper, T. (1983) 'Touch: a bonding gesture', in J. Wiemann and R. Harrison (eds), *Nonverbal interaction*, Sage, London.

—— and Patterson, M.L. (1982) *Nonverbal behavior and social psychology*, Plenum Press, New York.

Hewes, D. and Planalp, S. (1987) 'The individual's place in communication science', in C. Berger and S. Chaffee (eds), *Handbook of communication science*, Sage, London.

Hewgill, M. and Miller, G. (1965) 'Source credibility and response to fear-arousing communications', *Speech Monographs*, 32, 95–101.

Higgins, S.T. and Morris, E.K. (1985) 'A comment on contemporary definitions of reinforcement as a behavioral process', *Psychological Record*, 35, 81–8.

Highlen, P.S. and Baccus, G.K. (1977) 'Effects of reflection of feeling and probe on client self-referenced affect', *Journal of Counseling Psychology*, 24, 440–3.

—— and Nicholas, R.P. (1978) 'Effects of locus of control, instructions, and verbal conditioning on self-referenced affect in a counseling interview', *Journal of Counseling Psychology*, 25, 177–83.

Hildum, D.C. and Brown, R.W. (1956) 'Verbal reinforcement and interviewer bias', *Journal of Abnormal Psychology*, 53, 108–11.

Hill, C. (1989) *Therapist techniques and client outcomes*, Sage, Newbury Park.

—— (1992) 'Research on therapist techniques in brief individual therapy: implications for practitioners', *The Counseling Psychologist*, 20, 689–711.

—— and Gormally, J. (1977) 'Effects of reflection, restatement, probe and nonverbal behaviors on client affect', *Journal of Counseling Psychology*, 24, 92–7.

—— Helms, J., Tichenor, V., Spiegel, S., O'Grady, K. and Perry, E. (1988) 'Effects of therapist response modes in brief psychotherapy', *Journal of Counseling Psychology*, 35, 222–33.

—— and Stull, D.E. (1987) 'Gender and self-disclosure: strategies for exploring the issues', in V. Derlega and J. Berg (eds), *Self-disclosure: theory, research and therapy*, Plenum Press, New York.

Hiller, J. (1971) 'Verbal response indicators of conceptual vagueness', *American Educational Research Journal*, 8, 151–61.

—— Fisher, G. and Kaess, W. (1969) 'A computer investigation of verbal characteristics of effective classroom lecturing', *American Educational Research Journal*, 6, 661–75.

Hinton, P. (1993) *The psychology of interpersonal perception*, Routledge, London.

Hoffnung, R.J. (1969) 'Conditioning and transfer of affective self-references in a role-played counseling interview', *Journal of Consulting and Clinical Psychology*, 33, 527–31.

Hofling, C., Brotzman, E. and Calrymple, S. *et al.* (1966) 'An experimental study in nurse-physician relationships', *Journal of Nervous and Mental Disorders*, 143, 171–80.

Holahan, C.J. (1979) 'Redesigning physical environments to enhance social interactions', in R. Munoz, L. Snowden, J. Kelly *et al.* (eds), *Social and psychological research in community settings*, Jossey-Bass, San Francisco.

Hollander, E.P. (1978) *Leadership dynamics: a practical guide to effective relationships*, Free Press, New York.

—— (1985) 'Leadership and power', in G. Lindzey and E. Aronson (eds), *The handbook of social psychology*, Random House, New York.

—— and Offerman, L.R. (1990) 'Power and leadership in organizations', *American Psychologist*, 45, 179–89.

Holli, B. and Calabrese, R. (1991) *Communication and education skills: the dietitian's guide*, Lea and Febiger, Philadelphia.

Honey, P. (1988) *Face-to-face: a practical guide to interactive skills*, Gower, Aldershot.

Hopper, R., Bosma, J. and Ward, J. (1992) 'Dialogic teaching of medical terminology at the Cancer Information Service', *Journal of Language and Social Psychology*, 11, 63–74.

Hore, T. (1971) 'Assessment of teaching practice: an "attractive" hypothesis', *British Journal of Educational Psychology*, 41, 302–5.

Hosking, D.M. and Morley, I.E. (1986) 'The skills of leadership', Paper presented at Aston University Management Centre, Birmingham.

House, R.J. and Baetz, M. (1979) 'Leadership: some empirical generalizations and new research directions', in B. Straw and C. Cummings (eds), *Research in organizational behavior*, JAI Press, Greenwich, Conn.

Huling-Austin, L. (1992) 'Research on learning to teach: implications for teacher education and monitoring progress', *Journal of Teacher Education*, 43, 173–80.

Hulse, S., Edeth, H. and Deese, J. (1980) *The psychology of learning*, McGraw-Hill, New York.

Hutchins, P., Williams, R. and McLaughlin, T. (1989) 'Using group contingent free time to increase punctuality and preparedness of high school special education students', *Child and Family Therapy*, 11, 59–70.

Hyman, R.T. (1974) *Teaching: vantage points for study*, Lippincott Press, New York.

Ivey, A. (1988) *Intentional interviewing and counseling: facilitating client development*, Brooks/Cole, California.

—— and Authier, J. (1978) *Microcounseling: innovations in interviewing, counseling, psychotherapy and psychoeducation*, C.C. Thomas, Springfield, Illinois.

—— and Gluckstern, N. (1976) *Basic influencing skills: leader and participant manuals*, Microtraining Associates Inc., Mass.

Jackson, S. and Allen, M. (1987) 'Meta-analysis of the effectiveness of one-sided and two-sided argumentation', Paper presented at the annual conference of the International Communication Association, Montreal, Canada.

Jaffe, J., Anderson, S. and Stern, D. (1979) 'Conversational rhythms', in D. Aaronson and R. Rieber (eds), *Psycholinguistic research*, Lawrence Erlbaum, Hillsdale, NJ.

Janis, I. (1972) *Victims of groupthink: a psychological study of foreign policy decisions and fiascos*, Houghton Mifflin, Boston.

—— (1983) 'The role of social support in adherence to stressful decisions', *American Psychologist*, 38, 143–60.

—— and Mann, L. (1977) *Decision-making: a psychological analysis of conflict, choice and commitment*, Free Press, New York.

Jepson, C. and Chaiken, S. (1991) 'Chronic issue-specific fear inhibits systematic processing in persuasive communications', in M. Booth-Butterfield (ed.), *Communication, cognition and anxiety*, Sage, Newbury Park.

Johnson, C. and Dabbs, J. (1976) 'Self-disclosure in dyads as a function of distance and the subject-experimenter relationship', *Sociometry*, 39, 257–63.

Johnson, D.W. and Johnson, F.P. (1982) *Joining together* (2nd edition), Prentice-Hall, Englewood Cliffs, NJ.

Jones, E. (1990) *Interpersonal Perception*, Freeman & Co., New York.

Jones, S., Collins, K. and Hong, H. (1991) 'An audience effect on smile production in 10-month-old infants', *Psychological Science*, 2, 45–9.

Jones, S.E. and Yarbrough, A.E. (1985) 'A naturalistic study of the meanings of touch', *Communication Monographs*, 52, 19–56.

Jones, W.H., Hobbs, S.A. and Hockenbury, D. (1982) 'Loneliness and social skill deficits', *Journal of Personality and Social Psychology*, 42, 682–9.

Jourard, S.M. (1961) 'Religious denomination and self-disclosure', *Psychological Bulletin*, 8, 446.

—— (1964) *The transparent self*, Van Nostrand Reinhold, New York.

—— (1971) *Self-disclosure*, Wiley, New York.

Jucker, A.H. (1986) *News interviews – a pragmalinguistic perspective*, Benjamins, Amsterdam.

Kadunc, T. (1991) 'Teachers' nonverbal skills and communication research', *The Global Educator*, 11, 2–4.

Kahn, R. and Cannell, C. (1957) *The dynamics of interviewing*, Wiley, New York.

Kahn, S. (1981) 'Issues in the assessment and training of assertiveness with women', in J. Wine and M. Smye (eds), *Social competence*, Guilford Press, New York.

Kalma, A. (1992) 'Gazing in triads: a powerful signal in floor apportionment', *British Journal of Social Psychology*, 31, 21–39.

Katz, D. and Kahn, R.L. (1976) *The social psychology of organizations* (2nd edition), Academic Press, New York.

—— and Stotland, E. (1959) 'A preliminary statement to a theory of attitude structure and change', in S. Koch (ed.), *Psychology: a study of a science, Vol. 3*, McGraw-Hill, New York.

Kazdin, A. (1988) 'The token economy: a decade later', in G. Davey and C. Cullen (eds), *Human operant conditioning and behavior modification*, Wiley, Chichester.

Kellermann, K. (1992) 'Communication: inherently strategic and primarily automatic', *Communication Monographs*, 59, 288–300.

Kelley, H.H. and Thibaut, J.W. (1978) *Interpersonal relations: a theory of interdependence*, Wiley, New York.

Kelly, E.W. and True, J.H. (1980) 'Eye contact and communication of facilitation conditions', *Perceptual and Motor Skills*, 51, 815–20.

Kelly, J.A. (1982) *Social skills training: a practical guide for interventions*, Springer, New York.

Kendon, A. (1967) 'Some functions of gaze direction in social interaction', *Acta Psychologica*, 26, 22–63.

—— (1981) 'Geography of gesture', *Semiotica*, 37, 129–63.

—— (1984) 'Some use of gestures', in D. Tannen and M. Saville-Troike (eds), *Perspectives on silence*, Ablex, Norwood, NJ.

—— (1989) 'Gesture', *International Encyclopedia of Communications*, 2, 217–22, Oxford University Press.

—— and Ferber, A. (1973) 'A description of some human greetings', in R. Michael and J. Crook (eds), *Comparative ecology and behaviour of primates*, Academic Press, London.

Kennedy, J.J. and Zimmer, J.M. (1968) 'Reinforcing value of five stimulus conditions in a quasi-counseling situation', *Journal of Counseling Psychology*, 15, 357–62.

Kennedy, T.D., Timmons, E.O. and Noblin, C.D. (1971) 'Nonverbal maintenance of conditioned verbal behavior following interpretations, reflections and social reinforcers', *Journal of Personality and Social Psychology*, 20, 112–17.

Kennedy, W.A. and Willcutt, H.C. (1964) 'Praise and blame as incentives', *Psychological Bulletin*, 62, 323–32.

Kennelly, K.J. and Mount, S.A. (1985) 'Perceived contingency of reinforcements, helplessness, locus of control and academic performance', *Psychology in the Schools*, 22, 465–9.

Kern, J. (1982) 'Predicting the impact of assertive, empathic-assertive and non-assertive behavior: the assertiveness of the assertee', *Behavior Therapy*, 13, 486–98.

—— Cavell, T. and Beck, B. (1985) 'Predicting differential reactions to males' versus females' assertions, empathic assertions and nonassertions', *Behavior Therapy*, 16, 63–75.

Kestler, J. (1982) *Questioning techniques and tactics*, McGraw-Hill, Colorado Springs, Colorado.

Kiefer, F. (ed.) (1982) *Questions and answers*, D. Reidel, Dordrecht, Holland.

King, A. (1992) 'Comparison of self-questioning, summarizing and notetaking-review as strategies for learning from lectures', *American Educational Research Journal*, 29, 303–23.

King, G. (1972) 'Open and closed questions: the reference interview', *RQ-Reference and Adult Sciences Division*, 12, 157–60.

Kipling, R. (1902) 'The elephant child', in *Just-So Stories*, Macmillan, London.

Kleck, R.E. and Strenta, A.C. (1985) 'Physical deviance and the perception of social outcomes', in J.A. Graham and A.M. Kligman (eds), *The psychology of cosmetic treatments*, Praeger, New York.

Klein, K., Kaplan, K.J. and Firestone, I.J. (1975) 'Reciprocity, compensation and mediation in verbal and visual distancing', Paper presented at the 83rd Annual Meeting of the American Psychological Association, Chicago.

Kleinke, C.L. (1980) 'Interaction between gaze and legitimacy of request on compliance in a field setting', *Journal of Nonverbal Behavior*, 5, 3–12.

—— (1986a) *Meeting and understanding people*, W.H. Freeman, New York.

—— (1986b) 'Gaze and eye-contact: a research review', *Psychological Bulletin*, 100, 78–100.

—— Staneski, R.A. and Berger, D.E. (1975) 'Evaluation of an interviewer as a function of interviewer gaze, reinforcement of subject gaze and interviewer attractiveness', *Journal of Personality and Social Psychology*, 31, 15–22.

Klinger, E., Barta, S. and Maxeiner, M. (1981) 'Current concerns: assessing therapeutically relevant motivation', in P. Kendall and S. Hollon (eds), *Assessment strategies for cognitive behavioral interventions*, Academic Press, New York.

Knapp, M.L. (1972) *Nonverbal communication in human interaction*, Holt, Rinehart and Winston, New York.

—— and Hall J. (1992) *Nonverbal communication in human interaction* (3rd edition), Holt, Rinehart and Winston, New York.

—— Hart, R., Friedrich, G. and Schulman, G. (1973) 'The rhetoric of goodbye: verbal and nonverbal correlates of human leave-taking', *Speech Monographs*, 40, 182–98.

Knapper, C. (1981) 'Presenting and public speaking', in M. Argyle (ed.), *Social skills and work*, Methuen, London.

Koballa, T. (1986) 'Persuading teachers to re-examine the innovative elementary science programs of yesterday: the effect of anecdotal versus data-summary communication', *Journal of Research in Science Teaching*, 23, 437–49.

Kolotkin, R., Wielkiewicz, R., Judd, B. and Weisler, S. (1983) 'Behavioral components of assertion: comparison of univariate and multivariate assessment strategies', *Behavioral Assessment*, 6, 61–78.

Komaki, J. (1982) 'Managerial effectiveness: potential contributions of the behavioural approach', *Journal of Organizational Behaviour Management*, 3, 71–83.

Korda, M. (1976) *Power in the office*, Weidenfeld and Nicolson, London.

Krasner, L. (1958) 'Studies of the conditioning of verbal behaviour', *Psychological Bulletin*, 55, 148–70.

Krause, R., Steimer, E., Sanger-Alt, C. and Wagner, G. (1989) 'Facial expression of schizophrenic patients and their interaction partners', *Psychiatry*, 52, 1–12.

Kreps, G. (1988) 'The pervasive role of information in health and health care: implications for health communication policy', in J. Anderson (ed.), *Communication yearbook, II*. Sage, Beverly Hills.

—— and Thornton, B. (1992) *Health communication: theory and practice*, Waveland Press, Prospect Heights, Illinois.

Krivonos, P. and Knapp, M. (1975) 'Initiating communication: what do you say when you say hello?' *Central States Speech Journal*, 26, 115–25.

Kunda, Z. and Fong, G. (1993) 'Directional questions direct self-conceptions', *Journal of Experimental Social Psychology*, 29, 63–86.

Kuperminc, M. and Heimberg, R. (1983) 'Consequence probability and utility as factors in the decision to behave assertively', *Behavior Therapy*, 14, 673–46.

L'Abate, L. and Milan, M. (eds) (1985) *Handbook of social skills training and research*, Wiley, New York.

Lamb, R. (1988) 'Greetings and partings', in P. Marsh (ed.), *Eye to eye: your relationships and how they work*, Sidgwick and Jackson, London.

Land, M. (1984) 'Combined effect of two teacher clarity variables on student achievement', *Journal of Experimental Education*, 50, 14–17.

—— (1985) 'Vagueness and clarity in the classroom', in T. Husen and T. Postlethwaite (eds), *International encyclopedia of education: research studies*, Pergamon Press, Oxford.

Lang, G. and van der Molen, H. (1990) *Personal conversations: roles and skills for counsellors*, Routledge, London.

Lange, A. and Jakubowski, P. (1976) *Responsible assertive behavior*, Research Press, Champaign, Illinois.

Langer, E. (1992) 'Interpersonal mindlessness and language', *Communication Monographs*, 59, 324–7.

—— Blank, A. and Chanowitz, B. (1978) 'The mindlessness of ostensibly thoughtful action', *Journal of Personality and Social Psychology*, 36, 635–42.

Larson, C. and Sanders, R. (1975) 'Faith, mystery and data: an analysis of "scientific" studies of persuasion', *Quarterly Journal of Speech*, 61, 276–88.

Laver, J. (1981) 'Linguistic roles and politeness in greeting and parting', in F. Coulmas (ed.), *Conversational routine: explorations in standardized communication situations and prepatterned speech*, Mouton, The Hague.

—— and Hutcheson, S. (eds) (1972) *Communication in face-to-face interaction*, Penguin, Harmondsworth.

Lawler, E. (1983) 'Reward systems in organisations', in J. Lorsch (ed.), *Handbook of organizational behavior*, Prentice-Hall, Englewood Cliffs, NJ.

Lazarsfield, P. (1944) 'The controversy over detailed interviews – an offer for negotiation', *Public Opinion Quarterly*, 8, 38–60.

Lazarus, A. (1971) *Behavior therapy and beyond*, McGraw-Hill, New York.

Lazowski, L.E. and Andersen, S.M. (1991) 'Self-disclosure and social perception: the impact of private, negative and extreme communications', in M. Booth-Butterfield (ed.), *Communication, cognition and anxiety*, Sage, Newbury Park.

Lea, M. and Duck, S. (1982) 'A model for the role of similarity of values in friendship development', *British Journal of Social Psychology*, 21, 301–10.

Lepper, M. and Greene, D. (1978) 'Overjustification research and beyond: toward a means–ends analysis of intrinsic and extrinsic motivation', in M. Lepper and D. Greene (eds), *The hidden costs of reward: new perspectives on the psychology of human motivation*, Wiley, New York.

Leventhal, H., Safer, M. and Panagis, D. (1983) 'The impact of communication on the self-regulation of health beliefs, decisions and behavior', *Health Education Quarterly*, 10, 3–29.

Levin, M. (1977) 'Self-knowledge and the talking cure', *Review of Existential Psychology and Psychiatry*, 15, 95–111.

Levin, R.B. and Gross, A.M. (1987) 'Assertive style: effects on perceptions of assertive behavior', *Behavior Modification*, 11, 229–40.

Lewin, K., Lippitt, R. and White, R.K. (1939) 'Patterns of aggressive behaviour in experimentally created social climates', *Journal of Social Psychology*, 10, 271–99.

Lewis, P. and Gallois, C. (1984) 'Disagreements, refusals, or negative feelings: perception of negatively assertive messages from friends and strangers', *Behavior Therapy*, 15, 353–68.

Ley, P. (1983) 'Patients' understanding and recall in clinical communication failure', in D. Pendleton and J. Hasler (eds), *Doctor–patient communication*, Academic Press, London.

—— (1988) *Communicating with patients*, Chapman and Hall, London.

Lieberman, D. (1990) *Learning: behavior and cognition*, Wadsworth, California.

Likert, R. (1977) 'Management styles and the human component', *Management Review*, 66, 23–45.

Lind, E. (1982) 'The psychology of courtroom procedure', in N. Kerr and R. Bray (eds), *The psychology of the courtroom*, Academic Press, New York.

Lindzey, G. and Aronson, E. (1985) *The handbook of social psychology* (3rd edition), Random House, New York.

Linehan, M. and Egan, K. (1979) 'Assertion training for women', in A. Bellack and M. Hersen (eds), *Research and practice in social skills training*, Plenum, New York.

Littlejohn, S. (1989) *Theories of human communication* (2nd edition), Wadsworth, Belmont, California.

Livesey, P. (1986) *Partners in care: the consultation in general practice*, Heinemann, London.

Livingstone, C. and Borko, H. (1989) 'Expert–novice differences in teaching: a cognitive analysis and implications for teacher education', *Journal of Teacher Education*, 40, 36–42.

Locke, E. and Latham, G. (1984) *Goal-setting: a motivational technique*, Prentice-Hall, Englewood Cliffs, NJ.

Loftus, E. (1975) 'Leading questions and the eyewitness report', *Cognitive Psychology*, 7, 560–72.

—— (1982) 'Interrogating eyewitnesses – good questions and bad', in R. Hogarth (ed.), *Question framing and response consistency*, Jossey-Bass, San Francisco.

—— and Palmer, J. (1974) 'Reconstruction of automobile destruction: an example of the interaction between language and memory', *Journal of Verbal Learning and Verbal Behavior*, 13, 585–9.

—— and Zanni, G. (1975) 'Eyewitness testimony: the influence of the wording of a question', *Bulletin of the Psychonomic Society*, 5, 86–8.

Lombardo, J., Weiss, R. and Stich, M. (1973) 'Effectance reduction through speaking in reply and its relation to attraction', *Journal of Personality and Social Psychology*, 28, 325–32.

Long, L. and Long, T. (1976) 'Influence of religious status and religious attire on interviewees', *Psychological Reports*, 39, 25–6.

—— Paradise, L. and Long, T. (1981) *Questioning: skills for the helping process*, Brooks/Cole, Monterey, California.

Lott, A.J. and Lott, B.E. (1968) 'A learning theory approach to interpersonal attitudes', in A.G. Greenwald, T.C. Brock and T. McOstrom (eds), *Psychological foundations of attitudes*, Academic Press, New York.

Luft, J. (1970) *Group processes: an introduction to group dynamics*, National Press Books, Palo Alto, California.

—— (1984) *Group processes: an introduction to group dynamics* (2nd edition), Mayfield, San Francisco.

Lundsteen, S. (1971) *Listening: its impact on reading and other language acts*, National Council of Teachers of English, New York.

Lysakowski, R.S. and Walberg, H.J. (1981) 'Classroom reinforcement and learning. A quantitative synthesis', *Journal of Educational Research*, 75, 69–77.

Maguire, G.P. and Rutter, D. (1976) 'History taking for medical students', *Lancet*, 2, 556–8.

Maguire, P. (1984) 'Communication skills and patient care', in A. Steptoe and A. Mathews (eds), *Health care and human behaviour*, Academic Press, London.

—— (1985) 'Deficiencies in key interpersonal skills', in C. Kagan (ed.), *Interpersonal skills in nursing*, Croom Helm, London.

Maier, S. (1989) 'Learned helplessness: event covariation and cognitive changes', in S. Klein and R. Mowrer (eds), *Contemporary learning theory: instrumental conditioning theory and the impact of biological constraints on learning*, Lawrence Erlbaum, Hillsdale, NJ.

Margalit, B. and Mauger, P. (1985) 'Aggressiveness and assertiveness: a cross-cultural study of Israel and the United States', *Journal of CrossCultural Psychology*, 16, 497–511.

Marisi, D.Q. and Helmy, K. (1984) 'Intratask integration as a function of age and verbal praise', *Perceptual and Motor Skills*, 58, 936–9.

Markus, H. (1977) 'Self-schemata and processing information about the self', *Journal of Personality and Social Psychology*, 35, 63–78.

Marshall, K., Kurtz, D. and Associates (1982) *Interpersonal helping skills*, Jossey-Bass, London.

Martin, G. and Hrycaiko, D. (eds) (1983) *Behavior modification and coaching: principles, procedures and research*, C.C. Thomas, Springfield, Illinois.

Martin, J.R. (1970) *Explaining, understanding and teaching*, McGraw-Hill, New York.

Martinko, M.J. and Gardner, W.L. (1984) 'The observation of high-performing managers: methodological issues and managerial implications', in J.C. Hunt, D.M. Hosking, C.A. Schriesheim and R. Stewart (eds), *Leaders and managers: international perspectives on managerial behavior and leadership*, Pergamon Press, New York.

Marwell, G. and Schmitt, D. (1967) 'Dimensions of compliance-gaining behavior: an empirical analysis', *Sociometry*, 30, 350–64.

Maslow, A. (1954) *Motivation and personality*, Harper and Row, New York.
Massarik, F. (1972) 'Standards for group leadership', in L.N. Solomon and B. Berzon (eds), *New perspectives on encounter groups*, Jossey-Bass, San Francisco.
Matarazzo, J.D. and Wiens, A.N. (1972) *The interview: research on its anatomy and structure*, Aldine-Atherton, Chicago.
—— Wiens, A.N. and Saslow, G. (1965) 'Studies in interview speech behavior', in L. Krasner and L. Ullman (eds), *Research in behavior modification: new developments and implications*, Holt, Rinehart and Winston, New York.
Mayfield, E. (1972) 'Value of peer nominations in predicting life insurance', *Journal of Applied Psychology*, 46, 6–13.
Mayo, C. and Henley, N. (1981) 'Nonverbal behavior: barrier or agent for sex role change', in C. Mayo and N. Henley (eds), *Gender and nonverbal behavior*, Springer-Verlag, New York.
Mazur, A., Mazur, J. and Keating, C. (1984) 'Military rank attainment of a West Point class: effects of cadets' physical features', *American Journal of Sociology*, 36, 241–59.
McCall, M., Lombardo, M. and Morrison, A. (1988) *The lessons of experience: how successful executives develop on the job*, Levington, Massachusetts.
McCartan, P.J. and Hargie, O.D.W. (1990) 'Assessing assertive behaviour in student nurses: a comparison of assertion measures', *Journal of Advanced Nursing*, 15, 1370–6.
McEwan, H. (1992) 'Teaching and the interpretation of texts', *Educational Theory*, 42, 59–68.
McFall, M., Winnett, R., Bordewick, M. and Bornstein, P. (1982) 'Nonverbal components in the communication of assertiveness', *Behavior Modification*, 6, 121–40.
McGrade, B.J. (1966) 'Effectiveness of verbal reinforcers in relation to age and social class', *Journal of Personality and Social Psychology*, 4, 555–60.
McGregor, D. (1960) *The human side of enterprise*, McGraw-Hill, New York.
McGuire, J. and Priestley, P. (1981) *Life after school: a social skills curriculum*, Pergamon, Oxford.
McGuire, W. (1973) 'Persuasion, resistance and attitude change', in I. Pool (ed.), *Handbook of communication*, Rand McNally, Illinois.
—— (1989) 'Theoretical foundations of campaigns', in R. Rice and C. Atkin (eds), *Public communication campaigns* (2nd edition), Sage, Newbury Park.
McHenry, R. (1981) 'The selection interview', in M. Argyle (ed.), *Social skills and work*, Methuen, London.
McIntyre, T., Jeffrey, D. and McIntyre, S. (1984) 'Assertion training: the effectiveness of a contemporary cognitive-behavioral treatment package with professional nurses', *Behavior Research and Therapy*, 22, 311–18.
McKeown, R. (1977) 'Accountability in responding to classroom questions: impact on student achievement', *Journal of Experimental Education*, 45, 24–30.
McLaughlin, M. (1984) *Conversation: how talk is organised*, Sage, Beverly Hills.
—— Cody, M. and O'Hair, H. (1983) 'The management of failure events: some contextual determinants of accounting behaviour', *Human Communication Research*, 9, 208–24.
—— Cody, M. and Read, S. (eds) (1992) *Explaining one's self to others*, Lawrence Erlbaum, New Jersey.
Mehrabian, A. (1972) *Nonverbal communication*, Aldine-Atherton, Chicago.
—— and Ferris, S.R. (1967) 'Influence of attitudes from nonverbal communication in two channels', *Journal of Consulting Psychology*, 31, 248–52.
Meindl, J., Ehrlich, S. and Dukerich, J. (1985) 'The romance of leadership', *Administrative Science Quarterly*, 30, 78–102.

Melamed, J. and Bozionelos, N. (1992) 'Managerial promotion and height', *Psychological Reports*, 71, 587–93.

Merbaum, M. (1963) 'The conditioning of affective self-references by three classes of generalized reinforcers', *Journal of Personality*, 31, 179–91.

Metzler, K. (1977) *Creative interviewing: the writer's guide to gathering information by asking questions*, Prentice-Hall, Englewood Cliffs, NJ.

Meyer, M. (ed.) (1988) *Questions and questioning*, de Gruyter, New York and Berlin.

Meyer, W.V., Miggag, W. and Engler, U. (1986) 'Some effects of praise and blame on perceived ability and affect', *Social Cognition*, 4, 293–308.

Michelson, L., Sugai, D., Wood, R. and Kazdin, A. (1983) *Social skills assessment and training with children*, Plenum, New York.

Mikulineer, M. (1986) 'Attributional processes in the learned helplessness paradigm; behavioral effects of global attributions', *Journal of Personality and Social Psychology*, 51, 1248–56.

Millar, R., Crute, V. and Hargie, O. (1992) *Professional interviewing*, Routledge, London and New York.

Miller, G. (1983) 'On various ways of skinning symbolic cats: recent research on persuasive message strategies', *Journal of Language and Social Psychology*, 2, 123–40.

—— (1987) 'Persuasion', in C. Berger and S. Chaffee (eds), *Handbook of communication science*, Sage, Beverly Hills.

—— Boster, F., Roloff, M. and Seibold, D. (1977) 'Compliance–gaining message strategies: a typology and some findings concerning effects of situational differences', *Communication Monographs*, 44, 37–51.

—— and Burgoon, J. (1982) 'Factors affecting assessments of witness credibility', in N. Kerr and R. Bray (eds), *Psychology of the courtroom*, Academic Press, New York.

—— and Burgoon, M. (1978) 'Persuasion research: review and commentary', in B. Ruben (ed.), *Communication yearbook 2*, Transaction Books, New Brunswick.

—— Burgoon, M. and Burgoon, J. (1984) 'The functions of human communication in changing attitudes and gaining compliance', in C. Arnold and J. Bowers (eds), *Handbook of rhetorical and communication theory*, Allyn and Bacon, Boston.

Miller, J. and Eller, B.F. (1985) 'An examination of the effect of tangible and social reinforcers on intelligence test performance of middle school students', *Social Behaviour and Personality*, 13, 147–5.

Miller, K. and Monge, P. (1986) 'Participation, satisfaction and productivity: a meta-analytical view', *Academy of Management Journal*, 29, 727–53.

Miller, L. and Kenny, D. (1986) 'Reciprocity of self-disclosure at the individual and dyadic levels: a social relations analysis', *Journal of Personality and Social Psychology*, 50, 713–19.

—— Berg, J. and Archer, R. (1983) 'Openers: individuals who elicit intimate self-disclosure', *Journal of Personality and Social Psychology*, 44, 1234–44.

—— Cooke, L., Tsang, J. and Morgan, F. (1992) 'Nature and impact of positive and boastful disclosures for women and men', *Human Communication Research*, 18, 364–9.

Miller, N. (1963) 'Some reflections on the law of effect produce a new alternative to drive reduction', in M. Jones (ed.), Nebraska Symposium on Motivation, University of Nebraska, Lincoln.

—— Maruyama, G., Beaber, R. and Valone, K. (1976) 'Speed of speech and persuasion', *Journal of Personality and Social Psychology*, 34, 615–24.

Mills, H. (1991) *Negotiate: the art of winning*, BCA, London.

Mills, M.C. (1983) 'Adolescents' self-disclosure in individual and group theme-centred modelling, reflecting and probing interviews', *Psychological Reports*, 53, 691–701.

Miltz, R.J. (1972) 'Development and evaluation of a manual for improving teachers' explanations', *Technical Report 26*, Stanford University Center for Research and Development in Teaching, Stanford.

Mizes, J. (1985) 'The use of contingent reinforcement in the treatment of a conversion disorder: a multiple baseline study', *Journal of Behavior Therapy and Experimental Psychiatry*, 16, 341–5.

Montagu, M.F.A. (1971) *Touching: the human significance of the skin*, Columbia University Press, New York.

Montgomery, R. (1981) *Listening made easy*, AMACOM, New York.

Moos, R. (1973) 'Conceptualisations of human environments', *American Psychologist*, 28, 652–65.

Morley, I.E. and Hosking, D.M. (1985) 'The skills of leadership', Paper presented at the West European Conference on the Psychology of Work and Organization, Aachen, FRG, 1–3 April.

Morris, D., Collen, P., Marsh, P. and O'Shaughnessy, M. (1979) *Gestures: their origins and distribution*, Stein and Day, New York.

Morrow, N.C. and Hargie, O.D.W. (1987) 'An investigation of critical incidents in interpersonal communication in pharmacy practice', *Journal of Social and Administrative Pharmacy*, 4, 112–18.

—— Hargie, O.D.W., Donnelly, H. and Woodman, C. (1993a) 'Why do you ask? A study of questioning behaviour in community pharmacist–client consultations', *International Journal of Pharmacy Practice*, 2, 90–4.

—— Hargie, O.D.W. and Woodman C. (1993b) 'The advice-giving role of community pharmacists: a survey of consumer perceptions and attitudes', *Pharmaceutical Journal*, 251, 25–7.

Motley, M. (1992) 'Mindfulness in solving communicators' dilemmas', *Communication Monographs*, 59, 306–13.

Mucchielli, R. (1983) *Face-to-face in the counselling interview*, Macmillan, London.

Mullinix, S.B. and Galassi, J.P. (1981) 'Deriving the content of social skills training with a verbal response components approach', *Behavioral Assessment*, 3, 55–66.

Munn, W. and Gruner, C. (1981) '"Slick" jokes, speaker sex and informative speech', *Southern Speech Communication Journal*, 46, 411–18.

Munro, E.A., Manthei, R.J. and Small, J.J. (1983) *Counselling: a skills approach*, Methuen, New Zealand.

Myers, G. and Myers, M. (1985) *The dynamics of human communication*, McGraw-Hill, New York.

Nagata, D.K., Nay, W.R. and Seidman, E. (1983) 'Nonverbal and verbal content behaviors in the prediction of interviewer effectiveness', *Journal of Counseling Psychology*, 30, 83–6.

Naifeh, S. and Smith, G. (1984) *Why can't men open up?* Clarkson N. Potter, New York.

Naisbitt, J. (1982) *Megatrends: ten new directions transforming our lives*, Warner Books, New York.

Nelson-Gray, R., Haas, J., Romand, B., Herbert, J. and Herbert, D. (1989) 'Effects of open-ended versus close-ended questions on interviewees' problem related statements', *Perceptual and Motor Skills*, 69, 903–11.

Nelson-Jones, R. (1988) *Practical counselling and helping skills* (2nd edition), Holt, Rinehart and Winston, London.

—— (1989) *Effective thinking skills: preventing and managing personal problems*, Cassell, London.

Nemeth, C. (1992) 'Minority dissent as a stimulant to group performance', in S. Worchel, W. Wood and J. Simpson (eds), *Group process and productivity*, Sage, Newbury Park.

Nettles, R. and Bayton, J.A. (1988) 'Persons, situations, subjective expected utilities and assertive behavioral intentions', *The Journal of Psychology*, 122, 157–72.

Newman, H. (1982) 'The sounds of silence in communicative encounters', *Communication Quarterly*, 30, 142–9.

Nix, J., Lohr, J. and Mosesso, L. (1983) 'The relationship of sex-role characteristics to self-report and role-play measures of assertiveness in women', *Behavioral Assessment*, 6, 89–93.

Noller, P. (1980) 'Gaze in married couples', *Journal of Nonverbal Behavior*, 5, 115–29.

Norman, R. (1976) 'When what is said is important: a comparison of expert and attractive sources', *Journal of Experimental Social Psychology*, 12, 294–300.

Northouse, P. and Northouse, L. (1992) *Health communication: strategies for health professionals*, Prentice-Hall, Englewood Cliffs, NJ.

Norton, R. (1983) *Communicator style: theory, applications and measures*, Sage, Beverly Hills.

Novak, J.D., Ring, D.G. and Tanir, P. (1971) 'Interpretation of research findings in terms of Ausubel's Theory and implications for science education', *Science Education*, 55, 483–526.

Nuthall, G.A. (1968) 'Studies of teaching: 11 types of research on teaching', *New Zealand Journal of Educational Studies*, 3, 125–47.

O'Brien, J.S. and Holborn, S.W. (1979) 'Verbal and nonverbal expressions as reinforcers in verbal conditioning of adult conversation', *Journal of Behaviour Psychiatry*, 10, 267–9.

O'Connor, E.M. and Simms, C.M. (1990) 'Self-revelation and manipulation: the effects of sex and machiavellianism on self-disclosure', *Social Behaviour and Personality*, 18, 95–100.

O'Donnell, P.J., Kennedy, B. and McGill, P. (1983) 'Verbal operant conditioning, extinction trials and types of awareness statement', *Psychological Reports*, 53, 991–7.

Oguchi, T. (1991) 'Goal-based analysis of willingness of self-disclosure', *Japanese Psychological Research*, 33, 180–7.

O'Hair, D. and Friedrich, G. (1992) *Strategic communication in business and the professions*, Houghton Mifflin, Boston.

O'Keefe, D. (1990) *Persuasion: theory and research*, Sage, Newbury Park.

O'Leary, K. and O'Leary, S. (eds) (1977) *Classroom management: the successful use of behavior modification*, Pergamon, New York.

Oliver, L. (1974) 'The effects of verbal reinforcement on career choice realism', *Journal of Vocational Behavior*, 5, 275–84.

O'Neill, N. and O'Neill, G. (1977) 'Relationships', in B. Patton and K. Giffin (eds), *Interpersonal communication in action*, Harper and Row, New York.

O'Reilly, C. and Puffer, S. (1989) 'The impact on rewards and punishments in a social context: a laboratory and field experiment', *Journal of Occupational Psychology*, 62, 41–53.

Ostermeier, T. (1967) 'Effects of type and frequency of reference upon perceived source credibility and attitude change', *Speech Monographs*, 34, 137–44.

Owens, R.G. (1986) 'Handling strong emotions', in O. Hargie (ed.), *A handbook of communication skills*, Croom Helm, London/New York University Press, NY.

Pansa, M. (1979) 'Verbal conditioning of affect responses of process and reactive schizophrenics in a clinical interview situation', *British Journal of Medical Psychology*, 52, 175–82.

Papini, D., Farmer, F., Clark, S., Micka, J. and Barnett, J. (1990) 'Early adolescent age and gender differences in patterns of emotional self-disclosure to parents and friends', *Adolescence*, 25, 959–76.

Pardeck, J., Anderson, C., Gianino, E. and Miller, B. (1991) 'Assertiveness of social work students', *Psychological Reports*, 69, 589–90.

Park, B. and Kraus, S. (1992) 'Consensus in initial impressions as a function of verbal information', *Personality and Social Psychology Bulletin*, 182, 439–49.

Parrott, R., Greene, K. and Parker, R. (1992) 'Negotiating child health care routines during paediatrician–parent conversations', *Journal of Language and Social Psychology*, 11, 35–46.

Passons, W.R. (1975) *Gestalt approaches in counseling*, Holt, Rinehart and Winston, New York.

Patterson, C.H. (1986) *Theories of counseling and psychotherapy*, Harper and Row, New York.

Patterson, M. (1983) *Nonverbal behavior: a functional perspective*, Springer Verlag, New York.

Pattison, J. (1973) 'Effects of touch on self-exploration and the therapeutic relationship', *Journal of Consulting and Clinical Psychology*, 40, 170–5.

Pavlov, I.P. (1927) *Conditioned reflexes*, Dover Reprint, New York.

Pendleton, D. and Bochner, S. (1980) 'The communication of medical information in general practice consultations as a function of patients' social class', *Social Science and Medicine*, 14, 669–73.

Perrott, E. (1982) *Effective teaching*, Longman, London.

Pervin, L. (1978) 'Definitions, measurements and classifications of stimuli, situations and environments', *Human Ecology*, 6, 71–105.

—— (1989) *Goal concepts in personality and social psychology*, Lawrence Erlbaum, Hillsdale, NJ.

Petronio, S. and Bantz, C. (1991) 'Controlling the ramifications of disclosure: "don't tell anybody but. . ."' , *Journal of Language and Social Psychology*, 10, 263–70.

Petty, R. and Cacioppo, J. (1981) *Attitudes and persuasion: classic and contemporary approaches*, Wm. C. Brown: Dubuque, Iowa.

—— (1984) 'The effects of involvement on responses to argument quantity and quality: central and peripheral routes to persuasion', *Journal of Personality and Social Psychology*, 46, 69–81.

Phelps, S. and Austin, N. (1987) *The assertive woman: a new look*, Impact, San Luis Obispo, California.

Phillips, D. (1980) 'Airplane accidents, murder and the mass media: towards a theory of imitation and suggestion', *Social Forces*, 58, 1001–24.

—— and Cartensen, L. (1986) 'Clustering of teenage suicides after television news stories about suicide', *The New England Journal of Medicine*, 315, 685–9.

Phillips, E. (1978) *The social skills basis of psychopathology*, Grune and Stratton, New York.

Pietrofesa, J., Hoffman, A. and Splete, H. (1984) *Counseling: an introduction*, Houghton Mifflin, Boston.

Pinney, R.H. (1969) 'Presentational behaviors related to success in teaching', PhD thesis, Stanford University, *Dissertation Abstracts International*, 30, 1970.

Pope, B. (1979) *The mental health interview: research and applications*, Pergamon Press, Oxford.

—— (1986) *Social skills training for psychiatric nurses*, Harper and Row, London.

Poppleton, S. (1981) 'The social skills of selling', in M. Argyle (ed.), *Social skills and work*, Methuen, London.

Porritt, L. (1984) *Communication: choices for nurses*, Churchill Livingstone, Melbourne, Australia.

Powell, W.J. (1968) 'Differential effectiveness of interviewer interventions in an experimental interview', *Journal of Consulting and Clinical Psychology*, 32, 210–15.

Premack, D. (1965) 'Reinforcement theory', in D. Levine (ed.), *Nebraska Symposium on Motivation, Vol. 13*, University of Nebraska Press, Lincoln.

Prue, D. and Fairbank, J. (1981) 'Performance feedback in organizational behavior management: a review', *Journal of Organizational Behavior Management*, 3, 1–16.

Purvis, J., Dabbs, J. and Hopper, C. (1984) 'The "opener": skilled user of facial expression and speech pattern', *Personality and Social Psychology Bulletin*, 10, 61–6.

Quinn, R.E. and McGrath, M.R. (1982) 'Moving behind the single solution perspective', *Journal of Applied Behavioral Science*, 18, 463–72.

Rabin, C. and Zelner, D. (1992) 'The role of assertiveness in clarifying roles and strengthening job satisfaction of social workers in multidisciplinary mental health settings', *British Journal of Social Work*, 22, 17–32.

Rackham, N. and Carlisle, J. (1978) 'The effective negotiator – Part 1', *Journal of European Industrial Training*, 2, 6–10.

—— and Morgan, T. (1977) *Behaviour analysis in training*, McGraw-Hill, Maidenhead, Berks.

Ragan, S. (1990) 'Verbal play and multiple goals in the gynaecological exam interaction', *Journal of Language and Social Psychology*, 9, 67–84.

Rakos, R. (1986) 'Asserting and confronting', in O. Hargie (ed.) *A handbook of communication skills*, Croom Helm, London/New York University Press, NY.

—— (1991) *Assertive behavior: theory, research and training*, Routledge, London/New York.

Rapp, S., Carstensen, L. and Prue, D. (1983) 'Organizational behaviour management 1978–1982: an annotated bibliography', *Journal of Organizational Behaviour Management*, 5, 5–50.

Rauch, C.F. and Behling, O. (1984) 'Functionalism: basis for an alternative approach to the study of leadership', in J. Hunt, D. Hosking, C. Schriesheim and R. Stewart (eds), *Leaders and managers: international perspectives on managerial behavior and leadership*, Pergamon, New York.

Raven, B. (1988) 'Social power and compliance in health care', in S. Maes, C. Spielberger, P. Defares and I. Sarason (eds), *Topics in health psychology*, Wiley, New York.

—— and Haley, R. (1982) 'Social influences and compliance of hospital nurses with infection control policies', in J. Eiser (ed.), *Social psychology and behavioral medicine*, Wiley, Chichester.

—— and Rubin, J.Z. (1983) *Social psychology* (2nd edition), Wiley, New York.

Reardon, K. (1991) *Persuasion in practice*, Sage, Newbury Park.

Reece, M.M. and Whitman, R.N. (1962) 'Expressive movements, warmth and verbal reinforcement', *Journal of Abnormal and Social Psychology*, 64, 234–6.

Reid, L.S., Henneman, R. and Long, E. (1960) 'An experimental analysis of set: the effect of categorical instruction', *American Journal of Psychology*, 73, 568–72.

Reinard, J. (1988) 'The empirical study of the persuasive effects of evidence: the status after fifty years of research', *Human Communication Research*, 15, 3–59.

Reno, R.R. and Kenny, D.A. (1960) 'Effects of self-consciousness and social anxiety on self-disclosure among unacquainted individuals: an application of the social relations model', *Journal of Personality*, 60, 79–95.

Resnick, L. (1972) 'Teacher behaviour in an informal British infant school', *School Review*, 81, 63–83.

Reynolds, J.H. and Glaser, R. (1964) 'Effects of repetition and spaced review upon retention of a complex learning task', *Journal of Educational Psychology*, 5, 297–308.

Richardson, S. (1960) 'The use of leading questions in non-schedule interviews', *Human Organization*, 19, 86–9.

—— Dohrenwend, N. and Klein, D. (1965) *Interviewing: its forms and functions*, Basic Books, New York.

Rierdan, J. and Brooks, R. (1978) 'Verbal conditioning of male and female schizophrenics as a function of experimenter proximity', *Journal of Clinical Psychology*, 34, 33–6.

Riggio, R. and Friedman, H. (1986) 'Impression formation: the role of expressive behavior', *Journal of Personality and Social Psychology*, 50, 421–7.

Riseborough, M. (1981) 'Physiographic gestures as decoding facilitators: three experiments exploring a neglected facet of communication', *Journal of Nonverbal Behavior*, 5, 172–83.

Robinson, J. (1982) *An evaluation of health visiting*, CETHV, London.

Rogers, C.R. (1951) *Client-centered therapy*, Houghton Mifflin, Boston.

—— (1961) *On becoming a person: a therapist's view of psychotherapy*, Houghton Mifflin, Boston.

—— (1977) *On personal power: inner strength and its revolutionary impact*, Delacante Press, New York.

—— (1980) *A way of being*, Houghton Mifflin, Boston.

—— and Farson, R. (1973) 'Active listening', in R. Huseman, C. Logue and D. Freshley (eds), *Readings in interpersonal and organizational communication* (2nd edition), Holbrook Press, Boston, Mass.

Rogers, W. (1978) 'The contribution of kinesic illustrators toward the comprehension of verbal behavior within utterances', *Human Communication Research*, 5, 54–62.

Roloff, M. and Berger, C. (eds) (1982) *Social cognition and communication.* Sage, Beverly Hills.

Rose, Y. and Tryon, W. (1979) 'Judgements of assertive behavior as a function of speech loudness, latency, content, gestures, inflection and sex', *Behavior Modification*, 3, 112–23.

Rosenblatt, P.C. (1977) 'Cross-cultural perspective on attraction', in T.L. Huston (ed.), *Foundations of interpersonal attraction*, Academic Press, London.

Rosenfarb, I. (1992) 'A behaviour analytic interpretation of the therapeutic relationship', *The Psychological Record*, 42, 341–54.

Rosenfeld, H.M. (1981) 'Whither interactional synchrony?' in K. Bloom (ed.), *Prospective issues in infant research*, Lawrence Erlbaum, Hillsdale, NJ.

—— (1987) 'Conversational control functions of nonverbal behavior', in A. Siegman and S. Feldstein (eds), *Nonverbal behavior and communication*, Lawrence Erlbaum, Hillsdale, NJ.

—— and Hancks, M. (1980) 'The nonverbal context of verbal listener responses', in M. Kay (ed.), *The relationship of verbal and nonverbal communication*, Mouton, The Hague.

Rosenshine, B. (1968) 'Objectively measured behavioral predictors of effectiveness in explaining', *Technical Report 4*, Stanford University Center for Research and Development in Teaching, Stanford.

—— (1971) *Teaching behaviour and student achievement*, National Foundation for Educational Research in England and Wales, Windsor, Berks.

—— and Furst, N. (1973) 'The use of direct observation to study teaching', in R. Travers (ed.), *Second handbook of research on teaching*, Rand McNally, New York.

Roth, H.L. (1889) 'On salutations', *Journal of the Royal Anthropological Institute*, 19, 164–81.

Rothkopf, E.Z. (1972) 'Variable adjunct question schedules, interpersonal interaction and incidental learning from written material', *Journal of Educational Psychology*, 63, 87–92.

Rotter, J.B. (1966) 'Generalized expectancies for internal versus external control of reinforcement', *Psychological Monographs*, 80, No. 609.

Rousseau, E. and Redfield, D. (1980) 'Teacher questioning', *Evaluation in Education*, 4, 51–2.

Rowe, M. (1969) 'Science, silence and sanctions', *Science and Children*, 6, 11–13.
—— (1974a) 'Pausing phenomena: influence on the quality of instruction', *Journal of Psycholinguistic Research*, 3, 203–33
—— (1974b) 'Wait-time and rewards as instructional variables, their influence on language, logic, and fate control. Part One – wait-time', *Journal of Research in Science Teaching*, 11, 81–94.
Rozelle, R., Druckman, D. and Baxter, J. (1986) 'Nonverbal communication', in O. Hargie (ed.), *A handbook of communication skills*, Croom Helm, London/New York University Press, NY.
Ruffner, M. and Burgoon, M. (1981) *Interpersonal communication*, Holt, Rinehart and Winston, New York.
Russell, J.L. (1971) *Motivation*, W.C. Brown, Dubuque, Iowa.
Russo, N.F. (1975) 'Eye-contact, interpersonal distance, and the equilibrium theory', *Journal of Personality and Social Psychology*, 31, 497–502.
Rutter, D., Stephenson, G., Ayline, K. and White, P. (1978) 'The timing of looks in dyadic conversation', *British Journal of Social and Clinical Psychology*, 16, 191–2.
Saigh, P.A. (1981) 'Effects of nonverbal examiner praise on selected WAIS subtest performance of Lebanese undergraduates', *Journal of Nonverbal Behavior*, 6, 84–8.
Sajwaj, T. and Dillon, A. (1977) 'Complexities of an elementary behavior modification procedure: differential adult attention used for children's behavior disorders', in B. Etzel, J. Le Blanc and D. Baer (eds), *New developments in behavioral research: theory, method and application*, Lawrence Erlbaum, Hillsdale, NJ.
Saks, M. and Krupat, E. (1988) *Social psychology and its applications*, Harper and Row, New York.
Salmoni, A., Schmidt, R. and Walter, C. (1984) 'Knowledge of results and motor learning: a review and critical reappraisal', *Psychological Bulletin*, 95, 355–86.
Salter, A. (1949) *Conditioned reflex therapy*, Capricorn Books, New York.
Samaan, M. (1971) 'The differential effects of reinforcement and advice-giving on information seeking behavior in counseling', *Dissertation Abstracts International*, 32, 189A.
Samovar, L. and Mills, J. (1986) *Oral communication, message and response*, W.C. Brown, Dubuque, Iowa.
Sapolsky, A. (1960) 'Effect of interpersonal relationships upon verbal conditioning', *Journal of Abnormal and Social Psychology*, 60, 241–6.
Sarbin, T.R. and Allen, V.L. (1968) 'Role theory', in G. Lindzey and E. Aronson (eds), *Handbook of social psychology, Vol. 1*, Addison-Wesley, Reading, Mass.
Saunders, C. (1986) 'Opening and closing', in O. Hargie (ed.), A *handbook of communication skills*, Croom Helm, London/New York University Press, NY.
—— and Caves, R. (1986) 'An empirical approach to the identification of communication skills with reference to speech therapy', *Journal of Further and Higher Education*, 10, 29–44.
—— and Saunders, E.D. (1993) 'Expert teachers' perceptions of university teaching: the identification of teaching skills', in R. Ellis (ed.), *Quality Assurance for University Teaching*, Open University Press, Buckingham.
Schachter, S. and Singer, J. (1962) 'Cognitive, social, physiological determinants of emotional state', *Psychological Review*, 69, 379–99.
Schatzman, L. and Strauss, A. (1956) 'Social class and modes of communications', *American Journal of Sociology*, 60, 329–38.
Scheflen, A. (1974) *How behavior means*, Anchor, Garden City, NJ.
Schegloff, E.A. and Sacks, H. (1973) 'Opening-up closings', *Semiotica*, 8, 289–327.
Scheier, M.F. and Carver, C.S. (1985) 'The self-consciousness scale: a revised version for use with general populations', *Journal of Applied Social Psychology*, 15, 687–99.

Scherer, K. (1979) 'Acoustic concomitants of emotional dimensions: judging affect from synthesized tone sequences', in S. Weitz (ed.), *Nonverbal communication: readings with commentary* (2nd edition), Oxford University Press, New York.

—— and Ekman, P. (eds) (1982) *Handbook of methods in nonverbal behaviour research*, Cambridge University Press, Cambridge.

Schlenker, B. (1986) 'Self-identification: toward an integration of the private and public self', in R. Baumeister (ed.), *Public self and private self*, Springer-Verlag, New York.

—— and Weigold, M. (1989) 'Goals and the self-identification process: constructing desired identities', in L. Pervin (ed.), *Goal concepts in personality and social psychology*, Lawrence Erlbaum, Hillsdale, NJ.

Schleuder, J. and White, A. (1989) 'Priming effects of television news bumpers and teasers on attention and memory', Paper presented at the International Communication Association Conference, San Francisco.

Schlundt, D. and McFall, R. (1985) 'New directions in the assessment of social competence and social skills', in L. L'Abate and M. Milan (eds), *Handbook of social skills training and research*, Wiley, New York.

Schneider, D., Hastorf, A. and Ellsworth, P. (1979) *Person perception*, Addison-Wesley, Reading, Mass.

Schroth, M. (1992) 'The effect of delay of feedback on a delayed concept formation transfer task', *Contemporary Educational Psychology*, 17, 78–82.

Schuck, R.F. (1969) 'The effect of set induction upon pupil achievement, retention and assessment of effective teaching', *Educational Leadership*, 2, 785–93.

Schulman, L. (1979) *The skills of helping*, Peacock Publishers, Illinois.

Schultz, C.B. and Sherman, R.H. (1976) 'Social class, development and differences in reinforcer effectiveness', *Review of Educational Research*, 46, 25–59.

Schutz, W.C. (1955) 'What makes groups productive?' *Human Relations*, 8, 429–65.

Schwartz, B. (1989) *Psychology of learning and behavior*, Norton, New York.

Scofield, M.E. (1977) 'Verbal conditioning with a heterogeneous adolescent sample: the effects on two critical responses', *Psychology*, 14, 41–9.

Scott, M., McCroskey, J. and Sheahan, M. (1978) 'The development of a self-report measure of communication apprehension in organizational settings', *Journal of Communication*, 28, 104–11.

Secord, P.F. and Backman, C.W. (1974) *Social psychology*, McGraw-Hill, New York.

Segrin, C. (1992) 'Specifying the nature of social skill deficits associated with depression', *Human Communication Research*, 19, 89–123.

—— and Dillard, J. (1993) 'The complex link between social skill and dysphoria', *Communication Research*, 20, 76–104.

Seibold, D., Cantrill, J. and Meyers, R. (1985) 'Communication and interpersonal influence', in M. Knapp and G. Miller (eds), *Handbook of interpersonal communication*, Sage, Newbury Park.

Seligman, M.E.P. (1975) *Helplessness: on depression, development, and death*, W.H. Freeman, San Francisco.

Shaffer, D., Pegalis, L. and Cornell, D. (1992) 'Gender and self-disclosure revisited: personal and contextual variations in self-disclosure to same-sex acquaintants', *Journal of Social Psychology*, 132, 307–15.

Shamir, B. (1992) 'Attribution of influence and charisma to the leader: the romance of leadership revisited', *Journal of Applied Social Psychology*, 22, 386–407.

Shannon, C. and Weaver, W. (1949) *The mathematical theory of communication*, University of Illinois Press, Illinois.

Shaw, M.E. (1981) *Group dynamics: the psychology of small group behavior*, McGraw-Hill, New York.

Sherman, W. (1990) *Behavior modification*, Harper and Row, New York.

Showalter, J.T. (1974) 'Counselor nonverbal behavior as operant reinforcers for client self-references and expression of feelings', *Dissertation Abstracts International*, 35, 3435A.

Shutes, R. (1969) 'Verbal behaviors and instructional effectiveness', Stanford University, *Dissertation Abstracts International*, 30, 1970.

Shuy, R.W. (1983) 'Three types of interference to an effective exchange of information in the medical interview', in S. Fisher and A.D. Todd (eds), *Social organization of doctor–patient communication*, Center for Applied Linguistics, Washington, DC.

Siegel, J. (1980) 'Effects of objective evidence of expertness, nonverbal behavior and subject sex on client-perceived expertness', *Journal of Counseling Psychology*, 27, 117–21.

Siegman, A. (1985) 'Expressive correlates of affective states and traits', in A.W. Siegman and S. Feldstein (eds), *Multichannel integrations of nonverbal behavior*, Lawrence Erlbaum, New Jersey.

Sigal, J., Branden-Maguire, J., Hayden, M. and Mosley, N. (1985) 'The effect of presentation style and sex of lawyer on jury decision-making behavior', *Psychology: A Quarterly Journal of Human Behavior*, 22, 13–19.

Silver, R.J. (1970) 'Effects of subject status and interviewer response program on subject self-disclosure in standardized interviews', *Proceedings of the 78th Annual Convention*, APA, 5, 539–40.

Simms, M. and Smith, C. (1984) 'Teenage mothers: some views on health visitors', *Health Visitor*, 57, 269–70.

Simonson, N. (1973) 'Self-disclosure and psychotherapy', unpublished mimeo, University of Massachusetts.

Simpson, J. and Wood, W. (1992) 'Introduction: where is the group in social psychology?', in S. Worchel, W. Wood and J. Simpson (eds), *Group process and productivity*, Sage, Newbury Park.

Sinha, V. (1972) 'Age differences in self-disclosure', *Developmental Psychology*, 7, 257–8.

Skinner, B.F. (1953) *Science and human behaviour*, Collier-Macmillan, London.

—— (1957) *Verbal behavior*, Appleton-Century-Crofts, New York.

—— (1974) *About behaviorism*, Vintage Books, New York.

—— (1977) 'The force of coincidence', in B. Etzel, J. Le Blanc and D. Baer (eds), *New developments in behavioral research: theory, method and applications*, Lawrence Erlbaum, Hillsdale, NJ.

—— (1978) *Reflections on behaviorism and society*, Prentice-Hall, Englewood Cliffs, NJ.

Slobin, D., Miller, S. and Porter, L. (1968) 'Forms of address and social relations in a business organization', *Journal of Personality and Social Psychology*, 8, 289–92.

Smith, P. (1974) 'Aspects of the playgroup environment', in D. Canter and T. Lee (eds), *Psychology and the built environment*, Architectural Press, London.

Smith, R. and Smoll, F. (1990) 'Self-esteem and children's reactions to youth sport coaching behaviours: a field study of self-enhancement processes', *Developmental Psychology*, 26, 987–93.

Smith, V. (1986) 'Listening', in O. Hargie (ed.), *A handbook of communication skills*, Croom Helm, London/New York University Press, NY.

Snyder, M. (1987) *Public appearances private realities: the psychology of self-monitoring*, Freeman, New York.

Solano, C. and Dunnam, M. (1985) 'Two's company: self-disclosure and reciprocity in triads versus dyads', *Social Psychology Quarterly*, 48, 183–7.

Solomon, L.J., Brehony, K.A., Rothblum, E.D. and Kelly, J.A. (1982) 'Corporate managers' reaction to assertive social skills exhibited by males and females', *Journal of Organizational Behavior Management*, 4, 49–63.

Solomon, M. and Schopler, J. (1978) 'The relationship of physical attractiveness and punitiveness: is the linearity assumption out of line?' *Personality and Social Psychology Bulletin*, 4, 483–6.

—— (1982) 'Self consciousness and clothing', *Personality and Social Psychology Bulletin*, 8, 508–14.

Sommer, R. (1969) *Personal space*, Prentice-Hall, Englewood Cliffs, NJ.

Sorensen, G.A. and Beatty, M.J. (1988) 'The interactive effects of touch and touch avoidance on interpersonal evaluations', *Communication Research Reports*, 5, 84–90.

Spence, J. and Helmreich, R. (1978) *Masculinity and femininity: their psychological dimensions, correlates and antecedents*, University of Texas Press, Austin.

Spitzberg, B.H. and Cupach, W.R. (1984) *Interpersonal communication competence*, Sage, Beverly Hills.

Spooner, S.E. (1976) 'An investigation of the maintenance of specific counseling skills over time', *Dissertation Abstracts International*, February, 5840A.

Stang, D. and Wrightsman, L. (1981) *Dictionary of social behavior and social research methods*, Brooks Cole, Monterey, California.

Stasser, G. (1992) 'Pooling of unshared information during group discussion', in S. Worchel, W. Wood and J.A. Simpson (eds), *Group process and productivity*, Sage, Newbury Park.

Steel, L. (1991) 'Interpersonal correlates of trust and self-disclosure', *Psychological Reports*, 68, 1319–20.

Steil, L. (1991) 'Listening training: the key to success in today's organizations', in D. Borisoff and M. Purdy (eds), *Listening in everyday life*, University of America Press, Maryland.

—— Barker, L. and Watson, K. (1983) *Effective listening: key to your success*, Addison-Wesley, Reading, Mass.

Stenstroem, A. (1988) 'Questions in conversation', in M. Meyer (ed.), *Questions and questioning*, de Gruyter, New York and Berlin.

Sterling, B.S. and Owen, J.W. (1982) 'Perceptions of demanding versus reasoning male and female police officers', *Personality and Social Psychology Bulletin*, 8, 336–40.

Stewart, C.J. and Cash, W.B. (1988) *Interviewing: principles and practices* (5th edition), W.C. Brown, Dubuque, Iowa.

—— (1991) *Interviewing: principles and practices*, W.C. Brown, Dubuque, Iowa.

Stewart, J. (ed.) (1977) *Bridges, not walls*, Addison-Wesley, Reading, Mass.

Stewart, R., Powell, G. and Chetwynd, S. (1979) *Person perception and stereotyping*, Saxon House, Farnborough.

Stiles, W. and Putnam, S. (1982) 'Verbal exchanges in medical interviews: concepts and measurement', *Social Science and Medicine*, 35, 347–55.

St Lawrence, J.S. (1987) 'Assessment of assertion', in M. Hersen, R. Eisler and P. Miller (eds), *Progress in behavior modification*, Sage, Newbury Park.

—— Hansen, D.J., Cutts, T.F., Tisdelle, D.A. and Irish, J.D. (1985) 'Sex role orientation: a superordinate variable in social evaluation of assertive and unassertive behavior', *Behavior Modification*, 9, 387–96.

Stock, C.G. (1978) 'Effects of praise and its source on performance', *Perceptual and Motor Skills*, 47, 43–6.

Stogdill, R.M. (1948) 'Personal factors associated with leadership: a survey of the literature', *Journal of Psychology*, 25, 35–71.

—— (1950) 'Leadership, membership and organization', *Psychological Bulletin*, 47, 1–14.

—— (1974) *Handbook of leadership: a survey of theory and research*, Free Press, New York.

Stone, D. (1983) 'The effects of format and number of arguments on comprehension of text by college undergraduates', *Resources in Education*, 18, 33–5.

Stone, G. (1962) 'Appearance and the self', in A. Rose (ed.), *Human behavior and social processes*, Houghton Mifflin, Boston.

Strack, F. and Schwarz, N. (1992) 'Communication influences in standardised question situations: the case of implicit collaboration', in G. Semin and K. Fiedler (eds), *Language, interaction and social cognition*, Sage, London.

Stricker, G. (1990) 'Self-disclosure and psychotherapy', in G. Stricker and M. Fisher (eds), *Self-disclosure in the therapeutic relationship*, Plenum Press, New York.

—— and Fisher, M. (1990) (eds), *Self-disclosure in the therapeutic relationship*, Plenum Press, New York.

Strong, S., Taylor, R., Branon, J. and Loper, R. (1971) 'Nonverbal behavior and perceived counselor characteristics', *Journal of Counseling Psychology*, 18, 554–61.

Sudman, S. and Bradburn, N. (1982) *Asking questions*, Jossey-Bass, San Francisco.

Sue, D., Sue, D.M. and Ino, S. (1990) 'Assertiveness and social anxiety in Chinese-American women', *Journal of Psychology*, 124, 155–64.

Sullivan, H.S. (1953) *The interpersonal theory of psychiatry*, Norton, New York.

—— (1954) *The psychiatric interview*, Norton, New York.

Sutton, S. (1982) 'Fear arousing communication: a critical examination of theory and research', in J. Eiser (ed.), *Social psychology and behavioral medicine*, Wiley, New York.

Swann, W., Hixon, J., Stein-Seroussi, A. and Gilbert, D. (1990) 'The fleeting gleam of praise: cognitive processes underlying behavioral reactions to self-relevant feedback', *Journal of Personality and Social Psychology*, 59, 17–26.

Swenson, R., Nash, D. and Roos, E. (1984) 'Source credibility and perceived expertness of testimony in a simulated child-custody case', *Professional Psychology*, 15, 891–8.

Swift, J.N., Gooding, T. and Swift, P.R. (1988) 'Questions and wait time', in J.T. Dillon (ed.), *Questioning and discussion: a multidisciplinary study*, Ablex, Norwood, NJ.

Tajfel, J. (1981) *Human groups and social categories*, Cambridge University Press, London.

Tardy, C.H. (1988) 'Self-disclosure: objectives and methods of measurement', in C.H. Tardy (ed.), *A handbook for the study of human communication*, Ablex, Norwood, NJ.

Taylor, D. (1979) 'Motivational bases', in G. Chelune (ed.), *Self-disclosure*, Jossey-Bass, San Francisco.

Taylor, S. and Thompson, S. (1982) 'Stalking the elusive "vividness" effect', *Psychological Review*, 89, 155–81.

Tesser, A. (1978) 'Self-generated attitude change', in L. Berkowitz (ed.), *Advances in experimental social psychology, Vol. 11*, Academic Press, New York.

—— (1988) 'Toward a self-evaluation maintenance model of social behavior', in L. Berkowitz (ed.), *Advances in experimental social psychology, Vol. 21*, Academic Press, New York.

Thibaut, J. and Kelley, H. (1959) *The social psychology of groups*, Wiley, New York.

Thomas A. and Bull, P. (1981) 'The role of pre-speech posture change in dyadic interaction', *British Journal of Social Psychology*, 20, 105–11.

Thomlinson, D. (1991) 'Intercultural listening', in D. Borisoff and M. Purdy (eds), *Listening in everyday life*, University of America Press, Maryland.

Thyne, J. (1966) *The psychology of learning and techniques of teaching* (2nd edition), University of London Press, London.

Tizard, B., Hughes, M., Carmichael, H. and Pinkerton, G. (1983) 'Children's questions and adult answers', *Journal of Child Psychology and Psychiatry*, 24, 269–81.

Tjosvold, D. (1984) 'Effects of leader warmth and directiveness on subordinate performance on a subsequent task', *Journal of Applied Psychology*, 69, 422–7.

Tobin, K. (1987) 'The role of wait time in higher cognitive learning', *Review of Educational Research*, 57, 69–95.

Togo, D. and Hood, J. (1992) 'Quantitative information presentation and gender: an interaction effect', *The Journal of General Psychology*, 119, 161–7.

Tomkins, S.S. (1963) *Affect, imagery, consciousness*, Springer, New York.

Tracy, K. and Coupland, N. (1990) 'Multiple goals in discourse: an overview of issues', *Journal of Language and Social Psychology*, 9, 1–13.

Trower, P. (ed.) (1984) *Radical approaches to social skills training*, Croom Helm, London.

—— Bryant, B. and Argyle, M. (1978) *Social skills and mental health*, Methuen, London.

Tubbs, S. and Baird, J. (1976) *The open person. . . self-disclosure and personal growth*, Merrill, Columbus, Ohio.

Turk, C. (1985) *Effective speaking*, E. and F.N. Spon, London.

Turkat, I.D. and Alpher, V.S. (1984) 'Prediction versus reflection in therapist demonstrations of understanding: three analogue experiments', *British Journal of Medical Psychology*, 57, 235–40.

Turner, J. (1982) 'Managerial effectiveness: potential contributions of the behavioral approach', *Journal of Organizational Behavior Management*, 3, 71–83.

—— (1988) *A theory of social interaction*, Stanford University Press, California.

—— Hogg, M., Oakes, P., Reicher, S. and Wetherell, M. (1987) *Rediscovering the social group: a self-categorisation theory*, Blackwell, Oxford.

Turney, C., Owens, L., Hatton, N., Williams, G. and Cairns, L. (1976) *Sydney micro skills: series 2 handbook*, Sydney University Press, Sydney, Australia.

—— Ellis, K.J., Hatton, N., Owens, L.C., Towler, J. and Wright, R. (1983) *Sydney micro skills redeveloped: series 1 handbook*, Sydney University Press, Sydney, Australia.

Uhlemann, M.R., Lea, G.W. and Stone, G.L. (1976) 'Effect of instructions and modeling on trainees low in interpersonal communication skills', *Journal of Counseling Psychology*, 23, 509–13.

Vargas, A. and Borkowski, J. (1982) 'Physical attractiveness and counseling skills', *Journal of Counseling Psychology*, 29, 246–55.

Verner, C. and Dickinson, G. (1967) 'The lecture, an analysis and review of research', *Adult Education*, 17, 85–100.

Verplanck, W.S. (1955) 'The control of the content of conversation: reinforcement of statement of opinion', *Journal of Abnormal and Social Psychology*, 51, 668–76.

Von Cranach, M., Kalbermatten, V., Indermuhle, K. and Gugler, B. (1982) 'Goal-directed action', *European Monographs in Social Psychology, 30*, Academic Press, London.

Vondracek, F.W. (1969) 'The study of self-disclosure in experimental interviews', *Journal of Psychology*, 72, 55–9.

Vroom, V. (1964) *Work and motivation*, Wiley, New York.

Waldron, V., Cegala, D., Sharkey, F. and Teboul, B. (1990) 'Cognitive and tactical dimensions of coversational goal management', *Journal of Language and Social Psychology*, 9, 101–18.

Wallen, J., Waitzkin, H. and Stoeckle, J. (1979) 'Physicians' stereotypes about female health illness: a study of patients' sex and the information process during medical interviews', *Women and Health*, 4, 135–46.

Walton, L. and MacLeod Clark, J. (1986) 'Making contact', *Nursing Times*, 82, 28–32.

Warner, R.M., Maloy, D., Schneider, K., Knoth, R. and Wilder, B. (1987) 'Rhythmic organization of social interaction and observer ratings of positive affect and involvement', *Journal of Nonverbal Behavior*, 11, 57–74.

Washburn, P. and Hakel, M. (1973) 'Visual cues and verbal content as influences on impressions formed after simulated employment interviews', *Journal of Applied Psychology*, 58, 137–41.

Waskow, I.E. (1962) 'Reinforcement in a therapy-like situation through selective responding to feelings or content', *Journal of Consulting Psychology*, 26, 11–19.

Watson, K. and Barker, L. (1984) 'Listening behavior: definition and measurement', in R. Bostrom and B. Westley (eds), *Communication yearbook 8*, Sage, Beverly Hills, California.

Watzlawick, P. (1978) *The language of change*, Basic Books, New York.

—— Beavin, J. and Jackson, D. (1967) *Pragmatics of human communication*, W.W. Norton, New York.

Wearden, J. (1988) 'Some neglected problems in the analysis of human operant behavior', in G. Davey and C. Cullen (eds), *Human operant conditioning and behavior modification*, Wiley, New York.

Weaver, C. (1972) *Human listening: processes and behavior*, Bobbs-Merrill, Indianapolis, Indiana.

Weiner, M.F. (1978) *Therapist disclosure: the use of self in therapy*, Butterworth, Boston, Mass.

Weir, S. and Fine-Davis, M. (1989) '"Dumb blonde" and "temperamental redhead": the effect of hair colour on some attributed personality characteristics of women', *Irish Journal of Psychology*, 10, 11–19.

Weiss, R., Lombardo, J., Warren, D. and Kelley, K. (1971) 'Reinforcing effects of speaking in reply', *Journal of Personality and Social Psychology*, 20, 186–99.

West, C. (1981) *The social and psychological distortion of information*, Nelson-Hall, Chicago.

—— (1983) 'Ask me no questions. . . an analysis of queries and replies in physician–patient dialogues', in S. Fisher and A. Todd (eds), *The social organization of doctor–patient communication*, Center for Applied Linguistics, Washington, DC.

Wetzel, C.G. and Wright-Buckley, C. (1988) 'Reciprocity of self-disclosure: breakdowns of trust in cross-racial dyads', *Basic and Applied Social Psychology*, 9, 277–88.

Wheeless, L., Erickson, K. and Behrens, J. (1986) 'Cultural differences in disclosiveness as a function of locus of control', *Communication Monographs*, 53, 36–46.

Wheldall, K., Bevan, K. and Shortall, A. (1986) 'A touch of reinforcement: the effects of contingent teacher touch on the classroom behavior of young children', *Educational Review*, 38, 207–16.

—— and Glynn, T. (1989) *Effective classroom learning: a behavioural interactionist approach to teaching*, Basil Blackwell, Oxford.

Whetten, D.A. and Cameron, K.S. (1984) *Developing management skills*, Scott Foresman, Glenview, Illinois.

Whitcher, S.J. and Fisher, J.D. (1979) 'Multi-dimensional reaction to therapeutic touch in a hospital setting', *Journal of Personality and Social Psychology*, 37, 87–96.

White, B. and Saunders, S. (1986) 'The influence on patients' pain intensity ratings of antecedent reinforcement of pain talk or well talk', *Journal of Behaviour Therapy and Experimental Psychiatry*, 17, 155–9.

Whittington, D. (1986) 'Chairmanship', in O. Hargie (ed.), *A handbook of communication skills*, Croom Helm, London/New York University Press, NY.

Wiemann, J. and Giles, H. (1988) 'Interpersonal communication', in M. Hewstone, W.

Stroebe, J.-P. Codol and G. Stephenson (eds), *Introduction to social psychology*, Basil Blackwell, Oxford.

Wiener, M., Devoe, S., Rubinow, S. and Geller, J. (1972) 'Nonverbal behaviour and nonverbal communication', *Psychological Review*, 79, 185–214.

Wilensky, R. (1983) *Planning and understanding: a computational approach to human reasoning*, Addison-Wesley, Reading, Mass.

Wilke, H.A.M. (1991) 'Greed, efficiency and fairness in resource management situations', in W. Stroebe and M. Herostone (eds), *European Review of Social Psychology*, Wiley, Chichester.

—— and van Knippenberg, A. (1988) 'Group performance', in M. Hewstone, W. Stroebe, J.-P., Codel and G. Stephenson (eds), *Introduction to social psychology*, Basil Blackwell, Oxford.

—— and Meertens, R. (1994) *Group performance*, Routledge, London.

Willis, F. and Briggs, L. (1992) 'Relationship and touch in public settings', *Journal of Nonverbal Behavior*, 16, 55–63.

—— and Hamm, H. (1980) 'The use of interpersonal touch in securing compliance', *Journal of Nonverbal Behavior*, 5, 49–55.

Wilmot, W. (1987) *Dyadic communication*, Random House, New York.

Wilson, J. (1990) *Politically speaking: the pragmatic analysis of political language*, Basil Blackwell, Oxford.

Wilson, L.K. and Gallois, C. (1985) 'Perceptions of assertive behavior: sex combination, role appropriateness, and message type', *Sex Roles*, 12, 125–41.

—— and Gallois, C. (1993) *Assertion and its social context*, Pergamon, Oxford.

Wilson-Barnett, J. (1981) 'Communicating with patients in general wards', in W. Bridge and J. MacLeod Clark (eds), *Communication in nursing care*, Croom Helm, London.

Winograd, T. (1981) 'A framework for understanding discourse', in M. Just and P. Carpenter (eds), *Cognitive processes in comprehension*, Lawrence Erlbaum, Hillsdale, NJ.

Winton, W. (1990) 'Language and emotion', in H. Giles and W. Robinson (eds), *Handbook of language and social psychology*, Wiley, Chichester.

Witt, L. (1991) 'Person–situation effect on self-presentation on the telephone at work', *The Journal of Social Psychology*, 131, 213–18.

Wolff, F., Marsnik, N., Tacey, W. and Nichols, R. (1983) *Perceptive listening*, Holt, Rinehart and Winston, New York.

Wolpe, J. (1958) *Psychotherapy by reciprocal inhibition*, Stanford University Press, Stanford, California.

Wolvin, A. and Coakley, C. (1982) *Listening*, Wm C. Brown, Dubuque, Iowa.

—— (1988) *Listening* (3rd edition), Wm C. Brown, Dubuque, Iowa.

—— (1991) 'A survey of the status of listening training in some 500 corporations', *Communication Education*, 40, 152–64.

Woodall, G. and Burgoon, J. (1983) 'Talking fast and changing attitudes: a critique and clarification', *Journal of Nonverbal Behavior*, 8, 126–42.

Woodbury, H. (1984) 'The strategic use of questions in court', *Semiotica*, 48, 197–228.

Woodworth, R.S. and Marquis, D.G. (1949) *Psychology: a study of mental life*, Methuen, London.

Woolfolk, A. (1979) 'Self-disclosure in the classroom: an experimental study', *Contemporary Educational Psychology*, 4, 132–9.

Woolfolk, R.L. and Dever, S. (1979) 'Perceptions of assertion: an empirical analysis', *Behavior Therapy*, 10, 404–11.

Worchel, S. (1986) 'The influence of contextual variables on interpersonal spacing', *Journal of Nonverbal Behavior*, 10, 230–54.

—— Lee, J. and Adewole, A. (1975) 'Effects of supply and demand on ratings of objective value', *Journal of Personality and Social Psychology*, 32, 906–14.

Worthy, M., Gary, A. and Kahn, G. (1969) 'Self-disclosure as an exchange process', *Journal of Personality and Social Psychology*, 13, 59–64.

Wright, C. and Nuthall, G. (1970) 'Relationships between teacher behaviors and pupil achievement in three experimental elementary science lessons', *American Educational Research Journal*, 7, 477–93.

Wright, R., Wadley, V., Danner, M. and Phillips, P. (1992) 'Persuasion, reactance and judgements of interpersonal appeal', *European Journal of Social Psychology*, 22, 85–91.

Yager, G. and Beck, T. (1985) 'Beginning practicum: it only hurt until I laughed', *Counselor Education and Supervision*, 25, 149–56.

Yeschke, C. (1987) *Interviewing: an introduction to interrogation*, C.C. Thomas, Illinois.

Yukl, G.A. (1981) *Leadership in organizations*, Prentice-Hall, Englewood Cliffs, NJ.

Zahn, G.L. (1991) 'Face-to-face communication in an office setting: the effects of position, proximity and exposure', *Communication Research*, 18, 737–54.

Zaidel, S.F. and Mehrabian, A. (1969) 'The ability to communicate and infer positive and negative attitudes facially and vocally', *Journal of Experimental Research in Personality*, 3, 233–41.

Zajonc, R. (1980) 'Feeling and thinking', *American Psychologist*, 35, 151–75.

Zander, A. (1982) *Making groups effective*, Jossey-Bass, San Francisco.

Zimmer, J.M. and Anderson, S. (1968) 'Dimensions of positive regard and empathy', *Journal of Counseling Psychology*, 15, 417–26.

—— and Park, P. (1967) 'Factor analysis of counselor communications', *Journal of Counseling Psychology*, 14, 198–203.

Zollo, L.J., Heimberg, R.G. and Becker, R.E. (1985) 'Evaluations and consequences of assertive behavior', *Journal of Behavior Therapy and Experimental Psychiatry*, 16, 295–301.

Zuckerman, M., Spiegel, N., De Paulo, P. and Rosenthal, R. (1982) 'Nonverbal strategies for decoding deception', *Journal of Nonverbal Behavior*, 6, 171–87.

Zuker, E. (1983) *Mastering assertiveness skills*, AMACOM, New York.

Name index

Abele, A. 49
Abelson, R. 22
Abercrombie, M.L.J. 312
Abrami, P. 189
Adams, C. 258
Adelman, R.D. 213
Adler, R. 42
Agar, M. 162
Ainsworth-Vaughan, N. 214
Alberti, R. 268, 269, 270, 289
Alberts, J.K. 288
Allen, J.G. 219
Allen, K. 67
Allen, M. 235, 238
Allport, G. 248
Allwinn, S. 106
Alper, T. 42
Alpher, V.S. 125
Altman, I. 153
Anatol, K. 256
Andersen, S.M. 223, 224
Anderson, S. 125
Anthony, R.N. 304, 311
Applbaum, R. 256, 291, 298
Archer, R. 234, 241, 242
Argyle, M. 2, 3, 17, 18, 26, 30, 37, 50,
    58, 63, 134, 183, 292, 295
Armstrong, D. 195
Armstrong, S. 177, 178, 189
Aronson, E. 75, 90, 250
Arvey, R. 151
Ascani, K. 261
At Emery Air Freight 82
Atkins, M. 123, 265
Atkinson, J. 23
Atkinson, M. 265
Aubertine, H.E. 156
Auerswald, M.C. 127, 132

Austin, N. 268, 272, 282
Authier, J. 64, 78, 133, 190, 220, 222

Baccus, G.K. 138
Backman, C. 22, 76, 296, 303
Baetz, M. 250
Baird, J. 227
Bakhtar, M. 182
Bakken, D. 161
Baldock, J. 123
Baldwin, J.D. 68
Baldwin, J.I. 68
Baldwin, T. 269
Bales, R.F. 170, 293, 299, 300
Balsam, P.D. 66
Bandura, A. 4, 23, 69, 70, 72, 73, 87,
    88, 252, 253
Banks, D.L. 86
Bantz, C. 240
Bardovi-Harlie, K. 162
Barnabei, F. 138
Barnes, D. 57, 184
Barnlund, D. 20
Baron, R. 81, 296, 297, 301
Barry, B. 266
Bass, B.M. 250, 305, 310, 314
Bateman, T. 266
Baumeister, R. 80
Bavelas, A. 301, 303
Baxter, J. 54
Bayton, J.A. 286, 287
Beattie, G. 10, 48, 49
Beatty, M.J. 42
Beaumeister, R. 236
Beck, T. 229
Becker, H.S. 184
Becker, F.D. 52
Beezer, R. 108

Beharry, E.A. 126
Behling, O. 304
Beisecker, T. 246
Bell, R. 254
Benjamin, A. 123, 131, 165, 169
Benne, K.D. 298
Benson, P. 258
Berger, C. 14, 17, 22, 249
Berliner, D.C. 178
Bermann, E. 295
Berscheid, E. 16, 56, 258
Berg, J. 220
Berne, E. 172
Bernstein, B. 184
Bettinghaus, E. 265
Bickman, L. 58, 251
Bies, R. 246, 253
Bird, J. 102
Birdwhistell, R.L. 37
Black, J. 94
Blackman, D. 152
Blake, B.R. 307
Blanchard, K.H. 308
Bless, H. 110
Bligh, D. 114
Bochner, S. 184
Boddy, J. 82
Bond, M. 51
Bondy, A.S. 66
Boore, J. 177
Borden, M. 15
Borisoff, D. 194, 195, 203, 204
Borko, H. 178
Borkowski, J. 258
Bormann, E. 293, 297, 300
Boster, F. 263
Bostrom, R.N.194, 201, 217
Bower, G. 87, 88
Bowers, J. 25
Boy, A.V. 124
Bozionelos, N. 57
Bradac, J. 249
Bradburn, N. 94, 118
Brammer, L. 127, 128, 129, 136, 137, 139
Brehm, J. 77, 259
Brehm, S. 77, 259
Briggs, L. 13
Brigham, J. 22, 24, 248, 295
Brimer, M. 204
Brokaw, D.W. 76
Brooks, R. 86
Brooks, W. 11

Brophy, J. 75, 79, 80, 90, 91
Brown, A. 292
Brown, G. 115, 123, 177, 178, 180, 182, 189, 265
Brown, P. 17
Brown, R. 82, 294, 296
Brundage, L 239
Bruner, J. 35, 176
Bryan, A. 284
Bryman, A. 310
Buck, R. 52, 316
Buckwalter, A. 111
Bugental, D. 51, 172
Bull, P. 37, 48
Burger, J. 239
Burgoon, J. 256
Burgoon, M. 28, 246, 266
Burkhard, B. 7
Burley-Allen, M. 194, 215
Burton, M. 152
Busch, P. 145
Buss, A. 69, 272, 282
Butler, P.E. 282
Button, G. 162
Byrne, D. 75, 258, 260
Byrne, P. 165

Cacioppo, J. 253, 254, 262, 264
Cairns, L. 33, 79, 80
Calabrese, R. 10, 11
Cameron, G.T. 145
Cameron, K.S. 269
Campbell, D.T. 294
Campion, J. 151
Cannell, C.F. 75, 102
Canter, D. 60
Canter, L. 268
Canter, M. 255
Cantor, J. 22
Cappella, J.N. 40
Carkhuff, R.R. 141
Carlisle, J. 97, 229
Carson, R. 14
Cartensen, L. 253
Carter, K. 178
Carver, C.S. 237
Cartwright, D. 310, 312
Cary, M. 303
Cash, W.B. 123, 166
Catano, V. 81
Caves, R. 64
Chaikin, A. 221, 224, 228, 237, 243, 244, 254, 257, 258, 263

Chandler, P. 188
Chang, M. 257
Chelune, G. 220, 221
Chemers, M. 307
Chesner, S. 236
Cialdini, R. 248, 251, 252, 257, 261
Cianni-Surridge, M. 285
Cipani, E. 67
Citkowitz, R.D. 132
Clark, R.A. 253
Cline, R.J. 241
Cline, V.B. 126
Clore, G. 75, 258
Coakley, C. 194, 198, 203
Cody, M. 21, 265
Cohen-Cole, S.A. 102, 134, 159, 165
Collins, J. 4
Collins, M. 4
Conine, N. 217
Cook, M. 50, 55, 153
Cooley, C.H. 293
Cooper, R. 57
Corey, S. 94
Corner, J. 246
Coupland, J. 149, 234
Coupland, N. 27
Cozby, P. 219
Craig, K.D. 253
Cramer, R. 67
Crow, B. 214
Crowne, D. 82
Culley, S. 124, 128
Cupach, W. 3, 278

Dabbs, J. 51, 206, 242
Danish, S. 127, 222
Davey, G. 64, 87, 92
Davidhizar, R. 50
Davis, M. 231
Davison, G.C. 159
Davitz, J.R. 134
Dawley, H. 279, 280
Deaux, K. 297
De Bono, D. 257
Deci, E. 23, 24, 28
De Giovanni, I. 272
Del Greco, L. 272
Dell, D.M. 148
Derlega, V. 220, 221, 223, 224, 228, 237, 243, 244
De Paulo, B.M. 37
Dever, S. 276
De Vito, J.A. 11, 12, 231, 242

Dickinson, G. 181
Dickson, D.A. 1, 3, 10, 18, 20, 73, 83, 85, 92, 107, 122, 123, 132, 138, 155, 164, 177, 193, 251, 266
Dillard, J. 3, 24, 27, 28, 29, 263
Dillon, A. 89
Dillon, J.T. 94, 99, 105, 111, 117, 118, 119, 124, 131
Dimatteo, M. 65
Di Mattia, D.J. 132
Dimond, R. 234
DiNicola, D. 65
Dindia, K. 235, 238
Dinkmeyer, D. 29
Dittmar, H. 152
Dohrenwend, B. 104, 105, 108, 109
Domjan, M. 72
Dovidio, J.F. 49
Drachman, D. 260
Duck, S. 153, 259, 287
Dulany, D. 87
Duncan, S. 40, 48, 51, 85
Dunnam, M. 243

Eagly, A. 254, 308
Eder, R.W. 156
Efran, M. 258
Egan, G. 73, 124, 128, 136, 209
Egan, K. 275, 276, 282
Ehrlich, R.P. 138
Eisler, R. 4, 284
Ekman, P. 14, 37, 39, 44, 47, 48, 50, 51, 128, 133, 134
Eller, B.F. 80
Ellis, A. 10
Ellis, R. 1, 169
Ellison, C.W. 125
Emler, N. 224
Emmons, M. 15, 24, 268, 269, 270, 289
England, G.W. 305
Ennis, R. 177
Epling, W. 69
Eysenck, H. 25
Eysenck, S. 25

Fairbank, J. 72
Falcione, R. 256
Falk, D. 221
Fantino, E. 69
Faraone, S. 63
Farson, R. 216
Feigenbaum, W.M. 126
Feldman, R.S. 37, 45, 261, 294

Ferber, A. 142, 148
Ferris, S.R. 60
Festinger, L. 249, 295
Fiedler, F.E. 306, 307
Field, S. 148
Fillmore, C. 21
Fine-Davis, M. 154, 155
Firestone, I.J. 125
Fisch, H. 47
Fisher, B. 13
Fisher, D. 219, 241
Fisher, J. 43
Fisher, M. 220
Fisher, S. 72, 94, 228
Fiske, D.W. 40, 85
Fiske, J. 11, 12, 48, 51
Fitts, P. 33
Floyd, J. 194
Fong, M. 110, 226
Foot, H. 189, 257, 313
Forbes, R.J. 85
Forgas, J. 20, 34
Forsythe, S.M. 154
Fowler, F.J. 114
Foxman, R. 152
Franzoi, S. 231
Frederiksen, L.W. 4
French, P. 181
Fretz, B. 50
Frick, R. 208
Friedman, H. 38, 56, 189
Friedrich, G. 12
Friesen, W. 14, 40, 44, 133, 134
Fry, L. 278, 279
Furnham, A. 286
Furst, N. 180

Gage, N.L. 175, 179, 184
Galassi, J. 279, 283
Gall, M. 99
Gallagher, M. 138, 228
Gallois, C. 268, 276, 283, 284, 288
Garcia, J.E. 307
Gardner, W.L. 310
Garramone, G. 145
Gatewood, J.B. 47
Gervasio, A.H. 275
Giacolone, R. 73
Gibson, F. 235
Giles, H. 11, 25, 134, 256
Glaser, R. 164
Glass, D. 68
Gleason, J. 176

Gluckstern, N. 179, 185
Glueckauf, R.L. 288
Glynn, T. 74, 79, 80, 252
Goffman, E. 17, 41, 142, 161, 171
Goldberg, M. 266
Goldfried, M.R. 159
Goldman, M. 50, 82, 85, 86
Gonzales, M. 259
Gormally, J. 84, 132, 283, 288
Gorn, G. 266
Gouran, D. 11
Graesser, A. 94
Graham, J. 46
Green, R.T. 67
Greene, D. 87
Greenbaum, P. 148
Greenberg, M.A. 230
Greenspoon, J. 78
Gregg, V. 202
Grigsby, J. 235
Groce, S. 72, 94, 228
Gross, A.M. 283
Gruner, C. 257
Grzelak, J. 223
Gudjonsson, G. 94
Gudykunst, W. 11, 13, 33
Guetzkow, H. 301
Guirdham, M. 24
Gupta, S. 82
Gupton, T. 71

Haase, R.F. 132
Haines, J. 59
Hakel, M. 48
Halberstadt, A.G. 52
Haley, R. 247
Hall, E.T. 53
Hall, J. 27, 50, 61, 128
Halpin, A.W. 331
Hamm, H. 43
Hancks, M. 215
Hare, A.P. 293, 294
Hargie, O. 2, 3, 5, 18, 20, 21, 25, 29,
    61, 64, 98, 99, 106, 107, 138, 145,
    155, 169, 179, 195, 222, 228, 237,
    246, 268, 270
Harkness, C. 261
Harnack, R.V. 310
Harré, R. 18, 25
Harrigan, J. 211
Harris, C.W. 187
Harris, J. 110
Harris, M.B. 154

Hartford, B. 162
Haslett, B. 33
Hatton, N. 178
Hauer, A.L. 127
Hausknecht, D. 256
Heath, C. 182
Heath, R. 11
Heider, F. 34
Heimberg, R. 280
Hellkamp, D. 234
Helmreich, R. 135
Helmy, K. 80
Henley, N.M. 43, 153
Henry, S.E. 81
Hensley, W. 57, 258
Hersey, P. 308
Heslin, R. 42
Hewes, D. 21, 30, 31, 32
Hewgill, M. 255
Heywood, S. 46
Higgins, S.T. 72
Highlen, P.S. 138
Hildum, D.C. 82
Hilgard, E. 87, 88
Hill, C. 84, 125, 126, 131, 132, 133, 235
Hiller, J. 181, 182, 184
Hinton, P. 31
Ho, H. 51
Hoffnung, R.J. 132
Hofling, C. 251
Holahan, C.J. 152
Holborn, S.W. 78, 84, 85
Hollander, E.P. 304, 307
Holli, B. 10, 11
Honey, P. 300
Hood, J. 187
Hopper, R. 183
Horan, J. 285
Hore, T. 56, 258
Hosking, D.M. 304, 307, 308
House, R.J. 250
Hrycaiko, D. 64
Huling-Austin, L. 178
Hulse, S. 66
Hurtig, R. 63
Hutcheson, S. 32, 38
Hutchins, P. 71
Hyman, R.T. 177

Ivey, A. 64, 78, 122, 127, 133, 139,
    140, 141, 179, 185, 190, 220, 222

Jackson, P.R. 85

Jackson, S. 265
Jaffe, J. 60
Jakubowski, P. 269, 274
Janis, I. 31, 65, 297
Jepson, C. 263
Johnson, C. 242
Jones, E. 341
Jones, S. 52
Jones. W.H. 74
Jourard, S.M. 220, 236, 244
Jucker, A.H. 106

Kadunc, T. 45
Kahn, R. 102, 313
Kahn, S. 282
Kalma, A. 49
Katz, D. 24, 313
Kazdin, A. 69
Kellermann, K. 15, 28
Kelley, H.H. 241
Kelly, J. 2, 50, 269
Kendon, A. 44, 45, 50, 142, 148
Kennedy, J.J. 132
Kennedy, T.D. 126
Kennedy, W.A. 79
Kennelly, K.J. 76, 81
Kenny, D. 226
Kenny, D.A. 237
Kern, J. 280, 282, 288
Kestler, J. 94, 96, 104, 109
Kiefer, F. 94
King, A. 20
King, G. 100
Kipling, R. 97
Kleck, R. 55
Klein, K. 85
Kleinke, C.L. 43, 49, 75, 85, 149, 154
Klinger, E. 15
Knapp, M.L. 27, 48, 61, 128, 148, 162,
    165, 167, 170, 171, 172
Knapper, C. 189
Koballa, T. 262
Kolotkin, R. 272, 279
Komaki, J. 71, 252
Koran, S.J. 308
Korda, M. 59
Krasner, L. 84
Kraus, S. 156
Krause, R. 52
Kreps, G. 13, 30, 31
Krivonos, P. 148
Krupat, E. 293
Kunda, Z. 110

Kuperminc, M. 280

L'Abate, L. 1
Lamb, R. 25, 142, 151
Land, M. 180, 184
Lang, G. 29, 133, 134, 136, 159
Lange, A. 269, 274
Langer, E. 15, 16
Larson, C. 249
Latham, G. 28
Laver, J. 32, 38, 172
Lawler, E. 89
Lazarsfield, P. 106
Lazarus, A. 269
Lazowski, L.E. 223, 224
Lea, M. 259
Le Bow, M. 71
Lepper, M. 87
Leventhal, H. 263
Levin, M. 231
Levin, R.B. 283
Levinson, S. 17
Lewin, K. 309
Lewis, P. 283, 288
Ley, P. 177, 180, 181, 187, 193
Lieberman, D. 70, 74
Likert, R. 309
Lind, E. 265
Lindzey, G. 250
Linehan, M. 275, 276, 282
Littlejohn, S. 299
Livesey, P. 165
Livingstone, C. 178
Locke, E. 28
Loftus, E. 106, 109, 110, 111
Lombardo, J. 68
Long, L. 94, 236
Long, T. 236
Lott, A.J. 75
Luft, J. 233, 299
Lundsteen, S. 195
Lysakowski, R.S. 79

McCall, M. 253
McCartan, P.J. 5, 268
McEwan, H. 176
McFall, M. 271
McFall, R. 2
McGrade, B.J. 81
McGrath, M.R. 307
McGuire, J. 2, 262, 266
McHenry, R. 57, 58
McIntyre, T. 268

McKeown, R. 166
McLaughlin, M. 18, 21, 68, 178
McLemore, C.W. 76
MacLeod Clark, J. 115
McNeill, A. 237
Maguire, G.P. 148
Maguire, P. 97, 187
Maier, S. 88
Mangione, T.W. 114
Margalit, B. 286
Marisi, D.Q. 80
Markus, H. 22
Marlowe, D. 82
Marquis, D.G. 143
Marshall, K. 165
Marshall, P. 18, 20, 21, 25, 29
Martin, G. 64
Martin, J.R. 175
Martinko, M.J. 310
Marwell, G. 264
Maslow, A. 24
Massarik, F. 292
Matarazzo, J.D. 60, 78, 85
Mauger, P. 286
Mayfield, E. 57
Mayo, C. 153
Mazur, A. 57
Meertens, R. 299
Mehrabian, A. 47, 48, 51, 60, 86, 138, 172
Meindl, J. 304
Melamed, J. 57
Menlove, F. 253
Merrill, L. 204
Metts, S. 278
Metzler, K. 94
Meyer, M. 94
Meyer, W.V. 81, 89, 92
Michelson, L. 2
Mikulineer, M. 68
Milan, M. 1
Millar, R. 20, 25, 114, 155
Miller, D.R. 295
Miller, G. 246, 247, 255, 256, 260, 264
Miller, J. 80
Miller, K. 310
Miller, L. 223, 226, 238
Miller, N. 87
Mills, H. 122, 135, 137
Mills, J. 11
Mills, M.C. 126
Miltz, R.J. 184
Mizes, J. 70

Monge, P. 310
Mongeau, P. 263
Montagu, M.F.A. 42
Montgomery, R. 207
Moore, D. 256
Moos, R. 26, 27
Morgan, T. 148, 164, 199, 312, 313
Morley, I.E. 304, 307, 308
Morris, D. 45
Morris, E.K. 72
Morrow, N.C. 95, 101, 107, 164, 222,
    246, 268, 270
Motley, M. 16
Mount, S.A. 76, 81
Mouton, J.S. 307
Mucchielli, R. 124
Mullinix, S.B. 283
Munn, W. 257
Munro, E.A. 165
Myers, G. 14
Myers, M. 14

Nagata, D.K. 132, 138
Naifeh, S. 235
Naisbitt, J. 292
Nelson-Gray, R. 78
Nelson-Jones, R. 31, 86, 127, 136, 150,
    158, 166, 194
Nettles, R. 286, 287
Newman, H. 60
Nicholas, R.P. 138
Nix, J. 283
Noller, P. 50
Norman, R. 265
Northouse, L. 292, 293, 296
Northouse, P. 292, 293, 296
Norton, R. 123, 256
Novak, J.D. 157
Nuthall, G.A. 115, 164, 166, 179

O'Brien, J.S. 78, 84, 85
O'Connor, E.M. 237
O'Donnell, P.J. 77
Offerman, L.R. 307
Ogilvie, J. 33
Oguchi, T. 226
O'Hair, D. 12
O'Keefe, D. 246, 254, 266
O'Leary, K. 79, 89
O'Leary, S. 79, 89
Oliver, L. 78
O'Neill, G. 227
O'Neill, N. 227

O'Reilly, C. 73
O'Sullivan, M. 128
Oster, H. 48
Ostermeier, T. 255
Owen, J.W. 283
Owens, R.G. 206

Palmer, J. 111
Pansa, M. 84
Papini, D. 234
Pardeck, J. 268, 287
Park, B. 156
Park, P. 75
Parrott, R. 95
Parson, D. 246
Passons, W.R. 136
Patterson, E. 123, 258
Patterson, M. 43
Pattison, J. 43
Pavlov, I.P. 65
Pendleton, D. 184
Perlmann, R. 176
Perrott, E. 79, 83
Perry, M. 272, 282
Pervin, L. 23, 26
Petronio, S. 240
Petty, R. 253, 254, 262, 264
Phelps, S. 268, 272, 282
Phillips, D. 253
Phillips, E. 1, 2, 253
Pierce, W. 69
Pietrofesa, J. 128, 130, 134, 135
Pine, G.J. 124
Pinney, R.H. 187
Planalp, S. 21, 30, 31, 32
Pope, B. 158, 170
Poppleton, S. 97
Porac, J. 23, 28
Porritt, L. 195, 268
Posner, M. 33
Powell, W.J. 125
Premack, D. 71
Priestley, P. 2
Prior, D. 123
Prkachin, K.M. 253
Prue, D. 72
Puffer, S. 73
Purdy, M. 194, 195, 203
Purvis, J. 238
Putnam, S. 122

Quinn, R.E. 307
Quittner, A.L. 288

Rabin, C. 279
Rackham, N. 97, 148, 164, 199, 229, 312, 313
Ragan, S. 28
Rakos, R. 268, 277, 279, 280, 283, 286
Rapp, S. 64
Rauch, C.F. 304
Raven, B. 65, 75, 77, 247, 250, 301
Raynor, J. 23
Reardon, K. 246, 247, 266
Redfield, D. 99
Reece, M.M. 78
Reid, L.S. 156
Reinard, J. 255
Reno, R.R. 237
Resnick, L. 94
Reynolds, J.H. 164
Richardson, S. 3, 108, 109
Rierdan, J. 86
Riggio, R. 38, 56
Rime, B. 37
Riseborough, M. 46
Robinson, J. 148
Rogers, C.R. 96, 122, 158, 216
Rogers, W. 45
Roloff, M. 22
Rose, Y. 271, 278
Rosenblatt, P.C. 153
Rosenfarb, I. 83
Rosenfeld, H.M. 78
Rosenfeld, P. 47, 73, 148, 213
Rosenshine, B. 159, 180, 182, 185, 188, 189, 213
Rosenthal, R. 57
Rosenwein, R. 47
Roth, H.L. 142
Rothkopf, E.Z. 166
Rotter, J.B. 76
Rousseau, E. 99
Rowe, M. 117
Rozelle, R. 54, 226
Rubin, J.Z. 75, 77, 250, 301
Ruffner, M. 28
Russell, J.L. 80
Russo, N.F. 50
Rutter, D. 50, 148
Ryan, R. 23

Sacks, H. 162, 171
Saigh, P.A. 84, 89
Sajwaj, T. 89
Saks, M. 293
Salmoni, A. 33

Salter, A. 268
Samaan, M. 78
Samovar, L. 11
Sanders, R. 249
Sapolsky, A. 81
Saunders, C. 29, 64, 146, 150, 165
Saunders, E.D. 165
Saunders, S. 74
Schachter, S. 25
Schatzman, L. 105
Scheflen, A. 14
Schegloff, E.A. 162, 171
Scheier, M.F. 237
Scherer, K. 37, 60
Schlenker, B. 17, 29
Schleuder, J. 146
Schlundt, D. 2
Schmidt, L.D. 148
Schmitt, D. 264
Schneider, D. 59
Schopler, J. 58, 258
Schroth, M. 189
Schuck, R.F. 159, 160
Schulman, L. 167
Schultz, C.B. 80
Schutz, W.C. 295
Schwartz, N. 88
Schwarz, B. 65, 91, 93
Scofield, M.E. 85
Scott, M. 60
Secord, P.F. 22, 296, 303
Segrin, C. 1, 3
Seibold, D. 246
Seligman, M.E.P. 68
Shaffer, D. 235
Shamir, B. 304
Shannon, C. 11, 13
Shaw, M.E. 293, 301, 303
Sheats, P. 298
Sherman, W. 68, 80
Showalter, J.T. 84
Shukla, A. 82
Shutes, R. 190
Shuy, R.W. 149, 171
Siegel, J. 47
Siegman, A. 78
Sigal, J. 283
Silver, R.J. 125
Simms, C.M. 237
Simms, M. 152
Simon, H.A. 301
Simonson, N. 156
Simpson, J. 292

Singer, J. 25, 68
Sinha, V. 234
Skinner, B.F. 65, 66, 69, 70, 87, 92
Slobin, D. 225
Smith, C. 152
Smith, G. 235
Smith, P. 60
Smith, R. 64
Smith, V. 194, 201
Smoll, F. 64
Snyder, M. 35
Solano, C. 243
Solomon, L.J. 58, 258, 283
Sommer, R. 55
Sorensen, G.A. 42
Spence, J. 235
Spitzberg, B.H. 3
Spooner, S.E. 133
Stang, D. 247
Stangor, C. 263
Stasser, G. 308
St Clair, R. 134
Steel, L. 240
Steil, L. 194, 195
Stenstroem, A. 96
Sterling, B.S. 283
Stewart, C.J. 123, 166
Stewart, J. 181, 219
Stewart, R. 153
Stiles, W. 122
St Lawrence, J.S. 269, 283
Stock, C.G. 81
Stogdill, R.M. 304, 305
Stokes, T. 67
Stone, A.A. 230
Stone, D. 264
Stone, G. 304
Stotland, E. 24
Strack, F. 93
Strauss, A. 105
Street, R. 25, 256
Strenta, A.C. 55
Stricker, G. 220, 227, 231
Strong, S. 211
Stull, D.E. 235
Sudman, S. 94, 118
Sue, D. 286
Sullivan, H.S. 76, 149, 150
Sutton, S. 263
Swann, W. 76
Sweller, J. 188
Swenson, R. 255
Swift, J.N. 117

Taguiri, R. 35
Tajfel, J. 258
Tardy, C.H. 219, 221
Taylor, D. 239
Taylor, S. 262
Tesser, A. 22, 76
Thibaut, J. 241
Thomas, A. 48
Thomlinson, D. 285
Thompson, S. 262
Thornton, B. 13
Thyne, J. 175
Tizard, B. 94
Tjosvold, D. 311
Tobin, K. 117
Togo, D. 187
Tomkins, S.S. 134
Towne, N. 42
Tracy, K. 27
Trower, P. 1, 20, 74, 168
True, J. 50
Tryon, W. 271, 278
Tubbs, S. 227
Turk, C. 114, 156
Turkat, I.D. 125
Turner, J. 9, 246, 294
Turney, C. 64, 72, 104, 112, 146, 170,
    180, 311, 312

Uhlemann, M.R. 138

van der Molen, H. 29, 133, 134, 136,
    159
van Knippenberg, A. 296
Vargas, A. 258
Vartabedian, R. 239
Verner, C. 181
Verplanck, W.S. 84
Von Cranach, M. 28, 29
Vondracek, F.W. 126
Vroom, V. 23

Wagner, P. 221
Walberg, H.J. 79
Waldron, V. 29
Wallen, J. 177
Walster, E. 56, 258
Walton, L. 115
Warner, R.M. 47
Washburn, P. 48
Waskow, I.E. 132
Watzlawick, P. 14, 16, 61
Wearden, J. 88

Weatherley, D. 235
Weaver, C. 195
Weaver, W. 11, 13
Weigold, M. 29
Weiner, M.F. 220, 230
Weir, S. 154, 155
Weiss, R. 68
Wenrich, W. 279, 280
West, C. 94, 253
Wetzel, C.G. 239, 241
Wheeless, L. 236
Wheldall, K. 43, 74, 79, 80, 86, 252
Whetten, D.A. 269
White, A. 146
White, B. 74
Whitman, R.N. 78
Whittington, D. 1, 169, 311
Wiemann, J. 11
Wiener, M. 14
Wiens, A.N. 78, 85
Wilensky, R. 29
Wilke, H.A.M. 296, 299, 310, 314
Willcutt, H.C. 79
Willis, F. 13, 43
Wilmot, W. 18
Wilson, D. 145
Wilson, K. 268, 276, 283
Wilson, J. 106, 118
Wilson-Barnett, J. 177
Winer, B.J. 311
Winograd, T. 15
Winton, W. 25
Witt, L. 26

Wolff, F. 194, 195, 196, 198, 203, 205
Wolpe, J. 268
Wolvin, A. 194, 198, 203
Wood, W. 292
Woodall, G. 256
Woodbury, H. 93
Woodworth, R.S. 143
Woolfolk, A. 225
Woolfolk, R.L. 276
Wools, R. 60
Worchel, S. 55, 260
Worthy, M. 219
Wright, C. 115, 164, 166, 179
Wright, R. 258
Wright-Buckley, C. 239, 241
Wrightsman, L. 247, 297

Yager, G. 229
Yarbrough, A.E. 86
Yeschke, C. 238
Yukl, G.A. 305

Zahn, G.L. 54
Zaidel, S. 310, 312, 315
Zajonc, R. 33
Zander, A. 294, 310, 312, 315
Zanni, G. 109, 111
Zelner, D. 279
Zimmer, J.M. 75, 125, 132
Zollo, L.J. 289
Zucker, E. 214, 279, 290
Zuckerman, M. 220

Subject index

account 18
acoustic confusion 202
affect 25
age 25, 58, 80, 152, 173, 176, 234, 287
aggression 272
appearance 39, 41, 55, 251
assertiveness: and aggression 270–3;
    components of 277–82; contextual
    factors 282–9; covert processes
    279–81; definition 268–70; functions
    273–4; nonassertion 270–3;
    nonverbal element 281–2; personal
    factors 282–9; types of 274–7
attitude 24–5; change 249; definition
    248
attractiveness 74; familiarity 259;
    physical 56–7, 153, 239, 257–8, 259;
    praise and 81, 260–1; reciprocation
    and 261; scarcity 259–60; similarity
    239, 258–9
attribution 34, 81

banter 288
barristers 163
beliefs 280–1
business executives ix, 59, 253

careers officer ix, 159, 177, 183, 187
chairpersons 164, 170, 311, 313
channel 12
clergymen 43
client-centred counselling 158
closure: definition of 161–2; factual
    163–7; functions of 162–3;
    motivational 167–9; perceptual
    171–3; social 169–71
coaching 64
cognitive restructuring 280

communication 10
community workers 164
context 13
counselling 64, 106, 150, 159, 165–6,
    195, 231
counsellor ix, 50, 154, 156, 158, 167,
    185, 225, 226, 231
cueing: nonverbal 185–6; verbal 186–7
cultural factors 226, 235, 285–7

deception indicators 220, 226
dentist ix, 67, 151, 209
detective 102
doctor ix, 42, 43, 94, 95, 97, 98, 102,
    148, 149, 159, 165, 177, 181, 187,
    189, 195, 213, 225, 228, 251, 260,
    262

embarrassing predicaments 278
emotions 46, 47, 51, 60, 206–7
empathic understanding 238
environmental factors 38, 41, 59–60
explanation: aids to explanation 187–8;
    definition 175–6; demonstrations
    191–2; emphasis 185–7; functions
    176–7; gaining feedback 189–90;
    illustrations 179; planning 178–9;
    presenting 179–85; types 177–8;
    verbal examples 188–9
extroverts 25, 81, 204, 237
eye contact 50, 84, 85, 173, 284
eye-gaze 40, 48–50, 242
eye-witness testimony 110–12

face 17, 27
facial expression 50–2, 58
feedback 50, 170
fogging 276–7

gender 25, 80; and assertiveness 282–4;
   behavioural differences 153;
   listening differences 204; self-
   disclosure differences 235–6
gestures 44–6, 186
goals 23, 26, 27–9
gossip 224
greeting 142, 148
groups: communication networks
   301; conformity 297; definition
   293–4; dyadic and group interaction
   291; face-to-face interaction 293;
   functions 294–5; goals 294;
   groupthink 297; intra-group
   communication 298–303; norms
   295–6; primary and secondary 293;
   roles 297; size 293; status 297; task
   and psyche communication 299;
   types 292–3; see also leadership

head nods 48, 84, 85
health visitors 43, 50, 148, 152, 229

illustrators 40, 41, 44, 45, 46
implicit personality theories 35
influencing: and attitude 248–50, and
   attractiveness 257; and credibility
   254–7; definition 246–8; and power
   250–4
interpersonal attraction 74, 75, 153
interpersonal communication: code 14;
   definition 11; inevitable 14;
   irreversible 18; mindful and mindless
   15; multi-dimensional 16–18;
   purposeful 14–16; process 11–13;
   transactional 13–14
interpersonal distance 53–5
interview 64, 114, 155, 171, 179, 190;
   see also research interview,
   selection interview
interviewers 44, 48, 59, 165, 166
introverts 25, 204, 237

Johari Window 233
judges 163, 251

kinesics 43–4

lawyer 95, 96, 109, 183
leadership: definition 303–5; skills
   310–14; styles of 309–10; theories of
   305–8
learned helplessness 68

lecturers 115, 146, 165–6, 168, 170,
   188–9, 190, 209, 265
listening: active 196–8; definition
   195–6; facets of 203–9; functions of
   196; obstacles to 209–11; passive
   196–8; process of 199–203; and
   rationalisation 202; and reductionism
   201; types of 198–9
locus of control 76, 81

management 64, 71, 72, 82
medium 12
message 11–12; evidence in 262; fear
   appeals in 263–4; and structure 206;
   and use of arguments 264–7
metacognitions 32
motivation 23–4, 33, 203

negotiators 97, 229
nonverbal communication 32, 37, 83–8;
   definition 38; purposes 38–41
note-taking 201
nurses 9, 29, 43, 116, 164, 177, 268

paralanguage 41, 60–1
paraphrase see reflecting
pausing 117
perception 33–5; first impressions 153;
   selective nature of 197–8; social
   perception 281
personality 25, 153, 237
perspective taking 238
persuasion 47, 246–8
pharmacist ix, 64, 95, 101, 169, 228,
   268
physical characteristics 55–9
physical contact 41, 42–3, 173
physical therapy 217
politeness 17
politicians 39, 115, 163, 185
posture 46–8, 173
power 17; coercive 252; expert 251;
   information 253–4; legitimate 250;
   referent 252–3; reward 251–2
proxemics: definition 52; orientation
   57; proximity 53–5; territoriality
   52–3
psychiatrist 150
psychologist 145
public speakers 44, 163, 185
punishment 66

question: affective 106–7; closed

100–1; definition 93; distribution 117–18; functions 96–7; leading 107–12; multiple 115–16; open 101–2; and pauses 117; probes 112; probing 112–14; process 99–100; prompting 116; prosodic 93; recall 98–9; responses to 118–19; rhetorical 114–15; sequence of 102–4; status differences 95–6; structuring 116

reality testing 279
reflecting: definition 122; empathic understanding 125, 136; factual and affective communication 127–8; functions 128–9; guidelines 139–41; paraphrase 84, 85, 128, 129–33; positive regard 125; reflecting meaning 127; reflection of content 129; reflection of feeling 128, 133–8; restatement 127; summaries of content 140; summaries of feeling 140; versus alternative styles 123–7; versus other reinforcers 125–6
reinforcement 33; activity 71; appropriate use 88–9; behavioural consequences 65–6; conditioned 69; contingency 87, 89; discriminative stimulus 72; extinction 66; frequency 90; functions 73–7; Gain/Loss Theory 90; generalised 69, 70; genuineness 89; gestural 84–5; instrumental conditioning 65; intermittent 90; learned helplessness 68; mechanisms 87–8; minimal encouragers 78; negative 67–8; nonverbal components 48, 83–8; operant conditioning 65; partial 90; positive 66–7; praise 79–82; Premack principle 71; primary and secondary 68–9; and professional practice 63–5; proximity 86; punishment 66; response development 82–3; secondary 69; sensory 70; shaping 91; social 69–70; stimulus control 71–2; timing 90; token economy 69; variety 90; verbal components 77–83; vicarious 72–3
relationship development 228
research interview 104–5, 110, 159

salesmen 44, 57, 145, 149, 167

schema 22
selection interview 46, 57, 151, 156, 285
self-concept 20
self-disclosure: definition 219–20; elements of 223–6; features of 220–3; functions of 226–33; influencing factors 233–44; and reflecting 125–6; written 230
self-esteem 76
self-monitoring 35
self-presentation 17
set induction: cognitive aspects 155–60; definition 142–4; functions 144–5; motivational 145–7; perceptual 151–5; social 147–50
skill model of interpersonal interaction 19; feedback 13, 32–3; goal 23, 26, 27–9; mediating processes 29–32; perception 33–5; person–situation context 20–7; response 32
smiles 60, 84; see also facial expression
social class 80, 152
social cognitive theory 4
social skill 63; definitions 1–2; example of 5–7; features 2–4, 9; nature of 1, 316
social workers ix, 53, 59, 158, 208, 279
speech rate 61, 205
speech therapy 64
status 17, 46–7, 49, 54, 58, 225, 239; see also groups
stereotypes 22, 59
structuring 116
styles of interacting 123–7, 270
summaries of content 16, 140
summaries of feeling 140
summary 164–6, 312–13
sustaining 206

teachers ix, 39, 43, 44, 52, 53, 57, 58, 64, 72, 80, 82, 83, 94, 96, 99, 115, 117, 146, 156, 159, 164, 166, 168, 170, 176, 178–9, 182, 190, 225, 251, 259, 261, 262
television presenters 145–6, 163, 168, 172, 178, 185
therapists 131, 227, 230, 231
touch 42–3; see also physical contact
trainers 166
topic shifts 214
turn-taking 40, 49

warmth 74, 75, 85, 243, 311